THE DECLINE
AND FALL OF
THE ROMAN EMPIRE

The most majestic work of history ever written, *The Decline and Fall of the Roman Empire* bridges the abyss between the ancient and modern worlds. A masterful narrative ranging over Europe, Asia, and North Africa, it spans thirteen hundred years, encompassing the rise of two world religions and the ebb and flow of major social and legal institutions.

The first great investigation of the remote past to retain its authority, Gibbon's masterpiece is remarkable both for its scholarly erudition and its contribution to the study of history itself. Focusing throughout on the interplay of political forces and the achievements of the sciences, it traces a unifying thread animating historical incidents and giving them purpose and meaning. Carefully and coherently structured, embellished with elegance of detail, flashes of wit, and that most famous of Gibbon's qualities, "grave and temperate irony," *The Decline and Fall of the Roman Empire* remains a monumental achievement of the Enlightenment.

This three-volume paperbound edition was originally published in one volume by Harcourt, Brace & World, Inc., at $8.00.

WASHINGTON SQUARE PRESS
POCKET BOOKS • NEW YORK

THE DECLINE AND FALL OF THE ROMAN EMPIRE

Volume Three

EDWARD GIBBON

ABRIDGMENT BY D. M. LOW

THE DECLINE AND FALL OF THE ROMAN EMPIRE
VOLUME THREE

WASHINGTON SQUARE PRESS edition published May, 1962
3rd printing........................August, 1972

L

Published by
POCKET BOOKS, a division of Simon & Schuster, Inc.,
630 Fifth Avenue, New York, N.Y.

WASHINGTON SQUARE PRESS · editions are distributed
in the U.S. by Simon & Schuster, Inc., 630 Fifth Avenue,
New York, N.Y. 10020 and in Canada by Simon & Schuster of Canada, Ltd., Richmond Hill, Ontario, Canada.

Contents

The Crusades

The End of the Roman Empire

The Epilogue: Medieval Rome and the Dawn of the Renaissance

THE
DECLINE AND FALL
OF THE
ROMAN EMPIRE
Volume III

50.

DESCRIPTION OF ARABIA. CHARACTER AND RELIGION OF THE ARABS. THE RISE OF MAHOMET. HIS PRECEPTS. HIS FLIGHT FROM MECCA TO MEDINA. HIS DECLARATION OF WAR AGAINST THE INFIDELS. DEATH OF MAHOMET. HIS CHARACTER AND PRIVATE LIFE. ASSESSMENT OF HIS INFLUENCE

AFTER PURSUING above six hundred years the fleeting Cæsars of Constantinople and Germany, I now descend, in the reign of Heraclius, on the eastern borders of the Greek monarchy. While the state was exhausted by the Persian war, and the church was distracted by the Nestorian and Monophysite sects, Mahomet, with the sword in one hand and the Koran in the other, erected his throne on the ruins of Christianity and of Rome. The genius of the Arabian prophet, the manners of his nation, and the spirit of his religion, involve the causes of the decline and fall of the Eastern empire; and our eyes are curiously intent on one of the most memorable revolutions which have impressed a new and lasting character on the nations of the globe.[1]

In the vacant space between Persia, Syria, Egypt, and Ethiopia, the Arabian peninsula may be conceived as a triangle of spacious but irregular dimensions. From the northern point of Beles, on the Euphrates, a line of fifteen hundred miles is terminated by the Straits of Babelmandeb and the land of frankincense. About half this length may be allowed for the middle breadth, from east to west, from Bassora to Suez, from the Persian Gulf to the Red Sea. The sides of the triangle are gradually enlarged, and the southern basis pre-

[1] As in this and the following chapter I shall display much Arabic learning, I must profess my total ignorance of the Oriental tongues, and my gratitude to the learned interpreters, who have transfused their science into the Latin, French, and English languages. Their collections, versions, and histories, I shall occasionally notice.

sents a front of a thousand miles to the Indian Ocean. The entire surface of the peninsula exceeds in a fourfold proportion that of Germany or France; but the far greater part has been justly stigmatised with the epithets of the *stony* and the *sandy*. Even the wilds of Tartary are decked, by the hand of nature, with lofty trees and luxuriant herbage; and the lonesome traveller derives a sort of comfort and society from the presence of vegetable life. But in the dreary waste of Arabia a boundless level of sand is intersected by sharp and naked mountains; and the face of the desert, without shade or shelter, is scorched by the direct and intense rays of a tropical sun. Instead of refreshing breezes, the winds, particularly from the south-west, diffuse a noxious and even deadly vapour; the hillocks of sand which they alternately raise and scatter are compared to the billows of the ocean, and whole caravans, whole armies, have been lost and buried in the whirlwind. The common benefits of water are an object of desire and contest; and such is the scarcity of wood, that some art is requisite to preserve and propagate the element of fire. Arabia is destitute of navigable rivers, which fertilise the soil, and convey its produce to the adjacent regions: the torrents that fall from the hills are imbibed by the thirsty earth: the rare and hardy plants, the tamarind or the acacia that strike their roots into the clefts of the rocks, are nourished by the dews of the night: a scanty supply of rain is collected in cisterns and aqueducts: the wells and springs are the secret treasure of the desert; and the pilgrim of Mecca, after many a dry and sultry march, is disgusted by the taste of the waters which have rolled over a bed of sulphur or salt. Such is the general and genuine picture of the climate of Arabia. The experience of evil enhances the value of any local or partial enjoyments. A shady grove, a green pasture, a stream of fresh water, are sufficient to attract a colony of sedentary Arabs to the fortunate spots which can afford food and refreshment to themselves and their cattle, and which encourage their industry in the cultivation of the palm-tree and the vine. The highlands that border on the Indian Ocean are distinguished by their superior plenty of wood and water: the air is more temperate, the fruits are more delicious, the animals and the human race more numerous: the fertility of the soil invites and rewards the toil of the husbandman; and the peculiar gifts of frankincense and coffee have attracted in different

ages the merchants of the world. If it be compared with the
rest of the peninsula, this sequestered region may truly
deserve the appellation of the *happy;* and the splendid colour-
ing of fancy and fiction has been suggested by contrast and
countenanced by distance. It was for this earthly paradise that
nature had reserved her choicest favours and her most curious
workmanship: the incompatible blessings of luxury and innocence were ascribed to the natives: the soil was impregnated
with gold and gems, and both the land and sea were taught to
exhale the odours of aromatic sweets. This division of the
sandy, the *stony,* and the *happy,* so familiar to the Greeks
and Latins, is unknown to the Arabians themselves; and it is
singular enough, that a country whose language and inhabitants have ever been the same should scarcely retain a
vestige of its ancient geography. The maritime districts of
Bahrein and *Oman* are opposite to the realms of Persia. The
kingdom of *Yemen* displays the limits, or at least the situation,
of Arabia Felix: the name of *Neged* is extended over the
inland space; and the birth of Mahomet has illustrated the
province of *Hejaz* along the coast of the Red Sea.

The measure of population is regulated by the means of
subsistence; and the inhabitants of this vast peninsula might
be out-numbered by the subjects of a fertile and industrious
province. Along the shores of the Persian Gulf, of the ocean,
and even of the Red Sea, the *Ichthyophagi,* or fish-eaters,
continued to wander in quest of their precarious food. In
this primitive and abject state, which ill deserves the name of
society, the human brute, without arts or laws, almost without sense or language, is poorly distinguished from the rest
of the animal creation. Generations and ages might roll away
in silent oblivion, and the helpless savage was restrained
from multiplying his race by the wants and pursuits which
confined his existence to the narrow margin of the sea-coast.
But in an early period of antiquity the great body of the
Arabs had emerged from this scene of misery; and as the
naked wilderness could not maintain a people of hunters,
they rose at once to the more secure and plentiful condition
of the pastoral life. The same life is uniformly pursued by the
roving tribes of the desert; and in the portrait of the modern
Bedoweens we may trace the features of their ancestors, who,
in the age of Moses or Mahomet, dwelt under similar tents,
and conducted their horses, and camels, and sheep to the

same springs and the same pastures. Our toil is lessened, and our wealth is increased, by our dominion over the useful animals; and the Arabian shepherd had acquired the absolute possession of a faithful friend and a laborious slave. Arabia, in the opinion of the naturalist, is the genuine and original country of the *horse;* the climate most propitious, not indeed to the size, but to the spirit and swiftness, of that generous animal. The merit of the Barb, the Spanish, and the English breed is derived from a mixture of Arabian blood: the Bedoweens preserve, with superstitious care, the honours and the memory of the purest race: the males are sold at a high price, but the females are seldom alienated; and the birth of a noble foal was esteemed among the tribes as a subject of joy and mutual congratulation. These horses are educated in the tents, among the children of the Arabs, with a tender familiarity, which trains them in the habits of gentleness and attachment. They are accustomed only to walk and to gallop: their sensations are not blunted by the incessant abuse of the spur and the whip: their powers are reserved for the moments of flight and pursuit: but no sooner do they feel the touch of the hand or the stirrup, than they dart away with the swiftness of the wind; and if their friend be dismounted in the rapid career, they instantly stop till he has recovered his seat. In the sands of Africa and Arabia the *camel* is a sacred and precious gift. That strong and patient beast of burden can perform, without eating or drinking, a journey of several days; and a reservoir of fresh water is preserved in a large bag, a fifth stomach of the animal, whose body is imprinted with the marks of servitude: the larger breed is capable of transporting a weight of a thousand pounds; and the dromedary, of a lighter and more active frame, outstrips the fleetest courser in the race. Alive or dead, almost every part of the camel is serviceable to man: her milk is plentiful and nutritious: the young and tender flesh has the taste of veal: a valuable salt is extracted from the urine: the dung supplies the deficiency of fuel: and the long hair, which falls each year and is renewed, is coarsely manufactured into the garments, the furniture, and the tents of the Bedoweens. In the rainy seasons they consume the rare and insufficient herbage of the desert: during the heats of summer and the scarcity of winter they remove their encampments to the sea-coast, the hills of Yemen, or the neighbourhood of the Euphrates, and have often extorted the dangerous licence of visiting the banks of the Nile and the villages of Syria and Palestine. The life of a wandering Arab is a life of danger and distress; and though sometimes, by rapine or exchange, he may appropriate the fruits of industry, a private citizen in Europe is in the possession of more solid and pleasing luxury than the proudest emir who marches in the field at the head of ten thousand horse.

Yet an essential difference may be found between the hordes of Scythia and the Arabian tribes; since many of the latter were collected into towns, and employed in the labours of trade and agriculture. A part of their time and industry was still devoted to the management of their cattle: they mingled, in peace and war, with their brethren of the desert; and the Bedoweens derived from their useful intercourse some supply of their wants, and some rudiments of art and knowledge. Among the forty-two cities of Arabia, enumerated by Abulfeda, the most ancient and populous were situate in the *happy* Yemen: the towers of Saana, and the marvellous reservoir of Merab, were constructed by the kings of the Homerites; but their profane lustre was eclipsed by the prophetic glories of MEDINA and MECCA, near the Red Sea, and at the distance from each other of two hundred and seventy miles. The last of these holy places was known to the Greeks under the name of Macoraba; and the termination of the word is expressive of its greatness, which has not indeed, in the most flourishing period, exceeded the size and populousness of Marseilles. Some latent motive, perhaps of superstition, must have impelled the founders in the choice of a most unpromising situation. They erected their habitations of mud or stone in a plain about two miles long and one mile broad, at the foot of these barren mountains: the soil is a rock; the water even of the holy well of Zemzem is bitter or brackish; the pastures are remote from the city; and grapes are transported above seventy miles from the gardens of Tayef. The fame and spirit of the Koreishites, who reigned in Mecca, were conspicuous among the Arabian tribes; but their ungrateful soil refused the labours of agriculture, and their position was favourable to the enterprises of trade. By the seaport of Gedda, at the distance only of forty miles, they maintained an easy correspondence with Abyssinia; and that Christian kingdom afforded the first refuge to the disciples of Mahomet. The treasures of

Africa were conveyed over the peninsula to Gerrha or Katif, in the province of Bahrein, a city built, as it is said, of rock-salt, by the Chaldæan exiles; and from thence, with the native pearls of the Persian Gulf, they were floated on rafts to the mouth of the Euphrates. Mecca is placed almost at an equal distance, a month's journey, between Yemen on the right and Syria on the left hand. The former was the winter, the latter the summer, station of her caravans; and their seasonable arrival relieved the ships of India from the tedious and trouble-some navigation of the Red Sea. In the markets of Saana and Merab, in the harbours of Oman and Aden, the camels of the Koreishites were laden with a precious cargo of aromatics; a supply of corn and manufactures was purchased in the fairs of Bostra and Damascus; the lucrative exchange diffused plenty and riches in the streets of Mecca; and the noblest of her sons united the love of arms with the profession of merchandise.

CHARACTER OF THE ARABS

The perpetual independence of the Arabs has been the theme of praise among strangers and natives; and the arts of controversy transformed this singular event into a prophecy and a miracle in favour of the posterity of Ismael. Some exceptions, that can neither be dissembled nor eluded, render this mode of reasoning as indiscreet as it is superfluous; the kingdom of Yemen has been successively subdued by the Abyssinians, the Persians, the sultans of Egypt, and the Turks: the holy cities of Mecca and Medina have repeatedly bowed under a Scythian tyrant; and the Roman province of Arabia embraced the peculiar wilderness in which Ismael and his sons must have pitched their tents in the face of their brethren. Yet these exceptions are temporary or local; the body of the nation has escaped the yoke of the most powerful monarchies: the arms of Sesostris and Cyrus, of Pompey and Trajan, could never achieve the conquest of Arabia; the present sovereign of the Turks may exercise a shadow of jurisdiction, but his pride is reduced to solicit the friendship of a people whom it is dangerous to provoke and fruitless to attack. The obvious causes of their freedom are inscribed on the character and country of the Arabs. Many ages before Mahomet, their intrepid valour had been severely felt by their neighbours in offensive and defensive war. The patient and active virtues of a soldier are insensibly nursed in the habits and discipline of a pastoral life. The care of the sheep and camels is abandoned to the women of the tribe; but the martial youth, under the banner of the emir, is ever on horseback, and in the field, to practise the exercise of the bow, the javelin, and the scimitar. The long memory of their independence is the firmest pledge of its perpetuity, and succeeding generations are animated to prove their descent and to maintain their inheritance. Their domestic feuds are suspended on the approach of a common enemy; and in their last hostilities against the Turks, the caravan of Mecca was attacked and pillaged by fourscore thousand of the confederates. When they advance to battle, the hope of victory is in the front; in the rear, the assurance of a retreat. Their horses and camels, who in eight or ten days can perform a march of four or five hundred miles, disappear before the conqueror; the secret waters of the desert elude his search; and his victorious troops are consumed with thirst, hunger, and fatigue in the pursuit of an invisible foe, who scorns his efforts, and safely reposes in the heart of the burning solitude. The arms and deserts of the Bedoweens are not only the safeguards of their own freedom but the barriers also of the happy Arabia, whose inhabitants, remote from war, are enervated by the luxury of the soil and climate. The legions of Augustus melted away in disease and lassitude; and it is only by a naval power that the reduction of Yemen has been successfully attempted. When Mahomet erected his holy standard, that kingdom was a province of the Persian empire; yet seven princes of the Homerites still reigned in the mountains; and the vicegerent of Chosroes was tempted to forget his distant country and his unfortunate master. The historians of the age of Justinian represent the state of the independent Arabs, who were divided by interest or affection in the long quarrel of the East: the tribe of *Gassan* was allowed to encamp on the Syrian territory: the princes of *Hira* were permitted to form a city about forty miles to the southward of the ruins of Babylon. Their service in the field was speedy and vigorous; but their friendship was venal, their faith inconstant, their enmity capricious: it was an easier task to excite than to disarm these roving barbarians; and, in the familiar intercourse of war, they learned to see and to despise the splendid weakness both of Rome and of

Persia. From Mecca to the Euphrates, the Arabian tribes were confounded by the Greeks and Latins under the general appellation of SARACENS, a name which every Christian mouth has been taught to pronounce with terror and abhorrence.

The slaves of domestic tyranny may vainly exult in their national independence: but the Arab is personally free; and he enjoys, in some degree, the benefits of society, without forfeiting the prerogatives of nature. In every tribe, superstition, or gratitude, or fortune has exalted a particular family above the heads of their equals. The dignities of sheikh and emir invariably descend in this chosen race; but the order of succession is loose and precarious; and the most worthy or aged of the noble kinsmen are preferred to the simple though important office of composing disputes by their advice, and guiding valour by their example. Even a female of sense and spirit has been permitted to command the countrymen of Zenobia. The momentary junction of several tribes produces an army: their more lasting union constitutes a nation: and the supreme chief, the emir of emirs, whose banner is displayed at their head, may deserve, in the eyes of strangers, the honours of the kingly name. If the Arabian princes abuse their power, they are quickly punished by the desertion of their subjects, who had been accustomed to a mild and parental jurisdiction. Their spirit is free, their steps are unconfined, the desert is open, and the tribes and families are held together by a mutual and voluntary compact. The softer natives of Yemen supported the pomp and majesty of a monarch; but if he could not leave his palace without endangering his life, the active powers of government must have been devolved on his nobles and magistrates. The cities of Mecca and Medina present, in the heart of Asia, the form, or rather the substance, of a commonwealth. The grandfather of Mahomet, and his lineal ancestors, appear in foreign and domestic transactions as the princes of their country; but they reigned, like Pericles at Athens, or the Medici at Florence, by the opinion of their wisdom and integrity; their influence was divided with their patrimony; and the sceptre was transferred from the uncles of the prophet to a younger branch of the tribe of Koreish. On solemn occasions they convened the assembly of the people; and, since mankind must be either compelled or persuaded to obey, the use and reputation of oratory among the ancient Arabs is the clearest evidence of public freedom. But their simple freedom was of a very different cast from the nice and artificial machinery of the Greek and Roman republics, in which each member possessed an undivided share of the civil and political rights of the community. In the more simple state of the Arabs, the nation is free, because each of her sons disdains a base submission to the will of a master. His breast is fortified with the austere virtues of courage, patience, and sobriety; the love of independence prompts him to exercise the habits of self-command; and the fear of dishonour guards him from the meaner apprehension of pain, of danger, and of death. The gravity and firmness of the mind is conspicuous in his outward demeanour: his speech is slow, weighty, and concise; he is seldom provoked to laughter; his only gesture is that of stroking his beard, the venerable symbol of manhood; and the sense of his own importance teaches him to accost his equals without levity, and his superiors without awe. The liberty of the Saracens survived their conquests: the first caliphs indulged the bold and familiar language of their subjects: they ascended the pulpit to persuade and edify the congregation; nor was it before the seat of empire was removed to the Tigris that the Abbassides adopted the proud and pompous ceremonial of the Persian and Byzantine courts.

In the study of nations and men we may observe the causes that render them hostile or friendly to each other, that tend to narrow or enlarge, to mollify or exasperate, the social character. The separation of the Arabs from the rest of mankind has accustomed them to confound the ideas of stranger and enemy; and the poverty of the land has introduced a maxim of jurisprudence which they believe and practice to the present hour. They pretend that, in the division of the earth, the rich and fertile climates were assigned to the other branches of the human family; and that the posterity of the outlaw Ismael might recover, by fraud or force, the portion of inheritance of which he had been unjustly deprived. According to the remark of Pliny, the Arabian tribes are equally addicted to theft and merchandise: the caravans that traverse the desert are ransomed or pillaged; and their neighbours, since the remote times of Job and Sesostris, have been the victims of their rapacious spirit. If a Bedoween discovers from afar a solitary traveller, he rides furiously against him, crying, with a loud voice, "Undress thyself, thy aunt *(my wife)* is

without a garment." A ready submission entitles him to mercy;
resistance will provoke the aggressor, and his own blood
must expiate the blood which he presumes to shed in legitimate defence. A single robber, or a few associates, are branded
with their genuine name; but the exploits of a numerous
band assume the character of lawful and honourable war.
The temper of a people thus armed against mankind was
doubly inflamed by the domestic licence of rapine, murder,
and revenge. In the constitution of Europe, the right of peace
and war is now confined to a small, and the actual exercise
to a much smaller, list of respectable potentates; but each
Arab, with impunity and renown, might point his javelin
against the life of his countryman. The union of the nation
consisted only in a vague resemblance of language and manners; and in each community the jurisdiction of the magistrate
was mute and impotent. Of the time of ignorance which
preceded Mahomet, seventeen hundred battles are recorded
by tradition: hostility was embittered with rancour of civil
faction: and the recital, in prose or verse, of an obsolete feud,
was sufficient to rekindle the same passions among the
descendants of the hostile tribes. In private life every man, at
least every family, was the judge and avenger of its own
cause. The nice sensibility of honour, which weighs the insult
rather than the injury, sheds its deadly venom on the quarrels
of the Arabs: the honour of their women, and of their *beards*,
is most easily wounded; an indecent action, a contemptuous
word, can be expiated only by the blood of the offender; and
such is their patient inveteracy, that they expect whole months
and years the opportunity of revenge. A fine or compensation for murder is familiar to the barbarians of every age:
but in Arabia the kinsmen of the dead are at liberty to accept
the atonement, or to exercise with their own hands the law
of retaliation. The refined malice of the Arabs refuses even the
head of the murderer, substitutes an innocent to the guilty
person, and transfers the penalty to the best and most considerable of the race by whom they have been injured. If he
falls by their hands, they are exposed in their turn to the
danger of reprisals; the interest and principal of the bloody
debt are accumulated: the individuals of either family lead a
life of malice and suspicion, and fifty years may sometimes
elapse before the account of vengeance be finally settled.
This sanguinary spirit, ignorant of pity or forgiveness, had

been moderated, however, by the maxims of honour, which require in every private encounter some decent equality of age and strength, of numbers and weapons. An annual festival of two, perhaps of four, months, was observed by the Arabs before the time of Mahomet, during which their swords were religiously sheathed both in foreign and domestic hostility; and this partial truce is more strongly expressive of the habits of anarchy and warfare.

But the spirit of rapine and revenge was attempered by the milder influence of trade and literature. The solitary peninsula is encompassed by the most civilised nations of the ancient world; the merchant is the friend of mankind; and the annual caravans imported the first seeds of knowledge and politeness into the cities and even the camps of the desert. Whatever may be the pedigree of the Arabs, their language is derived from the same original stock with the Hebrew, the Syriac, and the Chaldæan tongues; the independence of the tribes was marked by their peculiar dialects; but each, after their own, allowed a just preference to the pure and perspicuous idiom of Mecca. In Arabia, as well as in Greece, the perfection of language outstripped the refinement of manners; and her speech could diversify the fourscore names of honey, the two hundred of a serpent, the five hundred of a lion, the thousand of a sword, at a time when this copious dictionary was intrusted to the memory of an illiterate people. The monuments of the Homerites were inscribed with an obsolete and mysterious character; but the Cufic letters, the groundwork of the present alphabet, were invented on the banks of the Euphrates; and the recent invention was taught at Mecca by a stranger who settled in that city after the birth of Mahomet. The arts of grammar, of metre, and of rhetoric were unknown to the freeborn eloquence of the Arabians; but their penetration was sharp, their fancy luxuriant, their wit strong and sententious, and their more elaborate compositions were addressed with energy and effect to the minds of their hearers. The genius and merit of a rising poet was celebrated by the applause of his own and the kindred tribes. A solemn banquet was prepared, and a chorus of women, striking their tymbals, and displaying the pomp of their nuptials, sung in the presence of their sons and husbands the felicity of their native tribe—that a champion had now appeared to vindicate their rights—that a herald had raised his voice to immortalise their renown. The distant or hostile tribes resorted to an annual fair, which was abolished by the fanaticism of the first Moslems—a national assembly that must have contributed to refine and harmonise the barbarians. Thirty days were employed in the exchange, not only of the corn and wine, but of eloquence and poetry. The prize was disputed by the generous emulation of the bards; the victorious performance was deposited in the archives of princes and emirs; and we may read in our own language the seven original poems which were inscribed in letters of gold, and suspended in the temple of Mecca. The Arabian poets were the historians and moralists of the age; and if they sympathised with the prejudices, they inspired and crowned the virtues, of their countrymen. The indissoluble union of generosity and valour was the darling theme of their song; and when they pointed their keenest satire against a despicable race, they affirmed, in the bitterness of reproach, that the men knew not how to give, nor the women to deny. The same hospitality which was practised by Abraham, and celebrated by Homer, is still renewed in the camps of the Arabs. The ferocious Bedoweens, the terror of the desert, embrace, without inquiry or hesitation, the stranger who dares to confide in their honour and to enter their tent. His treatment is kind and respectful: he shares the wealth or the poverty of his host; and, after a needful repose, he is dismissed on his way with thanks, with blessings, and perhaps with gifts. The heart and hand are more largely expanded by the wants of a brother or a friend; but the heroic acts that could deserve the public applause must have surpassed the narrow measure of discretion and experience. A dispute had arisen, who among the citizens of Mecca was entitled to the prize of generosity; and a successive application was made to the three who were deemed most worthy of the trial. Abdallah, the son of Abbas, had undertaken a distant journey, and his foot was in the stirrup, when he heard the voice of a suppliant, "O son of the uncle of the apostle of God, I am a traveller, and in distress!" He instantly dismounted to present the pilgrim with his camel, her rich caparison, and a purse of four thousand pieces of gold, accepting only the sword, either for its intrinsic value, or as the gift of an honoured kinsman. The servant of Kais informed the second suppliant that his master was asleep: but he immediately added, "Here is a purse of seven thousand pieces of gold (it is all we have in the house), and here is an order that will entitle you to a camel and a slave"; the master, as soon as he awoke, praised and enfranchised his faithful steward, with a gentle reproof, that by respecting his slumbers he had stinted his bounty. The third of the heroes, the blind Arabah, at the hour of prayer, was supporting his steps on the shoulders of two slaves. "Alas!" he replied, "my coffers are empty! but these you may sell; if you refuse, I renounce them." At these words, pushing away the youths, he groped along the wall with his staff. The character of Hatem is the perfect model of Arabian virtue: he was brave and liberal, an eloquent poet, and a successful robber: forty camels were roasted at his hospitable feast; and at the prayer of a suppliant enemy he restored both the captives and the spoil. The freedom of his countrymen disdained the laws of justice; they proudly indulged the spontaneous impulse of pity and benevolence.

THE RELIGION OF THE ARABS

The religion of the Arabs, as well as of the Indians, consisted in the worship of the sun, the moon, and the fixed stars; a primitive and specious mode of superstition. The bright luminaries of the sky display the visible image of a Deity: their number and distance convey to a philosophic, or even a vulgar, eye the idea of boundless space: the character of eternity is marked on these solid globes, that seem incapable of corruption or decay: the regularity of their motions may be ascribed to a principle of reason or instinct; and their real or imaginary influence encourages the vain belief that the earth and its inhabitants are the object of their peculiar care. The science of astronomy was cultivated at Babylon; but the school of the Arabs was a clear firmament and a naked plain. In their nocturnal marches they steered by the guidance of the stars; their names, and order, and daily station were familiar to the curiosity and devotion of the Bedoween; and he was taught by experience to divide in twenty-eight parts the zodiac of the moon, and to bless the constellations who refreshed with salutary rains the thirst of the desert. The reign of the heavenly orbs could not be extended beyond the visible sphere; and some metaphysical powers were necessary to sustain the transmigration of souls and the resurrection of bodies: a camel was left to perish on the grave, that he might serve his master in another life; and the invocation of departed spirits implies that they were still endowed with consciousness and power. I am ignorant, and I am careless, of the blind mythology of the barbarians—of the local deities, of the stars, the air, and the earth, of their sex or titles, their attributes or subordination. Each tribe, each family, each independent warrior, created and changed the rites and the object of his fantastic worship; but the nation, in every age, has bowed to the religion as well as to the language of Mecca. The genuine antiquity of the CAABA ascends beyond the Christian era; in describing the coast of the Red Sea the Greek historian Diodorus has remarked, between the Thamudites and the Sabæans, a famous temple, whose superior sanctity was revered by *all* the Arabians; the linen or silken veil, which is annually renewed by the Turkish emperor, was first offered by a pious king of the Homerites, who reigned seven hundred years before the time of Mahomet. A tent or a cavern might suffice for the worship of the savages, but an edifice of stone and clay has been erected in its place; and the art and power of the monarchs of the East have been confined to the simplicity of the original model. A spacious portico encloses the quadrangle of the Caaba—a square chapel twenty-four cubits long, twenty-three broad, and twenty-seven high: a door and a window admit the light; the double roof is supported by three pillars of wood; a spout (now of gold) discharges the rain-water, and the well Zemzem is protected by a dome from accidental pollution. The tribe of Koreish, by fraud or force, had acquired the custody of the Caaba: the sacerdotal office devolved through four lineal descents to the grandfather of Mahomet; and the family of the Hashemites, from whence he sprung, was the most respectable and sacred in the eyes of their country. The precincts of Mecca enjoyed the rights of sanctuary; and in the last month of each year the city and the temple were crowded with a long train of pilgrims, who presented their vows and offerings in the house of God. The same rites which are now accomplished by the faithful Musulman were invented and practised by the superstition of the idolaters. At an awful distance they cast away their garments: seven times with hasty steps they encircled the Caaba, and kissed the black stone: seven times they visited and adored the adjacent mountains: seven times they threw stones into the valley of Mina; and the pilgrimage was achieved as at the present hour, by a sacrifice of sheep and camels, and the burial of their hair and nails in the consecrated ground. Each tribe either found or introduced in the Caaba their domestic worship: the temple was adorned, or defiled, with three hundred and sixty idols of men, eagles, lions, and antelopes; and most conspicuous was the statue of Hebal, of red agate, holding in his hand seven arrows without heads or feathers, the instruments and symbols of profane divination. But this statue was a monument of Syrian arts: the devotion of the ruder ages was content with a pillar or a tablet; and the rocks of the desert were hewn into gods or altars in imitation of the black stone of Mecca, which is deeply tainted with the reproach of an idolatrous origin. From Japan to Peru the use of sacrifice has universally prevailed; and the votary has expressed his gratitude or fear by destroying or consuming, in honour of the gods, the dearest and most precious of their gifts. The life of a man is the most precious oblation to deprecate a public calamity: the altars of Phœnicia and Egypt, of Rome and Carthage, have been polluted with human gore: the cruel practice was long preserved among the Arabs; in the third century a boy was annually sacrificed by the tribe of the Dumatians; and a royal captive was piously slaughtered by the prince of the Saracens, the ally and soldier of the emperor Justinian. A parent who drags his son to the altar exhibits the most painful and sublime effort of fanaticism: the deed or the intention was sanctified by the example of saints and heroes; and the father of Mahomet himself was devoted by a rash vow, and hardly ransomed for the equivalent of an hundred camels. In the time of ignorance the Arabs, like the Jews and Egyptians, abstained from the taste of swine's flesh; they circumcised [1] their children at the age of puberty: the same customs, without the censure or the precept of the Koran, have been silently transmitted to their posterity and proselytes. It has been sagaciously conjectured that the artful legislator indulged the stubborn prejudices of his countrymen. It is more simple to believe that he adhered to the habits and opinions of his youth, without foreseeing that a practice congenial to the

---

[1] The Mahometan doctors are not fond of the subject; yet they hold circumcision necessary to salvation, and even pretend that Mahomet was miraculously born without a foreskin.

climate of Mecca might become useless or inconvenient on the
banks of the Danube or the Volga.

Arabia was free: the adjacent kingdoms were shaken by the
storms of conquest and tyranny, and the persecuted sects fled
to the happy land where they might profess what they thought,
and practise what they professed. The religions of the Sabians
and Magians, of the Jews and Christians, were disseminated
from the Persian Gulf to the Red Sea. In a remote period of
antiquity Sabianism was diffused over Asia by the science of
the Chaldæans and the arms of the Assyrians. From the observations of two thousand years the priests and astronomers
of Babylon deduced the eternal laws of nature and providence.
They adored the seven gods, or angels, who directed the
course of the seven planets, and shed their irresistible influence on the earth. The attributes of the seven planets, with
the twelve signs of the zodiac, and the twenty-four constellations of the northern and southern hemisphere, were represented by images and talismans; the seven days of the week
were dedicated to their respective deities; the Sabians prayed
thrice each day; and the temple of the moon at Haran was
the term of their pilgrimage. But the flexible genius of their
faith was always ready either to teach or to learn: in the
tradition of the creation, the deluge, and the patriarchs, they
held a singular agreement with their Jewish captives; they
appealed to the secret books of Adam, Seth, and Enoch; and
a slight infusion of the Gospel has transformed the last remnant of the Polytheists into the Christians of St. John, in
the territory of Bassora. The altars of Babylon were overturned by the Magians; but the injuries of the Sabians were
revenged by the sword of Alexander; Persia groaned above
five hundred years under a foreign yoke; and the purest disciples of Zoroaster escaped from the contagion of idolatry, and
breathed with their adversaries the freedom of the desert.
Seven hundred years before the death of Mahomet the Jews
were settled in Arabia; and a far greater multitude was expelled from the Holy Land in the wars of Titus and Hadrian.
The industrious exiles aspired to liberty and power: they
erected synagogues in the cities, and castles in the wilderness;
and their Gentile converts were confounded with the children
of Israel, whom they resembled in the outward mark of circumcision. The Christian missionaries were still more active
and successful: the Catholics asserted their universal reign;

the sects whom they oppressed successively retired beyond the limits of the Roman empire; the Marcionites and Manichæans dispersed their *fantastic* opinions and apocryphal gospels; the churches of Yemen, and the princes of Hira and Gassan, were instructed in a purer creed by the Jacobite and Nestorian bishops. The liberty of choice was presented to the tribes: each Arab was free to elect or to compose his private religion; and the rude superstition of his house was mingled with the sublime theology of saints and philosophers. A fundamental article of faith was inculcated by the consent of the learned strangers, the existence of one supreme God, who is exalted above the powers of heaven and earth, but who has often revealed himself to mankind by the ministry of his angels and prophets, and whose grace or justice has interrupted, by seasonable miracles, the order of nature. The most rational of the Arabs acknowledged his power, though they neglected his worship; and it was habit rather than conviction that still attached them to the relics of idolatry. The Jews and Christians were the people of the *Book;* the Bible was already translated into the Arabic language, and the volume of the Old Testament was accepted by the concord of these implacable enemies. In the story of the Hebrew patriarchs the Arabs were pleased to discover the fathers of their nation. They applauded the birth and promises of Ismael; revered the faith and virtue of Abraham; traced his pedigree and their own to the creation of the first man, and imbibed with equal credulity the prodigies of the holy text, and the dreams and traditions of the Jewish rabbis.

THE RISE OF MAHOMET

The base and plebeian origin of Mahomet is an unskilful calumny of the Christians, who exalt instead of degrading the merit of their adversary. His descent from Ismael was a national privilege or fable; but if the first steps of the pedigree are dark and doubtful, he could produce many generations of pure and genuine nobility: he sprung from the tribe of Koreish and the family of Hashem, the most illustrious of the Arabs, the princes of Mecca, and the hereditary guardians of the Caaba. The grandfather of Mahomet was Abdol Motalleb, the son of Hashem, a wealthy and generous citizen, who relieved the distress of famine with the supplies of commerce.

Mecca, which had been fed by the liberality of the father, was saved by the courage of the son. The kingdom of Yemen was subject to the Christian princes of Abyssinia: their vassal Abrahah was provoked by an insult to avenge the honour of the cross; and the holy city was invested by a train of elephants and an army of Africans. A treaty was proposed; and, in the first audience, the grandfather of Mahomet demanded the restitution of his cattle. "And why," said Abrahah, "do you not rather implore my clemency in favour of your temple, which I have threatened to destroy?" "Because," replied the intrepid chief, "the cattle is my own; the Caaba belongs to the gods, and *they* will defend their house from injury and sacrilege." The want of provisions, or the valour of the Koreish, compelled the Abyssinians to a disgraceful retreat: their discomfiture has been adorned with a miraculous flight of birds, who showered down stones on the heads of the infidels; and the deliverance was long commemorated by the era of the elephant. The glory of Abdol Motalleb was crowned with domestic happiness; his life was prolonged to the age of one hundred and ten years; and he became the father of six daughters and thirteen sons. His best beloved Abdallah was the most beautiful and modest of the Arabian youth; and in the first night, when he consummated his marriage with Amina, of the noble race of the Zahrites, two hundred virgins are said to have expired of jealousy and despair. Mahomet, or more properly Mohammed, the only son of Abdallah and Amina, was born at Mecca, four years after the death of Justinian, and two months after the defeat of the Abyssinians, whose victory would have introduced into the Caaba the religion of the Christians. In his early infancy he was deprived of his father, his mother, and his grandfather; his uncles were strong and numerous; and, in the division of the inheritance, the orphan's share was reduced to five camels and an Ethiopian maid-servant. At home and abroad, in peace and war, Abu Taleb, the most respectable of his uncles, was the guide and guardian of his youth; in his twenty-fifth year he entered into the service of Cadijah, a rich and noble widow of Mecca, who soon rewarded his fidelity with the gift of her hand and fortune. The marriage contract, in the simple style of antiquity, recites the mutual love of Mahomet and Cadijah; describes him as the most accomplished of the tribe of Koreish; and stipulates a dowry of twelve ounces of gold and twenty camels, which was supplied by the liberality of his uncle. By this alliance the son of Abdallah was restored to the station of his ancestors; and the judicious matron was content with his domestic virtues, till, in the fortieth year of his age, he assumed the title of a prophet, and proclaimed the religion of the Koran.

According to the tradition of his companions, Mahomet was distinguished by the beauty of his person, an outward gift which is seldom despised, except by those to whom it has been refused. Before he spoke, the orator engaged on his side the affections of a public or private audience. They applauded his commanding presence, his majestic aspect, his piercing eye, his gracious smile, his flowing beard, his countenance that painted every sensation of the soul, and his gestures that enforced each expression of the tongue. In the familiar offices of life he scrupulously adhered to the grave and ceremonious politeness of his country; his respectful attention to the rich and powerful was dignified by his condescension and affability to the poorest citizens of Mecca: the frankness of his manner concealed the artifice of his views; and the habits of courtesy were imputed to personal friendship or universal benevolence. His memory was capacious and retentive; his wit easy and social; his imagination sublime; his judgment clear, rapid, and decisive. He possessed the courage both of thought and action; and, although his designs might gradually expand with his success, the first idea which he entertained of his divine mission bears the stamp of an original and superior genius. The son of Abdallah was educated in the bosom of the noblest race, in the use of the purest dialect of Arabia; and the fluency of his speech was corrected and enhanced by the practice of discreet and seasonable silence. With these powers of eloquence, Mahomet was an illiterate barbarian: his youth had never been instructed in the arts of reading and writing; the common ignorance exempted him from shame or reproach, but he was reduced to a narrow circle of existence, and deprived of those faithful mirrors which reflect to our mind the minds of sages and heroes. Yet the book of nature and of man was open to his view; and some fancy has been indulged in the political and philosophical observations which are ascribed to the Arabian *traveller*. He compares the nations and the religions of the earth; discovers the weakness of the Persian and Roman monarchies; beholds with pity and indignation the degeneracy of the times; and resolves to unite under one God and one king the invincible spirit and primitive virtues of the Arabs. Our more accurate inquiry will suggest, that, instead of visiting the courts, the camps, the temples of the East, the two journeys of Mahomet into Syria were confined to the fairs of Bostra and Damascus; that he was only thirteen years of age when he accompanied the caravan of his uncle; and that his duty compelled him to return as soon as he had disposed of the merchandise of Cadijah. In these hasty and superficial excursions the eye of genius might discern some objects invisible to his grosser companions; some seeds of knowledge might be cast upon a fruitful soil; but his ignorance of the Syriac language must have checked his curiosity; and I cannot perceive in the life or writings of Mahomet that his prospect was far extended beyond the limits of the Arabian world. From every region of that solitary world the pilgrims of Mecca were annually assembled by the calls of devotion and commerce: in the free concourse of multitudes, a simple citizen, in his native tongue, might study the political state and character of the tribes, the theory and practice of the Jews and Christians. Some useful strangers might be tempted, or forced, to implore the rights of hospitality; and the enemies of Mahomet have named the Jew, the Persian, and the Syrian monk, whom they accuse of lending their secret aid to the composition of the Koran. Conversation enriches the understanding, but solitude is the school of genius; and the uniformity of a work denotes the hand of a single artist. From his earliest youth Mahomet was addicted to religious contemplation; each year, during the month of Ramadan, he withdrew from the world and from the arms of Cadijah: in the cave of Hera, three miles from Mecca, he consulted the spirit of fraud or enthusiasm, whose abode is not in the heavens, but in the mind of the prophet. The faith which, under the name of *Islam,* he preached to his family and nation, is compounded of an eternal truth and a necessary fiction, THAT THERE IS ONLY ONE GOD, AND THAT MAHOMET IS THE APOSTLE OF GOD.

It is the boast of the Jewish apologists, that, while the learned nations of antiquity were deluded by the fables of polytheism, their simple ancestors of Palestine preserved the knowledge and worship of the true God. The moral attributes of Jehovah may not easily be reconciled with the standard of

human virtue: his metaphysical qualities are darkly expressed;
but each page of the Pentateuch and the Prophets is an
evidence of his power: the unity of his name is inscribed in
the first table of the law; and his sanctuary was never defiled
by any visible image of the invisible essence. After the ruin
of the temple, the faith of the Hebrew exiles was purified,
fixed, and enlightened by the spiritual devotion of the synagogue; and the authority of Mahomet will not justify his
perpetual reproach that the Jews of Mecca or Medina adored
Ezra as the son of God. But the children of Israel had ceased
to be a people; and the religions of the world were guilty, at
least in the eyes of the prophet, of giving sons, or daughters,
or companions to the supreme God. In the rude idolatry of
the Arabs the crime is manifest and audacious: the Sabians
are poorly excused by the pre-eminence of the first planet,
or intelligence, in their celestial hierarchy; and in the Magian
system the conflict of the two principles betrays the imperfection of the conqueror. The Christians of the seventh century
had insensibly relapsed into a semblance of paganism; their
public and private vows were addressed to the relics and
images that disgraced the temples of the East: the throne of
the Almighty was darkened by a cloud of martyrs, and saints,
and angels, the objects of popular veneration; and the Colly-
ridian heretics, who flourished in the fruitful soil of Arabia,
invested the Virgin Mary with the name and honours of a
goddess. The mysteries of the Trinity and Incarnation *appear*
to contradict the principle of the divine unity. In their obvious
sense, they introduce three equal deities, and transform the
man Jesus into the substance of the Son of God: an orthodox
commentary will satisfy only a believing mind: intemperate
curiosity and zeal had torn the veil of the sanctuary: and
each of the Oriental sects was eager to confess that all, except
themselves, deserved the reproach of idolatry and polytheism.
The creed of Mahomet is free from suspicion or ambiguity;
and the Koran is a glorious testimony to the unity of God.
The prophet of Mecca rejected the worship of idols and men,
of stars and planets, on the rational principle that whatever
rises must set, that whatever is born must die, that whatever
is corruptible must decay and perish. In the Author of the
universe his rational enthusiasm confessed and adored an
infinite and eternal being, without form or place, without issue
or similitude, present to our most secret thoughts, existing

by the necessity of his own nature, and deriving from himself all moral and intellectual perfection. These sublime truths, thus announced in the language of the prophet, are firmly held by his disciples, and defined with metaphysical precision by the interpreters of the Koran. A philosophic theist might subscribe the popular creed of the Mahometans: a creed too sublime perhaps for our present faculties. What object remains for the fancy, or even the understanding, when we have abstracted from the unknown substance all ideas of time and space, of motion and matter, of sensation and reflection? The first principle of reason and revelation was confirmed by the voice of Mahomet: his proselytes, from India to Morocco, are distinguished by the name of *Unitarians;* and the danger of idolatry has been prevented by the interdiction of images. The doctrine of eternal decrees and absolute predestination is strictly embraced by the Mahometans; and they struggle with the common difficulties, *how* to reconcile the prescience of God with the freedom and responsibility of man; *how* to explain the permission of evil under the reign of infinite power and infinite goodness.

The God of nature has written his existence on all his works, and his law in the heart of man. To restore the knowledge of the one, and the practice of the other, has been the real or pretended aim of the prophets of every age: the liberality of Mahomet allowed to his predecessors the same credit which he claimed for himself; and the chain of inspiration was prolonged from the fall of Adam to the promulgation of the Koran. During that period some rays of prophetic light had been imparted to one hundred and twenty-four thousand of the elect, discriminated by their respective measure of virtue and grace; three hundred and thirteen apostles were sent with a special commission to recall their country from idolatry and vice; one hundred and four volumes have been dictated by the Holy Spirit; and six legislators of transcendent brightness have announced to mankind the six successive revelations of various rites, but of one immutable religion. The authority and station of Adam, Noah, Abraham, Moses, Christ, and Mahomet, rise in just gradation above each other; but whosoever hates or rejects any one of the prophets is numbered with the infidels. The writings of the patriarchs were extant only in the apocryphal copies of the Greeks and Syrians: the conduct of Adam had not entitled him to the gratitude of his children; the seven precepts of Noah were observed by an inferior and imperfect class of the proselytes of the synagogue; and the memory of Abraham was obscurely revered by the Sabians in his native land of Chaldæa: of the myriads of prophets, Moses and Christ alone lived and reigned; and the remnant of the inspired writings was comprised in the books of the Old and the New Testament. The miraculous story of Moses is consecrated and embellished in the Koran; and the captive Jews enjoy the secret revenge of imposing their own belief on the nations whose recent creeds they deride. For the author of Christianity, the Mahometans are taught by the prophet to entertain a high and mysterious reverence. "Verily, Christ Jesus, the son of Mary, is the apostle of God, and his word, which he conveyed unto Mary, and a Spirit proceeding from him: honourable in this world, and in the world to come; and one of those who approach near to the presence of God." The wonders of the genuine and apocryphal gospels are profusely heaped on his head; and the Latin church has not disdained to borrow from the Koran the immaculate conception [1] of his virgin mother. Yet Jesus was a mere mortal; and, at the day of judgment, his testimony will serve to condemn both the Jews, who reject him as a prophet, and the Christians, who adore him as the Son of God. The malice of his enemies aspersed his reputation, and conspired against his life; but their intention only was guilty; a phantom or a criminal was substituted on the cross; and the innocent saint was translated to the seventh heaven. During six hundred years the Gospel was the way of truth and salvation; but the Christians insensibly forgot both the laws and the example of their founder; and Mahomet was instructed by the Gnostics to accuse the church, as well as the synagogue, of corrupting the integrity of the sacred text. The piety of Moses and of Christ rejoiced in the assurance of a future Prophet, more illustrious than themselves: the evangelic promise of the *Paraclete,* or Holy Ghost, was prefigured in the name, and accomplished in the person, of Mahomet, the greatest and the last of the apostles of God.

The communication of ideas requires a similitude of

---

[1] It is darkly hinted in the Koran, and more clearly explained by the tradition of the Sonnites. In the xiith century, the immaculate conception was condemned by St. Bernard as a presumptuous novelty.

thought and language: the discourse of a philosopher would vibrate without effect on the ear of a peasant; yet how minute is the distance of *their* understandings, if it be compared with the contact of an infinite and a finite mind, with the word of God expressed by the tongue or the pen of a mortal? The inspiration of the Hebrew prophets, of the apostles and evangelists of Christ, might not be incompatible with the exercise of their reason and memory; and the diversity of their genius is strongly marked in the style and composition of the books of the Old and New Testament. But Mahomet was content with a character more humble, yet more sublime, of a simple editor; the substance of the Koran, according to himself or his disciples, is uncreated and eternal; subsisting in the essence of the Deity, and inscribed with a pen of light on the table of his everlasting decrees. A paper copy, in a volume of silk and gems, was brought down to the lowest heaven by the angel Gabriel, who, under the Jewish economy, had indeed been despatched on the most important errands; and this trusty messenger successively revealed the chapters and verses to the Arabian prophet. Instead of a perpetual and perfect measure of the divine will, the fragments of the Koran were produced at the discretion of Mahomet; each revelation is suited to the emergencies of his policy or passion; and all contradiction is removed by the saving maxim that any text of Scripture is abrogated or modified by any subsequent passage. The word of God and of the apostle was diligently recorded by his disciples on palm-leaves and the shoulder-bones of mutton; and the pages, without order or connection, were cast into a domestic chest in the custody of one of his wives. Two years after the death of Mahomet, the sacred volume was collected and published by his friend and successor Abubeker: the work was revised by the caliph Othman, in the thirtieth year of the Hegira; and the various editions of the Koran assert the same miraculous privilege of an uniform and incorruptible text. In the spirit of enthusiasm or vanity, the prophet rests the truth of his mission on the merit of his book; audaciously challenges both men and angels to imitate the beauties of a single page; and presumes to assert that God alone could dictate this incomparable performance. This argument is most powerfully addressed to a devout Arabian, whose mind is attuned to faith and rapture; whose ear is delighted by the music of sounds; and whose ignorance is incapable of comparing the productions of human genius. The harmony and copiousness of style will not reach, in a version, the European infidel: he will peruse with impatience the endless incoherent rhapsody of fable, and precept, and declamation, which seldom excites a sentiment or an idea, which sometimes crawls in the dust, and is sometimes lost in the clouds. The divine attributes exalt the fancy of the Arabian missionary; but his loftiest strains must yield to the sublime simplicity of the book of Job, composed in a remote age, in the same country, and in the same language. If the composition of the Koran exceed the faculties of a man, to what superior intelligence should we ascribe the Iliad of Homer, or the Philippics of Demosthenes? In all religions the life of the founder supplies the silence of his written revelation: the sayings of Mahomet were so many lessons of truth; his actions so many examples of virtue; and the public and private memorials were preserved by his wives and companions. At the end of two hundred years the *Sonna,* or oral law, was fixed and consecrated by the labours of Al Bochari, who discriminated seven thousand two hundred and seventy-five genuine traditions, from a mass of three hundred thousand reports of a more doubtful or spurious character. Each day the pious author prayed in the temple of Mecca, and performed his ablutions with the water of Zemzem: the pages were successively deposited on the pulpit and the sepulchre of the apostle; and the work has been approved by the four orthodox sects of the Sonnites.

The mission of the ancient prophets, of Moses and of Jesus, had been confirmed by many splendid prodigies; and Mahomet was repeatedly urged, by the inhabitants of Mecca and Medina, to produce a similar evidence of his divine legation; to call down from heaven the angel or the volume of his revelation, to create a garden in the desert, or to kindle a conflagration in the unbelieving city. As often as he is pressed by the demands of the Koreish, he involves himself in the obscure boast of vision and prophecy, appeals to the internal proofs of his doctrine, and shields himself behind the providence of God, who refuses those signs and wonders that would depreciate the merit of faith and aggravate the guilt of infidelity. But the modest or angry tone of his apologies betrays his weakness and vexation; and these passages of scandal established beyond suspicion the integrity of the Koran. The votaries of Mahomet are more assured than himself of his miraculous gifts; and their confidence and credulity increase as they are farther removed from the time and place of his spiritual exploits. They believe or affirm that trees went forth to meet him; that he was saluted by stones; that water gushed from his fingers; that he fed the hungry, cured the sick, and raised the dead; that a beam groaned to him; that a camel complained to him; that a shoulder of mutton informed him of its being poisoned; and that both animate and inanimate nature were equally subject to the apostle of God. His dream of a nocturnal journey is seriously described as a real and corporeal trans-action. A mysterious animal, the Borak, conveyed him from the temple of Mecca to that of Jerusalem: with his com-panion Gabriel he successively ascended the seven heavens, and received and repaid the salutations of the patriarchs, the prophets, and the angels, in their respective mansions. Beyond the seventh heaven Mahomet alone was permitted to proceed; he passed the veil of unity within two bow-shots of the throne, and felt a cold that pierced him to the heart, when his shoulder was touched by the hand of God. After this familiar though important conversation, he again descended to Jerusalem, remounted the Borak, returned to Mecca, and performed in the tenth part of a night the journey of many thousand years. According to another legend, the apostle confounded in a national assembly the malicious challenge of the Koreish. His resistless word split asunder the orb of the moon: the obedient planet stooped from her station in the sky, accom-plished the seven revolutions round the Caaba, saluted Ma-homet in the Arabian tongue, and, suddenly contracting her dimensions, entered at the collar, and issued forth through the sleeve, of his shirt. The vulgar are amused with these marvellous tales; but the gravest of the Musulman doctors imitate the modesty of their master, and indulge a latitude of faith or interpretation. They might speciously allege, that in preaching the religion it was needless to violate the har-mony of nature; that a creed unclouded with mystery may be excused from miracles; and that the sword of Mahomet was not less potent than the rod of Moses.

PRECEPTS OF MAHOMET

The polytheist is oppressed and distracted by the variety of superstition: a thousand rites of Egyptian origin were interwoven with the essence of the Mosaic law; and the spirit of the Gospel had evaporated in the pageantry of the church. The prophet of Mecca was tempted by prejudice, or policy, or patriotism, to sanctify the rites of the Arabians, and the custom of visiting the holy stone of the Caaba. But the precepts of Mahomet himself inculcate a more simple and rational piety: prayer, fasting, and alms are the religious duties of a Musulman; and he is encouraged to hope that prayer will carry him half way to God, fasting will bring him to the door of his palace, and alms will gain him admittance. I. According to the tradition of the nocturnal journey, the apostle, in his personal conference with the Deity, was commanded to impose on his disciples the daily obligation of fifty prayers. By the advice of Moses, he applied for an alleviation of this intolerable burden; the number was gradually reduced to five; without any dispensation of business or pleasure, or time or place: the devotion of the faithful is repeated at daybreak, at noon, in the afternoon, in the evening, and at the first watch of the night; and in the present decay of religious fervour, our travellers are edified by the profound humility and attention of the Turks and Persians. Cleanliness is the key of prayer: the frequent lustration of the hands, the face, and the body, which was practised of old by the Arabs, is solemnly enjoined by the Koran; and a permission is formally granted to supply with sand the scarcity of water. The words and attitudes of supplication, as it is performed either sitting, or standing, or prostrate on the ground, are prescribed by custom or authority; but the prayer is poured forth in short and fervent ejaculations; the measure of zeal is not exhausted by a tedious liturgy; and each Musulman for his own person is invested with the character of a priest. Among the theists, who reject the use of images, it has been found necessary to restrain the wanderings of the fancy, by directing the eye and the thought towards a *kebla* or visible point of the horizon. The prophet was at first inclined to gratify the Jews by the choice of Jerusalem; but he soon returned to a more natural partiality; and five times every day the eyes of the nations at Astracan, at Fez, at Delhi, are devoutly turned to the holy temple of Mecca. Yet every spot for the service of God is equally pure: the Mahometans indifferently pray in their chamber or in the street. As a distinction from the Jews and Christians, the Friday in each week is set apart for the useful institution of public worship: the people is assembled in the mosque; and the imam, some respectable elder, ascends the pulpit, to begin the prayer and pronounce the sermon. But the Mahometan religion is destitute of priesthood or sacrifice; and the independent spirit of fanaticism looks down with contempt on the ministers and the slaves of superstition. II. The voluntary penance of the ascetics, the torment and glory of their lives, was odious to a prophet who censured in his companions a rash vow of abstaining from flesh, and women, and sleep; and firmly declared that he would suffer no monks in his religion. Yet he instituted, in each year, a fast of thirty days; and strenuously recommended the observance as a discipline which purifies the soul and subdues the body, as a salutary exercise of obedience to the will of God and his apostle. During the month of Ramadan, from the rising to the setting of the sun, the Musulman abstains from eating, and drinking, and women, and baths, and perfumes; from all nourishment that can restore his strength, from all pleasure that can gratify his senses. In the revolution of the lunar year, the Ramadan coincides, by turns, with the winter cold and the summer heat; and the patient martyr, without assuaging his thirst with a drop of water, must expect the close of a tedious and sultry day. The interdiction of wine, peculiar to some orders of priests or hermits, is converted by Mahomet alone into a positive and general law; and a considerable portion of the globe has abjured, at his command, the use of that salutary, though dangerous liquor. These painful restraints are, doubtless, infringed by the libertine, and eluded by the hypocrite; but the legislator, by whom they are enacted, cannot surely be accused of alluring his proselytes by the indulgence of their sensual appetites. III. The charity of the Mahometans descends to the animal creation; and the Koran repeatedly inculcates, not as a merit, but as a strict and indispensable duty, the relief of the indigent and unfortunate. Mahomet, perhaps, is the only lawgiver who has defined the precise measure of charity: the standard may vary with the degree and nature of property, as it consists either in money, in corn or cattle, in fruits or merchandise: but the Musulman does not accomplish the law, unless he bestows a *tenth* of his revenue; and if his conscience accuses him of fraud or extortion, the tenth, under the idea of restitution, is enlarged to a *fifth*.[1] Benevolence is the foundation of justice, since we are forbid to injure those whom we are bound to assist. A prophet may reveal the secrets of heaven and of futurity: but in his moral precepts he can only repeat the lessons of our own hearts.

The two articles of belief, and the four practical duties, of Islam, are guarded by rewards and punishments; and the faith of the Musulman is devoutly fixed on the event of the judgment and the last day. The prophet has not presumed to determine the moment of that awful catastrophe, though he darkly announces the signs, both in heaven and earth, which will precede the universal dissolution, when life shall be destroyed, and the order of creation shall be confounded in the primitive chaos. At the blast of the trumpet new worlds will start into being; angels, genii, and men will arise from the dead, and the human soul will again be united to the body. The doctrine of the resurrection was first entertained by the Egyptians; and their mummies were embalmed, their pyramids were constructed, to preserve the ancient mansion of the soul during a period of three thousand years. But the attempt is partial and unavailing; and it is with a more philosophic spirit that Mahomet relies on the omnipotence of the Creator, whose word can re-animate the breathless clay, and collect the innumerable atoms that no longer retain their form or substance. The intermediate state of the soul it is hard to decide; and those who most firmly believe her immaterial nature, are at a loss to understand how she can think or act without the agency of the organs of sense.

The re-union of the soul and body will be followed by the final judgment of mankind; and in his copy of the Magian picture, the prophet has too faithfully represented the forms of proceeding, and even the slow and successive operations,

---

[1] The jealousy of Maracci prompts him to enumerate the more liberal alms of the Catholics of Rome. Fifteen great hospitals are open to many thousand patients and pilgrims; fifteen hundred maidens are annually portioned; fifty-six charity-schools are founded for both sexes; one hundred and twenty confraternities relieve the wants of their brethren, etc. The benevolence of London is still more extensive; but I am afraid that much more is to be ascribed to the humanity than to the religion of the people.

of an earthly tribunal. By his intolerant adversaries he is up-
braided for extending, even to themselves, the hope of
salvation; for asserting the blackest heresy, that every man
who believes in God, and accomplishes good works, may expect in the last day a favourable sentence. Such rational indifference is ill adapted to the character of a fanatic; nor is it
probable that a messenger from heaven should depreciate the
value and necessity of his own revelation. In the idiom of
the Koran, the belief of God is inseparable from that of Mahomet: the good works are those which he has enjoined; and
the two qualifications imply the profession of Islam, to which
all nations and all sects are equally invited. Their spiritual
blindness, though excused by ignorance and crowned with
virtue, will be scourged with everlasting torments; and the
tears which Mahomet shed over the tomb of his mother, for
whom he was forbidden to pray, display a striking contrast
of humanity and enthusiasm. The doom of the infidels is
common: the measure of their guilt and punishment is determined by the degree of evidence which they have rejected, by the magnitude of the errors which they have
entertained: the eternal mansions of the Christians, the Jews,
the Sabians, the Magians, and the idolators are sunk below
each other in the abyss: and the lowest hell is reserved for
the faithless hypocrites who have assumed the mask of
religion. After the greater part of mankind has been condemned for their opinions, the true believers only will be
judged by their actions. The good and evil of each Musulman
will be accurately weighed in a real or allegorical balance;
and a singular mode of compensation will be allowed for
the payment of injuries: the aggressor will refund an equivalent of his own good actions, for the benefit of the person
whom he has wronged; and if he should be destitute of any
moral property, the weight of his sins will be loaded with
an adequate share of the demerits of the sufferer. According
as the shares of guilt or virtue shall preponderate, the
sentence will be pronounced, and all, without distinction, will
pass over the sharp and perilous bridge of the abyss; but the
innocent, treading in the footsteps of Mahomet, will glorious-
ly enter the gates of paradise, while the guilty will fall into
the first and mildest of the seven hells. The term of expiation
will vary from nine hundred to seven thousand years; but
the prophet has judiciously promised that *all* his disciples,

whatever may be their sins, shall be saved, by their own faith and his intercession, from eternal damnation. It is not surprising that superstition should act most powerfully on the fears of her votaries, since the human fancy can paint with more energy the misery than the bliss of a future life. With the two simple elements of darkness and fire we create a sensation of pain, which may be aggravated to an infinite degree by the idea of endless duration. But the same idea operates with an opposite effect on the continuity of pleasure; and too much of our present enjoyments is obtained from the relief, or the comparison, of evil. It is natural enough that an Arabian prophet should dwell with rapture on the groves, the fountains, and the rivers of paradise; but instead of inspiring the blessed inhabitants with a liberal taste for harmony and science, conversation and friendship, he idly celebrates the pearls and diamonds, the robes of silk, palaces of marble, dishes of gold, rich wines, artificial dainties, numerous attendants, and the whole train of sensual and costly luxury, which becomes insipid to the owner, even in the short period of this mortal life. Seventy-two *Houris*, or black-eyed girls, of resplendent beauty, blooming youth, virgin purity, and exquisite sensibility, will be created for the use of the meanest believer; a moment of pleasure will be prolonged to a thousand years, and his faculties will be increased an hundred fold, to render him worthy of his felicity. Notwithstanding a vulgar prejudice, the gates of heaven will be open to both sexes; but Mahomet has not specified the male companions of the female elect, lest he should either alarm the jealousy of their former husbands, or disturb their felicity by the suspicion of an everlasting marriage. This image of a carnal paradise has provoked the indignation, perhaps the envy, of the monks: they declaim against the impure religion of Mahomet; and his modest apologists are driven to the poor excuse of figures and allegories. But the sounder and more consistent party adhere, without shame, to the literal interpretation of the Koran: useless would be the resurrection of the body, unless it were restored to the possession and exercise of its worthiest faculties; and the union of sensual and intellectual enjoyment is requisite to complete the happiness of the double animal, the perfect man. Yet the joys of the Mahometan paradise will not be confined to the indulgence of luxury and appetite; and the prophet has expressly declared that all meaner happiness will be forgotten and despised by the saints and martyrs, who shall be admitted to the beatitude of the divine vision.

MAHOMET'S FLIGHT FROM MECCA TO MEDINA

The first and most arduous conquests of Mahomet were those of his wife, his servant, his pupil, and his friend; since he presented himself as a prophet to those who were most conversant with his infirmities as a man. Yet Cadijah believed the words, and cherished the glory, of her husband; the obsequious and affectionate Zeid was tempted by the prospect of freedom; the illustrious Ali, the son of Abu Taleb, embraced the sentiments of his cousin with the spirit of a youthful hero; and the wealth, the moderation, the veracity of Abubeker, confirmed the religion of the prophet whom he was destined to succeed. By his persuasion ten of the most respectable citizens of Mecca were introduced to the private lessons of Islam; they yielded to the voice of reason and enthusiasm; they repeated the fundamental creed, "There is but one God, and Mahomet is the apostle of God"; and their faith, even in this life, was rewarded with riches and honours, with the command of armies and the government of kingdoms. Three years were silently employed in the conversion of fourteen proselytes, the first-fruits of his mission; but in the fourth year he assumed the prophetic office, and, resolving to impart to his family the light of divine truth, he prepared a banquet, a lamb, as it is said, and a bowl of milk, for the entertainment of forty guests of the race of Hashem. "Friends and kinsmen," said Mahomet to the assembly, "I offer you, and I alone can offer, the most precious of gifts, the treasures of this world and of the world to come. God has commanded me to call you to his service. Who among you will support my burden? Who among you will be my companion and my vizir?" No answer was returned, till the silence of astonishment, and doubt, and contempt was at length broken by the impatient courage of Ali, a youth in the fourteenth year of his age. "O prophet, I am the man: whosoever rises against thee, I will dash out his teeth, tear out his eyes, break his legs, rip up his belly. O prophet, I will be thy vizir over them." Mahomet accepted his offer with transport, and Abu Taleb was ironically exhorted to respect the superior dignity of his son. In a more serious tone, the father of Ali advised his nephew to relinquish his impracticable design. "Spare your remonstrances," replied the intrepid fanatic to his uncle and benefactor; "if they should place the sun on my right hand, and the moon on my left, they should not divert me from my course." He persevered ten years in the exercise of his mission; and the religion which has overspread the East and the West advanced with a slow and painful progress within the walls of Mecca. Yet Mahomet enjoyed the satisfaction of beholding the increase of his infant congregation of Unitarians, who revered him as a prophet, and to whom he seasonably dispensed the spiritual nourishment of the Koran. The number of proselytes may be esteemed by the absence of eighty-three men and eighteen women, who retired to Ethiopia in the seventh year of his mission; and his party was fortified by the timely conversion of his uncle Hamza, and of the fierce and inflexible Omar, who signalised in the cause of Islam the same zeal which he had exerted for its destruction. Nor was the charity of Mahomet confined to the tribe of Koreish, or the precincts of Mecca: on solemn festivals, in the days of pilgrimage, he frequented the Caaba, accosted the strangers of every tribe, and urged, both in private converse and public discourse, the belief and worship of a sole Deity. Conscious of his reason and of his weakness, he asserted the liberty of conscience, and disclaimed the use of religious violence: but he called the Arabs to repentance, and conjured them to remember the ancient idolaters of Ad and Thamud, whom the divine justice had swept away from the face of the earth.

The people of Mecca were hardened in their unbelief by superstition and envy. The elders of the city, the uncles of the prophet, affected to despise the presumption of an orphan, the reformer of his country: the pious orations of Mahomet in the Caaba were answered by the clamours of Abu Taleb. "Citizens and pilgrims, listen not to the tempter, hearken not to his impious novelties. Stand fast in the worship of Al Lâta and Al Uzzah." Yet the son of Abdallah was ever dear to the aged chief: and he protected the fame and person of his nephew against the assaults of the Koreishites, who had long been jealous of the pre-eminence of the family of Hashem. Their malice was coloured with the pretence of religion: in the age of Job the crime of impiety was punished by the

Arabian magistrate; and Mahomet was guilty of deserting and
denying the national deities. But so loose was the policy of
Mecca, that the leaders of the Koreish, instead of accusing a
criminal, were compelled to employ the measures of persuasion or violence. They repeatedly addressed Abu Taleb in
the style of reproach and menace. "Thy nephew reviles our
religion; he accuses our wise forefathers of ignorance and
folly; silence him quickly, lest he kindle tumult and discord
in the city. If he persevere, we shall draw our swords against
him and his adherents, and thou wilt be responsible for the
blood of thy fellow-citizens." The weight and moderation of
Abu Taleb eluded the violence of religious faction; the most
helpless or timid of the disciples retired to Ethiopia, and the
prophet withdrew himself to various places of strength in the
town and country. As he was still supported by his family,
the rest of the tribe of Koreish engaged themselves to renounce all intercourse with the children of Hashem—neither
to buy nor sell, neither to marry nor to give in marriage, but
to pursue them with implacable enmity, till they should deliver the person of Mahomet to the justice of the gods. The
decree was suspended in the Caaba before the eyes of the
nation: the messengers of the Koreish pursued the Musulman
exiles in the heart of Africa; they besieged the prophet and
his most faithful followers, intercepted their water, and inflamed their mutual animosity by the retaliation of injuries
and insults. A doubtful truce restored the appearances of
concord, till the death of Abu Taleb abandoned Mahomet to
the power of his enemies, at the moment when he was
deprived of his domestic comforts by the loss of his faithful
and generous Cadijah. Abu Sophian, the chief of the branch
of Ommiyah, succeeded to the principality of the republic of
Mecca. A zealous votary of the idols, a mortal foe of the line
of Hashem, he convened an assembly of the Koreishites and
their allies to decide the fate of the apostle. His imprison-
ment might provoke the despair of his enthusiasm; and the
exile of an eloquent and popular fanatic would diffuse the
mischief through the provinces of Arabia. His death was
resolved; and they agreed that a sword from each tribe should
be buried in his heart, to divide the guilt of his blood, and
baffle the vengeance of the Hashemites. An angel or a spy
revealed their conspiracy, and flight was the only resource
of Mahomet. At the dead of night, accompanied by his friend

Abubeker, he silently escaped from his house: the assassins watched at the door; but they were deceived by the figure of Ali, who reposed on the bed, and was covered with the green vestment, of the apostle. The Koreish respected the piety of the heroic youth; but some verses of Ali, which are still extant, exhibit an interesting picture of his anxiety, his tenderness, and his religious confidence. Three days Mahomet and his companion were concealed in the cave of Thor, at the distance of a league from Mecca; and in the close of each evening they received from the son and daughter of Abubeker a secret supply of intelligence and food. The diligence of the Koreish explored every haunt in the neighbourhood of the city: they arrived at the entrance of the cavern; but the providential deceit of a spider's web and a pigeon's nest is supposed to convince them that the place was solitary and inviolate. "We are only two," said the trembling Abubeker. "There is a third," replied the prophet; "it is God himself." No sooner was the pursuit abated than the two fugitives issued from the rock and mounted their camels: on the road to Medina they were overtaken by the emissaries of the Koreish; they redeemed themselves with prayers and promises from their hands. In this eventful moment the lance of an Arab might have changed the history of the world. The flight of the prophet from Mecca to Medina has fixed the memorable era of the *Hegira*, which, at the end of twelve centuries, still discriminates the lunar years of the Mahometan nations.

The religion of the Koran might have perished in its cradle had not Medina embraced with faith and reverence the holy outcasts of Mecca. Medina, or the *city*, known under the name of Yathreb before it was sanctified by the throne of the prophet, was divided between the tribes of the Charegites and the Awsites, whose hereditary feud was rekindled by the slightest provocations: two colonies of Jews, who boasted a sacerdotal race, were their humble allies, and, without converting the Arabs, they introduced the taste of science and religion, which distinguished Medina as the city of the Book. Some of her noblest citizens, in a pilgrimage to the Caaba, were converted by the preaching of Mahomet; on their return they diffused the belief of God and his prophet, and the new alliance was ratified by their deputies in two secret and nocturnal interviews on a hill in the suburbs of Mecca.

In the first, ten Charegites and two Awsites, united in faith
and love, protested, in the name of their wives, their children,
and their absent brethren, that they would for ever profess
the creed and observe the precepts of the Koran. The second
was a political association, the first vital spark of the empire
of the Saracens. Seventy-three men and two women of
Medina held a solemn conference with Mahomet, his kinsmen, and his disciples, and pledged themselves to each other
by a mutual oath of fidelity. They promised, in the name of
the city, that if he should be banished they would receive
him as a confederate, obey him as a leader, and defend him
to the last extremity, like their wives and children. "But if
you are recalled by your country," they asked with a flattering
anxiety, "will you not abandon your new allies?" "All things,"
replied Mahomet, with a smile, "are now common between
us; your blood is as my blood, your ruin as my ruin. We are
bound to each other by the ties of honour and interest. I am
your friend, and the enemy of your foes." "But if we are
killed in your service, what," exclaimed the deputies of
Medina, "will be our reward?" "PARADISE," replied the prophet. "Stretch forth thy hand." He stretched it forth, and
they reiterated the oath of allegiance and fidelity. Their treaty
was ratified by the people, who unanimously embraced the
profession of Islam; they rejoiced in the exile of the apostle,
but they trembled for his safety, and impatiently expected his
arrival. After a perilous and rapid journey along the sea-
coast, he halted at Koba, two miles from the city, and made
his public entry into Medina, sixteen days after his flight
from Mecca. Five hundred of the citizens advanced to meet
him; he was hailed with acclamations of loyalty and devotion;
Mahomet was mounted on a she-camel, an umbrella shaded
his head, and a turban was unfurled before him to supply
the deficiency of a standard. His bravest disciples, who had
been scattered by the storm, assembled round his person;
and the equal, though various, merit of the Moslems was
distinguished by the names of *Mohagerians* and *Ansars*,
the fugitives of Mecca, and the auxiliaries of Medina. To eradicate
the seeds of jealousy, Mahomet judiciously coupled his
principal followers with the rights and obligations of brethren;
and when Ali found himself without a peer, the prophet
tenderly declared that *he* would be the companion and brother
of the noble youth. The expedient was crowned with success;

the holy fraternity was respected in peace and war, and the two parties vied with each other in a generous emulation of courage and fidelity. Once only the concord was slightly ruffled by an accidental quarrel: a patriot of Medina arraigned the insolence of the strangers, but the hint of their expulsion was heard with abhorrence; and his own son most eagerly offered to lay at the apostle's feet the head of his father.

From his establishment at Medina Mahomet assumed the exercise of the regal and sacerdotal office; and it was impious to appeal from a judge whose decrees were inspired by the divine wisdom. A small portion of ground, the patrimony of two orphans, was acquired by gift or purchase; on that chosen spot he built a house and a mosque, more venerable in their rude simplicity than the palaces and temples of the Assyrian caliphs. His seal of gold, or silver, was inscribed with the apostolic title; when he prayed and preached in the weekly assembly, he leaned against the trunk of a palm-tree; and it was long before he indulged himself in the use of a chair or pulpit of rough timber. After a reign of six years, fifteen hundred Moslems, in arms and in the field, renewed their oath of allegiance; and their chief repeated the assurance of protection till the death of the last member, or the final dissolution of the party. It was in the same camp that the deputy of Mecca was astonished by the attention of the faithful to the words and looks of the prophet, by the eagerness with which they collected his spittle, a hair that dropped on the ground, the refuse water of his lustrations, as if they participated in some degree of the prophetic virtue. "I have seen," said he, "the Chosroes of Persia and the Cæsar of Rome, but never did I behold a king among his subjects like Mahomet among his companions." The devout fervour of enthusiasm acts with more energy and truth than the cold and formal servility of courts.

MAHOMET DECLARES WAR AGAINST THE INFIDEL

In the state of nature every man has a right to defend, by force of arms, his person and his possessions; to repel, or even to prevent, the violence of his enemies, and to extend his hostilities to a reasonable measure of satisfaction and retaliation. In the free society of the Arabs, the duties of subject and citizen imposed a feeble restraint; and Mahomet, in the exercise of a peaceful and benevolent mission, had been despoiled and banished by the injustice of his countrymen. The choice of an independent people had exalted the fugitive of Mecca to the rank of a sovereign; and he was invested with the just prerogative of forming alliances, and of waging offensive or defensive war. The imperfection of human rights was supplied and armed by the plenitude of divine power: the prophet of Medina assumed, in his new revelations a fiercer and more sanguinary tone, which proves that his former moderation was the effect of weakness: the means of persuasion had been tried, the season of forbearance was elapsed, and he was now commanded to propagate his religion by the sword, to destroy the monuments of idolatry, and, without regarding the sanctity of days or months, to pursue the unbelieving nations of the earth. The same bloody precepts, so repeatedly inculcated in the Koran, are ascribed by the author to the Pentateuch and the Gospel. But the mild tenor of the evangelic style may explain an ambiguous text, that Jesus did not bring peace on the earth, but a sword: his patient and humble virtues should not be confounded with the intolerant zeal of princes and bishops, who have disgraced the name of his disciples. In the prosecution of religious war, Mahomet might appeal with more propriety to the example of Moses, of the Judges, and the kings of Israel. The military laws of the Hebrews are still more rigid than those of the Arabian legislator.[1] The Lord of hosts marched in person before the Jews: if a city resisted their summons, the males, without distinction, were put to the sword: the seven nations of Canaan were devoted to destruction; and neither repentance nor conversion could shield them from the inevitable doom, that no creature within their precincts should be left alive. The fair option of friendship, or submission, or battle, was proposed to the enemies of Mahomet. If they professed the creed of Islam, they were admitted to all the temporal and spiritual benefits of his primitive disciples, and marched under the same banner to extend the religion which they had embraced. The clemency of the prophet was decided by his interest: yet he seldom

---

[1] The xth and xxth chapters of Deuteronomy, with the practical comments of Joshua, David, etc., are read with more awe than satisfaction by the pious Christians of the present age. But the bishops, as well as the rabbis of former times, have beat the drum-ecclesiastic with pleasure and success.

trampled on a prostrate enemy; and he seems to promise that on the payment of a tribute the least guilty of his unbelieving subjects might be indulged in their worship, or at least in their imperfect faith. In the first months of his reign he practised the lessons of holy warfare, and displayed his white banner before the gates of Medina: the martial apostle fought in person at nine battles or sieges; and fifty enterprises of war were achieved in ten years by himself or his lieutenants. The Arab continued to unite the professions of a merchant and a robber; and his petty excursions for the defence or the attack of a caravan insensibly prepared his troops for the conquest of Arabia. The distribution of the spoil was regulated by a divine law: the whole was faithfully collected in one common mass: a fifth of the gold and silver, the prisoners and cattle, the moveables and immoveables, was reserved by the prophet for pious and charitable uses; the remainder was shared in adequate portions by the soldiers who had obtained the victory or guarded the camp, the rewards of the slain devolved to their widows and orphans: and the increase of cavalry was encouraged by the allotment of a double share to the horse and to the man. From all sides the roving Arabs were allured to the standard of religion and plunder: the apostle sanctified the licence of embracing the female captives as their wives or concubines; and the enjoyment of wealth and beauty was a feeble type of the joys of paradise prepared for the valiant martyrs of the faith. "The sword," says Mahomet, "is the key of heaven and of hell: a drop of blood shed in the cause of God, a night spent in arms, is of more avail than two months of fasting or prayer: whosoever falls in battle, his sins are forgiven: at the day of judgment his wounds shall be resplendent as vermilion, and odoriferous as musk; and the loss of his limbs shall be supplied by the wings of angels and cherubim." The intrepid souls of the Arabs were fired with enthusiasm: the picture of the invisible world was strongly painted on their imagination; and the death which they had always despised became an object of hope and desire. The Koran inculcates, in the most absolute sense, the tenets of fate and predestination, which would extinguish both industry and virtue, if the actions of man were governed by his speculative belief. Yet their influence in every age has exalted the courage of the Saracens and Turks. The first companions of Mahomet advanced to battle with a fearless confidence: there is no danger where there is no chance: they were ordained to perish in their beds; or they were safe and invulnerable amidst the darts of the enemy.

Perhaps the Koreish would have been content with the flight of Mahomet, had they not been provoked and alarmed by the vengeance of an enemy who could intercept their Syrian trade as it passed and repassed through the territory of Medina. Abu Sophian himself, with only thirty or forty followers, conducted a wealthy caravan of a thousand camels; the fortune or dexterity of his march escaped the vigilance of Mahomet; but the chief of the Koreish was informed that the holy robbers were placed in ambush to await his return. He despatched a messenger ·to his brethren of Mecca, and they were roused, by the fear of losing their merchandise and their provisions, unless they hastened to his relief with the military force of the city. The sacred band of Mahomet was formed of three hundred and thirteen Moslems, of whom seventy-seven were fugitives, and the rest auxiliaries: they mounted by turns a train of seventy camels (the camels of Yathreb were formidable in war); but such was the poverty of his first disciples, that only two could appear on horseback in the field. In the fertile and famous vale of Beder, three stations from Medina, he was informed by his scouts of the caravan that approached on one side; of the Koreish, one hundred horse, eight hundred and fifty foot, who advanced on the other. After a short debate he sacrificed the prospect of wealth to the pursuit of glory and revenge; and a slight intrenchment was formed to cover his troops, and a stream of fresh water that glided through the valley. "O God," he exclaimed as the numbers of the Koreish descended from the hills, "O God, if these are destroyed, by whom wilt thou be worshipped on the earth?—Courage, my children; close your ranks; discharge your arrows, and the day is your own." At these words he placed himself, with Abubeker, on a throne or pulpit, and instantly demanded the succour of Gabriel and three thousand angels. His eye was fixed on the field of battle: the Musulmans fainted and were pressed: in that decisive moment the prophet started from his throne, mounted his horse, and cast a handful of sand into the air; "Let their faces be covered with confusion." Both armies heard the thunder of his voice: their fancy beheld the angelic warriors: the Koreish trembled and fled: seventy of the bravest were

·slain; and seventy captives adorned the first victory of the faithful. The dead bodies of the Koreish were despoiled and insulted: two of the most obnoxious prisoners were punished with death; and the ransom of the others, four thousand drachms of silver, compensated in some degree the escape of the caravan. But it was in vain that the camels of Abu Sophian explored a new road through the desert and along the Euphrates: they were overtaken by the diligence of the Musulmans; and wealthy must have been the prize, if twenty thousand drachms could be set apart for the fifth of the apostle. The resentment of the public and private loss stimulated Abu Sophian to collect a body of three thousand men, seven hundred of whom were armed with cuirasses, and two hundred were mounted on horseback; three thousand camels attended his march; and his wife Henda, with fifteen matrons of Mecca, incessantly sounded their timbrels to animate the troops, and to magnify the greatness of Hobal, the most popular deity of the Caaba. The standard of God and Mahomet was upheld by nine hundred and fifty believers: the disproportion of numbers was not more alarming than in the field of Beder; and their presumption of victory prevailed against the divine and human sense of the apostle. The second battle was fought on Mount Ohud, six miles to the north of Medina: the Koreish advanced in the form of a crescent; and the right wing of cavalry was led by Caled, the fiercest and most successful of the Arabian warriors. The troops of Mahomet were skilfully posted on the declivity of the hill; and their rear was guarded by a detachment of fifty archers. The weight of their charge impelled and broke the centre of the idolaters: but in the pursuit they lost the advantage of their ground: the archers deserted their station: the Musulmans were tempted by the spoil, disobeyed their general, and disordered their ranks. The intrepid Caled, wheeling his cavalry on their flank and rear, exclaimed, with a loud voice, that Mahomet was slain. He was indeed wounded in the face with a javelin: two of his teeth were shattered with a stone; yet, in the midst of tumult and dismay, he reproached the infidels with the murder of a prophet; and blessed the friendly hand that stanched his blood, and conveyed him to a place of safety. Seventy martyrs died for the sins of the people: they fell, said the apostle, in pairs, each brother embracing his lifeless companion; their bodies were mangled by the inhuman females of Mecca; and the wife of Abu Sophian tasted the entrails of Hamza, the uncle of Mahomet. They might applaud their superstition and satiate their fury; but the Musulmans soon rallied in the field, and the Koreish wanted strength or courage to undertake the siege of Medina. It was attacked the ensuing year by an army of ten thousand enemies; and this third expedition is variously named, from the *nations* which marched under the banner of Abu Sophian, from the *ditch* which was drawn before the city, and a camp of three thousand Musulmans. The prudence of Mahomet declined a general engagement: the valour of Ali was signalised in single combat; and the war was protracted twenty days, till the final separation of the confederates. A tempest of wind, rain, and hail overturned their tents: their private quarrels were fomented by an insidious adversary; and the Koreish, deserted by their allies, no longer hoped to subvert the throne, or to check the conquests, of their invincible exile.

The choice of Jerusalem for the first kebla of prayer discovers the early propensity of Mahomet in favour of the Jews; and happy would it have been for their temporal interest had they recognised in the Arabian prophet the hope of Israel and the promised Messiah. Their obstinacy converted his friendship into implacable hatred, with which he pursued that unfortunate people to the last moment of his life; and in the double character of an apostle and a conqueror, his persecution was extended to both worlds. The Kainoka dwelt at Medina under the protection of the city: he seized the occasion of an accidental tumult, and summoned them to embrace his religion, or contend with him in battle. "Alas," replied the trembling Jews, "we are ignorant of the use of arms, but we persevere in the faith and worship of our fathers; why wilt thou reduce us to the necessity of a just defence?" The unequal conflict was terminated in fifteen days; and it was with extreme reluctance that Mahomet yielded to the importunity of his allies, and consented to spare the lives of the captives. But their riches were confiscated, their arms became more effectual in the hands of the Musulmans; and a wretched colony of seven hundred exiles was driven with their wives and children to implore a refuge on the confines of Syria. The Nadhirites were more guilty, since they conspired in a friendly interview to assassinate the prophet. He besieged their castle, three miles from Medina; but their resolute defence obtained an honourable capitulation; and the garrison, sounding their trumpets and beating their drums, was permitted to depart with the honours of war. The Jews had excited and joined the war of the Koreish: no sooner had the *nations* retired from the *ditch,* than Mahomet, without laying aside his armour, marched on the same day to extirpate the hostile race of the children of Koraidha. After a resistance of twenty-five days they surrendered at discretion. They trusted to the intercession of their old allies of Medina: they could not be ignorant that fanaticism obliterates the feelings of humanity. A venerable elder, to whose judgment they appealed, pronounced the sentence of their death: seven hundred Jews were dragged in chains to the market-place of the city; they descended alive into the grave prepared for their execution and burial; and the apostle beheld with an inflexible eye the slaughter of his helpless enemies. Their sheep and camels were inherited by the Musulmans: three hundred cuirasses, five hundred .pikes, a thousand lances, composed the most useful portion of the spoil. Six days' journey to the northeast of Medina, the ancient and wealthy town of Chaibar was the seat of the Jewish power in Arabia: the territory, a fertile spot in the desert, was covered with plantations and cattle, and protected by eight castles, some of which were esteemed of impregnable strength. The forces of Mahomet consisted of two hundred horse and fourteen hundred foot: in the succession of eight regular and painful sieges they were exposed to danger, and fatigue, and hunger; and the most undaunted chiefs despaired of the event. The apostle revived their faith and courage by the example of Ali, on whom he bestowed the surname of the Lion of God: perhaps we may believe that an Hebrew champion of gigantic stature was cloven to the chest by his irresistible scimitar; but we cannot praise the modesty of romance, which represents him as tearing from its hinges the gate of a fortress and wielding the ponderous buckler in his left hand.[1] After the reduction of the castles the town of Chaibar submitted to the yoke. The chief of the tribe was tortured, in the presence of Mahomet, to force a confession of his hidden treasure: the industry of the shepherds and husbandmen was rewarded with a precarious tolera-

---

[1] Abu Rafe, the servant of Mahomet, is said to affirm that he himself and seven other men afterwards tried, without success, to move the same gate from the ground. Abu Rafe was an eye-witness, but who will be witness for Abu Rafe?

tion: they were permitted, so long as it should please the
conqueror, to improve their patrimony, in equal shares, for
his emolument and their own. Under the reign of Omar, the
Jews of Chaibar were transplanted to Syria; and the caliph
alleged the injunction of his dying master, that one and the
true religion should be professed in his native land of Arabia.

Five times each day the eyes of Mahomet were turned
towards Mecca, and he was urged by the most sacred and
powerful motives to revisit, as a conqueror, the city and the
temple from whence he had been driven as an exile. The
Caaba was present to his waking and sleeping fancy: an
idle dream was translated into vision and prophecy; he unfurled the holy banner; and a rash promise of success too
hastily dropped from the lips of the apostle. His march from
Medina to Mecca displayed the peaceful and solemn pomp of
a pilgrimage: seventy camels, chosen and bedecked for
sacrifice, preceded the van; the sacred territory was respected;
and the captives were dismissed without ransom to proclaim
his clemency and devotion. But no sooner did Mahomet
descend into the plain, within a day's journey of the city,
than he exclaimed, "They have clothed themselves with the
skins of tigers": the numbers and resolution of the Koreish
opposed his progress; and the roving Arabs of the desert
might desert or betray a leader whom they had followed for
the hopes of spoil. The intrepid fanatic sunk into a cool
and cautious politician: he waived in the treaty his title of
apostle of God; concluded with the Koreish and their allies
a truce of ten years; engaged to restore the fugitives of Mecca
who should embrace his religion; and stipulated only, for
the ensuing year, the humble privilege of entering the city as
a friend, and of remaining three days to accomplish the rites
of the pilgrimage. A cloud of shame and sorrow hung on the
retreat of the Musulmans, and their disappointment might
justly accuse the failure of a prophet who had so often appealed to the evidence of success. The faith and hope of the
pilgrims were rekindled by the prospect of Mecca: their
swords were sheathed: seven times in the footsteps of the
apostle they encompassed the Caaba: the Koreish had retired to the hills, and Mahomet, after the customary sacrifice,
evacuated the city on the fourth day. The people was edified
by his devotion; the hostile chiefs were awed, or divided, or
seduced; and both Caled and Amrou, the future conquerors

of Syria and Egypt, most seasonably deserted the sinking
cause of idolatry. The power of Mahomet was increased by
the submission of the Arabian tribes; ten thousand soldiers
were assembled for the conquest of Mecca; and the idolaters,
the weaker party, were easily convicted of violating the
truce. Enthusiasm and discipline impelled the march, and
preserved the secret, till the blaze of ten thousand fires proclaimed to the astonished Koreish the design, the approach,
and the irresistible force of the enemy. The haughty Abu
Sophian presented the keys of the city; admired the variety
of arms and ensigns that passed before him in review; observed
that the son of Abdallah had acquired a mighty kingdom;
and confessed, under the scimitar of Omar, that he was the
apostle of the true God. The return of Marius and Sulla was
stained with the blood of the Romans: the revenge of Mahomet was stimulated by religious zeal, and his injured
followers were eager to execute or to prevent the order of a
massacre. Instead of indulging their passions and his own,[1]
the victorious exile forgave the guilt, and united the factions,
of Mecca. His troops, in three divisions, marched into the
city: eight-and-twenty of the inhabitants were slain by the
sword of Caled; eleven men and six women were proscribed
by the sentence of Mahomet; but he blamed the cruelty of
his lieutenant; and several of the most obnoxious victims
were indebted for their lives to his clemency or contempt.
The chiefs of the Koreish were prostrate at his feet. "What
mercy can you expect from the man whom you have
wronged?" "We confide in the generosity of our kinsman."
"And you shall not confide in vain: begone! you are safe,
you are free." The people of Mecca deserved their pardon by
the profession of Islam; and after an exile of seven years,
the fugitive missionary was enthroned as the prince and
prophet of his native country. But the three hundred and sixty
idols of the Caaba were ignominiously broken: the house of
God was purified and adorned: as an example to future times,
the apostle again fulfilled the duties of a pilgrim; and a

---

[1] After the conquest of Mecca, the Mahomet of Voltaire imagines and
perpetrates the most horrid crimes. The poet confesses that he is not supported by the truth of history, and can only allege, que celui qui fait la
guerre à sa patrie au nom de Dieu est capable de tout. The maxim is
neither charitable nor philosophic; and some reverence is surely due to
the fame of heroes and the religion of nations. I am informed that a Turkish
ambassador at Paris was much scandalised at the representation of this
tragedy.

perpetual law was enacted that no unbeliever should dare to set his foot on the territory of the holy city.

The conquest of Mecca determined the faith and obedience of the Arabian tribes; who, according to the vicissitudes of fortune, had obeyed, or disregarded, the eloquence or the arms of the prophet. Indifference for rites and opinions still marks the character of the Bedoweens; and they might accept, as loosely as they hold, the doctrine of the Koran. Yet an obstinate remnant still adhered to the religion and liberty of their ancestors, and the war of Honain derived a proper appellation from the *idols,* whom Mahomet had vowed to destroy, and whom the confederates of Tayef had sworn to defend. Four thousand Pagans advanced with secrecy and speed to surprise the conqueror: they pitied and despised the supine negligence of the Koreish, but they depended on the wishes, and perhaps the aid, of a people who had so lately renounced their gods, and bowed beneath the yoke of their enemy. The banners of Medina and Mecca were displayed by the prophet; a crowd of Bedoweens increased the strength or numbers of the army, and twelve thousand Musulmans entertained a rash and sinful presumption of their invincible strength. They descended without precaution into the valley of Honain: the heights had been occupied by the archers and slingers of the confederates; their numbers were oppressed, their discipline was confounded, their courage was appalled, and the Koreish smiled at their impending destruction. The prophet, on his white mule, was encompassed by the enemies: he attempted to rush against their spears in search of a glorious death: ten of his faithful companions interposed their weapons and their breasts; three of these fell dead at his feet: "O my brethren," he repeatedly cried with sorrow and indignation, "I am the son of Abdallah, I am the apostle of truth! O man, stand fast in the faith! O God, send down thy succour!" His uncle Abbas, who, like the heroes of Homer, excelled in the loudness of his voice, made the valley resound with the recital of the gifts and promises of God: the flying Moslems returned from all sides to the holy standard; and Mahomet observed with pleasure that the furnace was again rekindled: his conduct and example restored the battle, and he animated his victorious troops to inflict a merciless revenge on the authors of their shame. From the field of Honain he marched without delay to the siege of Tayef, sixty miles to the south-east of Mecca, a fortress of strength, whose fertile lands produce the fruits of Syria in the midst of the Arabian desert. A friendly tribe, instructed (I know not how) in the art of sieges, supplied him with a train of battering-rams and military engines, with a body of five hundred artificers. But it was in vain that he offered freedom to the slaves of Tayef; that he violated his own laws by the extirpation of the fruit-trees; that the ground was opened by the miners; that the breach was assaulted by the troops. After a siege of twenty days the prophet sounded a retreat; but he retreated with a song of devout triumph, and affected to pray for the repentance and safety of the unbelieving city. The spoil of this fortunate expedition amounted to six thousand captives, twenty-four thousand camels, forty thousand sheep, and four thousand ounces of silver: a tribe who had fought at Honain redeemed their prisoners by the sacrifice of their idols: but Mahomet compensated the loss by resigning to the soldiers his fifth of the plunder, and wished, for their sake, that he possessed as many head of cattle as there were trees in the province of Tehama. Instead of chastising the disaffection of the Koreish, he endeavoured to cut out their tongues (his own expression), and to secure their attachment, by a superior measure of liberality: Abu Sophian alone was presented with three hundred camels and twenty ounces of silver; and Mecca was sincerely converted to the profitable religion of the Koran.

The *fugitives* and *auxiliaries* complained that they who had borne the burden were neglected in the season of victory. "Alas!" replied their artful leader, "suffer me to conciliate these recent enemies, these doubtful proselytes, by the gift of some perishable goods. To your guard I intrust my life and fortunes. You are the companions of my exile, of my kingdom, of my paradise." He was followed by the deputies of Tayef, who dreaded the repetition of a siege. "Grant us, O apostle of God! a truce of three years with the toleration of our ancient worship." "Not a month, not an hour." "Excuse us at least from the obligation of prayer." "Without prayer religion is of no avail." They submitted in silence: their temples were demolished, and the same sentence of destruction was executed on all the idols of Arabia. His lieutenants, on the shores of the Red Sea, the Ocean, and the Gulf of

Persia, were saluted by the acclamations of a faithful people; and the ambassadors who knelt before the throne of Medina were as numerous (says the Arabian proverb) as the dates that fall from the maturity of a palm-tree. The nation submitted to the God and the sceptre of Mahomet: the opprobrious name of tribute was abolished: the spontaneous or reluctant oblations of alms and tithes were applied to the service of religion; and one hundred and fourteen thousand Moslems accompanied the last pilgrimage of the apostle.

When Heraclius returned in triumph from the Persian war, he entertained, at Emesa, one of the ambassadors of Mahomet, who invited the princes and nations of the earth to the profession of Islam. On this foundation the zeal of the Arabians has supposed the secret conversion of the Christian emperor: the vanity of the Greeks has feigned a personal visit of the prince of Medina, who accepted from the royal bounty a rich domain, and a secure retreat, in the province of Syria. But the friendship of Heraclius and Mahomet was of short continuance: the new religion had inflamed rather than assuaged the rapacious spirit of the Saracens; and the murder of an envoy afforded a decent pretence for invading, with three thousand soldiers, the territory of Palestine, that extends to the eastward of the Jordan. The holy banner was intrusted to Zeid; and such was the discipline or enthusiasm of the rising sect, that the noblest chiefs served without reluctance under the slave of the prophet. On the event of his decease, Jaafar and Abdallah were successively substituted to the command; and if the three should perish in the war, the troops were authorised to elect their general. The three leaders were slain in the battle of Muta, the first military action which tried the valour of the Moslems against a foreign enemy. Zeid fell, like a soldier, in the foremost ranks: the death of Jaafar was heroic and memorable: he lost his right hand: he shifted the standard to his left: the left was severed from his body: he embraced the standard with his bleeding stumps, till he was transfixed to the ground with fifty honourable wounds. "Advance," cried Abdallah, who stepped into the vacant place, "advance with confidence: either victory or paradise is our own." The lance of a Roman decided the alternative; but the falling standard was rescued by Caled, the proselyte of Mecca: nine swords were broken in his hand; and his valour withstood and repulsed the superior numbers of the Christians. In the nocturnal council of the camp he was chosen to command: his skilful evolutions of the ensuing day secured either the victory or the retreat of the Saracens; and Caled is renowned among his brethren and his enemies by the glorious appellation of the *Sword of God.* In the pulpit, Mahomet described, with prophetic rapture, the crowns of the blessed martyrs; but in private he betrayed the feelings of human nature: he was surprised as he wept over the daughter of Zeid: "What do I see?" said the astonished votary. "You see," replied the apostle, "a friend who is deploring the loss of his most faithful friend." After the conquest of Mecca the sovereign of Arabia affected to prevent the hostile preparations of Heraclius; and solemnly proclaimed war against the Romans, without attempting to disguise the hardships and dangers of the enterprise. The Moslems were discouraged: they alleged the want of money, or horses, or provisions; the season of harvest, and the intolerable heat of the summer: "Hell is much hotter," said the indignant prophet. He disdained to compel their service: but on his return he admonished the most guilty, by an excommunication of fifty days. Their desertion enhanced the merit of Abubeker, Othman, and the faithful companions who devoted their lives and fortunes; and Mahomet displayed his banner at the head of ten thousand horse and twenty thousand foot. Painful indeed was the distress of the march: lassitude and thirst were aggravated by the scorching and pestilential winds of the desert: ten men rode by turns on the same camel; and they were reduced to the shameful necessity of drinking the water from the belly of that useful animal. In the mid-way, ten days' journey from Medina and Damascus, they reposed near the grove and fountain of Tabuc. Beyond that place Mahomet declined the prosecution of the war: he declared himself satisfied with the peaceful intentions; he was more probably daunted by the martial array, of the emperor of the East. But the active and intrepid Caled spread around the terror of his name; and the prophet received the submission of the tribes and cities, from the Euphrates to Ailah, at the head of the Red Sea. To his Christian subjects Mahomet readily granted the security of their persons, the freedom of their trade, the property of their goods, and the toleration of their worship. The weakness of their Arabian brethren had re-strained them from opposing his ambition; the disciples of Jesus were endeared to the enemy of the Jews; and it was the interest of a conqueror to propose a fair capitulation to the most powerful religion of the earth.

DEATH OF MAHOMET

Till the age of sixty-three years the strength of Mahomet was equal to the temporal and spiritual fatigues of his mission. His epileptic fits, an absurd calumny of the Greeks, would be an object of pity rather than abhorrence; but he seriously believed that he was poisoned at Chaibar by the revenge of a Jewish female. During four years the health of the prophet declined; his infirmities increased; but his mortal disease was a fever of fourteen days, which deprived him by intervals of the use of reason. As soon as he was conscious of his danger, he edified his brethren by the humility of his virtue or penitence. "If there be any man," said the apostle from the pulpit, "whom I have unjustly scourged, I submit my own back to the lash of retaliation. Have I aspersed the reputation of a Musulman? let him proclaim *my* faults in the face of the congregation. Has any one been despoiled of his goods? the little that I possess shall compensate the principal and the interest of the debt." "Yes," replied a voice from the crowd, "I am entitled to three drachms of silver." Mahomet heard the complaint, satisfied the demand, and thanked his creditor for accusing him in this world rather than at the day of judgment. He beheld with temperate firmness the approach of death; en-franchised his slaves (seventeen men, as they are named, and eleven women); minutely directed the order of his funeral; and moderated the lamentations of his weeping friends, on whom he bestowed the benediction of peace. Till the third day before his death he regularly performed the function of public prayer: the choice of Abubeker to supply his place appeared to mark that ancient and faithful friend as his successor in the sacerdotal and regal office; but he prudently declined the risk and envy of a more explicit nomination. At a moment when his faculties were visibly impaired, he called for pen and ink to write, or, more properly, to dictate, a divine book, the sum and accomplishment of all his revelations: a dispute arose in the chamber whether he should be allowed to supersede the authority of the Koran; and the prophet was forced to reprove the indecent vehemences of his disciples. If the slightest credit may be afforded to the traditions of his wives and companions, he maintained, in the bosom of his family, and to the last moments of his life, the dignity of an apostle, and the faith of an enthusiast; described the visits of Gabriel, who bid an everlasting farewell to the earth; and expressed his lively confidence, not only of the mercy, but of the favour, of the Supreme Being. In a familiar discourse he had mentioned his special prerogative, that the angel of death was not allowed to take his soul till he had respectfully asked the permission of the prophet. The request was granted; and Mahomet immediately fell into the agony of his dissolution: his head was reclined on the lap of Ayesha, the best beloved of all his wives; he fainted with the violence of pain; recovering his spirits, he raised his eyes towards the roof of the house, and, with a steady look, though a faltering voice, uttered the last broken, though articulate, words: "O God! . . . pardon my sins. . . . Yes, . . . I come, . . . among my fellow citizens on high"; and thus peaceably expired on a carpet spread upon the floor. An expedition for the conquest of Syria was stopped by this mournful event: the army halted at the gates of Medina; the chiefs were assembled round their dying master. The city, more especially the house, of the prophet, was a scene of clamorous sorrow or silent despair: fanaticism alone could suggest a ray of hope and consolation. "How can he be dead, our witness, our intercessor, our mediator, with God? By God he is not dead: like Moses and Jesus, he is wrapt in a holy trance, and speedily will he return to his faithful people." The evidence of sense was disregarded; and Omar, unsheathing his scimitar, threatened to strike off the heads of the infidels who should dare to affirm that the prophet was no more. The tumult was appeased by the weight and moderation of Abubeker. "Is it Mahomet," said he to Omar and the multitude, "or the God of Mahomet, whom you worship? The God of Mahomet liveth for ever; but the apostle was a mortal like ourselves, and, according to his own prediction, he has experienced the common fate of mortality." He was piously interred, by the hands of his nearest kinsman, on the same spot on which he

expired: Medina has been sanctified by the death and burial
of Mahomet; and the innumerable pilgrims of Mecca often
turn aside from the way, to bow, in voluntary devotion, before
the simple tomb of the prophet.

THE CHARACTER AND PRIVATE LIFE OF MAHOMET

At the conclusion of the life of Mahomet it may perhaps
be expected that I should balance his faults and virtues, that
I should decide whether the title of enthusiast or impostor
more properly belongs to that extraordinary man. Had I
been intimately conversant with the son of Abdallah, the task
would still be difficult, and the success uncertain: at the
distance of twelve centuries I darkly contemplate his shade
through a cloud of religious incense; and could I truly delineate
the portrait of an hour, the fleeting resemblance would not
equally apply to the solitary of Mount Hera, to the preacher
of Mecca, and to the conqueror of Arabia. The author of a
mighty revolution appears to have been endowed with a pious
and contemplative disposition: so soon as marriage had
raised him above the pressure of want, he avoided the paths
of ambition and avarice; and till the age of forty he lived with
innocence, and would have died without a name. The unity
of God is an idea most congenial to nature and reason; and
a slight conversation with the Jews and Christians would
teach him to despise and detest the idolatry of Mecca. It was
the duty of a man and a citizen to impart the doctrine of
salvation, to rescue his country from the dominion of sin
and error. The energy of a mind incessantly bent on the
same object would convert a general obligation into a particular call; the warm suggestions of the understanding of the
fancy would be felt as the inspirations of Heaven; the labour
of thought would expire in rapture and vision; and the in-
ward sensation, the invisible monitor, would be described
with the form and attributes of an angel of God. From
enthusiasm to imposture the step is perilous and slippery;
the dæmon of Socrates affords a memorable instance how
a wise man may deceive himself, how a good man may
deceive others, how the conscience may slumber in a mixed
and middle state between self-illusion and voluntary fraud.
Charity may believe that the original motives of Mahomet
were those of pure and genuine benevolence; but a human

missionary is incapable of cherishing the obstinate unbelievers who reject his claims, despise his arguments, and persecute his life; he might forgive his personal adversaries, he may lawfully hate the enemies of God; the stern passions of pride and revenge were kindled in the bosom of Mahomet, and he sighed, like the prophet of Nineveh, for the destruction of the rebels whom he had condemned. The injustice of Mecca and the choice of Medina transformed the citizen into a prince, the humble preacher into the leader of armies; but his sword was consecrated by the example of the saints; and the same God who afflicts a sinful world with pestilence and earthquakes might inspire for their conversion or chastisement the valour of his servants. In the exercise of political government he was compelled to abate of the stern rigour of fanaticism, to comply in some measure with the prejudices and passions of his followers, and to employ even the vices of mankind as the instruments of their salvation. The use of fraud and perfidy, of cruelty and injustice, were often subservient to the propagation of the faith; and Mahomet commanded or approved the assassination of the Jews and idolaters who had escaped from the field of battle. By the repetition of such acts the character of Mahomet must have been gradually stained; and the influence of such pernicious habits would be poorly compensated by the practice of the personal and social virtues which are necessary to maintain the reputation of a prophet among his sectaries and friends. Of his last years ambition was the ruling passion; and a politician will suspect that he secretly smiled (the victorious impostor!) at the enthusiasm of his youth, and the credulity of his proselytes.[1] A philosopher will observe that *their* credulity and *his* success would tend more strongly to fortify the assurance of his divine mission, that his interest and religion were inseparably connected, and that his conscience would be soothed by the persuasion that he alone was absolved by the Deity from the obligation of positive and moral laws. If he retained any vestige of his native innocence, the sins of Mahomet may be allowed as an evidence of his sincerity. In the support of truth, the arts of fraud and fiction may be deemed less criminal; and he would have started at the foulness of the

---

[1] In some passage of his voluminous writings, Voltaire compares the prophet, in his old age, to a fakir "qui détache la chaîne de son cou pour en donner sur les oreilles à ses confrères."

means, had he not been satisfied of the importance and
justice of the end. Even in a conqueror or a priest I can
surprise a word or action of unaffected humanity; and the
decree of Mahomet, that, in the sale of captives, the mothers
should never be separated from their children, may suspend,
or moderate, the censure of the historian.

The good sense of Mahomet despised the pomp of royalty;
the aspostle of God submitted to the menial offices of the
family; he kindled the fire, swept the floor, milked the ewes,
and mended with his own hands his shoes and his woollen
garment. Disdaining the penance and merit of an hermit, he
observed, without effort or vanity, the abstemious diet of an
Arab and a soldier. On solemn occasions he feasted his companions with rustic and hospitable plenty; but in his domestic
life many weeks would elapse without a fire being kindled
on the hearth of the prophet. The interdiction of wine was
confirmed by his example; his hunger was appeased with a
sparing allowance of barley-bread: he delighted in the taste
of milk and honey; but his ordinary food consisted of dates
and water. Perfumes and women were the two sensual enjoyments which his nature required, and his religion did not
forbid; and Mahomet affirmed that the fervour of his devotion
was increased by these innocent pleasures. The heat of the
climate inflames the blood of the Arabs, and their libidinous
complexion has been noticed by the writers of antiquity.
Their incontinence was regulated by the civil and religious
laws of the Koran: their incestuous alliances were blamed:
the boundless licence of polygamy was reduced to four legitimate wives or concubines; their rights both of bed and of
dowry were equitably determined; the freedom of divorce
was discouraged; adultery was condemned as a capital offence;
and fornication, in either sex, was punished with an hundred
stripes. Such were the calm and rational precepts of the
legislator; but in his private conduct Mahomet indulged the
appetites of a man, and abused the claims of a prophet. A
special revelation dispensed him from the laws which he had
imposed on his nation; the female sex, without reserve, was
abandoned to his desires; and this singular prerogative excited
the envy rather than the scandal, the veneration rather than
the envy, of the devout Musulmans. If we remember the
seven hundred wives and three hundred concubines of the
wise Solomon, we shall applaud the modesty of the Arabian,

who espoused no more than seventeen or fifteen wives; eleven
are enumerated who occupied at Medina their separate apartments round the house of the apostle, and enjoyed in their
turns the favour of his conjugal society. What is singular
enough, they were all widows, excepting only Ayesha, the
daughter of Abubeker. *She* was doubtless a virgin, since
Mahomet consummated his nuptials (such is the premature
ripeness of the climate) when she was only nine years of age.
The youth, the beauty, the spirit of Ayesha gave her a superior
ascendant: she was beloved and trusted by the prophet; and,
after his death, the daughter of Abubeker was long revered
as the mother of the faithful. Her behaviour had been
ambiguous and indiscreet: in a nocturnal march she was
accidentally left behind, and in the morning Ayesha returned
to the camp with a man. The temper of Mahomet was inclined
to jealousy; but a divine revelation assured him of her innocence: he chastised her accusers, and published a law of
domestic peace, that no woman should be condemned unless
four male witnesses had seen her in the act of adultery. In
his adventures with Zeineb, the wife of Zeid, and with Mary,
an Egyptian captive, the amorous prophet forgot the interest
of his reputation. At the house of Zeid, his freedman and
adopted son, he beheld, in a loose undress, the beauty of
Zeineb, and burst forth into an ejaculation of devotion and
desire. The servile, or grateful, freedman understood the hint,
and yielded without hesitation to the love of his benefactor.
But as the filial relation had excited some doubt and scandal,
the angel Gabriel descended from heaven to ratify the deed,
to annul the adoption, and gently to reprove the apostle for
distrusting the indulgence of his God. One of his wives,
Hafna, the daughter of Omar, surprised him on her own bed
in the embraces of his Egyptian captive: she promised secrecy
and forgiveness: he swore that he would renounce the possession of Mary. Both parties forgot their engagements; and
Gabriel again descended with a chapter of the Koran to
absolve him from his oath, and to exhort him freely to enjoy
his captives and concubines without listening to the clamours
of his wives. In a solitary retreat of thirty days he laboured
alone with Mary to fulfil the commands of the angel. When
his love and revenge were satiated, he summoned to his
presence his eleven wives, reproached their disobedience and
indiscretion, and threatened them with a sentence of divorce,

both in this world and in the next—a dreadful sentence, since those who had ascended the bed of the prophet were for ever excluded from the hope of a second marriage. Perhaps the incontinence of Mahomet may be palliated by the tradition of his natural or preternatural gifts:[1] he united the manly virtue of thirty of the children of Adam; and the apostle might rival the thirteenth labour of the Grecian Hercules. A more serious and decent excuse may be drawn from his fidelity to Cadijah. During the twenty-four years of their marriage her youthful husband abstained from the right of polygamy, and the pride or tenderness of the venerable matron was never insulted by the society of a rival. After her death he placed her in the rank of the four perfect women, with the sister of Moses, the mother of Jesus, and Fatima, the best beloved of his daughters. "Was she not old?" said Ayesha, with the insolence of a blooming beauty; "has not God given you a better in her place?" "No, by God," said Mahomet, with an effusion of honest gratitude, "there never can be a better! She believed in me when men despised me; she relieved my wants when I was poor and persecuted by the world."

In spite of his polygamy Mahomet left no heir. In 655 or 656 his son-in-law, Ali, became Commander of the Faithful, but his descendants did not retain power.

INFLUENCE OF MAHOMET

The talents of Mahomet are entitled to our applause; but his success has, perhaps, too strongly attracted our admiration. Are we surprised that a multitude of proselytes should embrace the doctrine and the passions of an eloquent fanatic? In the heresies of the church the same seduction has been tried and repeated from the time of the apostles to that of the reformers. Does it seem incredible that a private citizen should grasp the sword and the sceptre, subdue his native country, and erect a monarchy by his victorious arms? In the moving picture of the dynasties of the East, a hundred fortunate

---

[1] Sibi robur ad generationem, quantum triginta viri habent, inesse jactaret: ita ut unicâ horâ posset undecim fœminis *satisfacere*, ut ex Arabum libris refert S tus. Petrus Paschasius, c. 2 (Maracci). Al Jannabi records his own testimony, that he surpassed all men in conjugal vigour; and Abulfeda mentions the exclamation of Ali, who washed his body after his death, "O propheta, certe penis tuus cœlum versus erectus est."

usurpers have arisen from a baser origin, surmounted more formidable obstacles, and filled a larger scope of empire and conquest. Mahomet was alike instructed to preach and to fight; and the union of these opposite qualities, while it enhanced his merit, contributed to his success: the operation of force and persuasion, of enthusiasm and fear, continually acted on each other, till every barrier yielded to their irresistible power. His voice invited the Arabs to freedom and victory, to arms and rapine, to the indulgence of their darling passions in this world and the other: the restraints which he imposed were requisite to establish the credit of the prophet, and to exercise the obedience of the people; and the only objection to his success was his rational creed of the unity and perfections of God. It is not the propagation, but the permanency of his religion, that deserves our wonder: the same pure and perfect impression which he engraved at Mecca and Medina is preserved, after the revolutions of twelve centuries, by the Indian, the African, and the Turkish proselytes of the Koran. If the Christian apostles, St. Peter or St. Paul, could return to the Vatican, they might possibly inquire the name of the Deity who is worshipped with such mysterious rites in that magnificent temple: at Oxford or Geneva they would experience less surprise; but it might still be incumbent on them to peruse the catechism of the church, and to study the orthodox commentators on their own writings and the words of their Master. But the Turkish dome of St. Sophia, with an increase of splendour and size, represents the humble tabernacle erected at Medina by the hands of Mahomet. The Mahometans have uniformly withstood the temptation of reducing the object of their faith and devotion to a level with the senses and imagination of man. "I believe in one God, and Mahomet the apostle of God," is the simple and invariable profession of Islam. The intellectual image of the Deity has never been degraded by any visible idol; the honours of the prophet have never transgressed the measure of human virtue; and his living precepts have restrained the gratitude of his disciples within the bounds of reason and religion. The votaries of Ali have, indeed, consecrated the memory of their hero, his wife, and his children; and some of the Persian doctors pretend that the divine essence was incarnate in the person of the Imams; but their superstition is universally condemned by the Sonnites; and their impiety has afforded a seasonable warning against the worship of saints and martyrs. The metaphysical questions on the attributes of God, and the liberty of man, have been agitated in the schools of the Mahometans as well as in those of the Christians; but among the former they have never engaged the passions of the people, or disturbed the tranquillity of the state. The cause of this important difference may be found in the separation or union of the regal and sacerdotal characters. It was the interest of the caliphs, the successors of the prophet and commanders of the faithful, to repress and discourage all religious innovations; the order, the discipline, the temporal and spiritual ambition of the clergy, are unknown to the Moslems; and the sages of the law are the guides of their conscience and the oracles of their faith. From the Atlantic to the Ganges the Koran is acknowledged as the fundamental code, not only of theology but of civil and criminal jurisprudence; and the laws which regulate the actions and the property of mankind are guarded by the infallible and immutable sanction of the will of God. This religious servitude is attended with some practical disadvantage; the illiterate legislator had been often misled by his own prejudices and those of his country; and the institutions of the Arabian desert may be ill adapted to the wealth and numbers of Ispahan and Constantinople. On these occasions the Cadhi respectfully places on his head the holy volume, and substitutes a dexterous interpretation more apposite to the principles of equity and the manners and policy of the times.

His beneficial or pernicious influence on the public happiness is the last consideration in the character of Mahomet. The most bitter or most bigoted of his Christian or Jewish foes will surely allow that he assumed a false commission to inculcate a salutary doctrine, less perfect only than their own. He piously supposed, as the basis of his religion, the truth and sanctity of *their* prior revelations, the virtues and miracles of their founders. The idols of Arabia were broken before the throne of God; the blood of human victims was expiated by prayer, and fasting, and alms, the laudable or innocent arts of devotion; and his rewards and punishments of a future life were painted by the images most congenial to an ignorant and carnal generation. Mahomet was, perhaps, incapable of dictating a moral and political system for the use of his countrymen: but he breathed among the faithful a spirit of charity and friendship; recommended the practice of the social virtues; and checked, by his laws and precepts, the thirst of revenge, and the oppression of widows and orphans. The hostile tribes were united in faith and obedience, and the valour which had been idly spent in domestic quarrels was vigorously directed against a foreign enemy. Had the impulse been less powerful, Arabia, free at home, and formidable abroad, might have flourished under a succession of her native monarchs. Her sovereignty was lost by the extent and rapidity of conquest. The colonies of the nation were scattered over the East and West, and their blood was mingled with the blood of their converts and captives. After the reign of three caliphs, the throne was transported from Medina to the valley of Damascus and the banks of the Tigris; the holy cities were violated by impious war; Arabia was ruled by the rod of a subject, perhaps of a stranger; and the Bedoweens of the desert, awakening from their dream of dominion, resumed their old and solitary independence.

51.

THE FATE OF THE ALEXANDRIAN LIBRARY

Chapters 51 and 52 are omitted. They contain the narrative of the Arab conquests and the extension of their power and civilisation to Africa and Spain. Their advance into France was checked in 732 by the victory of Charles Martel. After they spread to the West these invasions lie, strictly speaking, outside the Roman Empire. One passage only from Chapter 51 is printed here. It describes the destruction of the Library at Alexandria. This deed was at least a symbol of the eclipse of the ancient culture, and, as Gibbon says, cannot be passed over. The story allowed him to pay a last salute to that literature which was the standard of his life and thought and from which as much as from anything he traced the decline and fall of civilisation. Nevertheless he tells the story critically and his scepticism is supported by modern opinion.

THE ALEXANDRIAN LIBRARY

I SHOULD DECEIVE the expectation of the reader if I passed in silence the fate of the Alexandrian library, as it is described by the learned Abulpharagius. The spirit of Amrou was more curious and liberal than that of his brethren, and in his leisure hours the Arabian chief was pleased with the conversation of John, the last disciple of Ammonius, and who derived the surname of *Philoponus* from his laborious studies of grammar and philosophy. Emboldened by this familiar intercourse, Philoponus presumed to solicit a gift, inestimable in *his* opinion, contemptible in that of the barbarians—the royal library, which alone, among the spoils of Alexandria, had not been appropriated by the visit and the seal of the conqueror. Amrou was inclined to gratify the wish of the grammarian, but his rigid integrity refused to alienate the minutest object without the consent of the caliph: and the

well-known answer of Omar was inspired by the ignorance
of a fanatic. "If these writings of the Greeks agree with the
book of God, they are useless and need not be preserved:
if they disagree, they are pernicious and ought to be destroyed."
The sentence was executed with blind obedience: the volumes
of paper or parchment were distributed to the four thousand
baths of the city; and such was their incredible multitude, that
six months were barely sufficient for the consumption of this
precious fuel. Since the Dynasties of Abulpharagius have been
given to the world in a Latin version, the tale has been
repeatedly transcribed; and every scholar, with pious indignation, has deplored the irreparable shipwreck of the learning,
the arts, and the genius of antiquity. For my own part, I
am strongly tempted to deny both the fact and the consequences. The fact is indeed marvellous. "Read and wonder!"
says the historian himself: and the solitary report of a stranger
who wrote at the end of six hundred years on the confines of
Media is overbalanced by the silence of two annalists of a
more early date, both Christians, both natives of Egypt, and
the most ancient of whom, the patriarch Eutychius, has amply
described the conquest of Alexandria. The rigid sentence of
Omar is repugnant to the sound and orthodox precept of the
Mahometan casuists: they expressly declare that the religious
books of the Jews and Christians, which are acquired by the
right of war, should never be committed to the flames; and
that the works of profane science, historians or poets, physicians or philosophers, may be lawfully applied to the faithful.
A more destructive zeal may perhaps be attributed to the
first successors of Mahomet; yet in this instance the conflagration would have speedily expired in the deficiency of
materials. I shall not recapitulate the disasters of the Alexandrian library, the involuntary flame that was kindled by
Cæsar in his own defence, or the mischievous bigotry of the
Christians, who studied to destroy the monuments of idolatry.
But if we gradually descend from the age of the Antonines to
that of Theodosius, we shall learn from a chain of contemporary witnesses that the royal palace and the temple of
Serapis no longer contained the four, or the seven, hundred
thousand volumes which had been assembled by the curiosity
and magnificence of the Ptolemies. Perhaps the church and
seat of the patriarchs might be enriched with a repository of
books; but if the ponderous mass of Arian and Monophysite

controversy were indeed consumed in the public baths, a philosopher may allow, with a smile, that it was ultimately devoted to the benefit of mankind. I sincerely regret the more valuable libraries which have been involved in the ruin of the Roman empire; but when I seriously compute the lapse of ages, the waste of ignorance, and the calamities of war, our treasures, rather than our losses, are the object of my surprise. Many curious and interesting facts are buried in oblivion: the three great historians of Rome have been transmitted to our hands in a mutilated state; and we are deprived of many pleasing compositions of the lyric, iambic, and dramatic poetry of the Greeks. Yet we should gratefully remember that the mischances of time and accident have spared the classic works to which the suffrage of antiquity had adjusted the first place of genius and glory: the teachers of ancient knowledge, who are still extant, had perused and compared the writings of their predecessors; nor can it fairly be presumed that any important truth, any useful discovery in art or nature, has been snatched away from the curiosity of modern ages.

53.

STATE OF THE EASTERN EMPIRE IN THE TENTH
CENTURY. WEALTH, MANUFACTURES, AND REVENUE
OF THE EMPIRE. THE IMPERIAL PALACE. OBLIVION OF
THE LATIN LANGUAGE. REVIVAL OF GREEK LEARNING.
DECAY OF TASTE

A RAY of historic light seems to beam from the darkness
of the tenth century. We open with curiosity and respect the
royal volumes of Constantine Porphyrogenitus, which he composed at a mature age for the instruction of his son, and
which promise to unfold the state of the Eastern empire, both
in peace and war, both at home and abroad. In the first of
these works he minutely describes the pompous ceremonies
of the church and palace of Constantinople, according to his
own practice and that of his predecessors. In the second he
attempts an accurate survey of the provinces, the *themes,* as
they were then denominated, both of Europe and Asia. The
system of Roman tactics, the discipline and order of the
troops, and the military operations by land and sea, are
explained in the third of these didactic collections, which
may be ascribed to Constantine or his father Leo. In the
fourth, of the administration of the empire, he reveals the
secrets of the Byzantine policy, in friendly or hostile intercourse with the nations of the earth. The literary labours of
the age, the practical systems of law, agriculture, and history,
might redound to the benefit of the subject, and the honour
of the Macedonian princes. The sixty books of the *Basilics,*
the code and pandects of civil jurisprudence, were gradually
framed in the three first reigns of that prosperous dynasty.
The art of agriculture had amused the leisure, and exercised
the pens, of the best and wisest of the ancients; and their
chosen precepts are comprised in the twenty books of the

Geoponics of Constantine. At his command the historical examples of vice and virtue were methodised in fifty-three books and every citizen might apply to his contemporaries or himself the lesson or the warning of past times. From the august character of a legislator, the sovereign of the East descends to the more humble office of a teacher and a scribe; and if his successors and subjects were regardless of his paternal cares, *we* may inherit and enjoy the everlasting legacy.

A closer survey will indeed reduce the value of the gift and the gratitude of posterity: in the possession of these Imperial treasures we may still deplore our poverty and ignorance; and the fading glories of their authors will be obliterated by indifference or contempt. The *Basilics* will sink to a broken copy, a partial and mutilated version in the Greek language, of the laws of Justinian; but the sense of the old civilians is often superseded by the influence of bigotry: and the absolute prohibition of divorce, concubinage, and interest for money, enslaves the freedom of trade and the happiness of private life. In the historical book a subject of Constantine might admire the inimitable virtues of Greece and Rome: he might learn to what a pitch of energy and elevation the human character had formerly aspired. But a contrary effect must have been produced by a new edition of the lives of the saints, which the great logothete, or chancellor of the empire, was directed to prepare; and the dark fund of superstition was enriched by the fabulous and florid legends of Simon the *Metaphrast*. The merits and miracles of the whole calendar are of less account in the eyes of a sage than the toil of a single husbandman, who multiplies the gifts of the Creator and supplies the food of his brethren. Yet the royal authors of the *Geoponics* were more seriously employed in expounding the precepts of the destroying art, which has been taught since the days of Xenophon as the art of heroes and kings. But the *Tactics* of Leo and Constantine are mingled with the baser alloy of the age in which they lived. It was destitute of original genius; they implicitly transcribe the rules and maxims which had been confirmed by victories. It was unskilled in the propriety of style and method; they blindly confound the most distant and discordant institutions, the phalanx of Sparta and that of Macedon, the legions of Cato and Trajan, of Augustus and Theodosius. Even the use, or at least the importance, of these military rudiments may be fairly questioned:

their general theory is dictated by reason; but the merit, as well as difficulty, consists in the application. The discipline of a soldier is formed by exercise rather than by study: the talents of a commander are appropriated to those calm, though rapid, minds, which nature produces to decide the fate of armies and nations: the former is the habit of a life, the latter the glance of a moment; and the battles won by lessons of tactics may be numbered with the epic poems created from the rules of criticism. The book of ceremonies is a recital, tedious yet imperfect, of the despicable pageantry which had infected the church and state since the gradual decay of the purity of the one and the power of the other. A review of the themes or provinces might promise such authentic and useful information as the curiosity of government only can obtain, instead of traditionary fables on the origin of the cities, and malicious epigrams on the vices of their inhabitants. Such information the historian would have been pleased to record; nor should his silence be condemned if the most interesting objects, the population of the capital and provinces, the amount of the taxes and revenues, the numbers of subjects and strangers who served under the Imperial standard, have been unnoticed by Leo the Philosopher and his son Constantine. His treatise of the public administration is stained with the same blemishes; yet it is discriminated by peculiar merit: the antiquities of the nations may be doubtful or fabulous; but the geography and manners of the barbaric world are delineated with curious accuracy. Of these nations the Franks alone were qualified to observe in their turn, and to describe, the metropolis of the East. The ambassador of the great Otho, a bishop of Cremona, has painted the state of Constantinople about the middle of the tenth century: his style is glowing, his narrative lively, his observation keen; and even the prejudices and passions of Liutprand are stamped with an original character of freedom and genius. From this scanty fund of foreign and domestic materials I shall investigate the form and substance of the Byzantine empire; the provinces and wealth, the civil government and military force, the character and literature, of the Greeks in a period of six hundred years, from the reign of Heraclius to the successful invasion of the Franks or Latins.

After the final division between the sons of Theodosius, the swarms of barbarians from Scythia and Germany over-

spread the provinces and extinguished the empire of ancient
Rome. The weakness of Constantinople was concealed by
extent of dominion; her limits were inviolate, or at least
entire; and the kingdom of Justinian was enlarged by the
splendid acquisition of Africa and Italy. But the possession
of these new conquests was transient and precarious, and
almost a moiety of the Eastern empire was torn away by
the arms of the Saracens. Syria and Egypt were oppressed
by the Arabian caliphs, and, after the reduction of Africa,
their lieutenants invaded and subdued the Roman province
which had been changed into the Gothic monarchy of Spain.
The islands of the Mediterranean were not inaccessible to their
naval powers; and it was from their extreme stations, the
harbours of Crete and the fortresses of Cilicia, that the faithful
or rebel emirs insulted the majesty of the throne and capital.
The remaining provinces, under the obedience of the emperors,
were cast into a new mould; and the jurisdiction of the
presidents, the consulars, and the counts was superseded by
the institution of the *themes,* or military governments, which
prevailed under the successors of Heraclius, and are described
by the pen of the royal author. Of the twenty-nine themes,
twelve in Europe and seventeen in Asia, the origin is obscure,
the etymology doubtful or capricious, the limits were arbitrary
and fluctuating; but some particular names that sound the most
strangely to our ear were derived from the character and
attributes of the troops that were maintained at the expense
and for the guard of the respective divisions. The vanity of
the Greek princes most eagerly grasped the shadow of conquest and the memory of lost dominion. A new Mesopotamia
was created on the western side of the Euphrates; the appellation and prætor of Sicily were transferred to a narrow slip
of Calabria; and a fragment of the duchy of Beneventum
was promoted to the style and title of the theme of Lombardy.
In the decline of the Arabian empire the successors of Constantine might indulge their pride in more solid advantages.
The victories of Nicephorus, John Zimisces, and Basil the
Second, revived the fame, and enlarged the boundaries, of
the Roman name; the province of Cilicia, the metropolis of
Antioch, the islands of Crete and Cyprus were restored to the
allegiance of Christ and Cæsar; one-third of Italy was annexed
to the throne of Constantinople, the kingdom of Bulgaria was
destroyed, and the last sovereigns of the Macedonian dynasty

extended their sway from the sources of the Tigris to the neighbourhood of Rome. In the eleventh century the prospect was again clouded by new enemies and new misfortunes; the relics of Italy were swept away by the Norman adventurers, and almost all the Asiatic branches were dissevered from the Roman trunk by the Turkish conquerors. After these losses the emperors of the Comnenian family continued to reign from the Danube to Peloponnesus, and from Belgrade to Nice, Trebizond, and the winding stream of the Meander. The spacious provinces of Thrace, Macedonia, and Greece were obedient to their sceptre; the possession of Cyprus, Rhodes, and Crete was accompanied by the fifty islands of the Ægean or Holy Sea, and the remnant of their empire transcends the measure of the largest of the European kingdoms.

WEALTH, MANUFACTURES, AND REVENUE OF THE EMPIRE

The same princes might assert, with dignity and truth, that of all the monarchs of Christendom they possessed the greatest city, the most ample revenue, the most flourishing and populous state. With the decline and fall of the empire the cities of the West had decayed and fallen; nor could the ruins of Rome, or the mud walls, wooden hovels, and narrow precincts of Paris and London, prepare the Latin stranger to contemplate the situation and extent of Constantinople, her stately palaces and churches, and the arts and luxury of an innumerable people. Her treasures might attract, but her virgin strength had repelled, and still promised to repel, the audacious invasion of the Persian and Bulgarian, the Arab and the Russian. The provinces were less fortunate and impregnable, and few districts, few cities, could be discovered which had not been violated by some fierce barbarian, impatient to despoil, because he was hopeless to possess. From the age of Justinian the Eastern empire was sinking below its former level; the powers of destruction were more active than those of improvement; and the calamities of war were embittered by the more permanent evils of civil and ecclesiastical tyranny. The captive who had escaped from the barbarians was often stripped and imprisoned by the ministers of his sovereign; the Greek superstition relaxed the mind by prayer, and emaciated the body by fasting; and the multitude of convents and festivals diverted many hands and many days

from the temporal service of mankind. Yet the subjects of the
Byzantine empire were still the most dexterous and diligent
of nations; their country was blessed by nature with every
advantage of soil, climate, and situation; and, in the support
and restoration of the arts, their patient and peaceful temper
was more useful than the warlike spirit and feudal anarchy
of Europe. The provinces that still adhered to the empire
were repeopled and enriched by the misfortunes of those which
were irrecoverably lost. From the yoke of the caliphs, the
Catholics of Syria, Egypt, and Africa retired to the allegiance
of their prince, to the society of their brethren; the moveable
wealth, which eludes the search of oppression, accompanied
and alleviated their exile, and Constantinople received into
her bosom the fugitive trade of Alexandria and Tyre. The
chiefs of Armenia and Scythia, who fled from hostile or
religious persecution, were hospitably entertained; their followers were encouraged to build new cities and to cultivate
waste lands; and many spots, both in Europe and Asia, preserved the name, the manners, or at least the memory, of
these national colonies. Even the tribes of barbarians who had
seated themselves in arms on the territory of the empire were
gradually reclaimed to the laws of the church and state, and,
as long as they were separated from the Greeks, their posterity
supplied a race of faithful and obedient soldiers. Did we
possess sufficient materials to survey the twenty-nine themes
of the Byzantine monarchy, our curiosity might be satisfied
with a chosen example: it is fortunate enough that the clearest
light should be thrown on the most interesting province, and
the name of PELOPONNESUS will awaken the attention of the
classic reader.

As early as the eighth century, in the troubled reign of the
Iconoclasts, Greece, and even Peloponnesus, were overrun by
some Sclavonian bands who outstripped the royal standard
of Bulgaria. The strangers of old, Cadmus, and Danaus, and
Pelops, had planted in that faithful soil the seeds of policy
and learning; but the savages of the north eradicated what
yet remained of their sickly and withered roots. In this
irruption the country and the inhabitants were transformed;
the Grecian blood was contaminated; and the proudest nobles
of Peloponnesus were branded with the names of foreigners
and *slaves*. By the diligence of succeeding princes, the land
was in some measure purified from the barbarians; and the

humble remnant was bound by an oath of obedience, tribute, and military service, which they often renewed and often violated. The siege of Patras was formed by a singular concurrence of the Sclavonians of Peloponnesus and the Saracens of Africa. In their last distress a pious fiction of the approach of the prætor of Corinth revived the courage of the citizens. Their sally was bold and successful; the strangers embarked, the rebels submitted, and the glory of the day was ascribed to a phantom or a stranger, who fought in the foremost ranks under the character of St. Andrew the Apostle. The shrine which contained his relics was decorated with the trophies of victory, and the captive race was for ever devoted to the service and vassalage of the metropolitan church of Patras. By the revolt of two Sclavonian tribes in the neighbourhood of Helos and Lacedæmon, the peace of the peninsula was often disturbed. They sometimes insulted the weakness, and sometimes resisted the oppression, of the Byzantine government, till at length the approach of their hostile brethren extorted a golden bull to define the rights and obligations of the Ezzerites and Milengi, whose annual tribute was defined at twelve hundred pieces of gold. From these strangers the Imperial geographer has accurately distinguished a domestic and perhaps original race, who, in some degree, might derive their blood from the much-injured Helots. The liberality of the Romans, and especially of Augustus, had enfranchised the maritime cities from the dominion of Sparta; and the continuance of the same benefit ennobled them with the title of *Eleuthero,* or Free-Laconians. In the time of Constantine Porphyrogenitus they had acquired the name of *Mainotes,* under which they dishonour the claim of liberty by the inhuman pillage of all that is shipwrecked on their rocky shores. Their territory, barren of corn but fruitful of olives, extended to the Cape of Malea: they accepted a chief or prince from the Byzantine prætor; and a light tribute of four hundred pieces of gold was the badge of their immunity rather than of their dependence. The freemen of Laconia assumed the character of Romans, and long adhered to the religion of the Greeks. By the zeal of the emperor Basil, they were baptized in the faith of Christ: but the altars of Venus and Neptune had been crowned by these rustic votaries five hundred years after they were proscribed in the Roman world. In the theme of Peloponnesus forty cities were still numbered, and the

declining state of Sparta, Argos, and Corinth may be suspended in the tenth century, at an equal distance, perhaps, between
their antique splendour and their present desolation. The duty
of military service, either in person or by substitute, was imposed on the lands or benefices of the province; a sum of
five pieces of gold was assessed on each of the substantial
tenants; and the same capitation was shared among several
heads of inferior value. On the proclamation of an Italian war,
the Peloponnesians excused themselves by a voluntary oblation of one hundred pounds of gold (four thousand pounds
sterling), and a thousand horses with their arms and trappings. The churches and monasteries furnished their con-
tingent; a sacrilegious profit was extorted from the sale of
ecclesiastical honours; and the indigent bishop of Leucadia
was made responsible for a pension of one hundred pieces of
gold.

But the wealth of the province, and the trust of the revenue,
were founded on the fair and plentiful produce of trade and
manufactures; and some symptoms of liberal policy may be
traced in a law which exempts from all personal taxes the
mariners of Peloponnesus, and the workmen in parchment and
purple. This denomination may be fairly applied or extended
to the manufactures of linen, woollen, and more especially of
silk: the two former of which had flourished in Greece since
the days of Homer; and the last was introduced perhaps as
early as the reign of Justinian. These arts, which were exercised at Corinth, Thebes, and Argos, afforded food and occupation to a numerous people: the men, women, and children
were distributed according to their age and strength; and if
many of these were domestic slaves, their masters, who directed the work and enjoyed the profit, were of a free and
honourable condition. The gifts which a rich and generous
matron of Peloponnesus presented to the emperor Basil, her
adopted son, were doubtless fabricated in the Grecian looms.
Danielis bestowed a carpet of fine wool, of a pattern which
imitated the spots of a peacock's tail, of a magnitude to overspread the floor of a new church, erected in the triple name
of Christ, of Michael the archangel, and of the prophet Elijah.
She gave six hundred pieces of silk and linen, of various use
and denomination: the silk was painted with the Tyrian dye,
and adorned by the labours of the needle; and the linen was
so exquisitely fine, that an entire piece might be rolled in the

hollow of a cane. In his description of the Greek manufactures, an historian of Sicily discriminates their price, according to the weight and quality of the silk, the closeness of the texture, the beauty of the colours, and the taste and materials of the embroidery. A single, or even a double or treble thread was thought sufficient for ordinary sale; but the union of six threads composed a piece of stronger and more costly workmanship. Among the colours, he celebrates, with affectation of eloquence, the fiery blaze of the scarlet, and the softer lustre of the green. The embroidery was raised either in silk or gold: the more simple ornament of stripes or circles was surpassed by the nicer imitation of flowers: the vestments that were fabricated for the palace or the altar often glittered with precious stones; and the figures were delineated in strings of Oriental pearls. Till the twelfth century, Greece alone, of all the countries of Christendom, was possessed of the insect who is taught by nature, and of the workmen who are instructed by art, to prepare this elegant luxury. But the secret had been stolen by the dexterity and diligence of the Arabs: the caliphs of the East and West scorned to borrow from the unbelievers their furniture and apparel; and two cities of Spain, Almeria and Lisbon, were famous for the manufacture, the use, and perhaps the exportation of silk. It was first introduced into Sicily by the Normans; and this emigration of trade distinguishes the victory of Roger from the uniform and fruitless hostilities of every age. After the sack of Corinth, Athens, and Thebes, his lieutenant embarked with a captive train of weavers and artificers of both sexes, a trophy glorious to their master and disgraceful to the Greek emperor. The king of Sicily was not insensible of the value of the present; and, in the restitution of the prisoners, he excepted only the male and female manufacturers of Thebes and Corinth, who labour, says the Byzantine historian, under a barbarous lord, like the old Eretrians in the service of Darius. A stately edifice, in the palace of Palermo, was erected for the use of this industrious colony; and the art was propagated by their children and disciples to satisfy the increasing demand of the western world. The decay of the looms of Sicily may be ascribed to the troubles of the island and the competition of the Italian cities. In the year thirteen hundred and fourteen, Lucca alone, among her sister republics, enjoyed the lucrative monopoly. A domestic revolution dispersed the manufacturers to Florence,

Bologna, Venice, Milan, and even the countries beyond the Alps; and thirteen years after this event, the statutes of Modena enjoin the planting of mulberry-trees and regulate the duties on raw silk. The northern climates are less propitious to the education of the silkworm; but the industry of France and England is supplied and enriched by the productions of Italy and China.

I must repeat the complaint that the vague and scanty memorials of the times will not afford any just estimate of the taxes, the revenue, and the resources of the Greek empire. From every province of Europe and Asia the rivulets of gold and silver discharged into the Imperial reservoir a copious and perennial stream. The separation of the branches from the trunk increased the relative magnitude of Constantinople; and the maxims of despotism contracted the state to the capital, the capital to the palace, and the palace to the royal person. A Jewish traveller, who visited the East in the twelfth century, is lost in his admiration of the Byzantine riches. "It is here," says Benjamin of Tudela, "in the queen of cities, that the tributes of the Greek empire are annually deposited, and the lofty towers are filled with precious magazines of silk, purple, and gold. It is said that Constantinople pays each day to her sovereign twenty thousand pieces of gold, which are levied on the shops, taverns, and markets, on the merchants of Persia and Egypt, of Russia and Hungary, of Italy and Spain, who frequent the capital by sea and land." In all pecuniary matters the authority of a Jew is doubtless respectable; but as the three hundred and sixty-five days would produce a yearly income exceeding seven millions sterling, I am tempted to retrench at least the numerous festivals of the Greek calendar. The mass of treasure that was saved by Theodora and Basil the Second will suggest a splendid, though indefinite, idea of their supplies and resources. The mother of Michael, before she retired to a cloister, attempted to check or expose the prodigality of her ungrateful son by a free and faithful account of the wealth which he inherited; one hundred and nine thousand pounds of gold and three hundred thousand of silver, the fruits of her own economy and that of her deceased husband. The avarice of Basil is not less renowned than his valour and fortune: his victorious armies were paid and rewarded without breaking into the mass of two hundred thousand pounds of gold (about eight millions sterling), which he had buried in the subterraneous vaults of the palace. Such accumulation of treasure is rejected by the theory and practice of modern policy; and we are more apt to compute the national riches by the use and abuse of the public credit. Yet the maxims of antiquity are still embraced by a monarch formidable to his enemies; by a republic respectable to her allies; and both have attained their respective ends of military power and domestic tranquillity.

THE IMPERIAL PALACE

Whatever might be consumed for the present wants or reserved for the future use of the state, the first and most sacred demand was for the pomp and pleasure of the emperor; and his discretion only could define the measure of his private expense. The princes of Constantinople were far removed from the simplicity of nature; yet, with the revolving seasons, they were led by taste or fashion to withdraw to a purer air from the smoke and tumult of the capital. They enjoyed, or affected to enjoy, the rustic festival of the vintage: their leisure was amused by the exercise of the chase and the calmer occupation of fishing; and in the summer heats they were shaded from the sun, and refreshed by the cooling breezes from the sea. The coasts and islands of Asia and Europe were covered with their magnificent villas; but instead of the modest art which secretly strives to hide itself and to decorate the scenery of nature, the marble structure of their gardens served only to expose the riches of the lord and the labours of the architect. The successive casualties of inheritance and forfeiture had rendered the sovereign proprietor of many stately houses in the city and suburbs, of which twelve were appropriated to the ministers of state; but the great palace, the centre of the Imperial residence, was fixed during eleven centuries to the same position, between the hippodrome, the cathedral of St. Sophia, and the gardens, which descended by many a terrace to the shores of the Propontis. The primitive edifice of the first Constantine was a copy, or rival, of ancient Rome; the gradual improvements of his successors aspired to emulate the wonders of the old world, and in the tenth century the Byzantine palace excited the admiration, at least of the Latins, by an unquestionable pre-eminence of strength, size, and magnificence. But the toil and treasure of so many ages had

produced a vast and irregular pile: each separate building
was marked with the character of the times and of the founder;
and the want of space might excuse the reigning monarch
who demolished, perhaps with secret satisfaction, the works
of his predecessors. The economy of the emperor Theophilus
allowed a more free and ample scope for his domestic luxury and splendour. A favorite ambassador, who had astonished
the Abbassides themselves by his pride and liberality, presented on his return the model of a palace which the caliph
of Bagdad had recently constructed on the banks of the
Tigris. The model was instantly copied and surpassed: the
new buildings of Theophilus were accompanied with gardens
and with five churches, one of which was conspicuous for
size and beauty: it was crowned with three domes, the roof
of gilt brass reposed on columns of Italian marble, and the
walls were incrusted with marbles of various colours. In the
face of the church a semicircular portico, of the figure and
name of the Greek *sigma*, was supported by fifteen columns
of Phrygian marble, and the subterraneous vaults were of
a similar construction. The square before the sigma was decorated with a fountain, and the margin of the basin was
lined and encompassed with plates of silver. In the beginning
of each season the basin, instead of water, was replenished
with the most exquisite fruits, which were abandoned to the
populace for the entertainment of the prince. He enjoyed
this tumultuous spectacle from a throne resplendent with
gold and gems, which was raised by a marble staircase to the
height of a lofty terrace. Below the throne were seated the
officers of his guards, the magistrates, the chiefs of the factions of the circus; the inferior steps were occupied by the
people, and the place below was covered with troops of danc-
ers, singers, and pantomimes. The square was surrounded by
the hall of justice, the arsenal, and the various offices of
business and pleasure; and the *purple* chamber was named
from the annual distribution of robes of scarlet and purple
by the hand of the empress herself. The long series of the
apartments was adapted to the seasons, and decorated with
marble and porphyry, with painting, sculpture, and mosaics,
with a profusion of gold, silver, and precious stones. His fan-
ciful magnificence employed the skill and patience of such
artists as the times could afford; but the taste of Athens would
have despised their frivolous and costly labours; a golden

tree, with its leaves and branches, which sheltered a multitude of birds warbling their artificial notes, and two lions of massy gold, and of the natural size, who looked and roared like their brethren of the forest. The successors of Theophilus, of the Basilian and Comnenian dynasties, were not less ambitious of leaving some memorial of their residence; and the portion of the palace most splendid and august was dignified with the title of the golden *triclinium*. With becoming modesty the rich and noble Greeks aspired to imitate their sovereign, and when they passed through the streets on horseback, in their robes of silk and embroidery, they were mistaken by the children for kings. A matron of Peloponnesus, who had cherished the infant fortunes of Basil the Macedonian, was excited by tenderness or vanity to visit the greatness of her adopted son. In a journey of five hundred miles from Patras to Constantinople, her age or indolence declined the fatigue of an horse or carriage; the soft litter or bed of Danielis was transported on the shoulders of ten robust slaves, and, as they were relieved at easy distances, a band of three hundred was selected for the performance of this service. She was entertained in the Byzantine palace with filial reverence and the honours of a queen; and whatever might be the origin of her wealth, her gifts were not unworthy of the regal dignity. I have already described the fine and curious manufactures of Peloponnesus, of linen, silk, and woollen; but the most acceptable of her presents consisted in three hundred beautiful youths, of whom one hundred were eunuchs; "for she was not ignorant," says the historian, "that the air of the palace is more congenial to such insects, than a shepherd's dairy to the flies of the summer." During her lifetime she bestowed the greater part of her estates in Peloponnesus, and her testament instituted Leo, the són of Basil, her universal heir. After the payment of the legacies, fourscore villas or farms were added to the Imperial domain, and three thousand slaves of Danielis were enfranchised by their new lord, and transplanted as a colony to the Italian coast. From this example of a private matron we may estimate the wealth and magnificence of the emperors. Yet our enjoyments are confined by a narrow circle, and, whatsoever may be its value, the luxury of life is possessed with more innocence and safety by the master of his own, than by the steward of the public, fortune.

In an absolute government, which levels the distinctions
of noble and plebeian birth, the sovereign is the sole fountain
of honour; and the rank, both in the palace and the empire,
depends on the titles and offices which are bestowed and resumed by his arbitrary will. Above a thousand years, from
Vespasian to Alexius Comnenus, the *Cæsar* was the second
person, or at least the second degree, after the supreme title
of *Augustus* was more freely communicated to the sons and
brothers of the reigning monarch. To elude without violating
his promise to a powerful associate, the husband of his sister,
and, without giving himself an equal, to reward the piety of
his brother Isaac, the crafty Alexius interposed a new and
supereminent dignity. The happy flexibility of the Greek
tongue allowed him to compound the names of Augustus and
Emperor (Sebastos and Autocrator), and the union produced
the sonorous title of *Sebastocrator*. He was exalted above the
Cæsar on the first step of the throne: the public acclamations
repeated his name; and he was only distinguished from the
sovereign by some peculiar ornaments of the head and feet.
The emperor alone could assume the purple or red buskins,
and the close diadem or tiara, which imitated the fashion of
the Persian kings. It was an high pyramidal cap of cloth or
silk, almost concealed by a profusion of pearls and jewels:
the crown was formed by an horizontal circle and two arches
of gold: at the summit, the point of their intersection, was
placed a globe or cross, and two strings or lappets of pearl
depended on either cheek. Instead of red, the buskins of the
Sebastocrator and Cæsar were green; and on their *open*
coronets, or crowns, the precious gems were more sparingly
distributed. Beside and below the Cæsar the fancy of Alexius
created the *Panhypersebastos* and the *Protosebastos*, whose
sound and signification will satisfy a Grecian ear. They imply
a superiority and a priority above the simple name of Augustus; and this sacred and primitive title of the Roman prince
was degraded to the kinsmen and servants of the Byzantine
court. The daughter of Alexius applauds with fond complacency this artful gradation of hopes and honours; but the
science of words is accessible to the meanest capacity; and
this vain dictionary was easily enriched by the pride of his
successors. To their favourite sons or brothers they imparted
the more lofty appellation of Lord or *Despot*, which was
illustrated with new ornaments and prerogatives, and placed

immediately after the person of the emperor himself. The five titles of, 1. *Despot;* 2. *Sebastocrator;* 3. *Cæsar;* 4. *Panhypersebastos;* and 5. *Protosebastos;* were usually confined to the princes of his blood: they were the emanations of his majesty; but as they exercised no regular functions, their existence was useless, and their authority precarious.

But in every monarchy the substantial powers of government must be divided and exercised by the ministers of the palace and treasury, the fleet and army. The titles alone can differ; and in the revolution of ages, the counts and prefects, the prætor and quæstor, insensibly descended, while their servants rose above their heads to the first honours of the state. 1. In a monarchy, which refers every object to the person of prince, the care and ceremonies of the palace form the most respectable department. The *Curopalata,* so illustrious in the age of Justinian, was supplanted by the *Protovestiare,* whose primitive functions were limited to the custody of the wardrobe. From thence his jurisdiction was extended over the numerous menials of pomp and luxury; and he presided with his silver wand at the public and private audience. 2. In the ancient system of Constantine, the name of *Logothete,* or accountant, was applied to the receivers of the finances: the principal officers were distinguished as the Logothetes of the domain, of the posts, the army, the private and public treasure; and the *great Logothete,* the supreme guardian of the laws and revenues, is compared with the chancellor of the Latin monarchies. His discerning eye pervaded the civil administration; and he was assisted, in due subordination, by the eparch or prefect of the city, the first secretary, and the keepers of the privy seal, the archives, and the red or purple ink which was reserved for the sacred signature of the emperor alone. The introductor and interpreter of foreign ambassadors were the great *Chiauss* and the *Dragoman,* two names of Turkish origin, and which are still familiar to the Sublime Porte. 3. From the humble style and service of guards, the *Domestics* insensibly rose to the station of generals; the military themes of the East and West, the legions of Europe and Asia, were often divided, till the *great Domestic* was finally invested with the universal and absolute command of the land forces. The *Protostrator,* in his original functions, was the assistant of the emperor when he mounted on horseback: he gradually became the lieutenant of the great Domestic in

the field; and his jurisdiction extended over the stables, the
cavalry, and the royal train of hunting and hawking. The
Stratopedarch was the great judge of the camp: the *Protospathaire* commanded the guards; the *Constable,* the *great
Æteriarch,* and the *Acolyth,* were the separate chiefs of the
Franks, the barbarians, and the Varangi, or English, the mercenary strangers, who, in the decay of the national spirit,
formed the nerve of the Byzantine armies. 4. The naval
powers were under the command of the *great Duke;* in his
absence they obeyed the *great Drungaire* of the fleet; and,
in *his* place, the *Emir,* or *Admiral,* a name of Saracen extrac-
tion, but which has been naturalised in all the modern languages of Europe. Of these officers, and of many more whom
it would be useless to enumerate, the civil and military hierarchy was framed. Their honours and emoluments, their dress
and titles, their mutual salutations, and respective pre-eminence, were balanced with more exquisite labour than would
have fixed the constitution of a free people; and the code was
almost perfect when this baseless fabric, the monument of
pride and servitude, was for ever buried in the ruins of the
empire.

The most lofty titles, and the most humble postures, which
devotion has applied to the Supreme Being, have been prostituted by flattery and fear to creatures of the same nature with
ourselves. The mode of *adoration,* of falling prostrate on the
ground and kissing the feet of the emperor, was borrowed
by Diocletian from Persian servitude; but it was continued
and aggravated till the last age of the Greek monarchy. Excepting only on Sundays, when it was waived, from a motive
of religious pride, this humiliating reverence was exacted from
all who entered the royal presence, from the princes invested
with the diadem and purple, and from the ambassadors who
represented their independent sovereigns, the caliphs of Asia,
Egypt, or Spain, the kings of France and Italy, and the Latin
emperors of ancient Rome. In his transactions of business,
Liutprand, bishop of Cremona, asserted the free spirit of a
Frank and the dignity of his master Otho. Yet his sincerity
cannot disguise the abasement of his first audience. When he
approached the throne, the birds of the golden tree began
to warble their notes, which were accompanied by the roar-
ings of the two lions of gold. With his two companions
Liutprand was compelled to bow and to fall prostrate; and

thrice he touched the ground with his forehead. He arose; but in the short interval the throne had been hoisted by an engine from the floor to the ceiling, the Imperial figure appeared in new and more gorgeous apparel, and the interview was concluded in haughty and majestic silence. In this honest and curious narrative the bishop of Cremona represents the ceremonies of the Byzantine court, which are still practised in the Sublime Porte, and which were preserved in the last age by the dukes of Muscovy or Russia. After a long journey by the sea and land, from Venice to Constantinople, the ambassador halted at the golden gate, till he was conducted by the formal officers to the hospitable palace prepared for his reception; but this palace was a prison, and his jealous keepers prohibited all social intercourse either with strangers or natives. At his first audience he offered the gifts of his master—slaves, and golden vases, and costly armour. The ostentatious payment of the officers and troops displayed before his eyes the riches of the empire: he was entertained at a royal banquet, in which the ambassadors of the nations were marshalled by the esteem or contempt of the Greeks: from his own table, the emperor, as the most signal favour, sent the plates which he had tasted; and his favourites were dismissed with a robe of honour. In the morning and evening of each day his civil and military servants attended their duty in the palace; their labour was repaid by the sight, perhaps by the smile, of their lord; his commands were signified by a nod or a sign: but all earthly greatness *stood* silent and submissive in his presence. In his regular or extraordinary processions through the capital, he unveiled his person to the public view: the rites of policy were connected with those of religion, and his visits to the principal churches were regulated by the festivals of the Greek calendar. On the eve of these processions the gracious or devout intention of the monarch was proclaimed by the heralds. The streets were cleared and purified; the pavement was strewed with flowers; the most precious furniture, the gold and silver plate and silken hangings, were displayed from the windows and balconies; and a severe discipline restrained and silenced the tumult of the populace. The march was opened by the military officers at the head of their troops: they were followed in long order by the magistrates and ministers of the civil government: the person of the emperor was guarded by his eunuchs and

domestics, and at the church door he was solemnly received
by the patriarch and his clergy. The task of applause was not
abandoned to the rude and spontaneous voices of the crowd.
The most convenient stations were occupied by the bands of
the blue and green factions of the circus; and their furious
conflicts, which had shaken the capital, were insensibly sunk
to an emulation of servitude. From either side they echoed
in responsive melody the praises of the emperor; their poets
and musicians directed the choir, and long life and victory
were the burden of every song. The same acclamations were
performed at the audience, the banquet, and the church; and
as an evidence of boundless sway, they were repeated in the
Latin, Gothic, Persian, French, and even English language,
by the mercenaries who sustained the real or fictitious character of those nations. By the pen of Constantine Porphyrogenitus this science of form and flattery has been reduced
into a pompous and trifling volume, which the vanity of
succeeding times might enrich with an ample supplement.
Yet the calmer reflection of a prince would surely suggest
that the same acclamations were applied to every character
and every reign: and if he had risen from a private rank, he
might remember that his own voice had been the loudest and
most eager in applause, at the very moment when he envied
the fortune, or conspired against the life, of his predecessor.

The princes of the North, of the nations, says Constantine,
without faith or fame, were ambitious of mingling their blood
with the blood of the Cæsars, by their marriage with a royal
virgin, or by the nuptials of their daughters with a Roman
prince. The aged monarch, in his instructions to his son,
reveals the secret maxims of policy and pride, and suggests
the most decent reasons for refusing these insolent and un-
reasonable demands. Every animal, says the discreet emperor,
is prompted by nature to seek a mate among the animals of
his own species; and the human species is divided into various
tribes, by the distinction of language, religion, and manners.
A just regard to the purity of descent preserves the harmony
of public and private life; but the mixture of foreign blood is
the fruitful source of disorder and discord. Such had ever
been the opinion and practice of the sage Romans: their
jurisprudence proscribed the marriage of a citizen and a
stranger: in the days of freedom and virtue a senator would
have scorned to match his daughter with a king: the glory of

Mark Antony was sullied by an Egyptian wife: and the emperor Titus was compelled, by popular censure, to dismiss with reluctance the reluctant Berenice.[1] This perpetual interdict was ratified by the fabulous sanction of the great Constantine. The ambassadors of the nations, more especially of the unbelieving nations, were solemnly admonished that such strange alliances had been condemned by the founder of the church and city. The irrevocable law was inscribed on the altar of St. Sophia; and the impious prince who should stain the majesty of the purple was excluded from the civil and ecclesiastical communion of the Romans. If the ambassadors were instructed by any false brethren in the Byzantine history, they might produce three memorable examples of the violation of this imaginary law: the marriage of Leo, or rather of his father Constantine the Fourth, with the daughter of the king of the Chazars, the nuptials of the granddaughter of Romanus with a Bulgarian prince, and the union of Bertha of France or Italy with young Romanus, the son of Constantine Porphyrogenitus himself.

*   *   *   *   *

OBLIVION OF THE LATIN LANGUAGE

By the well-known edict of Caracalla, his subjects, from Britain to Egypt, were entitled to the name and privileges of Romans, and their national sovereign might fix his occasional or permanent residence in any province of their common country. In the division of the East and West an ideal unity was scrupulously preserved, and in their titles, laws, and statutes the successors of Arcadius and Honorius announced themselves as the inseparable colleagues of the same office, as the joint sovereigns of the Roman world and city, which were bounded by the same limits. After the fall of the Western monarchy the majesty of the purple resided solely in the princes of Constantinople, and of these Justinian was the first who, after a divorce of sixty years, regained the dominion of ancient Rome, and asserted, by the right of conquest, the august title of Emperor of the Romans. A motive

---

[1] Berenicem invitus invitam dimisit (Suetonius in Tito, c. 7). Have I observed elsewhere that this Jewish beauty was at this time above fifty years of age? The judicious Racine has most discreetly suppressed both her age and her country.

of vanity or discontent solicited one of his successors, Constans the Second, to abandon the Thracian Bosphorus and to restore the pristine honours of the Tiber: an extravagant project (exclaims the malicious Byzantine), as if he had despoiled a beautiful and blooming virgin, to enrich, or rather to expose, the deformity of a wrinkled and decrepit matron. But the sword of the Lombards opposed his settlement in Italy; he entered Rome not as a conqueror, but as a fugitive, and, after a visit of twelve days, he pillaged and for ever deserted the ancient capital of the world. The final revolt and separation of Italy was accomplished about two centuries after the conquests of Justinian, and from his reign we may date the gradual oblivion of the Latin tongue. That legislator had composed his Institutes, his Code, and his Pandects in a language which he celebrates as the proper and public style of the Roman government, the consecrated idiom of the palace and senate of Constantinople, of the camps and tribunals of the East. But this foreign dialect was unknown to the people and soldiers of the Asiatic provinces, it was imperfectly understood by the greater part of the interpreters of the laws and the ministers of the state. After a short conflict, nature and habit prevailed over the obsolete institutions of human power: for the general benefit of his subjects Justinian promulgated his Novels in the two languages, the several parts of his voluminous jurisprudence were successively translated, the original was forgotten, the version was studied, and the Greek, whose intrinsic merit deserved indeed the preference, obtained a legal as well as popular establishment in the Byzantine monarchy. The birth and residence of succeeding princes estranged them from the Roman idiom; Tiberius by the Arabs, and Maurice by the Italians, are distinguished as the first of the Greek Cæsars, as the founders of a new dynasty and empire; the silent revolution was accomplished before the death of Heraclius, and the ruins of the Latin speech were darkly preserved in the terms of jurisprudence and the acclamations of the palace. After the restoration of the Western empire by Charlemagne and the Othos, the names of Franks and Latins acquired an equal signification and extent, and these haughty barbarians asserted, with some justice, their superior claim to the language and dominion of Rome. They insulted the aliens of the East who had renounced the dress and idiom of Romans, and their reasonable practice

will justify the frequent appellation of Greeks. But this contemptuous appellation was indignantly rejected by the prince
and people to whom it is applied. Whatsoever changes had
been introduced by the lapse of ages, they alleged a lineal
and unbroken succession from Augustus and Constantine;
and, in the lowest period of degeneracy and decay, the name
of ROMANS adhered to the last fragments of the empire of
Constantinople.

While the government of the East was transacted in Latin,
the Greek was the language of literature and philosophy, nor
could the masters of this rich and perfect idiom be tempted
to envy the borrowed learning and imitative taste of their
Roman disciples. After the fall of Paganism, the loss of
Syria and Egypt, and the extinction of the schools of Alexandria and Athens, the studies of the Greeks insensibly retired
to some regular monasteries, and, above all, to the royal
college of Constantinople, which was burnt in the reign of
Leo the Isaurian. In the pompous style of the age, the president of that foundation was named the Sun of Science; his
twelve associates, the professors in the different arts and
faculties, were the twelve signs of the zodiac; a library of
thirty-six thousand five hundred volumes was open to their
inquiries; and they could show an ancient manuscript of
Homer, on a roll of parchment one hundred and twenty feet
in length, the intestines, as it was fabled, of a prodigious serpent. But the seventh and eighth centuries were a period of
discord and darkness; the library was burnt, the college was
abolished, the Iconoclasts are represented as the foes of
antiquity, and a savage ignorance and contempt of letters
has disgraced the princes of the Heraclean and Isaurian
dynasties.

REVIVAL OF GREEK LEARNING

In the ninth century we trace the first dawnings of the
restoration of science. After the fanaticism of the Arabs had
subsided, the caliphs aspired to conquer the arts, rather than
the provinces, of the empire: their liberal curiosity rekindled
the emulation of the Greeks, brushed away the dust from
their ancient libraries, and taught them to know and reward
the philosophers, whose labours had been hitherto repaid by
the pleasure of study and the pursuit of truth. The Cæsar

Bardas, the uncle of Michael the Third, was the generous
protector of letters, a title which alone has preserved his
memory and excused his ambition. A particle of the treasures
of his nephew was sometimes diverted from the indulgence
of vice and folly; a school was opened in the palace of
Magnaura, and the presence of Bardas excited the emulation
of the masters and students. At their head was the philosopher
Leo, archbishop of Thessalonica; his profound skill in astronomy and the mathematics was admired by the strangers of
the East, and this occult science was magnified by vulgar
credulity, which modestly supposes that all knowledge superior
to its own must be the effect of inspiration or magic. At the
pressing entreaty of the Cæsar, his friend, the celebrated
Photius, renounced the freedom of a secular and studious
life, ascended the patriarchal throne, and was alternately
excommunicated and absolved by the synods of the East
and West. By the confession even of priestly hatred, no art
or science, except poetry, was foreign to this universal
scholar, who was deep in thought, indefatigable in reading,
and eloquent in diction. Whilst he exercised the office of
protospathaire, or captain of the guards, Photius was sent
ambassador to the caliph of Bagdad. The tedious hours of
exile, perhaps of confinement, were beguiled by the hasty
composition of his *Library,* a living monument of erudition
and criticism. Two hundred and fourscore writers, historians,
orators, philosophers, theologians, are reviewed without any
regular method; he abridges their narrative or doctrine, ap-
preciates their style and character, and judges even the fathers
of the church with a discreet freedom which often breaks
through the superstition of the times. The emperor Basil,
who lamented the defects of his own education, intrusted to
the care of Photius his son and successor Leo the Philosopher,
and the reign of that prince and of his son Constantine
Porphyrogenitus forms one of the most prosperous eras of
the Byzantine literature. By their munificence the treasures
of antiquity were deposited in the Imperial library; by their
pens, or those of their associates, they were imparted in such
extracts and abridgments as might amuse the curiosity, without oppressing the indolence, of the public. Besides the
Basilics, or code of laws, the arts of husbandry and war,
of feeding or destroying the human species, were propagated
with equal diligence; and the history of Greece and Rome

was digested into fifty-three heads or titles, of which two only (of embassies, and of virtues and vices) have escaped the injuries of time. In every station the reader might contemplate the image of the past world, apply the lesson or warning of each page, and learn to admire, perhaps to imitate, the examples of a brighter period. I shall not expatiate on the works of the Byzantine Greeks, who, by the assiduous study of the ancients, have deserved, in some measure, the remembrance and gratitude of the moderns. The scholars of the present age may still enjoy the benefit of the philosophical commonplace-book of Stobæus, the grammatical and historic lexicon of Suidas, the Chiliads of Tzetzes, which comprise six hundred narratives in twelve thousand verses, and the commentaries on Homer of Eustathius, archbishop of Thessalonica, who, from his horn of plenty, has poured the names and authorities of four hundred writers. From these originals, and from the numerous tribe of scholiasts and critics, some estimate may be formed of the literary wealth of the twelfth century. Constantinople was enlightened by the genius of Homer and Demosthenes, of Aristotle and Plato; and in the enjoyment or neglect of our present riches we must envy the generation that could still peruse the history of Theopompus, the orations of Hyperides, the comedies of Menander, and the odes of Alcæus and Sappho. The frequent labour of illustration attests not only the existence but the popularity of the Grecian classics; the general knowledge of the age may be deduced from the example of two learned females, the empress Eudocia and the princess Anna Comnena, who cultivated, in the purple, the arts of rhetoric and philosophy. The vulgar dialect of the city was gross and barbarous: a more correct and elaborate style distinguished the discourse, or at least the compositions, of the church and palace, which sometimes affected to copy the purity of the Attic models.

THE DECAY OF TASTE

In our modern education, the painful though necessary attainment of two languages which are no longer living may consume the time and damp the ardour of the youthful student. The poets and orators were long imprisoned in the barbarous dialects of our Western ancestors, devoid of harmony or grace; and their genius, without precept or example, was abandoned to the rude and native powers of their judgment and fancy. But the Greeks of Constantinople, after purging away the impurities of their vulgar speech, acquired the free use of their ancient language, the most happy composition of human art, and a familiar knowledge of the sublime masters who had pleased or instructed the first of nations. But these advantages only tend to aggravate the reproach and shame of a degenerate people. They held in their lifeless hands the riches of their fathers, without inheriting the spirit which had created and improved that sacred patrimony: they read, they praised, they compiled, but their languid souls seemed alike incapable of thought and action. In the revolution of ten centuries, not a single discovery was made to exalt the dignity or promote the happiness of mankind. Not a single idea has been added to the speculative systems of antiquity, and a succession of patient disciples became in their turn the dogmatic teachers of the next servile generation. Not a single composition of history, philosophy, or literature, has been saved from oblivion by the intrinsic beauties of style or sentiment, of original fancy, or even of successful imitation. In prose, the least offensive of the Byzantine writers are absolved from censure by their naked and unpresuming simplicity: but the orators, most eloquent in their own conceit, are the farthest removed from the models whom they affect to emulate. In every page our taste and reason are wounded by the choice of gigantic and obsolete words, a stiff and intricate phraseology, the discord of images, the childish play of false or unseasonable ornament, and the painful attempt to elevate themselves, to astonish the reader, and to involve a trivial meaning in the smoke of obscurity and exaggeration. Their prose is soaring to the vicious affectation of poetry: their poetry is sinking below the flatness and insipidity of prose. The tragic, epic, and lyric muses were silent and inglorious: the bards of Constantinople seldom rose above a riddle or epigram, a panegyric or tale; they forgot even the rules of prosody; and with the melody of Homer yet sounding in their ears, they confounded all measure of feet and syllables in the impotent strains which have received the name of *political* or city verses. The minds of the Greeks were bound in the fetters of a base and imperious superstition, which extends her dominion round the circle of profane science. Their understandings were bewildered in metaphysical controversy: in the belief of visions and miracles they had lost all principles of moral evidence, and their taste was vitiated by the homilies of the monks, an absurd medley of declamation and Scripture. Even these contemptible studies were no longer dignified by the abuse of superior talents: the leaders of the Greek church were humbly content to admire and copy the oracles of antiquity, nor did the schools or pulpit produce any rivals of the fame of Athanasius and Chrysostom.

In all the pursuits of active and speculative life, the emulation of states and individuals is the most powerful spring of the efforts and improvements of mankind. The cities of ancient Greece were cast in the happy mixture of union and independence, which is repeated on a larger scale, but in a looser form, by the nations of modern Europe: the union of language, religion, and manners, which renders them the spectators and judges of each other's merit: the independence of government and interest, which asserts their separate freedom, and excites them to strive for pre-eminence in the career of glory. The situation of the Romans was less favourable; yet in the early ages of the republic, which fixed the national character, a similar emulation was kindled among the states of Latium and Italy; and in the arts and sciences they aspired to equal or surpass their Grecian masters. The empire of the Cæsars undoubtedly checked the activity and progress of the human mind: its magnitude might indeed allow some scope for domestic competition; but when it was gradually reduced, at first to the East, and at last to Greece and Constantinople, the Byzantine subjects were degraded to an abject and languid temper, the natural effect of their solitary and insulated state. From the North they were oppressed by nameless tribes of barbarians, to whom they scarcely imparted the appellation of men. The language and religion of the more polished Arabs were an insurmountable bar to all social intercourse. The conquerors of Europe were their brethren in the Christian faith; but the speech of the Franks or Latins was unknown, their manners were rude, and they were rarely connected, in peace or war, with the successors of Heraclius. Alone in the universe, the self-satisfied pride of the Greeks was not disturbed by the comparison of foreign merit; and it is no wonder if they fainted in the race, since they had neither competitors to urge their speed, nor

judges to crown their victory. The nations of Europe and
Asia were mingled by the expeditions to the Holy Land;
and it is under the Comnenian dynasty that a faint emulation
of knowledge and military virtue was rekindled in the Byzantine empire.

*In Chapter 54, Gibbon describes the rise and persecution
of the Paulicians (A.D. 600–880), a Gnostic sect, and indicates
that in some way they foreshadowed the ideas of the Reformation. In Chapter 55 he describes the establishment of the
Bulgarians, Croats, and Hungarians in the old provinces of
the Danube, the origin of the Russian monarchy and the
conversion of the Russians and northern Europeans to Christianity.*

56.

CONFLICT OF THE SARACENS, FRANKS AND
GREEKS IN ITALY. THE COMING OF THE NORMANS.
CONQUESTS OF ROBERT GUISCARD

THE THREE GREAT nations of the world, the Greeks, the
Saracens, and the Franks, encountered each other on the
theatre of Italy. The southern provinces, which now compose the kingdom of Naples, were subject, for the most part,
to the Lombard dukes and princes of Beneventum—so powerful in war, that they checked for a moment the genius of
Charlemagne—so liberal in peace, that they maintained in
their capital an academy of thirty-two philosophers and grammarians. The division of this flourishing state produced the
rival principalities of Benevento, Salerno, and Capua; and
the thoughtless ambition or revenge of the competitors invited
the Saracens to the ruin of their common inheritance. During a calamitous period of two hundred years Italy was
exposed to a repetition of wounds, which the invaders were
not capable of healing by the union and tranquillity of a
perfect conquest. Their frequent and almost annual squadrons
issued from the port of Palermo, and were entertained with
too much indulgence by the Christians of Naples: the more
formidable fleets were prepared on the African coast; and
even the Arabs of Andalusia were sometimes tempted to assist
or oppose the Moslems of an adverse sect. In the revolution
of human events a new ambuscade was concealed in the
Caudine forks, the fields of Cannæ were bedewed a second
time with the blood of the Africans, and the sovereign of
Rome again attacked or defended the walls of Capua and
Tarentum. A colony of Saracens had been planted at Bari,
which commands the entrance of the Adriatic Gulf; and their
impartial depredations provoked the resentment and concili-
ated the union of the two emperors. An offensive alliance
was concluded between Basil the Macedonian, the first of

his race, and Lewis the great-grandson of Charlemagne; and
each party supplied the deficiencies of his associate. It would
have been imprudent in the Byzantine monarch to transport
his stationary troops of Asia to an Italian campaign; and the
Latin arms would have been insufficient if *his* superior navy
had not occupied the mouth of the Gulf. The fortress of Bari
was invested by the infantry of the Franks, and by the
cavalry and galleys of the Greeks; and, after a defence of
four years, the Arabian emir submitted to the clemency of
Lewis, who commanded in person the operations of the siege.
This important conquest had been achieved by the concord of
the East and West; but their recent amity was soon embittered
by the mutual complaints of jealousy and pride. The Greeks
assumed as their own the merit of the conquest and the pomp
of the triumph, extolled the greatness of their powers, and
affected to deride the intemperance and sloth of the handful
of barbarians who appeared under the banners of the Carlovingian prince. His reply is expressed with the eloquence of
indignation and truth: "We confess the magnitude of your
preparations," says the great-grandson of Charlemagne. "Your
armies were indeed as numerous as a cloud of summer locusts,
who darken the day, flap their wings, and, after a short flight,
tumble weary and breathless to the ground. Like them, ye
sunk after a feeble effort; ye were vanquished by your own
cowardice, and withdrew from the scene of action to injure
and despoil our Christian subjects of the Sclavonian coast. We
were few in number, and why were we few? because, after
a tedious expectation of your arrival, I had dismissed my host,
and retained only a chosen band of warriors to continue the
blockade of the city. If they indulged their hospitable feasts
in the face of danger and death, did these feasts abate the
vigour of their enterprise? Is it by your fasting that the walls
of Bari have been overturned? Did not these valiant Franks,
diminished as they were by languor and fatigue, intercept and
vanquish the three most powerful emirs of the Saracens? and
did not their defeat precipitate the fall of the city? Bari is
now fallen; Tarentum trembles; Calabria will be delivered;
and, if we command the sea, the island of Sicily may be
rescued from the hands of the infidels. My brother" (a name
most offensive to the vanity of the Greek), "accelerate your
naval succours, respect your allies, and distrust your flatterers."
These lofty hopes were soon extinguished by the death of

Lewis, and the decay of the Carlovingian house; and whoever might deserve the honour, the Greek emperors, Basil and his son Leo, secured the advantage, of the reduction of Bari. The Italians of Apulia and Calabria were persuaded or compelled to acknowledge their supremacy, and an ideal line from Mount Garganus to the bay of Salerno leaves the far greater part of the kingdom of Naples under the dominion of the Eastern empire. Beyond that line the dukes or republics of Amalfi and Naples, who had never forfeited their voluntary allegiance, rejoiced in the neighbourhood of their lawful sovereign; and Amalfi was enriched by supplying Europe with the produce and manufactures of Asia. But the Lombard princes of Benevento, Salerno, and Capua were reluctantly torn from the communion of the Latin world, and too often violated their oaths of servitude and tribute. The city of Bari rose to dignity and wealth as the metropolis of the new theme or province of Lombardy; the title of patrician, and afterwards the singular name of *Catapan,* was assigned to the supreme governor; and the policy both of the church and state was modelled in exact subordination to the throne of Constantinople. As long as the sceptre was disputed by the princes of Italy, their efforts were feeble and adverse; and the Greeks resisted or eluded the forces of Germany which descended from the Alps under the Imperial standard of the Othos. The first and greatest of those Saxon princes was compelled to relinquish the siege of Bari: the second, after the loss of his stoutest bishops and barons, escaped with honour from the bloody field of Crotona. On that day the scale of war was turned against the Franks by the valour of the Saracens. These corsairs had indeed been driven by the Byzantine fleets from the fortresses and coasts of Italy; but a sense of interest was more prevalent than superstition or resentment, and the caliph of Egypt had transported forty thousand Moslems to the aid of his Christian ally. The successors of Basil amused themselves with the belief that the conquest of Lombardy had been achieved, and was still preserved, by the justice of their laws, the virtues of their ministers, and the gratitude of a people whom they had rescued from anarchy and oppression. A series of rebellions might dart a ray of truth into the palace of Constantinople; and the illusions of flattery were dispelled by the easy and rapid success of the Norman adventurers.

The revolution of human affairs had produced in Apulia and Calabria a melancholy contrast between the age of Pythagoras and the tenth century of the Christian era. At the former period the coast of Great Greece (as it was then styled) was planted with free and opulent cities: these cities were peopled with soldiers, artists, and philosophers; and the military strength of Tarentum, Sybaris, or Crotona was not inferior to that of a powerful kingdom. At the second era these once flourishing provinces were clouded with ignorance, impoverished by tyranny, and depopulated by barbarian war: nor can we severely accuse the exaggeration of a contemporary, that a fair and ample district was reduced to the same desolation which had covered the earth after the general deluge. Among the hostilities of the Arabs, the Franks, and the Greeks in the southern Italy, I shall select two or three anecdotes expressive of their national manners. 1. It was the amusement of the Saracens to profane, as well as to pillage, the monasteries and churches. At the siege of Salerno a Musulman chief spread his couch on the communion-table, and on that altar sacrificed each night the virginity of a Christian nun. As he wrestled with a reluctant maid, a beam in the roof was accidentally or dexterously thrown down on his head; and the death of the lustful emir was imputed to the wrath of Christ, which was at length awakened for the defence of his faithful spouse. 2. The Saracens besieged the cities of Beneventum and Capua: after a vain appeal to the successors of Charlemagne, the Lombards implored the clemency and aid of the Greek emperor. A fearless citizen dropped from the walls, passed the intrenchments, accomplished his commission, and fell into the hands of the barbarians as he was returning with the welcome news. They commanded him to assist their enterprise, and deceive his countrymen, with the assurance that wealth and honours should be the reward of his falsehood, and that his sincerity would be punished with immediate death. He affected to yield, but as soon as he was conducted within hearing of the Christians on the rampart, "Friends and brethren," he cried with a loud voice, "be bold and patient; maintain the city; your sovereign is informed of your distress, and your deliverers are at hand. I know my doom, and commit my wife and children to your gratitude." The rage of the Arabs confirmed his evidence; and the self-devoted patriot was transpierced with an hundred spears. He deserves to live in the memory of the virtuous, but the repetition of the same story in ancient and modern times may sprinkle some doubts on the reality of this generous deed.[1] 3. The recital of the third incident may provoke a smile amidst the horrors of war. Theobald, marquis of Camerino and Spoleto, supported the rebels of Beneventum; and his wanton cruelty was not incompatible in that age with the character of an hero. His captives of the Greek nation or party were castrated without mercy, and the outrage was aggravated by a cruel jest, that he wished to present the emperor with a supply of eunuchs, the most precious ornaments of the Byzantine court. The garrison of a castle had been defeated in a sally, and the prisoners were sentenced to the customary operation. But the sacrifice was disturbed by the intrusion of a frantic female, who, with bleeding cheeks, dishevelled hair, and importunate clamours, compelled the marquis to listen to her complaint. "Is it thus," she cried, "ye magnanimous heroes, that ye wage war against women, against women who have never injured ye, and whose only arms are the distaff and the loom?" Theobald denied the charge, and protested that, since the Amazons, he had never heard of a female war. "And how," she furiously exclaimed, "can you attack us more directly, how can you wound us in a more vital part, than by robbing our husbands of what we most dearly cherish, the source of our joys, and the hope of our posterity? The plunder of our flocks and herds I have endured without a murmur, but this fatal injury, this irreparable loss, subdues my patience, and calls aloud on the justice of heaven and earth." A general laugh applauded her eloquence; the savage Franks, inaccessible to pity, were moved by her ridiculous, yet rational, despair; and with the deliverance of the captives she obtained the restitution of her effects. As she returned in triumph to the castle she was overtaken by a messenger, to inquire, in the name of Theobald, what punishment should be inflicted on her husband, were he again taken in arms? "Should such," she answered without

---

[1] In the year 663 the same tragedy is described by Paul the Deacon under the walls of the same city of Beneventum. But the actors are different, and the guilt is imputed to the Greeks themselves, which in the Byzantine edition is applied to the Saracens. In the late modern war in Germany, M. d'Assas, a French officer of the regiment of Auvergne, *is said* to have devoted himself in a similar manner. His behaviour is the more heroic, as mere silence was required by the enemy who had made him prisoner (Voltaire, Siècle de Louis XV, c. 33).

hesitation, "be his guilt and misfortune, he has eyes, and a nose, and hands, and feet. These are his own, and these he may deserve to forfeit by his personal offences. But let my lord be pleased to spare what his little handmaid presumes to claim as her peculiar and lawful property."[1]

THE COMING OF THE NORMANS

The establishment of the Normans in the kingdoms of Naples and Sicily is an event most romantic in its origin, and in its consequences most important both to Italy and the Eastern empire. The broken provinces of the Greeks, Lombards, and Saracens were exposed to every invader, and every sea and land were invaded by the adventurous spirit of the Scandinavian pirates. After a long indulgence of rapine and slaughter, a fair and ample territory was accepted, occupied, and named, by the Normans of France: they renounced their gods for the God of the Christians; and the dukes of Normandy acknowledged themselves the vassals of the successors of Charlemagne and Capet. The savage fierceness which they had brought from the snowy mountains of Norway was refined, without being corrupted, in a warmer climate; the companions of Rollo insensibly mingled with the natives; they imbibed the manners, language, and gallantry of the French nation; and, in a martial age, the Normans might claim the palm of valour and glorious achievements. Of the fashionable superstitions, they embraced with ardour the pilgrimages of Rome, Italy, and the Holy Land. In this active devotion their minds and bodies were invigorated by exercise: danger was the incentive, novelty the recompense; and the prospect of the world was decorated by wonder, credulity, and ambitious hope. They confederated for their mutual defence; and the robbers of the Alps, who had been allured by the garb of a pilgrim, were often chastised by the arm of a warrior. In one of these pious visits to the cavern of Mount Garganus in Apulia, which had been sanctified by the apparition of the archangel Michael, they were accosted by a stranger in the Greek habit, but who soon revealed himself as a rebel, a

---

[1] Liutprand. Should the licentiousness of the tale be questioned, I may exclaim, with poor Sterne, that it is hard if I may not transcribe with caution what a bishop could write without scruple. What if I had translated, ut viris certetis testiculos amputare, in quibus nostri corporis refocillatio, etc.?

fugitive, and a mortal foe of the Greek empire. His name was
Melo; a noble citizen of Bari, who, after an unsuccessful
revolt, was compelled to seek new allies and avengers of his
country. The bold appearance of the Normans revived his
hopes and solicited his confidence: they listened to the complaints, and still more to the promises, of the patriot. The
assurance of wealth demonstrated the justice of his cause;
and they viewed, as the inheritance of the brave, the fruitful land which was oppressed by effeminate tyrants. On their
return to Normandy they kindled a spark of enterprise, and a
small but intrepid band was freely associated for the deliverance of Apulia. They passed the Alps by separate roads,
and in the disguise of pilgrims; but in the neighbourhood of
Rome they were·saluted by the chief of Bari, who supplied
the more indigent with arms and horses, and instantly led
them to the field of action. In the first conflict their valour
prevailed; but in the second engagement they were overwhelmed by the numbers and military engines of the Greeks,
and indignantly retreated with their faces to the enemy. The
unfortunate Melo ended his life a suppliant at the court of
Germany: his Norman followers, excluded from their native
and their promised land, wandered among the hills and
valleys of Italy, and earned their daily subsistence by the
sword. To that formidable sword the princes of Capua,
Beneventum, Salerno, and Naples alternately appealed in their
domestic quarrels; the superior spirit and discipline of the
Normans gave victory to the side which they espoused; and
their cautious policy observed the balance of power, lest
the preponderance of any rival state should render their aid
less important and their service less profitable. Their first
asylum was a strong camp in the depth of the marshes of
Campania; but they were soon endowed by the liberality of
the duke of Naples with a more plentiful and permanent seat.
Eight miles from his residence, as a bulwark against Capua,
the town of Aversa was built and fortified for their use; and
they enjoyed as their own the corn and fruits, the meadows
and groves, of that fertile district. The report of their success
attracted every year new swarms of pilgrims and soldiers: the
poor were urged by necessity; the rich were excited by hope;
and the brave and active spirits of Normandy were impatient
of ease and ambitious of renown. The independent standard
of Aversa afforded shelter and encouragement to the outlaws

of the province, to every fugitive who had escaped from
the injustice or justice of his superiors; and these foreign associates were quickly assimilated in manners and language to
the Gallic colony. The first leader of the Normans was Count
Rainulf; and, in the origin of society, pre-eminence of rank
is the reward and the proof of superior merit.

Since the conquest of Sicily by the Arabs, the Grecian
emperors had been anxious to regain that valuable possession;
but their efforts, however strenuous, had been opposed by the
distance and the sea. Their costly armaments, after a gleam
of success, added new pages of calamity and disgrace to the
Byzantine annals: twenty thousand of their best troops were
lost in a single expedition; and the victorious Moslems derided
the policy of a nation which entrusted eunuchs not only with
the custody of their women, but with the command of their
men. After a reign of two hundred years, the Saracens were
ruined by their divisions. The emir disclaimed the authority
of the king of Tunis; the people rose against the emir; the
cities were usurped by the chiefs; each meaner rebel was
independent in his village or castle; and the weaker of two
rival brothers implored the friendship of the Christians. In
every service of danger the Normans were prompt and useful;
and five hundred *knights,* or warriors on horseback, were enrolled by Arduin, the agent and interpreter of the Greeks,
under the standard of Maniaces, governor of Lombardy. Before their landing the brothers were reconciled; the union
of Sicily and Africa was restored; and the island was guarded
to the water's edge. The Normans led the van, and the Arabs
of Messina felt the valour of an untried foe. In a second action
the emir of Syracuse was unhorsed and transpierced by the
iron arm of William of Hauteville. In a third engagement his
intrepid companions discomfited the host of sixty thousand
Saracens, and left the Greeks no more than the labour of the
pursuit: a splendid victory; but of which the pen of the
historian may divide the merit with the lance of the Normans.
It is, however, true, that they essentially promoted the success
of Maniaces, who reduced thirteen cities, and the greater part
of Sicily, under the obedience of the emperor. But his military
fame was sullied by ingratitude and tyranny. In the division
of the spoil the deserts of his brave auxiliaries were forgotten;
and neither their avarice nor their pride could brook this in-
jurious treatment. They complained by the mouth of their

interpreter: their complaint was disregarded; their interpreter was scourged; the sufferings were *his;* the insult and resentment belonged to *those* whose sentiments he had delivered. Yet they dissembled till they had obtained, or stolen, a safe passage to the Italian continent: their brethren of Aversa sympathised in their indignation, and the province of Apulia was invaded as the forfeit of the debt. Above twenty years after the first emigration, the Normans took the field with no more than seven hundred horse and five hundred foot; and after the recall of the Byzantine legions from the Sicilian war, their numbers are magnified to the amount of threescore thousand men. Their herald proposed the option of battle or retreat; "Of battle," was the unanimous cry of the Normans; and one of their stoutest warriors, with a stroke of his fist, felled to the ground the horse of the Greek messenger. He was dismissed with a fresh horse; the insult was concealed from the Imperial troops; but in two successive battles they were more fatally instructed of the prowess of their adversaries. In the plains of Cannæ the Asiatics fled before the adventurers of France; the duke of Lombardy was made prisoner; the Apulians acquiesced in a new dominion; and the four places of Bari, Otranto, Brundusium, and Tarentum were alone saved in the shipwreck of the Grecian fortunes. From this era we may date the establishment of the Norman power, which soon eclipsed the infant colony of Aversa. Twelve counts were chosen by the popular suffrage; and age, birth, and merit were the motives of their choice. The tributes of their peculiar districts were appropriated to their use; and each count erected a fortress in the midst of his lands, and at the head of his vassals. In the centre of the province the common habitation of Melphi was reserved as the metropolis and citadel of the republic; an house and separate quarter was allotted to each of the twelve counts; and the national concerns were regulated by this military senate. The first of his peers, their president and general, was entitled Count of Apulia; and this dignity was conferred on William of the iron arm, who, in the language of the age, is styled a lion in battle, a lamb in society, and an angel in council. The manners of his countrymen are fairly delineated by a contemporary and national historian. "The Normans," says Malaterra, "are a cunning and revengeful people; eloquence and dissimulation appear to be their hereditary qualities: they can stoop to flatter; but, unless they are curbed by the restraint of law, they indulge the licentiousness of nature and passion. Their princes affect the praise of popular munificence; the people observe the medium, or rather blend the extremes, of avarice and prodigality; and in their eager thirst of wealth and dominion, they despise whatever they possess, and hope whatever they desire. Arms and horses, the luxury of dress, the exercises of hunting and hawking are the delight of the Normans; but, on pressing occasions, they can endure with incredible patience the inclemency of every climate, and the toil of a military life."

The Normans of Apulia were seated on the verge of the two empires, and, according to the policy of the hour, they accepted the investiture of their lands from the sovereigns of Germany or Constantinople. But the firmest title of these adventurers was the right of conquest; they neither loved nor trusted; they were neither trusted nor beloved; the contempt of the princes was mixed with fear, and the fear of the natives was mingled with hatred and resentment. Every object of desire, a horse, a woman, a garden, tempted and gratified the rapaciousness of the strangers, and the avarice of their chiefs was only coloured by the more specious names of ambition and glory. The twelve counts were sometimes joined in a league of injustice; in their domestic quarrels they disputed the spoils of the people; the virtues of William were buried in his grave; and Drogo, his brother and successor, was better qualified to lead the valour, than to restrain the violence, of his peers. Under the reign of Constantine Monomachus, the policy, rather than benevolence, of the Byzantine court attempted to relieve Italy from this adherent mischief, more grievous than a flight of barbarians; and Argyrus, the son of Melo, was invested for this purpose with the most lofty titles and the most ample commission. The memory of his father might recommend him to the Normans, and he had already engaged their voluntary service to quell the revolt of Maniaces, and to avenge their own and the public injury. It was the design of Constantine to transplant this warlike colony from the Italian provinces to the Persian war, and the son of Melo distributed among the chiefs the gold and manufactures of Greece as the first-fruits of the Imperial bounty. But his arts were baffled by the sense and spirit of the conquerors of Apulia: his gifts, or at least his proposals, were rejected, and they unanimously refused to relinquish their possessions and their hopes for the distant prospect of Asiatic fortune. After the means of persuasion had failed, Argyrus resolved to compel or to destroy: the Latin powers were solicited against the common enemy, and an offensive alliance was formed of the pope and the two emperors of the East and West. The throne of St. Peter was occupied by Leo the Ninth, a simple saint, of a temper most apt to deceive himself and the world, and whose venerable character would consecrate with the name of piety the measures least compatible with the practice of religion. His humanity was affected by the complaints, perhaps the calumnies, of an injured people; the impious Normans had interrupted the payment of tithes, and the temporal sword might be lawfully unsheathed against the sacrilegious robbers who were deaf to the censures of the church. As a German of noble birth and royal kindred, Leo had free access to the court and confidence of the emperor Henry the Third, and in search of arms and allies his ardent zeal transported him from Apulia to Saxony, from the Elbe to the Tiber. During these hostile preparations, Argyrus indulged himself in the use of secret and guilty weapons: a crowd of Normans became the victims of public or private revenge, and the valiant Drogo was murdered in a church. But his spirit survived in his brother Humphrey, the third count of Apulia. The assassins were chastised, and the son of Melo, overthrown and wounded, was driven from the field to hide his shame behind the walls of Bari, and to await the tardy succour of his allies.

But the power of Constantine was distracted by a Turkish war, the mind of Henry was feeble and irresolute, and the pope, instead of repassing the Alps with a German army, was accompanied only by a guard of seven hundred Swabians and some volunteers of Lorraine. In his long progress from Mantua to Beneventum a vile and promiscuous multitude of Italians was enlisted under the holy standard; the priest and the robber slept in the same tent, the pikes and crosses were intermingled in the front, and the martial saint repeated the lessons of his youth in the order of march, of encampment, and of combat. The Normans of Apulia could muster in the field no more than three thousand horse, with a handful of infantry; the defection of the natives intercepted their provisions and retreat; and their spirit, incapable of fear, was chilled for a moment by superstitious awe. On the hostile approach of Leo, they knelt, without disgrace or reluctance, before their spiritual father. But the pope was inexorable; his lofty Germans affected to deride the diminutive stature of their adversaries; and the Normans were informed that death or exile was their only alternative. Flight they disdained, and, as many of them had been three days without tasting food, they embraced the assurance of a more easy and honourable death. They climbed the hill of Civitella, descended into the plain, and charged in three divisions the army of the pope. On the left, and in the centre, Richard count of Aversa, and Robert the famous Guiscard, attacked, broke, routed, and pursued the Italian multitudes, who fought without discipline and fled without shame. A harder trial was reserved for the valour of Count Humphrey, who led the cavalry of the right wing. The Germans have been described as unskilful in the management of the horse and lance, but on foot they formed a strong and impenetrable phalanx, and neither man, nor steed, nor armour could resist the weight of their long and two-handed swords. After a severe conflict they were encompassed by the squadrons returning from the pursuit, and died in their ranks with the esteem of their foes and the satisfaction of revenge. The gates of Civitella were shut against the flying pope, and he was overtaken by the pious conquerors, who kissed his feet to implore his blessing and the absolution of their sinful victory. The soldiers beheld in their enemy and captive the vicar of Christ; and, though we may suppose the policy of the chiefs, it is probable that they were infected by the popular superstition. In the calm of retirement the well-meaning pope deplored the effusion of Christian blood which must be imputed to his account; he felt that he had been the author of sin and scandal; and, as his undertaking had failed, the indecency of his military character was universally condemned. With these dispositions he listened to the offers of a beneficial treaty, deserted an alliance which he had preached as the cause of God, and ratified the past and future conquests of the Normans. By whatever hands they had been usurped, the provinces of Apulia and Calabria were a part of the donation of Constantine and the patrimony of St. Peter: the grant and the acceptance confirmed the mutual claims of the pontiff and the adventurers. They promised to support each other with spiritual and temporal arms; a tribute or quit-rent of twelve pence was afterwards stipulated for every plough-land, and since this memorable transaction the kingdom of Naples has remained above seven hundred years a fief of the Holy See.

CONQUESTS OF ROBERT GUISCARD

The pedigree of Robert Guiscard is variously deduced from the peasants and the dukes of Normandy: from the peasants, by the pride and ignorance of a Grecian princess; from the dukes, by the ignorance and flattery of the Italian subjects. His genuine descent may be ascribed to the second or middle order of private nobility. He sprang from a race of *valvassors* or *bannerets*, of the diocese of Coutances, in the Lower Normandy; the castle of Hauteville was their honourable seat; his father Tancred was conspicuous in the court and army of the duke, and his military service was furnished by ten soldiers or knights. Two marriages, of a rank not unworthy of his own, made him the father of twelve sons, who were educated at home by the impartial tenderness of his second wife. But a narrow patrimony was insufficient for this numerous and daring progeny; they saw around the neighbour-hood the mischiefs of poverty and discord, and resolved to seek in foreign wars a more glorious inheritance. Two only remained to perpetuate the race and cherish their father's age; their ten brothers, as they successively attained the vigour of manhood, departed from the castle, passed the Alps, and joined the Apulian camp of the Normans. The elder were prompted by native spirit: their success encouraged their younger brethren; and the three first in seniority, William, Drogo, and Humphrey, deserved to be the chiefs of their nation and the founders of the new republic. Robert was the eldest of the seven sons of the second marriage, and even the reluctant praise of his foes has endowed him with the heroic qualities of a soldier and a statesman. His lofty stature surpassed the tallest of his army; his limbs were cast in the true proportion of strength and gracefulness; and to the decline of life he maintained the patient vigour of health and the commanding dignity of his form. His complexion was ruddy, his shoulders were broad, his hair and beard were long and of a flaxen colour, his eyes sparkled with fire, and his voice, like that of Achilles, could impress obedience and terror

amidst the tumult of battle. In the ruder ages of chivalry
such qualifications are not below the notice of the poet or historian; they may observe that Robert, at once, and with equal
dexterity, could wield in the right hand his sword, his lance
in the left; that in the battle of Civitella he was thrice unhorsed, and that in the close of that memorable day he was
adjudged to have borne away the prize of valour from the
warriors of the two armies. His boundless ambition was
founded on the consciousness of superior worth; in the pursuit of greatness he was never arrested by the scruples of
justice, and seldom moved by the feelings of humanity; though
not insensible of fame, the choice of open or clandestine
means was determined only by his present advantage. The
surname of *Guiscard* was applied to this master of political
wisdom, which is too often confounded with the practice of
dissimulation and deceit, and Robert is praised by the Apulian
poet for excelling the cunning of Ulysses and the eloquence
of Cicero. Yet these arts were disguised by an appearance
of military frankness; in his highest fortune he was accessible
and courteous to his fellow-soldiers; and while he indulged
the prejudices of his new subjects, he affected in his dress and
manners to maintain the ancient fashion of his country. He
grasped with a rapacious, that he might distribute with a
liberal, hand; his primitive indigence had taught the habits of
frugality; the gain of a merchant was not below his attention;
and his prisoners were tortured with slow and unfeeling cruelty
to force a discovery of their secret treasure. According to the
Greeks, he departed from Normandy with only five followers
on horseback and thirty on foot; yet even this allowance appears too bountiful; the sixth son of Tancred of Hauteville
passed the Alps as a pilgrim, and his first military band was
levied among the adventurers of Italy. His brothers and
countrymen had divided the fertile lands of Apulia, but they
guarded their shares with the jealousy of avarice; the aspiring
youth was driven forwards to the mountains of Calabria, and
in his first exploits against the Greeks and the natives it is
not easy to discriminate the hero from the robber. To surprise
a castle or a convent, to ensnare a wealthy citizen, to plunder
the adjacent villages for necessary food, were the obscure
labours which formed and exercised the powers of his mind
and body. The volunteers of Normandy adhered to his stand-

ard, and, under his command, the peasants of Calabria assumed the name and character of Normans.

As the genius of Robert expanded with his fortune, he awakened the jealousy of his elder brother, by whom, in a transient quarrel, his life was threatened and his liberty restrained. After the death of Humphrey the tender age of his sons excluded them from the command; they were reduced to a private estate by the ambition of their guardian and uncle; and Guiscard was exalted on a buckler, and saluted count of Apulia and general of the republic. With an increase of authority and of force, he resumed the conquest of Calabria, and soon aspired to a rank that should raise him for ever above the heads of his equals. By some acts of rapine or sacrilege he had incurred a papal excommunication: but Nicholas the Second was easily persuaded that the divisions of friends could terminate only in their mutual prejudice; that the Normans were the faithful champions of the Holy See; and it was safer to trust the alliance of a prince than the caprice of an aristocracy. A synod of one hundred bishops was convened at Melphi; and the count interrupted an important enterprise to guard the person and execute the decrees of the Roman pontiff. His gratitude and policy conferred on Robert and his posterity the ducal title, with the investiture of Apulia, Calabria, and all the lands, both in Italy and Sicily, which his sword could rescue from the schismatic Greeks and the unbelieving Saracens. This apostolic sanction might justify his arms: but the obedience of a free and victorious people could not be transferred without their consent; and Guiscard dissembled his elevation till the ensuing campaign had been illustrated by the conquest of Consenza and Reggio. In the hour of triumph he assembled his troops and solicited the Normans to confirm by their suffrage the judgment of the vicar of Christ: the soldiers hailed with joyful acclamations their valiant duke; and the counts, his former equals, pronounced the oath of fidelity with hollow smiles and secret indignation. After this inauguration, Robert styled himself, "By the grace of God and St. Peter, duke of Apulia, Calabria, and hereafter of Sicily"; and it was the labour of twenty years to deserve and realise these lofty appellations. Such tardy progress, in a narrow space, may seem unworthy of the abilities of the chief and the spirit of the nation: but the Normans were few in number; their resources were scanty;

their service was voluntary and precarious. The bravest designs of the duke were sometimes opposed by the free voice of his parliament of barons: the twelve counts of popular election conspired against his authority; and against their perfidious uncle the sons of Humphrey demanded justice and revenge. By his policy and vigour Guiscard discovered their plots, suppressed their rebellions, and punished the guilty with death or exile; but in these domestic feuds his years, and the national strength, were unprofitably consumed. After the defeat of his foreign enemies, the Greeks, Lombards, and Saracens, their broken forces retreated to the strong and populous cities of the sea-coast. They excelled in the arts of fortification and defence; the Normans were accustomed to serve on horseback in the field, and their rude attempts could only succeed by the efforts of persevering courage. The resistance of Salerno was maintained above eight months: the siege or blockade of Bari lasted near four years. In these actions the Norman duke was the foremost in every danger, in every fatigue the last and most patient. As he pressed the citadel of Salerno an huge stone from the rampart shattered one of his military engines, and by a splinter he was wounded in the breast. Before the gates of Bari he lodged in a miserable hut or barrack, composed of dry branches, and thatched with straw—a perilous station, on all sides open to the inclemency of the winter and the spears of the enemy.

The Italian conquests of Robert correspond with the limits of the present kingdom of Naples; and the countries united by his arms have not been disssevered by the revolutions of seven hundred years. The monarchy has been composed of the Greek provinces of Calabria and Apulia, of the Lombard principality of Salerno, the republic of Amalphi, and the inland dependencies of the large and ancient duchy of Beneventum. Three districts only were exempted from the common law of subjection—the first for ever, and the two last till the middle of the succeeding century. The city and immediate territory of Benevento had been transferred, by gift or exchange, from the German emperor to the Roman pontiff; and although this holy land was sometimes invaded, the name of St. Peter was finally more potent than the sword of the Normans. Their first colony of Aversa subdued and held the state of Capua, and her princes were reduced to beg their bread before the palace of their fathers. The dukes of Naples, the present metropolis, maintained the popular freedom under the shadow of the Byzantine empire. Among the new acquisitions of Guiscard the science of Salerno and the trade of Amalphi may detain for a moment the curiosity of the reader. I. Of the learned faculties jurisprudence implies the previous establishment of laws and property; and theology may perhaps be superseded by the full light of religion and reason. But the savage and the sage must alike implore the assistance of physic; and if *our* diseases are inflamed by luxury, the mischiefs of blows and wounds would be more frequent in the ruder ages of society. The treasures of Grecian medicine had been communicated to the Arabian colonies of Africa, Spain, and Sicily; and in the intercourse of peace and war a spark of knowledge had been kindled and cherished at Salerno, an illustrious city, in which the men were honest and the women beautiful. A school, the first that arose in the darkness of Europe, was consecrated to the healing art: the conscience of monks and bishops was reconciled to that salutary and lucrative profession; and a crowd of patients of the most eminent rank and most distant climates invited or visited the physicians of Salerno. They were protected by the Norman conquerors; and Guiscard, though bred in arms, could discern the merit and value of a philosopher. After a pilgrimage of thirty-nine years, Constantine, an African Christian, returned from Bagdad, a master of the language and learning of the Arabians; and Salerno was enriched by the practice, the lessons, and the writings of the pupil of Avicenna. The school of medicine has long slept in the name of an university; but her precepts are abridged in a string of aphorisms, bound together in the Leonine verses, or Latin rhymes, of the twelfth century. II. Seven miles to the west of Salerno, and thirty to the south of Naples, the obscure town of Amalphi displayed the power and rewards of industry. The land, however fertile, was of narrow extent; but the sea was accessible and open: the inhabitants first assumed the office of supplying the western world with the manufactures and productions of the East; and this useful traffic was the source of their opulence and freedom. The government was popular, under the administration of a duke and the supremacy of the Greek emperor. Fifty thousand citizens were numbered in the walls of Amalphi; nor was any city more abundantly provided with gold, silver, and the objects of precious luxury.

The mariners who swarmed in her port excelled in the theory and practice of navigation and astronomy; and the discovery of the compass, which has opened the globe, is due to their ingenuity or good fortune. Their trade was extended to the coasts, or at least to the commodities, of Africa, Arabia, and India; and their settlements in Constantinople, Antioch, Jerusalem, and Alexandria acquired the privileges of independent colonies. After three hundred years of prosperity Amalphi was oppressed by the arms of the Normans, and sacked by the jealousy of Pisa; but the poverty of one thousand fishermen is yet dignified by the remains of an arsenal, a cathedral, and the palaces of royal merchants.

Roger, the twelfth and last of the sons of Tancred, had been long detained in Normandy by his own and his father's age. He accepted the welcome summons; hastened to the Apulian camp; and deserved at first the esteem, and afterwards the envy, of his elder brother. Their valour and ambition were equal; but the youth, the beauty, the elegant manners, of Roger, engaged the disinterested love of the soldiers and people. So scanty was his allowance, for himself and forty followers, that he descended from conquest to robbery, and from robbery to domestic theft; and so loose were the notions of property, that, by his own historian, at his special command, he is accused of stealing horses from a stable at Melphi. His spirit emerged from poverty and disgrace: from these base practices he rose to the merit and glory of a holy war; and the invasion of Sicily was seconded by the zeal and policy of his brother Guiscard. After the retreat of the Greeks, the *idolaters,* a most audacious reproach of the Catholics, had retrieved their losses and possessions; but the deliverance of the island, so vainly undertaken by the forces of the Eastern empire, was achieved by a small and private band of adventurers. In the first attempt Roger braved, in an open boat, the real and fabulous dangers of Scylla and Charybdis; landed with only sixty soldiers on a hostile shore, drove the Saracens to the gates of Messina; and safely returned with the spoils of the adjacent country. In the fortress of Trani his active and patient courage were equally conspicuous. In his old age he related with pleasure, that, by the distress of the siege, himself, and the countess his wife, had been reduced to a single cloak or mantle, which they wore alternately: that in a sally his horse had been slain, and he was dragged away by the

Saracens; but that he owed his rescue to his good sword, and had retreated with his saddle on his back, lest the meanest trophy might be left in the hands of the miscreants. In the siege of Trani, three hundred Normans withstood and repulsed the forces of the island. In the field of Ceramio fifty thousand horse and foot were overthrown by one hundred and thirty-six Christian soldiers, without reckoning St. George, who fought on horseback in the foremost ranks. The captive banners, with four camels, were reserved for the successor of St. Peter; and had these barbaric spoils been exposed not in the Vatican, but in the Capitol, they might have revived the memory of the Punic triumphs. These insufficient numbers of the Normans most probably denote their knights, the soldiers of honourable and equestrian rank, each of whom was attended by five or six followers in the field; yet, with the aid of this interpretation, and after every fair allowance on the side of valour, arms, and reputation, the discomfiture of so many myriads will reduce the prudent reader to the alternative of a miracle or a fable. The Arabs of Sicily derived a frequent and powerful succour from their countrymen of Africa: in the siege of Palermo the Norman cavalry was assisted by the galleys of Pisa; and, in the hour of action, the envy of the two brothers was sublimed to a generous and invincible emulation. After a war of thirty years, Roger, with the title of great count, obtained the sovereignty of the largest and most fruitful island of the Mediterranean; and his administration displays a liberal and enlightened mind above the limits of his age and education. The Moslems were maintained in the free enjoyment of their religion and property: a philosopher and physician of Mazara, of the race of Mahomet, harangued the conqueror, and was invited to court; his geography of the seven climates was translated into Latin; and Roger, after a diligent perusal, preferred the work of the Arabian to the writings of the Grecian Ptolemy. A remnant of Christian natives had promoted the success of the Normans: they were rewarded by the triumph of the cross. The island was restored to the jurisdiction of the Roman pontiff; new bishops were planted in the principal cities; and the clergy was satisfied by a liberal endowment of churches and monasteries. Yet the Catholic hero asserted the rights of the civil magistrate. Instead of resigning the investiture of benefices, he dexterously applied to his own profit the papal claims: the

supremacy of the crown was secured and enlarged by the
singular bull which declares the princes of Sicily hereditary
and perpetual legates of the Holy Sea.

To Robert Guiscard the conquest of Sicily was more
glorious than beneficial: the possession of Apulia and Calabria
was inadequate to his ambition; and he resolved to embrace or
create the first occasion of invading, perhaps of subduing,
the Roman empire of the East. From his first wife, the
partner of his humble fortunes, he had been divorced under
the pretence of consanguinity; and her son Bohemond was
destined to imitate, rather than to succeed, his illustrious
father. The second wife of Guiscard was the daughter of the
princes of Salerno; the Lombards acquiesced in the lineal
succession of their son Roger; their five daughters were given
in honourable nuptials, and one of them was betrothed, in
a tender age, to Constantine, a beautiful youth, the son and
heir of the emperor Michael. But the throne of Constantinople
was shaken by a revolution: the Imperial family of Ducas was
confined to the palace or the cloister; and Robert deplored
and resented the disgrace of his daughter and the expulsion
of his ally. A Greek, who styled himself the father of Constantine, soon appeared at Salerno, and related the adventures of his fall and flight. That unfortunate friend was
acknowledged by the duke, and adorned with the pomp and
titles of Imperial dignity: in his triumphal progress through
Apulia and Calabria, Michael was saluted with the tears and
acclamations of the people; and pope Gregory the Seventh
exhorted the bishops to preach, and the Catholics to fight, in
the pious work of his restoration. His conversations with
Robert were frequent and familiar; and their mutual promises
were justified by the valour of the Normans and the treasures
of the East. Yet this Michael, by the confession of the
Greeks and Latins, was a pageant and an impostor; a monk
who had fled from his convent, or a domestic who had served
in the palace. The fraud had been contrived by the subtle
Guiscard; and he trusted that, after this pretender had given
a decent colour to his arms, he would sink, at the nod of the
conqueror, into his primitive obscurity. But victory was the
only argument that could determine the belief of the Greeks;
and the ardour of the Latins was much inferior to their
credulity: the Norman veterans wished to enjoy the harvest of
their toils, and the unwarlike Italians trembled at the known

and unknown dangers of a transmarine expedition. In his new levies Robert exerted the influence of gifts and promises, the terrors of civil and ecclesiastical authority; and some acts of violence might justify the reproach that age and infancy were pressed without distinction into the service of their unrelenting prince. After two years' incessant preparations the land and naval forces were assembled at Otranto, at the heel, or extreme promontory, of Italy; and Robert was accompanied by his wife, who fought by his side, his son Bohemond, and the representative of the emperor Michael. Thirteen hundred knights of Norman race or discipline formed the sinews of the army, which might be swelled to thirty thousand followers of every denomination. The men, the horses, the arms, the engines, the wooden towers covered with raw hides, were embarked on board one hundred and fifty vessels: the transports had been built in the ports of Italy, and the galleys were supplied by the alliance of the republic of Ragusa.

At the mouth of the Adriatic Gulf the shores of Italy and Epirus incline towards each other. The space between Brundusium and Durazzo, the Roman passage, is no more than one hundred miles; at the last station of Otranto it is contracted to fifty; and this narrow distance had suggested to Pyrrhus and Pompey the sublime or extravagant idea of a bridge. Before the general embarkation the Norman duke despatched Bohemond with fifteen galleys to seize or threaten the isle of Corfu, to survey the opposite coast, and to secure an harbour in the neighbourhood of Vallona for the landing of the troops. They passed and landed without perceiving an enemy; and this successful experiment displayed the neglect and decay of the naval power of the Greeks. The islands of Epirus and the maritime towns were subdued by the arms or the name of Robert, who led his fleet and army from Corfu (I use the modern appellation) to the siege of Durazzo. That city, the western key of the empire, was guarded by ancient renown and recent fortifications, by George Palæologus, a patrician, victorious in the Oriental wars, and a numerous garrison of Albanians and Macedonians, who, in every age, have maintained the character of soldiers. In the prosecution of his enterprise the courage of Guiscard was assailed by every form of danger and mischance. In the most propitious season of the year, as his fleet passed along the coast, a storm of wind and snow unexpectedly arose: the Adriatic was

swelled by the raging blast of the south, and a new shipwreck confirmed the old infamy of the Acroceraunian rocks.
The sails, the masts, and the oars were shattered or torn away;
the sea and shore were covered with the fragments of vessels,
with arms and dead bodies; and the greatest part of the
provisions were either drowned or damaged. The ducal galley
was laboriously rescued from the waves, and Robert halted
seven days on the adjacent cape to collect the relics of his
loss and revive the drooping spirits of his soldiers. The Normans were no longer the bold and experienced mariners who
had explored the ocean from Greenland to Mount Atlas, and
who smiled at the petty dangers of the Mediterranean. They
had wept during the tempest; they were alarmed by the hostile
approach of the Venetians, who had been solicited by the
prayers and promises of the Byzantine court. The first day's
action was not disadvantageous to Bohemond, a beardless
youth, who led the naval powers of his father. All night the
galleys of the republic lay on their anchors in the form of a
crescent; and the victory of the second day was decided by
the dexterity of their evolutions, the station of their archers,
the weight of their javelins, and the borrowed aid of the
Greek fire. The Apulian and Ragusian vessels fled to the
shore, several were cut from their cables and dragged away
by the conqueror; and a sally from the town carried slaughter
and dismay to the tents of the Norman duke. A seasonable
relief was poured into Durazzo, and, as soon as the besiegers
had lost the command of the sea, the islands and maritime
towns withdrew from the camp the supply of tribute and
provision. That camp was soon afflicted with a pestilential
disease; five hundred knights perished by an inglorious death;
and the list of burials (if all could obtain a decent burial)
amounted to ten thousand persons. Under these calamities the
mind of Guiscard alone was firm and invincible; and while
he collected new forces from Apulia and Sicily, he battered,
or scaled, or sapped, the walls of Durazzo. But his industry
and valour were encountered by equal valour and more
perfect industry. A moveable turret, of a size and capacity
to contain five hundred soldiers, had been rolled forwards to
the foot of the rampart; but the descent of the door or drawbridge was checked by an enormous beam, and the wooden
structure was instantly consumed by artificial flames.

While the Roman empire was attacked by the Turks in the

East, and the Normans in the West, the aged successor of
Michael surrendered the sceptre to the hands of Alexius, an
illustrious captain, and the founder of the Comnenian dynasty.
The princess Anne, his daughter and historian, observes, in
her affected style, that even Hercules was unequal to a
double combat; and, on this principle, she approves an hasty
peace with the Turks, which allowed her father to undertake
in person the relief of Durazzo. On his accession, Alexius
found the camp without soldiers, and the treasury without
money; yet such were the vigour and activity of his measures,
that in six months he assembled an army of seventy thousand
men, and performed a march of five hundred miles. His
troops were levied in Europe and Asia, from Peloponnesus
to the Black Sea; his majesty was displayed in the silver
arms and rich trappings of the companies of horseguards;
and the emperor was attended by a train of nobles and
princes, some of whom, in rapid succession, had been clothed
with the purple, and were indulged by the lenity of the times
in a life of affluence and dignity. Their youthful ardour might
animate the multitude; but their love of pleasure and contempt of subordination were pregnant with disorder and
mischief; and their importunate clamours for speedy and
decisive action disconcerted the prudence of Alexius, who
might have surrounded and starved the besieging army. The
enumeration of provinces recalls a sad comparison of the
past and present limits of the Roman world: the raw levies
were drawn together in haste and terror; and the garrisons
of Anatolia, or Asia Minor, had been purchased by the evacua-
tion of the cities which were immediately occupied by the
Turks. The strength of the Greek army consisted in the
Varangians, the Scandinavian guards, whose numbers were
recently augmented by a colony of exiles and volunteers from
the British island of Thule. Under the yoke of the Norman
conqueror, the Danes and English were oppressed and united:
a band of adventurous youths resolved to desert a land of
slavery; the sea was open to their escape; and, in their long
pilgrimage, they visited every coast that afforded any hope
of liberty and revenge. They were entertained in the service of
the Greek emperor; and their first station was in a new
city on the Asiatic shore: but Alexius soon recalled them to
the defence of his person and palace; and bequeathed to his
successors the inheritance of their faith and valour. The name

of a Norman invader revived the memory of their wrongs:
they marched with alacrity against the national foe, and
panted to regain in Epirus the glory which they had lost in
the battle of Hastings. The Varangians were supported by
some companies of Franks or Latins; and the rebels who had
fled to Constantinople from the tyranny of Guiscard were
eager to signalize their zeal and gratify their revenge. In this
emergency the emperor had not disdained the impure aid
of the Paulicians or Manichæans of Thrace and Bulgaria;
and these heretics united with the patience of martyrdom
the spirit and discipline of active valour. The treaty with the
sultan had procured a supply of some thousand Turks; and the
arrows of the Scythian horse were opposed to the lances of
the Norman cavalry. On the report and distant prospect of
these formidable numbers, Robert assembled a council of his
principal officers. "You behold," said he, "your danger: it is
urgent and inevitable. The hills are covered with arms and
standards; and the emperor of the Greeks is accustomed to
wars and triumphs. Obedience and union are our only safety;
and I am ready to yield the command to a more worthy
leader." The vote and acclamation, even of his secret enemies,
assured him, in that perilous moment, of their esteem and
confidence; and the duke thus continued: "Let us trust in
the rewards of victory, and deprive cowardice of the means
of escape. Let us burn our vessels and our baggage, and give
battle on this spot, as if it were the place of our nativity and
our burial." The resolution was unanimously approved; and,
without confining himself to his lines, Guiscard awaited
in battle-array the nearer approach of the enemy. His rear
was covered by a small river; his right wing extended to the
sea; his left to the hills: nor was he conscious, perhaps, that on
the same ground Cæsar and Pompey had formerly disputed
the empire of the world.

Against the advice of his wisest captains, Alexius resolved
to risk the event of a general action, and exhorted the garrison
of Durazzo to assist their own deliverance by a well-timed
sally from the town. He marched in two columns to surprise
the Normans before daybreak on two different sides: his light
cavalry was scattered over the plain; the archers formed the
second line; and the Varangians claimed the honours of the
vanguard. In the first onset the battle-axes of the strangers
made a deep and bloody impression on the army of Guiscard,

which was now reduced to fifteen thousand men. The Lombards and Calabrians ignominiously turned their backs; they fled towards the river and the sea; but the bridge had been broken down to check the sally of the garrison, and the coast was lined with the Venetian galleys, who played their engines among the disorderly throng. On the verge of ruin, they were saved by the spirit and conduct of their chiefs. Gaita, the wife of Robert, is painted by the Greeks as a warlike Amazon, a second Pallas; less skilful in arts, but not less terrible in arms, than the Athenian goddess: though wounded by an arrow, she stood her ground, and strove, by her exhortation and example, to rally the flying troops. Her female voice was seconded by the more powerful voice and arm of the Norman duke, as calm in action as he was magnanimous in council: "Whither," he cried aloud, "whither do ye fly? Your enemy is implacable; and death is less grievous than servitude." The moment was decisive: as the Varangians advanced before the line, they discovered the nakedness of their flanks: the main battle of the duke, of eight hundred knights, stood firm and entire; they couched their lances, and the Greeks deplore the furious and irresistible shock of the French cavalry. Alexius was not deficient in the duties of a soldier or a general; but he no sooner beheld the slaughter of the Varangians, and the flight of the Turks, than he despised his subjects, and despaired of his fortune. The princess Anne, who drops a tear on this melancholy event, is reduced to praise the strength and swiftness of her father's horse, and his vigorous struggle when he was almost overthrown by the stroke of a lance which had shivered the Imperial helmet. His desperate valour broke through a squadron of Franks who opposed his flight; and after wandering two days and as many nights in the mountains, he found some repose, of body, though not of mind, in the walls of Lychnidus. The victorious Robert reproached the tardy and feeble pursuit which had suffered the escape of so illustrious a prize: but he consoled his disappointment by the trophies and standards of the field, the wealth and luxury of the Byzantine camp, and the glory of defeating an army five times more numerous than his own. A multitude of Italians had been the victims of their own fears; but only thirty of his knights were slain in this memorable day. In the Roman host, the loss of Greeks, Turks, and English amounted to five or six thousand: the plain of

Durazzo was stained with noble and royal blood; and the end of the impostor Michael was more honourable than his life.

It is more than probable that Guiscard was not afflicted by the loss of a costly pageant, which had merited only the contempt and derision of the Greeks. After their defeat they still persevered in the defence of Durazzo; and a Venetian commander supplied the place of George Palæologus, who had been imprudently called away from his station. The tents of the besiegers were converted into barracks, to sustain the inclemency of the winter; and in answer to the defiance of the garrison, Robert insinuated that his patience was at least equal to their obstinacy. Perhaps he already trusted to his secret correspondence with a Venetian noble, who sold the city for a rich and honourable marriage. At the dead of night several rope-ladders were dropped from the walls; the light Calabrians ascended in silence; and the Greeks were awakened by the name and trumpets of the conqueror. Yet they defended the streets three days against an enemy already master of the rampart; and near seven months elapsed between the first investment and the final surrender of the place. From Durazzo the Norman duke advanced into the heart of Epirus or Albania; traversed the first mountains of Thessaly; surprised three hundred English in the city of Castoria; approached Thessalonica; and made Constantinople tremble. A more pressing duty suspended the prosecution of his ambitious designs. By shipwreck, pestilence, and the sword, his army was reduced to a third of the original numbers; and instead of being recruited from Italy, he was informed, by plaintive epistles, of the mischiefs and dangers which had been produced by his absence: the revolt of the cities and barons of Apulia; the distress of the pope; and the approach or invasion of Henry king of Germany. Highly presuming that his person was sufficient for the public safety, he repassed the sea in a single brigantine, and left the remains of the army under the command of his son and the Norman counts, exhorting Bohemond to respect the freedom of his peers, and the counts to obey the authority of their leader. The son of Guiscard trod in the footsteps of his father; and the two destroyers are compared by the Greeks to the caterpillar and the locust, the last of whom devours whatever has escaped the teeth of the former. After winning two battles against the emperor, he descended into the plain of Thessaly, and besieged Larissa, the fabulous realm of Achilles, which contained the treasure and magazines of the Byzantine camp. Yet a just praise must not be refused to the fortitude and prudence of Alexius, who bravely struggled with the calamities of the times. In the poverty of the state, he presumed to borrow the superfluous ornaments of the churches: the desertion of the Manichæans was supplied by some tribes of Moldavia: a reinforcement of seven thousand Turks replaced and revenged the loss of their brethren; and the Greek soldiers were exercised to ride, to draw the bow, and to the daily practice of ambuscades and evolutions. Alexius had been taught by experience that the formidable cavalry of the Franks on foot was unfit for action, and almost incapable of motion; his archers were directed to aim their arrows at the horse rather than the man; and a variety of spikes and snares were scattered over the ground on which he might expect an attack. In the neighbourhood of Larissa the events of war were protracted and balanced. The courage of Bohemond was always conspicuous, and often successful; but his camp was pillaged by a stratagem of the Greeks; the city was impregnable; and the venal or discontented counts deserted his standard, betrayed their trusts, and enlisted in the service of the emperor. Alexius returned to Constantinople with the advantage, rather than the honour, of victory. After evacuating the conquests which he could no longer defend, the son of Guiscard embarked for Italy, and was embraced by a father who esteemed his merit, and sympathised in his misfortune.

Of the Latin princes, the allies of Alexius and enemies of Robert, the most prompt and powerful was Henry the Third or Fourth, king of Germany and Italy, and future emperor of the West. The epistle of the Greek monarch to his brother is filled with the warmest professions of friendship, and the most lively desire of strengthening their alliance by every public and private tie. He congratulates Henry on his success in a just and pious war, and complains that the prosperity of his own empire is disturbed by the audacious enterprises of the Norman Robert. The list of his presents expresses the manners of the age—a radiated crown of gold, a cross set with pearls to hang on the breast, a case of relics with the names and titles of the saints, a vase of crystal, a vase of sardonyx, some balm, most probably of Mecca, and one hundred pieces of purple. To these he added a more solid present, of one hundred and forty-four thousand Byzantines of gold, with a farther assurance of two hundred and sixteen thousand, so soon as Henry should have entered in arms the Apulian territories, and confirmed by an oath the league against the common enemy. The German, who was already in Lombardy at the head of an army and a faction, accepted these liberal offers, and marched towards the south: his speed was checked by the sound of the battle of Durazzo; but the influence of his arms, or name, in the hasty return of Robert, was a full equivalent for the Grecian bribe. Henry was the sincere adversary of the Normans, the allies and vassals of Gregory the Seventh, his implacable foe. The long quarrel of the throne and mitre had been recently kindled by the zeal and ambition of that haughty priest: the king and the pope had degraded each other; and each had seated a rival on the temporal or spiritual throne of his antagonist. After the defeat and death of his Swabian rebel, Henry descended into Italy, to assume the Imperial crown, and to drive from the Vatican the tyrant of the church. But the Roman people adhered to the cause of Gregory: their resolution was fortified by supplies of men and money from Apulia; and the city was thrice ineffectually besieged by the king of Germany. In the fourth year he corrupted, as it is said, with Byzantine gold, the nobles of Rome, whose estates and castles had been ruined by the war. The gates, the bridges, and fifty hostages were delivered into his hands: the anti-pope, Clement the Third, was consecrated in the Lateran: the grateful pontiff crowned his protector in the Vatican; and the emperor Henry fixed his residence in the Capitol, as the lawful successor of Augustus and Charlemagne. The ruins of the Septizonium were still defended by the nephew of Gregory: the pope himself was invested in the castle of St. Angelo; and his last hope was in the courage and fidelity of his Norman vassal. Their friendship had been interrupted by some reciprocal injuries and complaints; but, on this pressing occasion, Guiscard was urged by the obligation of his oath, by his interest, more potent than oaths, by the love of fame, and his enmity to the two emperors. Unfurling the holy banner, he resolved to fly to the relief of the prince of the apostles: the most numerous of his armies, six thousand horse and thirty thousand foot, was instantly assembled; and his march from Salerno to Rome was animated by the public applause and the promise of the

divine favour. Henry, invincible in sixty-six battles, trembled
at his approach; recollected some indispensable affairs that
required his presence in Lombardy; exhorted the Romans to
persevere in their allegiance; and hastily retreated three days
before the entrance of the Normans. In less than three years
the son of Tancred of Hauteville enjoyed the glory of delivering the pope, and of compelling the two emperors, of the
East and West, to fly before his victorious arms. But the
triumph of Robert was clouded by the calamities of Rome. By
the aid of the friends of Gregory the walls had been perforated
or scaled; but the Imperial faction was still powerful and
active; on the third day the people rose in a furious tumult;
and an hasty word of the conqueror, in his defence or revenge,
was the signal of fire and pillage. The Saracens of Sicily,
the subjects of Roger, and auxiliaries of his brother, embraced
this fair occasion of rifling and profaning the holy city of the
Christians; many thousands of the citizens, in the sight and by
the allies of their spiritual father, were exposed to violation,
captivity, or death; and a spacious quarter of the city, from
the Lateran to the Coliseum, was consumed by the flames,
and devoted to perpetual solitude. From a city where he was
now hated, and might be no longer feared, Gregory retired
to end his days in the palace of Salerno. The artful pontiff
might flatter the vanity of Guiscard with the hope of a
Roman or Imperial crown; but this dangerous measure, which
would have inflamed the ambition of the Norman, must for
ever have alienated the most faithful princes of Germany.

*The remainder of this chapter summarises the further con-
flicts between the Normans and the East and West. Roger
King of Sicily invaded Greece and rescued Louis VII of
France in 1146. In return the Emperor Manuel repulsed the
Normans and carried an offensive into Apulia and Calabria
(1148–1155). His design of recovering the Empire in the
West went no further. In 1194 the Emperor Henry VI con-
quered Sicily and by 1204 the power of the Normans in the
Mediterranean area was at an end.*

57.

THE KINGDOM OF ROUM.
THE TURKISH CONQUEST OF JERUSALEM

The Seljuk Turks were the first to appear of the nations destined to achieve the final overthrow of the Roman empire. After expeditions into Hindustan and the subjection of Persia, they invaded the Asiatic provinces. In 1071, under Alp Arslan, they defeated the Romans, capturing the emperor, Romanus Diogenes. Over the next twenty years the Seljukian empire reached its height of prosperity under Alp Arslan's son, Malek Shah. The Roman provinces of Asia Minor came under the power of Soliman, a direct descendant of Seljuk.

THE KINGDOM OF ROUM

SINCE the first conquests of the caliphs, the establishment of the Turks in Anatolia or Asia Minor was the most deplorable loss which the church and empire had sustained. By the propagation of the Moslem faith, Soliman deserved the name of *Gazi*, a holy champion; and his new kingdom of the Romans, or of *Roum*, was added to the tables of Oriental geography. It is described as extending from the Euphrates to Constantinople, from the Black Sea to the confines of Syria; pregnant with mines of silver and iron, of alum and copper, fruitful in corn and wine, and productive of cattle and excellent horses. The wealth of Lydia, the arts of the Greeks, the splendour of the Augustan age, existed only in books and ruins, which were equally obscure in the eyes of the Scythian conquerors. Yet in the present decay Anatolia still contains *some* wealthy and populous cities; and, under the Byzantine empire, they were far more flourishing in numbers, size, and opulence. By the choice of the sultan, Nice, the metropolis of Bithynia, was preferred for his palace and fortress: the seat of the Seljukian dynasty of Roum was planted one hundred miles from Constantinople; and the divinity of Christ was denied and derided in the same temple in which it had been pronounced by the first general synod of the Catholics. The unity of God, and the mission of Mahomet, were preached in the mosques; the Arabian learning was taught in the schools; the Cadhis judged according to the law of the Koran; the Turkish manners and language prevailed in the cities; and Turkman camps were scattered over the plains and mountains of Anatolia. On the hard conditions of tribute and servitude, the Greek Christians might enjoy the exercise of their religion; but their most holy churches were profaned, their priests and bishops were insulted, they were compelled to suffer the triumph of the *pagans* and the apostacy of their brethren, many thousand children were marked by the knife of circumcision, and many thousand captives were devoted to the service of the pleasures of their masters. After the loss of Asia, Antioch still maintained her primitive allegiance to Christ and Cæsar; but the solitary province was separated from all Roman aid, and surrounded on all sides by the Mahometan powers. The despair of Philaretus the governor prepared the sacrifice of his religion and loyalty, had not his guilt been prevented by his son, who hastened to the Nicene palace, and offered to deliver this valuable prize into the hands of Soliman. The ambitious sultan mounted on horse-back, and in twelve nights (for he reposed in the day) performed a march of six hundred miles. Antioch was oppressed by the speed and secrecy of his enterprise; and the dependent cities, as far as Laodicea and the confines of Aleppo, obeyed the example of the metropolis. From Laodicea to the Thracian Bosphorus, or arm of St. George, the conquests and reign of Soliman extended thirty days' journey in length, and in breadth about ten or fifteen, between the rocks of Lycia and the Black Sea. The Turkish ignorance of navigation protected for a while the inglorious safety of the emperor; but no sooner had a fleet of two hundred ships been constructed by the hands of the captive Greeks, than Alexius trembled behind the walls of his capital. His plaintive epistles were dispersed over Europe to excite the compassion of the Latins, and to paint the danger, the weakness, and the riches of the city of Constantine.

TURKISH CONQUEST OF JERUSALEM

But the most interesting conquest of the Seljukian Turks was that of Jerusalem, which soon became the theatre of nations. In their capitulation with Omar, the inhabitants had stipulated the assurance of their religion and property, but the articles were interpreted by a master against whom it was dangerous to dispute; and in the four hundred years of the reign of the caliphs the political climate of Jerusalem was exposed to the vicissitudes of storms and sunshine. By the increase of proselytes and population the Mahometans might excuse their usurpation of three-fourths of the city: but a peculiar quarter was reserved for the patriarch with his clergy and people; a tribute of two pieces of gold was the price of protection; and the sepulchre of Christ, with the church of the Resurrection, was still left in the hands of his votaries. Of these votaries the most numerous and respectable portion were strangers to Jerusalem; the pilgrimages to the Holy Land had been stimulated, rather than suppressed, by the conquest of the Arabs; and the enthusiasm which had always prompted these perilous journeys was nourished by the congenial passions of grief and indignation. A crowd of pilgrims from the East and West continued to visit the holy sepulchre and the adjacent sanctuaries, more especially at the festival of Easter; and the Greeks and Latins, the Nestorians and Jacobites, the Copts and Abyssinians, the Armenians and Georgians, maintained the chapels, the clergy, and the poor of their respective communions. The harmony of prayer in so many various tongues, the worship of so many nations in the common temple of their religion, might have afforded a spectacle of edification and peace; but the zeal of the Christian sects was embittered by hatred and revenge; and in the kingdom of a suffering Messiah, who had pardoned his enemies, they aspired to command and persecute their spiritual brethren. The pre-eminence was asserted by the spirit and numbers of the Franks, and the greatness of Charlemagne protected both the Latin pilgrims and the Catholics of the East. The poverty of Carthage, Alexandria, and Jerusalem was relieved by the alms of that pious emperor, and many monasteries of Palestine were founded or restored by his liberal devotion. Harun Alrashid, the greatest of the Abbassides, esteemed in his

Christian brother a similar supremacy of genius and power:
their friendship was cemented by a frequent intercourse of
gifts and embassies; and the caliph, without resigning the substantial dominion, presented the emperor with the keys of the
holy sepulchre, and perhaps of the city of Jerusalem. In the
decline of the Carlovingian monarchy the republic of Amalphi
promoted the interest of trade and religion in the East. Her
vessels transported the Latin pilgrims to the coasts of Egypt
and Palestine, and deserved, by their useful imports, the
favour and alliance of the Fatimite caliphs: an annual fair
was instituted on Mount Calvary; and the Italian merchants
founded the convent and hospital of St. John of Jerusalem,
the cradle of the monastic and military order which has since
reigned in the isles of Rhodes and of Malta. Had the Christian pilgrims been content to revere the tomb of a prophet,
the disciples of Mahomet, instead of blaming, would have
imitated, their piety; but these rigid *Unitarians* were scan-
dalized by a worship which represents the birth, death, and
resurrection of a God; the Catholic images were branded with
the name of idols; and the Moslems smiled with indignation
at the miraculous flame which was kindled on the eve of
Easter in the holy sepulchre. This pious fraud, first devised
in the ninth century, was devoutly cherished by the Latin
crusaders, and is annually repeated by the clergy of the
Greek, Armenian, and Coptic sects, who impose on the
credulous spectators for their own benefit and that of their
tyrants. In every age a principle of toleration has been fortified
by a sense of interest, and the revenue of the prince and his
emir was increased each year by the expense and tribute of
so many thousand strangers.

The revolution which transferred the sceptre from the
Abbassides to the Fatimites was a benefit rather than an
injury to the Holy Land. A sovereign resident in Egypt was
more sensible of the importance of Christian trade; and the
emirs of Palestine were less remote from the justice and
power of the throne. But the third of these Fatimite caliphs
was the famous Hakem, a frantic youth, who was delivered by
his impiety and despotism from the fear either of God or
man, and whose reign was a wild mixture of vice and folly.
Regardless of the most ancient customs of Egypt, he imposed
on the women an absolute confinement; the restraint excited
the clamours of both sexes; their clamours provoked his fury;

a part of Old Cairo was delivered to the flames, and the
guards and citizens were engaged many days in a bloody
conflict. At first the caliph declared himself a zealous Musulman, the founder or benefactor of mosques and colleges:
twelve hundred and ninety copies of the Koran were transcribed at his expense in letters of gold, and his edict extirpated
the vineyards of the Upper Egypt. But his vanity was soon
flattered by the hope of introducing a new religion; he aspired
above the fame of a prophet, and styled himself the visible
image of the Most High God, who, after nine apparitions on
earth, was at length manifest in his royal person. At the
name of Hakem, the lord of the living and the dead, every
knee was bent in religious adoration; his mysteries were performed on a mountain near Cairo; sixteen thousand converts
had signed his profession of faith; and at the present hour a
free and warlike people, the Druses of Mount Libanus, are
persuaded of the life and divinity of a madman and tyrant.
In his divine character Hakem hated the Jews and Christians,
as the servants of his rivals, while some remains of prejudice
still pleaded in favour of the law of Mahomet. Both in Egypt
and Palestine his cruel and wanton persecution made some
martyrs and many apostates; the common rights and special
privileges of the sectaries were equally disregarded, and a
general interdict was laid on the devotion of strangers and
natives. The temple of the Christian world, the church of the
Resurrection, was demolished to its foundations; the luminous
prodigy of Easter was interrupted; and much profane labour
was exhausted to destroy the cave in the rock which properly
constitutes the holy sepulchre. At the report of this sacrilege
the nations of Europe were astonished and afflicted: but, instead of arming in the defence of the Holy Land, they contented themselves with burning or banishing the Jews, as the
secret advisers of the impious barbarian. Yet the calamities
of Jerusalem were in some measure alleviated by the in-
constancy or repentance of Hakem himself; and the royal
mandate was sealed for the restitution of the churches when
the tyrant was assassinated by the emissaries of his sister. The
succeeding caliphs resumed the maxims of religion and policy:
a free toleration was again granted; with the pious aid of the
emperor of Constantinople the holy sepulchre arose from its
ruins; and, after a short abstinence, the pilgrims returned with

an increase of appetite to the spiritual feast. In the sea-voyage of Palestine the dangers were frequent, and the opportunities rare; but the conversion of Hungary opened a safe communication between Germany and Greece. The charity of St. Stephen, the apostle of his kingdom, relieved and conducted his itinerant brethren; and from Belgrade to Antioch they traversed fifteen hundred miles of a Christian empire. Among the Franks the zeal of pilgrimage prevailed beyond the example of former times, and the roads were covered with multitudes of either sex and of every rank, who professed their contempt of life so soon as they should have kissed the tomb of their Redeemer. Princes and prelates abandoned the care of their dominions, and the numbers of these pious caravans were a prelude to the armies which marched in the ensuing age under the banner of the cross. About thirty years before the first crusade, the archbishop of Mentz, with the bishops of Utrecht, Bamberg, and Ratisbon, undertook this laborious journey from the Rhine to the Jordan, and the multitude of their followers amounted to seven thousand persons. At Constantinople they were hospitably entertained by the emperor, but the ostentation of their wealth provoked the assault of the wild Arabs; they drew their swords with scrupulous reluctance, and sustained a siege in the village of Capernaum till they were rescued by the venal protection of the Fatimite emir. After visiting the holy places they embarked for Italy, but only a remnant of two thousand arrived in safety in their native land. Ingulphus, a secretary of William the Conqueror, was a companion of this pilgrimage; he observes that they sallied from Normandy thirty stout and well-appointed horsemen; but that they repassed the Alps twenty miserable palmers, with the staff in their hand, and the wallet at their back.

After the defeat of the Romans the tranquillity of the Fatimite caliphs was invaded by the Turks. One of the lieutenants of Malek Shah, Atsiz the Carizmian, marched into Syria at the head of a powerful army, and reduced Damascus by famine and the sword. Hems, and the other cities of the province, acknowledged the caliph of Bagdad and the sultan of Persia; and the victorious emir advanced without resistance to the banks of the Nile: the Fatimite was preparing to fly into the heart of Africa; but the negroes of his guard and the inhabitants of Cairo made a desperate sally, and repulsed the Turk from the confines of Egypt. In his retreat he indulged the licence of slaughter and rapine: the judge and notaries of Jerusalem were invited to his camp; and their execution was followed by the massacre of three thousand citizens. The cruelty or the defeat of Atsiz was soon punished by the sultan Toucush, the brother of Malek Shah, who, with a higher title and more formidable powers, asserted the dominion of Syria and Palestine. The house of Seljuk reigned about twenty years in Jerusalem; but the hereditary command of the holy city and territory was intrusted or abandoned to the emir Ortok, the chief of a tribe of Turkmans, whose children, after their expulsion from Palestine, formed two dynasties on the borders of Armenia and Assyria. The Oriental Christians and the Latin pilgrims deplored a revolution which, instead of the regular government and old alliance of the caliphs, imposed on their necks the iron yoke of the strangers of the North. In his court and camp the great sultan had adopted in some degree the arts and manners of Persia; but the body of the Turkish nation, and more especially the pastoral tribes, still breathed the fierceness of the desert. From Nice to Jerusalem the western countries of Asia were a scene of foreign and domestic hostility; and the shepherds of Palestine, who held a precarious sway on a doubtful frontier, had neither leisure nor capacity to await the slow profits of commercial and religious freedom. The pilgrims, who, through innumerable perils, had reached the gates of Jerusalem, were the victims of private rapine or public oppression, and often sunk under the pressure of famine and disease, before they were permitted to salute the holy sepulchre. A spirit of native barbarism, or recent zeal, prompted the Turkmans to insult the clergy of every sect: the patriarch was dragged by the hair along the pavement and cast into a dungeon, to extort a ransom from the sympathy of his flock; and the divine worship in the church of the Resurrection was often disturbed by the savage rudeness of its masters. The pathetic tale excited the millions of the West to march under the standard of the cross to the relief of the Holy Land; and yet how trifling is the sum of these accumulated evils, if compared with the single act of the sacrilege of Hakem, which had been so patiently endured by the Latin Christians! A slighter provocation inflamed the more irascible temper of their descendants: a new spirit had arisen of religious chivalry and papal dominion; a nerve was touched of exquisite feeling; and the sensation vibrated to the heart of Europe.

59.

ST. LOUIS AND THE SIXTH AND SEVENTH CRUSADES. THE LOSS OF ANTIOCH. THE LOSS OF ACRE AND THE HOLY LAND

The capture of Jerusalem by the Turks stimulated both the spiritual and temporal enthusiasm in Western Europe which led to the crusades. In 1099 Jerusalem was retaken by Godfrey de Bouillon and a kingdom established there. Saladin conquered Jerusalem in 1187 and brought the kingdom to an end. Subsequent efforts to recapture the city were unsuccessful.

Gibbon begins his account of the crusades in Chapter 58. He reserves his description of the Fourth Crusade, which had a very direct bearing on the fate of the Roman Empire, for a subsequent chapter, (c. 60), which is included in full.

ST. LOUIS AND THE SIXTH AND SEVENTH CRUSADES

OF THE SEVEN CRUSADES, the two last were undertaken by Louis the Ninth, king of France, who lost his liberty in Egypt, and his life on the coast of Africa. Twenty-eight years after his death he was canonised at Rome, and sixty-five miracles were readily found and solemnly attested to justify the claim of the royal saint. The voice of history renders a more honourable testimony, that he united the virtues of a king, an hero, and a man; that his martial spirit was tempered by the love of private and public justice; and that Louis was the father of his people, the friend of his neighbours, and the terror of the infidels. Superstition alone, in all the extent of her baleful influence, corrupted his understanding and his heart; his devotion stooped to admire and imitate the begging friars of Francis and Dominic; he pursued with blind and cruel zeal the enemies of the faith; and the best of kings twice descended from his throne to seek the adventures of a spiritual knight-errant. A monkish historian would have been content to applaud the most despicable part of his character; but the noble and gallant Joinville, who shared the friendship and captivity of Louis, has traced with the pencil of nature the free portrait of his virtues as well as of his failings. From this intimate knowledge we may learn to suspect the political views of depressing their great vassals, which are so often imputed to the royal authors of the crusades. Above all the princes of the middle ages Louis the Ninth successfully laboured to restore the prerogatives of the crown; but it was at home, and not in the East, that he acquired these for himself and his posterity; his vow was the result of enthusiasm and sickness; and if he were the promoter, he was likewise the victim, of this holy madness. For the invasion of Egypt, France was exhausted of her troops and treasures; he covered the sea of Cyprus with eighteen hundred sails; the most modest enumeration amounts to fifty thousand men; and, if we might trust his own confession, as it is reported by Oriental vanity, he disembarked nine thousand five hundred horse, and one hundred and thirty thousand foot, who performed their pilgrimage under the shadow of his power.

In complete armour, the oriflamme waving before him, Louis leaped foremost on the beach; and the strong city of Damietta, which had cost his predecessors a siege of sixteen months, was abandoned on the first assault by the trembling Moslems. But Damietta was the first and the last of his conquests; and in the fifth and sixth crusades the same causes, almost on the same ground, were productive of similar calamities. After a ruinous delay, which introduced into the camp the seeds of an epidemical disease, the Franks advanced from the sea-coast towards the capital of Egypt, and strove to surmount the unseasonable inundation of the Nile which opposed their progress. Under the eye of their intrepid monarch, the barons and knights of France displayed their invincible contempt of danger and discipline; his brother, the count of Artois, stormed with inconsiderate valour the town of Massoura; and the carrier pigeons announced to the inhabitants of Cairo that all was lost. But a soldier, who afterwards usurped the sceptre, rallied the flying troops: the main body of the Christians was far behind their vanguard, and Artois was overpowered and slain. A shower of Greek fire was incessantly poured on the invaders; the Nile was commanded by the Egyptian galleys, the open country by the Arabs; all provisions were intercepted; each day aggravated the sickness and famine; and about the same time a retreat was found to be necessary and impracticable. The Oriental writers confess that Louis might have escaped if he would have deserted his subjects: he was made prisoner, with the greatest part of his nobles; all who could not redeem their lives by service or ransom were inhumanly massacred, and the walls of Cairo were decorated with a circle of Christian heads. The king of France was loaded with chains, but the generous victor, a great-grandson of the brother of Saladin, sent a robe of honour to his royal captive, and his deliverance, with that of his soldiers, was obtained by the restitution of Damietta and the payment of four hundred thousand pieces of gold. In a soft and luxurious climate the degenerate children of the companions of Noureddin and Saladin were incapable of resisting the flower of European chivalry; they triumphed by the arms of their slaves or Mamalukes, the hardy natives of Tartary, who at a tender age had been purchased of the Syrian merchants, and were educated in the camp and palace of the sultan. But Egypt soon afforded a new example of the danger of prætorian bands; and the rage of these ferocious animals, who had been let loose on the strangers, was provoked to devour their benefactor. In the pride of conquest, Touran Shaw, the last of his race, was murdered by his Mamalukes; and the most daring of the assassins entered the chamber of the captive king, with drawn scimitars, and their hands imbrued in the blood of their sultan. The firmness of Louis commanded their respect; their avarice prevailed over cruelty and zeal, the treaty was accomplished, and the king of France, with the relics of his army, was permitted to embark for Palestine. He wasted four years within the walls of Acre, unable to visit Jerusalem, and unwilling to return without glory to his native country.

The memory of his defeat excited Louis, after sixteen years of wisdom and repose, to undertake the seventh and last of the crusades. His finances were restored, his kingdom was enlarged; a new generation of warriors had arisen, and he embarked with fresh confidence at the head of six thousand horse and thirty thousand foot. The loss of Antioch had provoked the enterprise; a wild hope of baptizing the king of

Tunis tempted him to steer for the African coast; and the report of an immense treasure reconciled his troops to the delay of their voyage to the Holy Land. Instead of a proselyte, he found a siege; the French panted and died on the burning sands; St. Louis expired in his tent; and no sooner had he closed his eyes than his son and successor gave the signal of the retreat. "It is thus," says a lively writer, "that a Christian king died near the ruins of Carthage, waging war against the sectaries of Mahomet, in a land to which Dido had introduced the deities of Syria."

THE LOSS OF ANTIOCH

A more unjust and absurd constitution cannot be devised than that which condemns the natives of a country to perpetual servitude under the arbitrary dominion of strangers and slaves. Yet such has been the state of Egypt above five hundred years. The most illustrious sultans of the Baharite and Borgite dynasties were themselves promoted from the Tartar and Circassian bands; and the four-and-twenty beys, or military chiefs, have ever been succeeded, not by their sons, but by their servants. They produce the great charter of their liberties, the treaty of Selim the First with the republic; and the Othman emperor still accepts from Egypt a slight acknowledgment of tribute and subjection. With some breathing intervals of peace and order, the two dynasties are marked as a period of rapine and bloodshed; but their throne, however shaken, reposed on the two pillars of discipline and valour; their sway extended over Egypt, Nubia, Arabia, and Syria; their Mamalukes were multiplied from eight hundred to twenty-five thousand horse; and their numbers were increased by a provincial militia of one hundred and seven thousand foot, and the occasional aid of sixty-six thousand Arabs. Princes of such power and spirit could not long endure on their coast an hostile and independent nation; and if the ruin of the Franks was postponed about forty years, they were indebted to the cares of an unsettled reign, to the invasion of the Mogols, and to the occasional aid of some warlike pilgrims. Among these the English reader will observe the name of our first Edward, who assumed the cross in the lifetime of his father Henry. At the head of a thousand soldiers the future conqueror of Wales and Scotland delivered Acre from a siege; marched as far as Nazareth with an army of nine thousand men; emulated the fame of his uncle Richard; extorted, by his valour, a ten years' truce; and escaped, with a dangerous wound, from the dagger of a fanatic *assassin*. Antioch, whose situation had been less exposed to the calamities of the holy war, was finally occupied and ruined by Bondocdar, or Bibars, sultan of Egypt and Syria; the Latin principality was extinguished; and the first seat of the Christian name was dispeopled by the slaughter of seventeen, and the captivity of one hundred, thousand of her inhabitants. The maritime towns of Laodicea, Gabala, Tripoli, Berytus, Sidon, Tyre, and Jaffa, and the stronger castles of the Hospitalers and Templars, successively fell; and the whole existence of the Franks was confined to the city and colony of St. John of Acre, which is sometimes described by the more classic title of Ptolemais.

THE LOSS OF ACRE AND THE HOLY LAND

After the loss of Jerusalem, Acre, which is distant about seventy miles, became the metropolis of the Latin Christians, and was adorned with strong and stately buildings, with aqueducts, an artificial port, and a double wall. The population was increased by the incessant streams of pilgrims and fugitives; in the pauses of hostility the trade of the East and West was attracted to this convenient station, and the market could offer the produce of every clime and the interpreters of every tongue. But in this conflux of nations every vice was propagated and practised: of all the disciples of Jesus and Mahomet, the male and female inhabitants of Acre were esteemed the most corrupt, nor could the abuse of religion be corrected by the discipline of law. The city had many sovereigns and no government. The kings of Jerusalem and Cyprus, of the house of Lusignan, the princes of Antioch, the counts of Tripoli and Sidon, the great masters of the hospital, the temple, and the Teutonic order, the republics of Venice, Genoa, and Pisa, the pope's legate, the kings of France and England, assumed an independent command; seventeen tribunals exercised the power of life and death; every criminal was protected in the adjacent quarter; and the perpetual jealousy of the nations often burst forth in acts of violence and blood. Some adventurers, who disgraced the ensign of the cross, compensated their want of pay by the plunder of the Mahometan villages; nineteen Syrian merchants, who traded under the public faith, were despoiled and hanged by the Christians, and the denial of satisfaction justified the arms of the sultan Khalil. He marched against Acre at the head of sixty thousand horse and one hundred and forty thousand foot; his train of artillery (if I may use the word) was numerous and weighty; the separate timbers of a single engine were transported in one hundred waggons; and the royal historian Abulfeda, who served with the troops of Hamah, was himself a spectator of the holy war. Whatever might be the vices of the Franks, their courage was rekindled by enthusiasm and despair; but they were torn by the discord of seventeen chiefs, and overwhelmed on all sides by the powers of the sultan. After a siege of thirty-three days the double wall was forced by the Moslems; the principal tower yielded to their engines; the Mamalukes made a general assault; the city was stormed, and death or slavery was the lot of sixty thousand Christians. The convent, or rather fortress, of the Templars resisted three days longer; but the great master was pierced with an arrow, and, of five hundred knights, only ten were left alive, less happy than the victims of the sword, if they lived to suffer on a scaffold in the unjust and cruel proscription of the whole order. The king of Jerusalem, the patriarch, and the great master of the hospital effected their retreat to the shore; but the sea was rough, the vessels were insufficient, and great numbers of the fugitives were drowned before they could reach the isle of Cyprus, which might comfort Lusignan for the loss of Palestine. By the command of the sultan the churches and fortifications of the Latin cities were demolished: a motive of avarice or fear still opened the holy sepulchre to some devout and defenceless pilgrims; and a mournful and solitary silence prevailed along the coast which had so long resounded with the WORLD'S DEBATE.

60.

SCHISM AND ENMITY OF THE GREEKS AND LATINS.
THE FOURTH CRUSADE. ALLIANCE OF THE FRENCH
AND VENETIANS AND THEIR VOYAGE TO
CONSTANTINOPLE. CONQUEST AND PILLAGE OF
CONSTANTINOPLE BY THE LATINS

THE RESTORATION of the Western empire by Charlemagne was
speedily followed by the separation of the Greek and Latin
churches. A religious and national animosity still divides the
two largest communions of the Christian world; and the
schism of Constantinople, by alienating her most useful allies,
and provoking her most dangerous enemies, has precipitated
the decline and fall of the Roman empire in the East.

In the course of the present history the aversion of the
Greeks for the Latins has been often visible and conspicuous.
It was originally derived from the disdain of servitude, inflamed, after the time of Constantine, by the pride of equality
or dominion, and finally exasperated by the preference which
their rebellious subjects had given to the alliance of the Franks.
In every age the Greeks were proud of their superiority in
profane and religious knowledge: they had first received the
light of Christianity; they had pronounced the decrees of the
seven general councils; they alone possessed the language of
Scripture and philosophy: nor should the barbarians, immersed in the darkness of the West, presume to argue on the
high and mysterious questions of theological science. Those
barbarians despised in their turn the restless and subtle levity
of the Orientals, the authors of every heresy, and blessed
their own simplicity, which was content to hold the tradition
of the apostolic church. Yet in the seventh century the synods
of Spain, and afterwards of France, improved or corrupted
the Nicene creed, on the mysterious subject of the third person of the Trinity. In the long controversies of the East the
nature and generation of the Christ had been scrupulously
defined; and the well-known relation of father and son seemed

to convey a faint image to the human mind. The idea of birth was less analogous to the Holy Spirit, who, instead of a divine gift or attribute, was considered by the Catholics as a substance, a person, a god; he was not begotten, but in the orthodox style he *proceeded*. Did he proceed from the Father alone, perhaps *by* the Son? or from the Father *and* the Son? The first of these opinions was asserted by the Greeks, the second by the Latins; and the addition to the Nicene creed of the word *filioque* kindled the flame of discord between the Oriental and the Gallic churches. In the origin of the dispute the Roman pontiffs affected a character of neutrality and moderation: they condemned the innovation, but they acquiesced in the sentiment, of their Transalpine brethren; they seemed desirous of casting a veil of silence and charity over the superfluous research; and in the correspondence of Charlemagne and Leo the Third, the pope assumes the liberality of a statesman, and the prince descends to the passions and prejudices of a priest. But the orthodoxy of Rome spontaneously obeyed the impulse of her temporal policy; and the *filioque*, which Leo wished to erase, was transcribed in the symbol and chanted in the liturgy of the Vatican. The Nicene and Athanasian creeds are held as the Catholic faith, without which none can be saved; and both Papists and Protestants must now sustain and return the anathemas of the Greeks, who deny the procession of the Holy Ghost from the Son as well as from the Father. Such articles of faith are not susceptible of treaty; but the rules of discipline will vary in remote and independent churches; and the reason, even of divines, might allow that the difference is inevitable and harmless. The craft or superstition of Rome has imposed on her priests and deacons the rigid obligation of celibacy; among the Greeks it is confined to the bishops; the loss is compensated by dignity or annihilated by age; and the parochial clergy, the papas, enjoy the conjugal society of the wives whom they have married before their entrance into holy orders. A question concerning the *Azyms* was fiercely debated in the eleventh century, and the essence of the Eucharist was supposed in the East and West to depend on the use of leavened or unleavened bread. Shall I mention in a serious history the furious reproaches that were urged against the Latins, who for a long while remained on the defensive? They neglected to abstain, according to the apostolical decree, from things strangled, and from blood: they fasted, a Jewish observance! on the Saturday of each week: during the first week of Lent they permitted the use of milk and cheese; their infirm monks were indulged in the taste of flesh; and animal grease was substituted for the want of vegetable oil: the holy chrism or unction in baptism was reserved to the episcopal order; the bishops, as the bridegrooms of their churches, were decorated with rings; their priests shaved their faces, and baptized by a single immersion. Such were the crimes which provoked the zeal of the patriarchs of Constantinople, and which were justified with equal zeal by the doctors of the Latin church.

Bigotry and national aversion are powerful magnifiers of every object of dispute; but the immediate cause of the schism of the Greeks may be traced in the emulation of the leading prelates, who maintained the supremacy of the old metropolis, superior to all, and of the reigning capital, inferior to none, in the Christian world. About the middle of the ninth century, Photius, an ambitious layman, the captain of the guards and principal secretary, was promoted by merit and favour to the more desirable office of patriarch of Constantinople. In science, even ecclesiastical science, he surpassed the clergy of the age; and the purity of his morals has never been impeached: but his ordination was hasty, his rise was irregular; and Ignatius, his abdicated predecessor, was yet supported by the public compassion and the obstinacy of his adherents. They appealed to the tribunal of Nicholas the First, one of the proudest and most aspiring of the Roman pontiffs, who embraced the welcome opportunity of judging and condemning his rival of the East. Their quarrel was embittered by a conflict of jurisdiction over the king and nation of the Bulgarians; nor was their recent conversion to Christianity of much avail to either prelate, unless he could number the proselytes among the subjects of his power. With the aid of his court the Greek patriarch was victorious; but in the furious contest he deposed in his turn the successor of St. Peter, and involved the Latin church in the reproach of heresy and schism. Photius sacrificed the peace of the world to a short and precarious reign: he fell with his patron, the Cæsar Bardas; and Basil the Macedonian performed an act of justice in the restoration of Ignatius, whose age and dignity had not been sufficiently respected. From his monastery, or prison,

Photius solicited the favour of the emperor by pathetic complaints and artful flattery; and the eyes of his rival were scarcely closed when he was again restored to the throne of Constantinople. After the death of Basil he experienced the vicissitudes of courts and the ingratitude of a royal pupil: the patriarch was again deposed, and in his last solitary hours he might regret the freedom of a secular and studious life. In each revolution the breath, the nod, of the sovereign had been accepted by a submissive clergy; and a synod of three hundred bishops was always prepared to hail the triumph, or to stigmatise the fall, of the holy, or the execrable, Photius. By a delusive promise of succour or reward, the popes were tempted to countenance these various proceedings; and the synods of Constantinople were ratified by their epistles or legates. But the court and the people, Ignatius and Photius, were equally adverse to their claims; their ministers were insulted or imprisoned; the procession of the Holy Ghost was forgotten; Bulgaria was for ever annexed to the Byzantine throne; and the schism was prolonged by their rigid censure of all the multiplied ordinations of an irregular patriarch. The darkness and corruption of the tenth century suspended the intercourse, without reconciling the minds, of the two nations. But when the Norman sword restored the churches of Apulia to the jurisdiction of Rome, the departing flock was warned, by a petulant epistle of the Greek patriarch, to avoid and abhor the errors of the Latins. The rising majesty of Rome could no longer brook the insolence of a rebel; and Michael Cerularius was excommunicated in the heart of Constantinople by the pope's legates. Shaking the dust from their feet, they deposited on the altar of St. Sophia a direful anathema, which enumerates the seven mortal heresies of the Greeks, and devotes the guilty teachers, and their unhappy sectaries, to the eternal society of the devil and his angels. According to the emergencies of the church and state, a friendly correspondence was sometimes resumed; the language of charity and concord was sometimes affected; but the Greeks have never recanted their errors, the popes have never repealed their sentence; and from this thunderbolt we may date the consummation of the schism. It was enlarged by each ambitious step of the Roman pontiffs: the emperors blushed and trembled at the ignominious fate of their royal brethren of Germany; and the people was scandalised by the temporal power and military life of the Latin clergy.

ENMITY OF THE GREEKS AND LATINS

The aversion of the Greeks and Latins was nourished and manifested in the three first expeditions to the Holy Land. Alexius Comnenus contrived the absence at least of the formidable pilgrims: his successors, Manuel and Isaac Angelus, conspired with the Moslems for the ruin of the greatest princes of the Franks; and their crooked and malignant policy was seconded by the active and voluntary obedience of every order of their subjects. Of this hostile temper a large portion may doubtless be ascribed to the difference of language, dress, and manners, which severs and alienates the nations of the globe. The pride as well as the prudence of the sovereign was deeply wounded by the intrusion of foreign armies that claimed a right of traversing his dominions, and passing under the walls of his capital: his subjects were insulted and plundered by the rude strangers of the West: and the hatred of the pusillanimous Greeks was sharpened by secret envy of the bold and pious enterprises of the Franks. But these profane causes of national enmity were fortified and inflamed by the venom of religious zeal. Instead of a kind embrace, an hospitable reception from their Christian brethren of the East, every tongue was taught to repeat the names of schismatic and heretic, more odious to an orthodox ear than those of Pagan and infidel: instead of being loved for the general conformity of faith and worship, they were abhorred for some rules of discipline, some questions of theology, in which themselves or their teachers might differ from the Oriental church. In the crusade of Louis the Seventh the Greek clergy washed and purified the altars which had been defiled by the sacrifice of a French priest. The companions of Frederic Barbarossa deplore the injuries which they endured, both in word and deed, from the peculiar rancour of the bishops and monks. Their prayers and sermons excited the people against the impious barbarians; and the patriarch is accused of declaring that the faithful might obtain the redemption of all their sins by the extirpation of the schismatics. An enthusiast named Dorotheus alarmed the fears and restored the confidence of the emperor by a prophetic assurance that the German heretic,

after assaulting the gate of Blachernæ, would be made a
signal example of the divine vengeance. The passage of these
mighty armies were rare and perilous events; but the crusades introduced a frequent and familiar intercourse between
the two nations, which enlarged their knowledge without
abating their prejudices. The wealth and luxury of Constantinople demanded the productions of every climate: these
imports were balanced by the art and labour of her numerous inhabitants; her situation invites the commerce of the
world; and, in every period of her existence, that commerce
has been in the hands of foreigners. After the decline of
Amalphi, the Venetians, Pisans, and Genoese introduced
their factories and settlements into the capital of the empire:
their services were rewarded with honours and immunities;
they acquired the possession of lands and houses, their families
were multiplied by marriages with the natives, and, after the
toleration of a Mahometan mosque, it was impossible to interdict the churches of the Roman rite. The two wives of
Manuel Comnenus were of the race of the Franks: the first,
a sister-in-law of the emperor Conrad; the second, a daughter
of the prince of Antioch: he obtained for his son Alexius a
daughter of Philip Augustus king of France; and he bestowed
his own daughter on a marquis of Montferrat, who was educated and dignified in the palace of Constantinople. The
Greek encountered the arms, and aspired to the empire, of
the West: he esteemed the valour, and trusted the fidelity,
of the Franks; their military talents were unfitly recompensed
by the lucrative offices of judges and treasurers; the policy of
Manuel had solicited the alliance of the pope; and the popular voice accused him of a partial bias to the nation and
religion of the Latins. During his reign and that of his successor Alexius, they were exposed at Constantinople to the
reproach of foreigners, heretics, and favourites; and this triple
guilt was severely expiated in the tumult which announced
the return and elevation of Andronicus. The people rose in
arms: from the Asiatic shore the tyrant despatched his troops
and galleys to assist the national revenge; and the hopeless
resistance of the strangers served only to justify the rage
and sharpen the daggers of the assassins. Neither age, nor
sex, nor the ties of friendship or kindred, could save the victims of national hatred, and avarice, and religious zeal: the
Latins were slaughtered in their houses and in the streets;

their quarter was reduced to ashes; the clergy were burnt in their churches, and the sick in their hospitals; and some estimate may be formed of the slain from the clemency which sold above four thousand Christians in perpetual slavery to the Turks. The priests and monks were the loudest and most active in the destruction of the schismatics; and they chanted a thanksgiving to the Lord when the head of a Roman cardinal, the pope's legate, was severed from his body, fastened to the tail of a dog, and dragged, with savage mockery, through the city. The more diligent of the strangers had retreated, on the first alarm, to their vessels; and escaped through the Hellespont from the scene of blood. In their flight they burnt and ravaged two hundred miles of the sea-coast, inflicted a severe revenge on the guiltless subjects of the empire, marked the priests and monks as their peculiar enemies, and compensated, by the accumulation of plunder, the loss of their property and friends. On their return they exposed to Italy and Europe the wealth and weakness, the perfidy and malice of the Greeks, whose vices were painted as the genuine characters of heresy and schism. The scruples of the first crusaders had neglected the fairest opportunities of securing, by the possession of Constantinople, the way to the Holy Land: a domestic revolution invited, and almost compelled, the French and Venetians to achieve the conquest of the Roman empire of the East.

In the series of the Byzantine princes I have exhibited the hypocrisy and ambition, the tyranny and fall, of Andronicus, the last male of the Comnenian family who reigned at Constantinople. The revolution which cast him headlong from the throne saved and exalted Isaac Angelus, who descended by the females from the same Imperial dynasty. The successor of a second Nero might have found it an easy task to deserve the esteem and affection of his subjects: they sometimes had reason to regret the administration of Andronicus. The sound and vigorous mind of the tyrant was capable of discerning the connection between his own and the public interest; and while he was feared by all who could inspire him with fear, the unsuspected people, and the remote provinces, might bless the inexorable justice of their master. But his successor was vain and jealous of the supreme power, which he wanted courage and abilities to exercise: his vices were pernicious, his virtues (if he possessed any virtues) were useless, to mankind; and the Greeks, who imputed their calamities to his negligence, denied him the merit of any transient or accidental benefits of the times. Isaac slept on the throne, and was awakened only by the sound of pleasure: his vacant hours were amused by comedians and buffoons, and even to these buffoons the emperor was an object of contempt: his feasts and buildings exceeded the examples of royal luxury: the number of his eunuchs and domestics amounted to twenty thousand; and a daily sum of four thousand pounds of silver would swell to four millions sterling the annual expense of his household and table. His poverty was relieved by oppression; and the public discontent was inflamed by equal abuses in the collection and the application of the revenue. While the Greeks numbered the days of their servitude, a flattering prophet, whom he rewarded with the dignity of patriarch, assured him of a long and victorious reign of thirty-two years, during which he should extend his sway to Mount Libanus, and his conquests beyond the Euphrates. But his only step towards the accomplishment of the prediction was a splendid and scandalous embassy to Saladin, to demand the restitution of the holy sepulchre, and to propose an offensive and defensive league with the enemy of the Christian name. In these unworthy hands, of Isaac and his brother, the remains of the Greek empire crumbled into dust. The island of Cyprus, whose name excites the ideas of elegance and pleasure, was usurped by his namesake, a Comnenian prince; and by a strange concatenation of events, the sword of our English Richard bestowed that kingdom on the house of Lusignan, a rich compensation for the loss of Jerusalem.

The honour of the monarchy and the safety of the capital were deeply wounded by the revolt of the Bulgarians and Wallachians. Since the victory of the second Basil, they had supported, above an hundred and seventy years, the loose dominion of the Byzantine princes; but no effectual measures had been adopted to impose the yoke of laws and manners on these savage tribes. By the command of Isaac, their sole means of subsistence, their flocks and herds, were driven away to contribute towards the pomp of the royal nuptials; and their fierce warriors were exasperated by the denial of equal rank and pay in the military service. Peter and Asan, two powerful chiefs, of the race of the ancient kings, asserted their own rights and the national freedom: their demoniac impostors proclaimed to the crowd that their glorious patron St. Demetrius had for ever deserted the cause of the Greeks: and the conflagration spread from the banks of the Danube to the hills of Macedonia and Thrace. After some faint efforts, Isaac Angelus and his brother acquiesced in their independence; and the Imperial troops were soon discouraged by the bones of their fellow-soldiers that were scattered along the passes of Mount Hæmus. By the arms and policy of John, or Joannices, the second kingdom of Bulgaria was firmly established. The subtle barbarian sent an embassy to Innocent the Third to acknowledge himself a genuine son of Rome in descent and religion, and humbly received from the pope the licence of coining money, the royal title, and a Latin archbishop or patriarch. The Vatican exulted in the spiritual conquest of Bulgaria, the first object of the schism; and if the Greeks could have preserved the prerogatives of the church, they would gladly have resigned the rights of the monarchy.

The Bulgarians were malicious enough to pray for the long life of Isaac Angelus, the surest pledge of their freedom and prosperity. Yet their chiefs could involve in the same indiscriminate contempt the family and nation of the emperor. "In all the Greeks," said Asan to his troops, "the same climate, and character, and education, will be productive of the same fruits. Behold my lance," continued the warrior, "and the long streamers that float in the wind. They differ only in colour; they are formed of the same silk, and fashioned by the same workman; nor has the stripe that is stained in purple any superior price or value above its fellows." Several of these candidates for the purple successively rose and fell under the empire of Isaac: a general who had repelled the fleets of Sicily was driven to revolt and ruin by the ingratitude of the prince; and his luxurious repose was disturbed by secret conspiracies and popular insurrections. The emperor was saved by accident, or the merit of his servants: he was at length oppressed by an ambitious brother, who, for the hope of a precarious diadem, forgot the obligations of nature, of loyalty, and of friendship. While Isaac in the Thracian valleys pursued the idle and solitary pleasures of the chase, his brother, Alexius Angelus, was invested with the purple by the unanimous suffrage of the camp: the capital and the clergy subscribed to their choice; and the vanity of the new sovereign rejected the name of his fathers for the lofty and royal appellation of the Comnenian race. On the despicable character of Isaac I have exhausted the language of contempt, and can only add that in a reign of eight years the baser Alexius was supported by the masculine vices of his wife Euphrosyne. The first intelligence of his fall was conveyed to the late emperor by the hostile aspect and pursuit of the guards, no longer his own: he fled before them above fifty miles as far as Stagyra in Macedonia; but the fugitive, without an object or a follower, was arrested, brought back to Constantinople, deprived of his eyes, and confined in a lonesome tower, on a scanty allowance of bread and water. At the moment of the revolution, his son Alexius, whom he educated in the hope of empire, was twelve years of age. He was spared by the usurper, and reduced to attend his triumph both in peace and war; but as the army was encamped on the sea-shore, an Italian vessel facilitated the escape of the royal youth; and, in the disguise of a common sailor, he eluded the search of his enemies, passed the Hellespont, and found a secure refuge in the isle of Sicily. After saluting the threshold of the apostles, and imploring the protection of Pope Innocent the Third, Alexius accepted the kind invitation of his sister Irene, the wife of Philip of Swabia, king of the Romans. But in his passage through Italy he heard that the flower of Western chivalry was assembled at Venice for the deliverance of the Holy Land; and a ray of hope was kindled in his bosom that their invincible swords might be employed in his father's restoration.

THE FOURTH CRUSADE

About ten or twelve years after the loss of Jerusalem, the nobles of France were again summoned to the holy war by the voice of a third prophet, less extravagant, perhaps than Peter the Hermit, but far below St. Bernard in the merit of an orator and a statesman. An illiterate priest of the neighbourhood of Paris, Fulk of Neuilly, forsook his parochial duty, to assume the more flattering character of a popular and itinerant missionary. The fame of his sanctity and miracles was spread over the land: he declaimed, with severity and vehemence, against the vices of the age; and his sermons, which he preached in the streets of Paris, converted the rob-

bers, the usurers, the prostitutes, and even the doctors and
scholars of the university. No sooner did Innocent the Third
ascend the chair of St. Peter than he proclaimed in Italy,
Germany, and France, the obligation of a new crusade. The
eloquent pontiff described the ruin of Jerusalem, the triumph
of the Pagans, and the shame of Christendom: his liberality
proposed the redemption of sins, a plenary indulgence to all
who should serve in Palestine, either a year in person, or two
years by a substitute: and among his legates and orators who
blew the sacred trumpet, Fulk of Neuilly was the loudest
and most successful. The situation of the principal monarchs
was averse to the pious summons. The emperor Frederic the
Second was a child; and his kingdom of Germany was disputed by the rival houses of Brunswick and Swabia, the
memorable factions of the Guelphs and Ghibelines. Philip
Augustus of France had performed, and could not be persuaded to renew, the perilous vow; but as he was not less ambitious of praise than of power, he cheerfully instituted a
perpetual fund for the defence of the Holy Land. Richard
of England was satiated with the glory and misfortunes of
his adventure, and he presumed to deride the exhortations of
Fulk of Neuilly, who was not abashed in the presence of kings.
"You advise me," said Plantagenet, "to dismiss my three
daughters, pride, avarice, and incontinence: I bequeath them
to the most deserving; my pride to the knights-templars, my
avarice to the monks of Cisteaux, and my incontinence to
the prelates." But the preacher was heard and obeyed by the
great vassals, the princes of the second order; and Theobald,
or Thibaut, count of Champagne, was the foremost in the
holy race. The valiant youth, at the age of twenty-two years,
was encouraged by the domestic examples of his father, who
marched in the second crusade, and of his elder brother, who
had ended his days in Palestine with the title of King of
Jerusalem: two thousand two hundred knights owed service
and homage to his peerage: the nobles of Champagne excelled
in all the exercises of war; and, by his marriage with the
heiress of Navarre, Thibaut could draw a band of hardy Gas-
cons from either side of the Pyrenæan mountains. His companion in arms was Louis, count of Blois and Chartres; like
himself of regal lineage, for both the princes were nephews,
at the same time, of the kings of France and England. In a
crowd of prelates and barons, who imitated their zeal, I dis-

tinguish the birth and merit of Matthew of Montmorency; the famous Simon of Montfort, the scourge of the Albigeois; and a valiant noble, Jeffrey of Villehardouin, marshal of Champagne, who has condescended, in the rude idiom of his age and country, to write or dictate an original narrative of the councils and actions in which he bore a memorable part. At the same time, Baldwin count of Flanders, who had married the sister of Thibaut, assumed the cross at Bruges, with his brother Henry and the principal knights and citizens of that rich and industrious province. The vow which the chiefs had pronounced in churches, they ratified in tournaments: the operations of the war were debated in full and frequent assemblies: and it was resolved to seek the deliverance of Palestine in Egypt, a country, since Saladin's death, which was almost ruined by famine and civil war. But the fate of so many royal armies displayed the toils and perils of a land expedition; and if the Flemings dwelt along the ocean, the French barons were destitute of ships and ignorant of navigation. They embraced the wise resolution of choosing six deputies or representatives of whom Villehardouin was one, with a discretionary trust to direct the motions, and to pledge the faith, of the whole confederacy. The maritime states of Italy were alone possessed of the means of transporting the holy warriors with their arms and horses; and the six deputies proceeded to Venice to solicit, on motives of piety or interest, the aid of that powerful republic.

In the invasion of Italy by Attila, I have mentioned the flight of the Venetians from the fallen cities of the continent, and their obscure shelter in the chain of islands that line the extremity of the Adriatic Gulf. In the midst of the waters, free, indigent, laborious, and inaccessible, they gradually coalesced into a republic: the first foundations of Venice were laid in the island of Rialto; and the annual election of the twelve tribunes was superseded by the permanent office of a duke or doge. On the verge of the two empires, the Venetians exult in the belief of primitive and perpetual independence. Against the Latins their antique freedom has been asserted by the sword, and may be justified by the pen. Charlemagne himself resigned all claims of sovereignty to the islands of the Adriatic Gulf: his son Pepin was repulsed in the attacks of the *lagunas* or canals, too deep for the cavalry, and too shallow for the vessels; and in every age, under the

German Cæsars, the lands of the republic have been clearly
distinguished from the kingdom of Italy. But the inhabitants
of Venice were considered by themselves, by strangers, and
by their sovereigns, as an inalienable portion of the Greek
empire; in the ninth and tenth centuries the proofs of their
subjection are numerous and unquestionable; and the vain
titles, the servile honours, of the Byzantine court, so am-
bitiously solicited by their dukes, would have degraded the
magistrates of a free people. But the bands of this dependence,
which was never absolute or rigid, were imperceptibly relaxed
by the ambition of Venice and the weakness of Constantinople.
Obedience was softened into respect, privilege ripened into
prerogative, and the freedom of domestic government was
fortified by the independence of foreign dominion. The maritime cities of Istria and Dalmatia bowed to the sovereigns
of the Adriatic; and when they armed against the Normans
in the cause of Alexius, the emperor applied, not to the duty
of his subjects, but to the gratitude and generosity of his
faithful allies. The sea was their patrimony: the western
parts of the Mediterranean, from Tuscany to Gibraltar, were
indeed abandoned to their rivals of Pisa and Genoa; but the
Venetians acquired an early and lucrative share of the commerce of Greece and Egypt. Their riches increased with the
increasing demand of Europe: their manufacture of silk and
glass, perhaps the institution of their bank, are of high antiquity; and they enjoyed the fruits of their industry in the
magnificence of public and private life. To assert her flag, to
avenge her injuries, to protect the freedom of navigation, the
republic could launch and man a fleet of an hundred galleys;
and the Greeks, the Saracens, and the Normans were encountered by her naval arms. The Franks of Syria were assisted by the Venetians in the reduction of the sea-coast; but
their zeal was neither blind nor disinterested; and in the conquest of Tyre they shared the sovereignty of a city, the first
seat of the commerce of the world. The policy of Venice was
marked by the avarice of a trading, and the insolence of a
maritime power; yet her ambition was prudent: nor did she
often forget that, if armed galleys were the effect and safeguard, merchant vessels were the cause and supply, of her
greatness. In her religion she avoided the schism of the Greeks,
without yielding a servile obedience to the Roman pontiff;
and a free intercourse with the infidels of every clime appears

to have allayed betimes the fever of superstition. Her primitive government was a loose mixture of democracy and monarchy: the doge was elected by the votes of the general assembly; as long as he was popular and successful, he reigned with the pomp and authority of a prince: but in the frequent revolutions of the state, he was deposed, or banished, or slain, by the justice or injustice of the multitude. The twelfth century produced the first rudiments of the wise and jealous aristocracy, which has reduced the doge to a pageant, and the people to a cipher.

ALLIANCE OF THE FRENCH AND VENETIANS

When the six ambassadors of the French pilgrims arrived at Venice, they were hospitably entertained in the palace of St. Mark, by the reigning duke: his name was Henry Dandolo; and he shone in the last period of human life as one of the most illustrious characters of the times. Under the weight of years, and after the loss of his eyes, Dandolo retained a sound understanding and a manly courage; the spirit of an hero, ambitious to signalise his reign by some memorable exploits; and the wisdom of a patriot, anxious to build his fame on the glory and advantage of his country. He praised the bold enthusiasm and liberal confidence of the barons and their deputies: in such a cause, and with such associates, he should aspire, were he a private man, to terminate his life; but he was the servant of the republic, and some delay was requisite to consult, on this arduous business, the judgment of his colleagues. The proposal of the French was first debated by the six *sages* who had been recently appointed to control the administration of the doge: it was next disclosed to the forty members of the council of state; and finally communicated to the legislative assembly of four hundred and fifty representatives, who were annually chosen in the six quarters of the city. In peace and war the doge was still the chief of the republic; his legal authority was supported by the personal reputation of Dandolo; his arguments of public interest were balanced and approved; and he was authorised to inform the ambassadors of the following conditions of the treaty. It was proposed that the crusaders should assemble at Venice on the feast of St. John of the ensuing year; that flat-bottomed vessels should be prepared for four thousand five

hundred horses and nine thousand squires, with a number of
ships sufficient for the embarkation of four thousand five
hundred knights and twenty thousand foot: that during a term
of nine months they should be supplied with provisions,
and transported to whatsoever coast the service of God and
Christendom should require; and that the republic should
join the armament with a squadron of fifty galleys. It was
required that the pilgrims should pay, before their departure,
a sum of eighty-five thousand marks of silver; and that all
conquests, by sea and land, should be equally divided between
the confederates. The terms were hard; but the emergency
was pressing, and the French barons were not less profuse of
money than of blood. A general assembly was convened to
ratify the treaty: the stately chapel and place of St. Mark
were filled with ten thousand citizens; and the noble deputies
were taught a new lesson of humbling themselves before the
majesty of the people. "Illustrious Venetians," said the marshal of Champagne, "we are sent by the greatest and most
powerful barons of France to implore the aid of the masters
of the sea for the deliverance of Jerusalem. They have enjoined us to fall prostrate at your feet; nor will we rise from
the ground till you have promised to avenge with us the injuries of Christ." The eloquence of their words and tears,
their martial aspect and suppliant attitude, were applauded
by an universal shout; as it were, says Jeffrey, by the sound
of an earthquake. The venerable doge ascended the pulpit to
urge their request by those motives of honour and virtue
which alone can be offered to a popular assembly: the treaty
was transcribed on parchment, attested with oaths and seals,
mutually accepted by the weeping and joyful representatives
of France and Venice, and despatched to Rome for the approbation of Pope Innocent the Third. Two thousand marks
were borrowed of the merchants for the first expenses of the
armament. Of the six deputies, two repassed the Alps to announce their success, while their four companions made a
fruitless trial of the zeal and emulation of the republics of
Genoa and Pisa.

The execution of the treaty was still opposed by unfore-
seen difficulties and delays. The marshal, on his return to
Troyes, was embraced and approved by Thibaut count of
Champagne, who had been unanimously chosen general of
the confederates. But the health of that valiant youth already

declined, and soon became hopeless; and he deplored the untimely fate which condemned him to expire, not in a field of battle, but on a bed of sickness. To his brave and numerous vassals the dying prince distributed his treasures: they swore in his presence to accomplish his vow and their own; but some there were, says the marshal, who accepted his gifts and forfeited their word. The more resolute champions of the cross held a parliament at Soissons for the election of a new general but such was the incapacity, or jealousy, or reluctance, of the princes of France, that none could be found both able and willing to assume the conduct of the enterprise. They acquiesced in the choice of a stranger, of Boniface, marquis of Montferrat, descended of a race of heroes, and himself of conspicuous fame in the wars and negociations of the times; nor could the piety or ambition of the Italian chief decline this honourable invitation. After visiting the French court, where he was received as a friend and kinsman, the marquis, in the church of Soissons, was invested with the cross of a pilgrim and the staff of a general; and immediately repassed the Alps, to prepare for the distant expedition of the East. About the festival of the Pentecost he displayed his banner, and marched towards Venice at the head of the Italians: he was preceded or followed by the counts of Flanders and Blois and the most respectable barons of France; and their numbers were swelled by the pilgrims of Germany, whose object and motives were similar to their own. The Venetians had fulfilled, and even surpassed, their engagements: stables were constructed for the horses, and barracks for the troops; the magazines were abundantly replenished with forage and provisions; and the fleet of transports, ships, and galleys, was ready to hoist sail as soon as the republic had received the price of the freight and armament. But that price far exceeded the wealth of the crusaders who were assembled at Venice. The Flemings, whose obedience to their count was voluntary and precarious, had embarked in their vessels for the long navigation of the ocean and Mediterranean; and many of the French and Italians had preferred a cheaper and more convenient passage from Marseilles and Apulia to the Holy Land. Each pilgrim might complain that, after he had furnished his own contribution, he was made responsible for the deficiency of his absent brethren; the gold and silver plate of the chiefs, which they freely delivered to the treasury of

St. Mark, was a generous but inadequate sacrifice; and after
all their efforts, thirty-four thousand marks were still wanting
to complete the stipulated sum. The obstacle was removed
by the policy and patriotism of the doge, who proposed to
the barons that, if they would join their arms in reducing
some revolted cities of Dalmatia, he would expose his person
in the holy war, and obtain from the republic a long indulgence, till some wealthy conquest should afford the means of
satisfying the debt. After much scruple and hesitation, they
chose rather to accept the offer than to relinquish the enterprise; and the first hostilities of the fleet and army were directed against Zara, a strong city of the Sclavonian coast,
which had renounced its allegiance to Venice, and implored
the protection of the king of Hungary. The crusaders burst
the chain or boom of the harbour; landed their horses, troops,
and military engines; and compelled the inhabitants, after a
defence of five days, to surrender at discretion: their lives
were spared, but the revolt was punished by the pillage of
their houses and the demolition of their walls. The season
was far advanced; the French and Venetians resolved to pass
the winter in a secure harbour and plentiful country; but
their repose was disturbed by national and tumultuous quarrels
of the soldiers and mariners. The conquest of Zara had scattered the seeds of discord and scandal: the arms of the allies
had been stained in their outset with the blood, not of infidels,
but of Christians: the king of Hungary and his new subjects
were themselves enlisted under the banner of the cross; and
the scruples of the devout were magnified by the fear or lassitude of the reluctant pilgrims. The pope had excommunicated the false crusaders who had pillaged and massacred their
brethren, and only the marquis Boniface and Simon of Montfort escaped these spiritual thunders; the one by his absence
from the siege, the other by his final departure from the camp.
Innocent might absolve the simple and submissive penitents
of France; but he was provoked by the stubborn reason of
the Venetians, who refused to confess their guilt, to accept
their pardon, or to allow, in their temporal concerns, the interposition of a priest.

The assembly of such formidable powers by sea and land
had revived the hopes of young Alexius, and both at Venice
and Zara he solicited the arms of the crusaders for his own
restoration and his father's deliverance. The royal youth was

recommended by Philip, king of Germany; his prayers and presence excited the compassion of the camp, and his cause was embraced and pleaded by the marquis of Montferrat and the doge of Venice. A double alliance, and the dignity of Cæsar, had connected with the Imperial family the two elder brothers of Boniface; he expected to derive a kingdom from the important service; and the more generous ambition of Dandolo was eager to secure the inestimable benefits of trade and dominion that might accrue to his country. Their influence procured a favourable audience for the ambassadors of Alexius; and if the magnitude of his offers excited some suspicion, the motives and rewards which he displayed might justify the delay and diversion of those forces which had been consecrated to the deliverance of Jerusalem. He promised, in his own and his father's name, that, as soon as they should be seated on the throne of Constantinople, they would terminate the long schism of the Greeks, and submit themselves and their people to the lawful supremacy of the Roman church. He engaged to recompense the labours and merits of the crusaders by the immediate payment of two hundred thousand marks of silver; to accompany them in person to Egypt; or, if it should be judged more advantageous, to maintain, during a year, ten thousand men, and, during his life, five hundred knights, for the service of the Holy Land. These tempting conditions were accepted by the republic of Venice, and the eloquence of the doge and marquis persuaded the counts of Flanders, Blois, and St. Pol, with eight barons of France, to join in the glorious enterprise. A treaty of offensive and defensive alliance was confirmed by their oaths and seals; and each individual, according to his situation and character, was swayed by the hope of public or private advantage; by the honour of restoring an exiled monarch; or by the sincere and probable opinion that their efforts in Palestine would be fruitless and unavailing, and that the acquisition of Constantinople must precede and prepare the recovery of Jerusalem. But they were the chiefs or equals of a valiant band of freemen and volunteers, who thought and acted for themselves: the soldiers and clergy were divided; and, if a large majority subscribed to the alliance, the numbers and arguments of the dissidents were strong and respectable. The boldest hearts were appalled by the report of the naval power and impregnable strength of Constantinople, and their apprehensions

were disguised to the world, and perhaps to themselves, by
the more decent objections of religion and duty. They alleged
the sanctity of a vow which had drawn them from their
families and homes to the rescue of the holy sepulchre; nor
should the dark and crooked counsels of human policy divert
them from a pursuit, the event of which was in the hands of
the Almighty. Their first offence, the attack of Zara, had been
severely punished by the reproach of their conscience and
the censures of the pope, nor would they again imbrue their
hands in the blood of their fellow Christians. The apostle of
Rome had pronounced; nor would they usurp the right of
avenging with the sword the schism of the Greeks and the
doubtful usurpation of the Byzantine monarch. On these
principles or pretences many pilgrims, the most distinguished
for their valour and piety, withdrew from the camp; and their
retreat was less pernicious than the open or secret opposition
of a discontented party that laboured, on every occasion, to
separate the army and disappoint the enterprise.

THE VOYAGE TO CONSTANTINOPLE

Notwithstanding this defection, the departure of the fleet
and army was vigorously pressed by the Venetians, whose
zeal for the service of the royal youth concealed a just resentment to his nation and family. They were mortified by the
recent preference which had been given to Pisa, the rival of
their trade; they had a long arrear of debt and injury to liqui-
date with the Byzantine court; and Dandolo might not discourage the popular tale that he had been deprived of his eyes
by the emperor Manuel, who perfidiously violated the sanctity
of an ambassador. A similar armament, for ages, had not
rode the Adriatic: it was composed of one hundred and twenty
flat-bottomed vessels or *palanders* for the horses, two hundred
and forty transports filled with men and arms, seventy storeships laden with provisions, and fifty stout galleys well prepared for the encounter of an enemy. While the wind was
favourable, the sky serene, and the water smooth, every eye
was fixed with wonder and delight on the scene of military
and naval pomp which overspread the sea. The shields of the
knights and squires, at once an ornament and a defence, were
arranged on either side of the ships; the banners of the nations
and families were displayed from the stern; our modern artil-

lery was supplied by three hundred engines for casting stones and darts; the fatigues of the way were cheered with the sound of music; and the spirits of the adventurers were raised by the mutual assurance that forty thousand Christian heroes were equal to the conquest of the world. In the navigation from Venice and Zara the fleet was successfully steered by the skill and experience of the Venetian pilots: at Durazzo the confederates first landed on the territories of the Greek empire; the isle of Corfu afforded a station and repose; they doubled, without accident, the perilous cape of Malea, the southern point of Peloponnesus or the Morea; made a descent in the islands of Negropont and Andros; and cast anchor at Abydus on the Asiatic side of the Hellespont. These preludes of conquest were easy and bloodless; the Greeks of the provinces, without patriotism or courage, were crushed by an irresistible force; the presence of the lawful heir might justify their obedience, and it was rewarded by the modesty and discipline of the Latins. As they penetrated through the Hellespont, the magnitude of their navy was compressed in a narrow channel, and the face of the waters was darkened with innumerable sails. They again expanded in the basin of the Propontis, and traversed that placid sea, till they approached the European shore at the abbey of St. Stephen, three leagues to the west of Constantinople. The prudent doge dissuaded them from dispersing themselves in a populous and hostile land; and, as their stock of provisions was reduced, it was resolved, in the season of harvest, to replenish their storeships in the fertile islands of the Propontis. With this resolution they directed their course; but a strong gale and their own impatience drove them to the eastward, and so near did they run to the shore and the city, that some volleys of stones and darts were exchanged between the ships and the rampart. As they passed along, they gazed with admiration on the capital of the East, or, as it should seem, of the earth, rising from her seven hills, and towering over the continents of Europe and Asia. The swelling domes and lofty spires of five hundred palaces and churches were gilded by the sun and reflected in the waters; the walls were crowded with soldiers and spectators, whose numbers they beheld, of whose temper they were ignorant; and each heart was chilled by the reflection that, since the beginning of the world, such an enterprise had never been undertaken by such a handful of warriors. But the momentary apprehension was dispelled by hope and valour; and every man, says the marshal of Champagne, glanced his eye on the sword or lance which he must speedily use in the glorious conflict. The Latins cast anchor before Chalcedon; the mariners only were left in the vessels; the soldiers, horses, and arms were safely landed; and, in the luxury of an Imperial palace, the barons tasted the first fruits of their success. On the third day the fleet and army moved towards Scutari, the Asiatic suburb of Constantinople: a detachment of five hundred Greek horse was surprised and defeated by fourscore French knights; and in a halt of nine days the camp was plentifully supplied with forage and provisions.

In relating the invasion of a great empire, it may seem strange that I have not described the obstacles which should have checked the progress of the strangers. The Greeks, in truth, were an unwarlike people; but they were rich, industrious, and subject to the will of a single man: had that man been capable of fear when his enemies were at a distance, or of courage when they approached his person. The first rumour of his nephew's alliance with the French and Venetians was despised by the usurper Alexius: his flatterers persuaded him that in this contempt he was bold and sincere; and each evening, in the close of the banquet, he thrice discomfited the barbarians of the West. These barbarians had been justly terrified by the report of his naval power; and the sixteen hundred fishing-boats of Constantinople could have manned a fleet to sink them in the Adriatic, or stop their entrance in the mouth of the Hellespont. But all force may be annihilated by the negligence of the prince and the venality of his ministers. The great duke or admiral made a scandalous, almost a public, auction of the sails, the masts, and the rigging; the royal forests were reserved for the more important purpose of the chase; and the trees, says Nicetas, were guarded by the eunuchs like the groves of religious worship. From his dream of pride Alexius was awakened by the siege of Zara and the rapid advances of the Latins; as soon as he saw the danger was real, he thought it inevitable, and his vain presumption was lost in abject despondency and despair. He suffered these contemptible barbarians to pitch their camp in the sight of the palace, and his apprehensions were thinly disguised by the pomp and menace of a suppliant embassy.

The sovereign of the Romans was astonished (his ambassadors were instructed to say) at the hostile appearance of the strangers. If these pilgrims were sincere in their vow for the deliverance of Jerusalem, his voice must applaud, and his treasures should assist, their pious design; but should they dare to invade the sanctuary of empire, their numbers, were they ten times more considerable, should not protect them from his just resentment. The answer of the doge and barons was simple and magnanimous. "In the cause of honour and justice," they said, "we despise the usurper of Greece, his threats, and his offers. *Our* friendship and *his* allegiance are due to the lawful heir, to the young prince who is seated among us, and to his father the emperor Isaac, who has been deprived of his sceptre, his freedom, and his eyes by the crime of an ungrateful brother. Let that brother confess his guilt and implore forgiveness, and we ourselves will intercede that he may be permitted to live in affluence and security. But let him not insult us by a second message: our reply will be made in arms, in the palace of Constantinople."

On the tenth day of their encampment at Scutari the crusaders prepared themselves, as soldiers and as Catholics, for the passage of the Bosphorus. Perilous indeed was the adventure: the stream was broad and rapid; in a calm the current of the Euxine might drive down the liquid and unextinguishable fires of the Greeks, and the opposite shores of Europe were defended by seventy thousand horse and foot in formidable array. On this memorable day, which happened to be bright and pleasant, the Latins were distributed in six battles or divisions; the first, or vanguard, was led by the count of Flanders, one of the most powerful of the Christian princes in the skill and number of his cross-bows. The four successive battles of the French were commanded by his brother Henry, the counts of St. Pol and Blois, and Matthew of Montmorency, the last of whom was honoured by the marshal and nobles of Champagne. The sixth division, the rear-guard and reserve of the army, was conducted by the marquis of Montferrat, at the head of the Germans and Lombards. The chargers, saddled, with their long caparisons dragging on the ground, were embarked in the flat *palanders*, and the knights stood by the side of their horses, in complete armour, their helmets laced, and their lances in their hands. Their numerous train of *serjeants* and archers occupied the transports, and each transport was towed by the strength and swiftness of a galley. The six divisions traversed the Bosphorus without encountering an enemy or an obstacle; to land the foremost was the wish, to conquer or die was the resolution, of every division and of every soldier. Jealous of the pre-eminence of danger, the knights in their heavy armour leaped into the sea when it rose as high as their girdle; the serjeants and archers were animated by their valour; and the squires, letting down the drawbridges of the palanders, led the horses to the shore. Before the squadrons could mount, and form, and couch their lances, the seventy thousand Greeks had vanished from their sight; the timid Alexius gave the example to his troops, and it was only by the plunder of his rich pavilions that the Latins were informed that they had fought against an emperor. In the first consternation of the flying enemy, they resolved, by a double attack, to open the en-trance of the harbour. The tower of Galata, in the suburb of Pera, was attacked and stormed by the French, while the Venetians assumed the more difficult task of forcing the boom or chain that was stretched from that tower to the Byzantine shore. After some fruitless attempts their intrepid persever-ance prevailed; twenty ships of war, the relics of the Grecian navy, were either sunk or taken; the enormous and massy links of iron were cut asunder by the shears or broken by the weight of the galleys; and the Venetian fleet, safe and trium-phant, rode at anchor in the port of Constantinople. By these daring achievements a remnant of twenty thousand Latins solicited the licence of besieging a capital which contained above four hundred thousand inhabitants, able, though not willing, to bear arms in the defence of their country. Such an account would indeed suppose a population of near two millions: but whatever abatement may be required in the numbers of the Greeks, the *belief* of those numbers will equal-ly exalt the fearless spirit of their assailants.

THE CONQUEST OF CONSTANTINOPLE BY THE LATINS

In the choice of the attack the French and Venetians were divided by their habits of life and warfare. The former affirmed with truth that Constantinople was most accessible on the side of the sea and the harbour. The latter might assert with honour that they had long enough trusted their lives and fortunes to a frail bark and a precarious element, and loudly demanded a trial of knighthood, a firm ground, and a close onset, either on foot or horseback. After a prudent compromise of employing the two nations by sea and land in the service best suited to their character, the fleet covering the army, they both proceeded from the entrance to the extremity of the harbour: the stone bridge of the river was hastily repaired; and the six battles of the French formed their encampment against the front of the capital, the basis of the triangle which runs about four miles from the port to the Propontis. On the edge of a broad ditch, at the foot of a lofty rampart, they had leisure to contemplate the difficulties of their enterprise. The gates to the right and left of their narrow camp poured forth frequent sallies of cavalry and light infantry, which cut off their stragglers, swept the country of provisions, sounded the alarm five or six times in the course of each day, and compelled them to plant a palisade and sink an entrenchment for their immediate safety. In the supplies and convoys the Venetians had been too sparing, or the Franks too voracious: the usual complaints of hunger and scarcity were heard, and perhaps felt: their stock of flour would be exhausted in three weeks; and their disgust of salt meat tempted them to taste the flesh of their horses. The trembling usurper was supported by Theodore Lascaris, his son-in-law, a valiant youth, who aspired to save and to rule his country; the Greeks, regardless of that country, were awakened to the defence of their religion; but their firmest hope was in the strength and spirit of the Varangian guards, of the Danes and English, as they are named in the writers of the times. After ten days' incessant labour the ground was levelled, the ditch filled, the approaches of the besiegers were regularly made, and two hundred and fifty engines of assault exercised their various powers to clear the rampart, to batter the walls, and to sap the foundations. On the first appearance of a breach the scaling-ladders were applied: the numbers that defended the vantage-ground repulsed and oppressed the adventurous Latins: but they admired the resolution of fifteen knights and serjeants, who had gained the ascent, and maintained their perilous station till they were precipitated or made prisoners by the Imperial guards. On the side of the harbour the naval attack was more successfully conducted by the Venetians; and that industrious people employed every resource that was known and practised before the invention of gunpowder. A double line, three bow-shots in front, was formed by the galleys and ships; and the swift motion of the former was supported by the weight and loftiness of the latter, whose decks, and poops, and turret, were the platform of military engines, that discharged their shot over the heads of the first line. The soldiers, who leaped from the galleys on shore, immediately planted and ascended their scaling-ladders, while the large ships, advancing more slowly into the intervals, and lowering a drawbridge, opened a way through the air from their masts to the rampart. In the midst of the conflict the doge, a venerable and conspicuous form, stood aloft in complete armour on the prow of his galley. The great standard of St. Mark was displayed before him; his threats, promises, and exhortations urged the diligence of the rowers; his vessel was the first that struck; and Dandolo was the first warrior on the shore. The nations admired the magnanimity of the blind old man, without reflecting that his age and infirmities diminished the price of life and enhanced the value of immortal glory. On a sudden, by an invisible hand (for the standard-bearer was probably slain), the banner of the republic was fixed on the rampart: twenty-five towers were rapidly occupied; and, by the cruel expedient of fire, the Greeks were driven from the adjacent quarter. The doge had despatched the intelligence of his success, when he was checked by the danger of his confederates. Nobly declaring that he would rather die with the pilgrims than gain a victory by their destruction, Dandolo relinquished his advantage, recalled his troops and hastened to the scene of action. He found the six weary diminutive *battles* of the French encompassed by sixty squadrons of the Greek cavalry, the least of which was more numerous than the largest of their divisions. Shame and despair had provoked Alexius to the last effort of a general sally; but he was awed by the firm order and manly aspect of the Latins; and, after skirmishing at a distance, withdrew his troops in the close of the evening. The silence or tumult of the night exasperated his fears; and the timid usurper, collecting a treasure of ten thousand pounds of gold, basely deserted his wife, his people, and his fortune; threw himself into a bark; stole through the Bosphorus; and landed in shameful safety in an obscure harbour of Thrace. As soon as they were apprised of his flight, the Greek nobles sought pardon and peace in the dungeon where the blind Isaac expected each hour the visit of the executioner. Again saved and exalted by the vicissitudes of fortune, the captive in his Imperial robes was replaced on the throne, and surrounded with prostrate slaves, whose real terror and affected joy he was incapable of discerning. At the dawn of day hostilities were suspended, and the Latin chiefs were surprised by a message from the lawful and reigning emperor, who was impatient to embrace his son and to reward his generous deliverers.

But these generous deliverers were unwilling to release their hostage till they had obtained from his father the payment, or at least the promise, of their recompense. They chose four ambassadors, Matthew of Montmorency, our historian the marshal of Champagne, and two Venetians, to congratulate the emperor. The gates were thrown open on their approach, the streets on both sides were lined with the battle-axes of the Danish and English guard: the presence-chamber glittered with gold and jewels, the false substitutes of virtue and power: by the side of the blind Isaac his wife was seated, the sister of the king of Hungary: and, by her appearance, the noble matrons of Greece were drawn from their domestic retirement and mingled with the circle of senators and soldiers. The Latins, by the mouth of the marshal, spoke like men conscious of their merits, but who respected the work of their own hands; and the emperor clearly understood that his son's engagements with Venice and the pilgrims must be ratified without hesitation or delay. Withdrawing into a private chamber with the empress, a chamberlain, an interpreter, and the four ambassadors, the father of young Alexius inquired with some anxiety into the nature of his stipulations. The submission of the Eastern empire to the pope, the succour of the Holy Land, and a present contribution of two hundred thousand marks of silver.—"These conditions are weighty," was his prudent reply: "they are hard to accept, and difficult to perform. But no conditions can exceed the measure of your services and deserts." After this satisfactory assurance, the barons mounted on horseback and introduced the heir of Constantinople to the city and palace: his youth and marvellous adventures engaged every heart in his favour, and Alexius was solemnly crowned with his father in the dome of St. Sophia. In the first days of his reign, the people, already blessed with the restoration of plenty and peace, was delighted by the joyful catastrophe of the tragedy; and the discontent of the nobles, their regret, and their fears, were covered by the polished surface of pleasure and loyalty. The mixture of two discordant nations in the same capital might have been pregnant with mischief and danger; and the suburb of Galata, or Pera, was assigned for the quarters of the French and Venetians. But the liberty of trade and familiar intercourse was allowed between the friendly nations; and each day the pilgrims were tempted by devotion or curiosity to visit the churches and palaces of Constantinople. Their rude minds, insensible perhaps of the finer arts, were astonished by the magnificent scenery: and the poverty of their native towns enhanced the populousness and riches of the first metropolis of Christendom. Descending from his state, young Alexius was prompted by interest and gratitude to repeat his frequent and familiar visits to his Latin allies; and in the freedom of the table the gay petulance of the French sometimes forgot the emperor of the East. In their more serious conferences it was agreed that the re-union of the two churches must be the result of patience and time; but avarice was less tractable than zeal; and a large sum was instantly disbursed to appease the wants, and silence the importunity, of the crusaders. Alexius was alarmed by the approaching hour of their departure: their absence might have relieved him from the engagement which he was yet incapable of performing; but his friends would have left him, naked and alone, to the caprice and prejudices of a perfidious nation. He wished to bribe their stay, the delay of a year, by undertaking to defray their expense, and to satisfy, in their name, the freight of the Venetian vessels. The offer was agitated in the council of the barons; and, after a repetition of their debates and scruples, a majority of votes again acquiesced in the advice of the doge and the prayer of the young emperor. At the price of sixteen hundred pounds of gold, he prevailed on the marquis of Montferrat to lead him with an army round the provinces of Europe; to establish his authority, and pursue his uncle, while Constantinople was awed by the presence of Baldwin and his confederates of France and Flanders. The expedition was successful: the blind emperor exulted in the success of his arms, and listened to the predictions of his flatterers, that the same Providence which had raised him from the dungeon to the throne would heal his gout, restore his sight, and watch over the long prosperity of his reign. Yet the mind of the suspicious old man was tormented by the rising glories of his son; nor could his pride conceal from his envy, that, while his own name was pronounced in faint and reluctant acclamations, the royal youth was the theme of spontaneous and universal praise.

By the recent invasion the Greeks were awakened from a dream of nine centuries; from the vain presumption that the capital of the Roman empire was impregnable to foreign arms. The strangers of the West had violated the city, and bestowed the sceptre, of Constantine: their Imperial clients soon became as unpopular as themselves: the well-known vices of Isaac were rendered still more contemptible by his infirmities, and the young Alexius was hated as an apostate who had renounced the manners and religion of his country. His secret covenant with the Latins was divulged or suspected; the people, and especially the clergy, were devoutly attached to their faith and superstition; and every convent, and every shop, resounded with the danger of the church and the tyranny of the pope. An empty treasury could ill supply the demands of regal luxury and foreign extortion: the Greeks refused to avert, by a general tax, the impending evils of servitude and pillage; the oppression of the rich excited a more dangerous and personal resentment; and if the emperor melted the plate and despoiled the images of the sanctuary, he seemed to justify the complaints of heresy and sacrilege. During the absence of marquis Boniface and his Imperial pupil, Constantinople was visited with a calamity which might be justly imputed to the zeal and indiscretion of the Flemish pilgrims. In one of their visits to the city they were scandalised by the aspect of a mosque or synagogue, in which one God was worshipped, without a partner or a son. Their effectual mode of controversy was to attack the infidels with the sword, and their habitation with fire: but the infidels, and some Christian neighbours, presumed to defend their lives and properties; and the flames which bigotry had kindled consumed the most orthodox and innocent structures. During eight days and nights the conflagration spread above a league in front, from the harbour to the Propontis, over the thickest and most populous regions of the city. It is not easy to count the stately churches and palaces that were reduced to a

smoking ruin, to value the merchandise that perished in the
trading streets, or to number the families that were involved
in the common destruction. By this outrage, which the doge
and the barons in vain affected to disclaim, the name of the
Latins became still more unpopular; and the colony of that
nation, above fifteen thousand persons, consulted their safety
in a hasty retreat from the city to the protection of their
standard in the suburb of Pera. The emperor returned in
triumph; but the firmest and most dexterous policy would
have been insufficient to steer him through the tempest which
overwhelmed the person and government of that unhappy
youth. His own inclination, and his father's advice, attached
him to his benefactors; but Alexius hesitated between gratitude
and patriotism, between the fear of his subjects and of his
allies. By his feeble and fluctuating conduct he lost the
esteem and confidence of both; and, while he invited the
marquis of Montferrat to occupy the palace, he suffered the
nobles to conspire, and the people to arm, for the deliverance
of their country. Regardless of his painful situation, the Latin
chiefs repeated their demands, resented his delays, suspected
his intentions, and exacted a decisive answer of peace or war.
The haughty summons was delivered by three French knights
and three Venetian deputies, who girded their swords, mounted
their horses, pierced through the angry multitude, and entered,
with a fearless countenance, the palace and presence of the
Greek emperor. In a peremptory tone they recapitulated their
services and his engagements; and boldly declared that, unless
their just claims were fully and immediately satisfied, they
should no longer hold him either as a sovereign or a friend.
After this defiance, the first that had ever wounded an Imperial ear, they departed without betraying any symptoms of
fear; but their escape from a servile palace and a furious
city astonished the ambassadors themselves; and their return
to the camp was the signal of mutual hostility.

Among the Greeks all authority and wisdom were over-
borne by the impetuous multitude, who mistook their rage
for valour, their numbers for strength, and their fanaticism
for the support and inspiration of Heaven. In the eyes of both
nations Alexius was false and contemptible: the base and
spurious race of the Angeli was rejected with clamorous disdain; and the people of Constantinople encompassed the
senate to demand at their hands a more worthy emperor. To

every senator, conspicuous by his birth or dignity, they successively presented the purple: by each senator the deadly garment was repulsed: the contest lasted three days; and we may learn from the historian Nicetas, one of the members of the assembly, that fear and weakness were the guardians of their loyalty. A phantom, who vanished in oblivion, was forcibly proclaimed by the crowd: but the author of the tumult, and the leader of the war, was a prince of the house of Ducas; and his common appellation of Alexius must be discriminated by the epithet of Mourzoufle, which in the vulgar idiom expressed the close junction of his black and shaggy eyebrows. At once a patriot and a courtier, the perfidious Mourzoufle, who was not destitute of cunning and courage, opposed the Latins both in speech and action, inflamed the passions and prejudices of the Greeks, and insinuated himself into the favour and confidence of Alexius, who trusted him with the office of great chamberlain, and tinged his buskins with the colours of royalty. At the dead of night he rushed into the bed-chamber with an affrighted aspect, exclaiming that the palace was attacked by the people and betrayed by the guards. Starting from his couch, the unsuspecting prince threw himself into the arms of his enemy, who had contrived his escape by a private staircase. But that staircase terminated in a prison: Alexius was seized, stripped, and loaded with chains; and, after tasting some days the bitterness of death, he was poisoned, or strangled, or beaten with clubs, at the command, and in the presence, of the tyrant. The emperor Isaac Angelus soon followed his son to the grave; and Mourzoufle, perhaps, might spare the superfluous crime of hastening the extinction of impotence and blindness.

THE PILLAGE OF CONSTANTINOPLE

The death of the emperors, and the usurpation of Mourzoufle, had changed the nature of the quarrel. It was no longer the disagreement of allies who overvalued their services, or neglected their obligations: the French and Venetians forgot their complaints against Alexius, dropped a tear on the untimely fate of their companion, and swore revenge against the perfidious nation who had crowned his assassin. Yet the prudent doge was still inclined to negociate: he asked as a debt, a subsidy, or a fine, fifty thousand pounds of gold,

about two millions sterling; nor would the conference have
been abruptly broken if the zeal, or policy, of Mourzoufle
had not refused to sacrifice the Greek church to the safety
of the state. Amidst the invectives of his foreign and domestic
enemies, we may discern that he was not unworthy of the
character which he had assumed, of the public champion:
the second siege of Constantinople was far more laborious
than the first; the treasury was replenished, and discipline
was restored, by a severe inquisition into the abuses of the
former reign; and Mourzoufle, an iron mace in his hand,
visiting the posts, and affecting the port and aspect of a
warrior, was an object of terror to his soldiers, at least, and
to his kinsmen. Before and after the death of Alexius, the
Greeks made two vigorous and well-conducted attempts to
burn the navy in the harbour; but the skill and courage of
the Venetians repulsed the fire-ships; and the vagrant flames
wasted themselves without injury in the sea. In a nocturnal
sally the Greek emperor was vanquished by Henry, brother
of the count of Flanders: the advantages of number and
surprise aggravated the shame of his defeat: his buckler was
found on the field of battle; and the Imperial standard, a
divine image of the Virgin, was presented, as a trophy and a
relic, to the Cistercian monks, the disciples of St. Bernard.
Near three months, without excepting the holy season of
Lent, were consumed in skirmishes and preparations, before
the Latins were ready or resolved for a general assault. The
land fortifications had been found impregnable; and the
Venetian pilots represented, that, on the shore of the Propontis, the anchorage was unsafe, and the ships must be
driven by the current far away to the straits of the Hellespont;
a prospect not unpleasing to the reluctant pilgrims, who sought
every opportunity of breaking the army. From the harbour,
therefore, the assault was determined by the assailants and
expected by the besieged; and the emperor had placed his
scarlet pavilions on a neighbouring height, to direct and
animate the efforts of his troops. A fearless spectator, whose
mind could entertain the ideas of pomp and pleasure, might
have admired the long array of two embattled armies, which
extended above half a league, the one on the ships and galleys,
the other on the walls and towers raised above the ordinary
level by several stages of wooden turrets. Their first fury was
spent in the discharge of darts, stones, and fire, from the

engines; but the water was deep; the French were bold; the Venetians were skilful; they approached the walls; and a desperate conflict of swords, spears, and battle-axes, was fought on the trembling bridges that grappled the floating to the stable batteries. In more than a hundred places the assault was urged and the defence was sustained; till the superiority of ground and numbers finally prevailed, and the Latin trumpets sounded a retreat. On the ensuing days the attack was renewed with equal vigour and a similar event; and, in the night, the doge and the barons held a council, apprehensive only for the public danger: not a voice pronounced the words of escape or treaty; and each warrior, according to his temper, embraced the hope of victory or the assurance of a glorious death. By the experience of the former siege the Greeks were instructed, but the Latins were animated; and the knowledge that Constantinople *might* be taken was of more avail than the local precautions which that knowledge had inspired for its defence. In the third assault two ships were linked together to double their strength; a strong north wind drove them on the shore; the bishops of Troyes and Soissons led the van; and the auspicious names of the *Pilgrim* and the *Paradise* resounded along the line. The episcopal banners were displayed on the walls; a hundred marks of silver had been promised to the first adventurers; and if their reward was intercepted by death, their names have been immortalised by fame. Four towers were scaled; three gates were burst open; and the French knights, who might tremble on the waves, felt themselves invincible on horseback on the solid ground. Shall I relate that the thousands who guarded the emperor's person fled on the approach, and before the lance, of a single warrior? Their ignominious flight is attested by their countryman Nicetas: an army of phantoms marched with the French hero, and he was magnified to a giant in the eyes of the Greeks. While the fugitives deserted their posts and cast away their arms, the Latins entered the city under the banners of their leaders: the streets and gates opened for their passage; and either design or accident kindled a third conflagration, which consumed in a few hours the measure of three of the largest cities of France. In the close of evening the barons checked their troops and fortified their stations: they were awed by the extent and populousness of the capital, which might yet require the labour of a month, if the churches and palaces were conscious of their internal strength. But in the morning a suppliant procession, with crosses and images, announced the submission of the Greeks and deprecated the wrath of the conquerors: the usurper escaped through the golden gate: the palaces of Blachernæ and Boucoleon were occupied by the count of Flanders and the marquis of Montferrat; and the empire, which still bore the name of Constantine and the title of Roman, was subverted by the arms of the Latin pilgrims.

Constantinople had been taken by storm; and no restraints except those of religion and humanity were imposed on the conquerors by the laws of war. Boniface, marquis of Montferrat, still acted as their general; and the Greeks, who revered his name as that of their future sovereign, were heard to exclaim in a lamentable tone, "Holy marquis-king, have mercy upon us!" His prudence or compassion opened the gates of the city to the fugitives, and he exhorted the soldiers of the cross to spare the lives of their fellow-Christians. The streams of blood that flow down the pages of Nicetas may be reduced to the slaughter of two thousand of his unresisting countrymen; and the greater part was massacred, not by the strangers, but by the Latins who had been driven from the city, and who exercised the revenge of a triumphant faction. Yet of these exiles, some were less mindful of injuries than of benefits; and Nicetas himself was indebted for his safety to the generosity of a Venetian merchant. Pope Innocent the Third accuses the pilgrims of respecting, in their lust, neither age, nor sex, nor religious profession; and bitterly laments that the deeds of darkness, fornication, adultery, and incest, were perpetrated in open day; and that noble matrons and holy nuns were polluted by the grooms and peasants of the Catholic camp. It is indeed probable that the licence of victory prompted and covered a multitude of sins: but it is certain that the capital of the East contained a stock of venal or willing beauty sufficient to satiate the desires of twenty thousand pilgrims, and female prisoners were no longer subject to the right or abuse of domestic slavery. The marquis of Montferrat was the patron of discipline and decency: the count of Flanders was the mirror of chastity: they had forbidden, under pain of death, the rape of married women, or virgins, or nuns; and the proclamation was sometimes invoked by the vanquished and respected by the victors. Their cruelty and lust were moderated by the authority of the chiefs and feelings of the soldiers; for we are no longer describing an irruption of the northern savages; and however ferocious they might still appear, time, policy, and religion had civilised the manners of the French, and still more of the Italians. But a free scope was allowed to their avarice, which was glutted, even in the holy week, by the pillage of Constantinople. The right of victory, unshackled by any promise or treaty, had confiscated the public and private wealth of the Greeks; and every hand, according to its size and strength, might lawfully execute the sentence and seize the forfeiture. A portable and universal standard of exchange was found in the coined and uncoined metals of gold and silver, which each captor, at home or abroad, might convert into the possessions most suitable to his temper and situation. Of the treasures which trade and luxury had accumulated, the silks, velvets, furs, the gems, spices, and rich moveables, were the most precious, as they could not be procured for money in the ruder countries of Europe. An order of rapine was instituted; nor was the share of each individual abandoned to industry or chance. Under the tremendous penalties of perjury—excommunication and death—the Latins were bound to deliver their plunder into the common stock: three churches were selected for the deposit and distribution of the spoil: a single share was allotted to a foot soldier, two for a serjeant on horseback, four to a knight, and larger proportions according to the rank and merit of the barons and princes. For violating this sacred engagement, a knight belonging to the count of St. Paul was hanged with his shield and coat of arms round his neck: his example might render similar offenders more artful and discreet, but avarice was more powerful than fear, and it is generally believed that the secret far exceeded the acknowledged plunder. Yet the magnitude of the prize surpassed the largest scale of experience or expectation. After the whole had been equally divided between the French and Venetians, fifty thousand marks were deducted to satisfy the debts of the former and the demands of the latter. The residue of the French amounted to four hundred thousand marks of silver, about eight hundred thousand pounds sterling; nor can I better appreciate the value of that sum in the public and private transactions of the age than by defining it as seven times the annual revenue of the kingdom of England.

In this great revolution we enjoy the singular felicity of comparing the narratives of Villehardouin and Nicetas, the opposite feelings of the marshal of Champagne and the Byzantine senator. At the first view it should seem that the wealth of Constantinople was only transferred from one nation to another, and that the loss and sorrow of the Greeks is exactly balanced by the joy and advantage of the Latins. But in the miserable account of war the gain is never equivalent to the loss, the pleasure to the pain; the smiles of the Latins were transient and fallacious; the Greeks for ever wept over the ruins of their country, and their real calamities were aggravated by sacrilege and mockery. What benefits accrued to the conquerors from the three fires which annihilated so vast a portion of the buildings and riches of the city? What a stock of such things as could neither be used nor transported was maliciously or wantonly destroyed! How much treasure was idly wasted in gaming, debauchery, and riot! And what precious objects were bartered for a vile price by the impatience or ignorance of the soldiers, whose reward was stolen by the base industry of the last of the Greeks! These alone who had nothing to lose might derive some profit from the revolution; but the misery of the upper ranks of society is strongly painted in the personal adventures of Nicetas himself. His stately palace had been reduced to ashes in the second conflagration; and the senator, with his family and friends, found an obscure shelter in another house which he possessed near the church of St. Sophia. It was the door of this mean habitation that his friend the Venetian merchant guarded, in the disguise of a soldier, till Nicetas could save by a precipitate flight the relics of his fortune and the chastity of his daughter. In a cold wintry season these fugitives, nursed in the lap of prosperity, departed on foot; his wife was with child; the desertion of their slaves compelled them to carry their baggage on their own shoulders; and their women, whom they placed in the centre, were exhorted to conceal their beauty with dirt, instead of adorning it with paint and jewels. Every step was exposed to insult and danger: the threats of the strangers were less painful than the taunts of the plebeians, with whom they were now levelled; nor did the exiles breathe in safety till their mournful pilgrimage was concluded at Selymbria, above forty miles from the capital.

On the way they overtook the patriarch, without attendance and almost without apparel, riding on an ass, and reduced to a state of apostolical poverty, which, had it been voluntary, might perhaps have been meritorious. In the meanwhile his desolate churches were profaned by the licentiousness and party zeal of the Latins. After stripping the gems and pearls, they converted the chalices into drinking-cups; their tables, on which they gamed and feasted, were covered with the pictures of Christ and the saints; and they trampled under foot the most venerable objects of the Christian worship. In the cathedral of St. Sophia the ample veil of the sanctuary was rent asunder for the sake of the golden fringe; and the altar, a monument of art and riches, was broken in pieces and shared among the captors. Their mules and horses were laden with the wrought silver and gilt carvings which they tore down from the doors and pulpit; and if the beasts stumbled under the burden, they were stabbed by their impatient drivers, and the holy pavement streamed with their impure blood. A prostitute was seated on the throne of the patriarch; and that daughter of Belial, as she is styled, sung and danced in the church to ridicule the hymns and processions of the Orientals. Nor were the repositories of the royal dead secure from violation: in the church of the Apostles the tombs of the emperors were rifled; and it is said that after six centuries the corpse of Justinian was found without any signs of decay or putrefaction. In the streets the French and Flemings clothed themselves and their horses in painted robes and flowing headdresses of linen; and the coarse intemperance of their feasts insulted the splendid sobriety of the East. To expose the arms of a people of scribes and scholars, they affected to display a pen, an inkhorn, and a sheet of paper, without discerning that the instruments of science and valour were *alike* feeble and useless in the hands of the modern Greeks.

Their reputation and their language encouraged them, however, to despise the ignorance and to overlook the progress of the Latins. In the love of the arts the national difference was still more obvious and real; the Greeks preserved with reverence the works of their ancestors, which they could not imitate; and, in the destruction of the statues of Constantinople, we are provoked to join in the complaints and invectives of the Byzantine historian. We have seen how the rising city was adorned by the vanity and despotism of the Imperial founder: in the ruins of paganism some gods and heroes were saved from the axe of superstition; and the forum and hippodrome were dignified with the relics of a better age. Several of these are described by Nicetas in a florid and affected style; and from his descriptions I shall select some interesting particulars. 1. The victorious charioteers were cast in bronze, at their own, or the public, charge, and fitly placed in the hippodrome: they stood aloft in their chariots wheeling round the goal: the spectators could admire their attitude and judge of the resemblance; and of these figures, the most perfect might have been transported from the Olympic stadium. 2. The sphinx, river-horse, and crocodile, denote the climate and manufacture of Egypt and the spoils of that ancient province. 3. The she-wolf suckling Romulus and Remus, a subject alike pleasing to the *old* and the *new* Romans, but which could rarely be treated before the decline of the Greek sculpture. 4. An eagle holding and tearing a serpent in his talons—a domestic monument of the Byzantines, which they ascribed, not to a human artist, but to the magic power of the philosopher Apollonius, who, by this talisman, delivered the city from such venomous reptiles. 5. An ass and his driver, which were erected by Augustus in his colony of Nicopolis, to commemorate a verbal omen of the victory of Actium. 6. An equestrian statue, which passed in the vulgar opinion for Joshua, the Jewish conqueror, stretching out his hand to stop the course of the descending sun. A more classical tradition recognised the figures of Bellerophon and Pegasus; and the free attitude of the steed seemed to mark that he trod on air rather than on the earth. 7. A square and lofty obelisk of brass; the sides were embossed with a variety of picturesque and rural scenes: birds singing, rustics labouring or playing on their pipes, sheep bleating, lambs skipping, the sea, and a scene of fish and fishing, little naked Cupids laughing, playing, and pelting each other with apples, and on the summit a female figure turning with the slightest breath, and thence denominated *the wind's attendant*. 8. The Phrygian shepherd presenting to Venus the prize of beauty, the apple of discord. 9. The incomparable statue of Helen, which is delineated by Nicetas in the words of admiration and love: her well-turned feet, snowy arms, rosy lips, bewitching smiles, swimming eyes, arched eyebrows, the harmony of her shape, the lightness of her drapery, and her flowing locks that waved in the wind—a beauty that might have moved her barbarian destroyers to pity and remorse. 10. The manly, or divine, form of Hercules, as he was restored to life by the master-hand of Lysippus, of such magnitude that his thumb was equal to the waist, his leg to the stature, of a common man: his chest ample, his shoulders broad, his limbs strong and muscular, his hair curled, his aspect commanding. Without his bow, or quiver, or club, his lion's skin carelessly thrown over him, he was seated on an osier basket, his right leg and arm stretched to the utmost, his left knee bent and supporting his elbow, his head reclining on his left hand, his countenance indignant and pensive. 11. A colossal statue of Juno, which had once adorned her temple of Samos; the enormous head by four yoke of oxen was laboriously drawn to the palace. 12. Another colossus, of Pallas or Minerva, thirty feet in height, and representing with admirable spirit the attributes and character of the martial maid. Before we accuse the Latins, it is just to remark that this Pallas was destroyed after the first siege by the fear and superstition of the Greeks themselves. The other statues of brass which I have enumerated were broken and melted by the unfeeling avarice of the crusaders: the cost and labour were consumed in a moment; the soul of genius evaporated in smoke, and the remnant of base metal was coined into money for the payment of the troops. Bronze is not the most durable of monuments: from the marble forms of Phidias and Praxiteles the Latins might turn aside with stupid contempt; but unless they were crushed by some accidental injury, those useless stones stood secure on their pedestals. The most enlightened of the strangers, above the gross and sensual pursuits of their countrymen, more piously exercised the right of conquest in the search and seizure of the relics of the saints. Immense was the supply of heads and bones, crosses and images, that were scattered by this revolution over the churches of Europe; and such was the increase of pilgrimage and oblation, that no branch, perhaps, of more lucrative plunder was imported from the East. Of the writings of antiquity many that still existed in the twelfth century are now lost. But the pilgrims were not solicitous to save or transport the volumes of an unknown tongue: the perishable substance of paper or parchment can only be preserved by the multiplicity of copies; the literature of the Greeks had almost centred in the metropolis; and, without computing the extent of our loss, we may drop a tear over the libraries that have perished in the triple fire of Constantinople.

61.

**BALDWIN II AND THE HOLY CROWN OF THORNS.
RECOVERY OF CONSTANTINOPLE BY THE GREEKS.
GENERAL CONSEQUENCES OF THE CRUSADES**

*The capture of Constantinople by the Latins in 1204 was
followed by the establishment there of the so called Latin
Emperors, Baldwin I and his four successors. At the same
time Greek claimants to the empire were established at Nicæa
and Trebizond. The rule of the Latin Emperors was incom-
petent and disastrous, and the last of them, Baldwin II, made
a public appeal for help to the West.*

BALDWIN II AND THE HOLY CROWN OF THORNS

IT WAS ONLY in the age of chivalry that valour could ascend
from a private station to the thrones of Jerusalem and Constantinople. The titular kingdom of Jerusalem had devolved
to Mary, the daughter of Isabella and Conrad of Montferrat,
and the granddaughter of Almeric or Amaury. She was given
to John of Brienne, of a noble family in Champagne, by the
public voice, and the judgment of Philip Augustus, who named
him as the most worthy champion of the Holy Land. In the
fifth crusade he led an hundred thousand Latins to the conquest of Egypt: by him the siege of Damietta was achieved;
and the subsequent failure was justly ascribed to the pride
and avarice of the legate. After the marriage of his daughter
with Frederic the Second he was provoked by the emperor's
ingratitude to accept the command of the army of the church;
and though advanced in life, and despoiled of royalty, the
sword and spirit of John of Brienne were still ready for the
service of Christendom. In the seven years of his brother's
reign, Baldwin of Courtenay had not emerged from a state
of childhood, and the barons of Romania felt the strong
necessity of placing the sceptre in the hands of a man and

an hero. The veteran king of Jerusalem might have disdained the name and office of regent; they agreed to invest him for his life with the title and prerogatives of emperor, on the sole condition that Baldwin should marry his second daughter, and succeed at a mature age to the throne of Constantinople. The expectation, both of the Greeks and Latins, was kindled by the renown, the choice, and the presence of John of Brienne; and they admired his martial aspect, his green and vigorous age of more than fourscore years, and his size and stature, which surpassed the common measure of mankind. But avarice, and the love of ease, appear to have chilled the ardour of enterprise: his troops were disbanded, and two years rolled away without action or honour, till he was awakened by the dangerous alliance of Vataces, emperor of Nice, and of Azan king of Bulgaria. They besieged Constantinople by sea and land, with an army of one hundred thousand men, and a fleet of three hundred ships of war; while the entire force of the Latin emperor was reduced to one hundred and sixty knights, and a small addition of serjeants and archers. I tremble to relate, that, instead of defending the city, the hero made a sally at the head of his cavalry; and that, of forty-eight squadrons of the enemy, no more than three escaped from the edge of his invincible sword. Fired by his example, the infantry and the citizens boarded the vessels that anchored close to the walls; and twenty-five were dragged in triumph into the harbour of Constantinople. At the summons of the emperor, the vassals and allies armed in her defence; broke through every obstacle that opposed their passage; and, in the succeeding year, obtained a second victory over the same enemies. By the rude poets of the age John of Brienne is compared to Hector, Roland, and Judas Maccabæus: but their credit, and his glory, receives some abatement from the silence of the Greeks. The empire was soon deprived of the last of her champions; and the dying monarch was ambitious to enter paradise in the habit of a Franciscan friar.

In the double victory of John of Brienne I cannot discover the name or exploits of his pupil Baldwin, who had attained the age of military service, and who succeeded to the imperial dignity on the decease of his adoptive father. The royal youth was employed on a commission more suitable to his temper; he was sent to visit the Western courts, of the pope more

especially, and of the king of France; to excite their pity by
the view of his innocence and distress; and to obtain some
supplies of men or money for the relief of the sinking empire.
He thrice repeated these mendicant visits, in which he seemed
to prolong his stay, and postpone his return; of the five-and-
twenty years of his reign, a greater number were spent abroad
than at home; and in no place did the emperor deem himself
less free and secure than in his native country and his capital.
On some public occasions, his vanity might be soothed by
the title of Augustus, and by the honours of the purple; and
at the general council of Lyons, when Frederic the Second was
excommunicated and deposed, his Oriental colleague was
enthroned on the right hand of the pope. But how often was
the exile, the vagrant, the Imperial beggar, humbled with
scorn, insulted with pity, and degraded in his own eyes and
those of the nations! In his first visit to England he was
stopped at Dover by a severe reprimand, that he should
presume, without leave, to enter an independent kingdom.
After some delay, Baldwin, however, was permitted to pursue his journey, was entertained with cold civility, and
thankfully departed with a present of seven hundred marks.
From the avarice of Rome he could only obtain the proclamation of a crusade, and a treasure of indulgences: a coin whose
currency was depreciated by too frequent and indiscriminate
abuse. His birth and misfortunes recommended him to the
generosity of his cousin Louis the Ninth; but the martial zeal
of the saint was diverted from Constantinople to Egypt and
Palestine; and the public and private poverty of Baldwin was
alleviated, for a moment, by the alienation of the marquisate
of Namur and the lordship of Courtenay, the last remains
of his inheritance. By such shameful or ruinous expedients he
once more returned to Romania, with an army of thirty thousand soldiers, whose numbers were doubled in the apprehension of the Greeks. His first despatches to France and England
announced his victories and his hopes: he had reduced the
country round the capital to the distance of three days'
journey; and if he succeeded against an important, though
nameless, city (most probably Chiorli), the frontier would be
safe and the passage accessible. But these expectations (if
Baldwin was sincere) quickly vanished like a dream: the
troops and treasures of France melted away in his unskilful
hands: and the throne of the Latin emperor was protected by

a dishonourable alliance with the Turks and Comans. To
secure the former, he consented to bestow his niece on the
unbelieving sultan of Cogni; to please the latter, he complied
with their pagan rites; a dog was sacrificed between the two
armies; and the contracting parties tasted each other's blood,
as a pledge of their fidelity. In the palace, or prison, of Constantinople, the successor of Augustus demolished the vacant
houses for winter-fuel, and stripped the lead from the churches
for the daily expense of his family. Some usurious loans were
dealt with a scanty hand by the merchants of Italy; and
Philip, his son and heir, was pawned at Venice as the security
for a debt. Thirst, hunger, and nakedness are positive evils:
but wealth is relative; and a prince, who would be rich in a
private station, may be exposed by the increase of his wants
to all the anxiety and bitterness of poverty.

But in this abject distress the emperor and empire were
still possessed of an ideal treasure, which drew its fantastic
value from the superstition of the Christian world. The merit
of the true cross was somewhat impaired by its frequent
division; and a long captivity among the infidels might shed
some suspicion on the fragments that were produced in the
East and West. But another relic of the Passion was preserved
in the Imperial chapel of Constantinople; and the crown of
thorns which had been placed on the head of Christ was
equally precious and authentic. It had formerly been the
practice of the Egyptian debtors to deposit, as a security, the
mummies of their parents; and both their honour and religion
were bound for the redemption of the pledge. In the same
manner, and in the absence of the emperor, the barons of
Romania borrowed the sum of thirteen thousand one hundred
and thirty-four pieces of gold on the credit of the holy crown:
they failed in the performance of their contract; and a rich
Venetian, Nicholas Querini, undertook to satisfy their impatient creditors, on condition that the relic should be lodged
at Venice, to become his absolute property if it were not redeemed within a short and definite term. The barons apprised
their sovereign of the hard treaty and impending loss; and as
the empire could not afford a ransom of seven thousand
pounds sterling, Baldwin was anxious to snatch the prize
from the Venetians, and to vest it with more honour and
emolument in the hands of the most Christian king. Yet the
negociation was attended with some delicacy. In the purchase

of relics the saint would have started at the guilt of simony; but if the mode of expression were changed, he might lawfully repay the debt, accept the gift, and acknowledge the obligation. His ambassadors, two Dominicans, were despatched to Venice to redeem and receive the holy crown, which had escaped the dangers of the sea and the galleys of Vataces. On opening a wooden box they recognised the seals of the doge and barons, which were applied on a shrine of silver; and within this shrine the monument of the Passion was enclosed in a golden vase. The reluctant Venetians yielded to justice and power; the emperor Frederic granted a free and honourable passage; the court of France advanced as far as Troyes in Champagne to meet with devotion this inestimable relic: it was borne in triumph through Paris by the king himself, barefoot, and in his shirt; and a free gift of ten thousand marks of silver reconciled Baldwin to his loss. The success of this transaction tempted the Latin emperor to offer with the same generosity the remaining furniture of his chapel; a large and authentic portion of the true cross; the baby-linen of the Son of God; the lance, the sponge, and the chain of his Passion; the rod of Moses; and part of the skull of St. John the Baptist. For the reception of these spiritual treasures twenty thousand marks were expended by St. Louis on a stately foundation, the holy chapel of Paris, on which the muse of Boileau has bestowed a comic immortality. The truth of such remote and ancient relics, which cannot be proved by any human testimony, must be admitted by those who believe in the miracles which they have performed. About the middle of the last age, an inveterate ulcer was touched and cured by an holy prickle of the holy crown: the prodigy is attested by the most pious and enlightened Christians of France; nor will the fact be easily disproved, except by those who are armed with a general antidote against religious credulity.

RECOVERY OF CONSTANTINOPLE BY THE GREEKS

The Latins of Constantinople were on all sides encompassed and pressed: their sole hope, the last delay of their ruin, was in the division of their Greek and Bulgarian enemies; and of this hope they were deprived by the superior arms and policy of Vataces, emperor of Nice. From the Propontis to the

rocky coast of Pamphylia, Asia was peaceful and prosperous
under his reign; and the events of every campaign extended
his influence in Europe. The strong cities of the hills of Macedonia and Thrace were rescued from the Bulgarians, and their
kingdom was circumscribed by its present and proper limits
along the southern banks of the Danube. The sole emperor of
the Romans could no longer brook that a lord of Epirus, a
Comnenian prince of the West, should presume to dispute or
share the honours of the purple; and the humble Demetrius
changed the colour of his buskins, and accepted with gratitude
the appellation of despot. His own subjects were exasperated
by his baseness and incapacity; they implored the protection
of their supreme lord. After some resistance, the kingdom of
Thessalonica was united to the empire of Nice; and Vataces
reigned without a competitor from the Turkish borders to the
Adriatic gulf. The princes of Europe revered his merit and
power; and had he subscribed an orthodox creed, it should
seem that the pope would have abandoned without reluctance
the Latin throne of Constantinople. But the death of Vataces,
the short and busy reign of Theodore his son, and the helpless
infancy of his grandson John, suspended the restoration of
the Greeks. In the next chapter I shall explain their domestic
revolutions; in this place it will be sufficient to observe that
the young prince was oppressed by the ambition of his
guardian and colleague Michael Palæologus, who displayed
the virtues and vices that belong to the founder of a new
dynasty. The emperor Baldwin had flattered himself that he
might recover some provinces or cities by an impotent
negociation. His ambassadors were dismissed from Nice with
mockery and contempt. At every place which they named
Palæologus alleged some special reason which rendered it
dear and valuable in his eyes: in the one he was born; in
another he had been first promoted to military command;
and in a third he had enjoyed, and hoped long to enjoy,
the pleasures of the chase. "And what then do you propose
to give us?" said the astonished deputies. "Nothing," replied
the Greek; "not a foot of land. If your master be desirous of
peace, let him pay me, as an annual tribute, the sum which
he receives from the trade and customs of Constantinople.
On these terms I may allow him to reign. If he refuses, it is
war. I am not ignorant of the art of war, and I trust the
event to God and my sword." An expedition against the despot

of Epirus was the first prelude of his arms. If a victory was
followed by a defeat, if the race of the Comneni or Angeli
survived in those mountains his efforts and his reign, the
captivity of Villehardouin prince of Achaia deprived the Latins
of the most active and powerful vassal of their expiring
monarchy. The republics of Venice and Genoa disputed, in
the first of their naval wars, the command of the sea and the
commerce of the East. Pride and interest attached the Venetians to the defence of Constantinople; their rivals were
tempted to promote the designs of her enemies, and the alliance of the Genoese with the schismatic conqueror provoked
the indignation of the Latin church.

Intent on his great object, the emperor Michael visited in
person and strengthened the troops and fortifications of
Thrace. The remains of the Latins were driven from their
last possessions: he assaulted without success the suburb of
Galata, and corresponded with a perfidious baron, who
proved unwilling, or unable, to open the gates of the metropolis. The next spring his favourite general, Alexius Stratego-
pulus, whom he had decorated with the title of Cæsar, passed
the Hellespont with eight hundred horse and some infantry on
a secret expedition. His instructions enjoined him to approach, to listen, to watch, but not to risk any doubtful or
dangerous enterprise against the city. The adjacent territory
between the Propontis and the Black Sea was cultivated by
an hardy race of peasants and outlaws, exercised in arms,
uncertain in their allegiance, but inclined by language, religion,
and present advantage, to the party of the Greeks. They were
styled the *volunteers,* and by their free service the army of
Alexius, with the regulars of Thrace and the Coman auxiliaries, was augmented to the number of five-and-twenty thousand men. By the ardour of the volunteers, and by his own
ambition, the Cæsar was stimulated to disobey the precise
orders of his master, in the just confidence that success would
plead his pardon and reward. The weakness of Constantinople
and the distress and terror of the Latins were familiar to the
observation of the volunteers; and they represented the present
moment as the most propitious to surprise and conquest. A
rash youth, the new governor of the Venetian colony, had
sailed away with thirty galleys and the best of the French
knights on a wild expedition to Daphnusia, a town on the
Black Sea, at the distance of forty leagues, and the remaining

Latins were without strength or suspicion. They were informed that Alexius had passed the Hellespont; but their apprehensions were lulled by the smallness of his original numbers, and their imprudence had not watched the subsequent
increase of his army. If he left his main body to second and
support his operations, he might advance unperceived in the
night with a chosen detachment. While some applied scaling-
ladders to the lowest part of the walls, they were secure of an
old Greek who would introduce their companions through
a subterraneous passage into his house; they could soon on
the inside break an entrance through the golden gate, which
had been long obstructed; and the conqueror would be in the
heart of the city before the Latins were conscious of their
danger. After some debate, the Cæsar resigned himself to the
faith of the volunteers; they were trusty, bold, and successful;
and, in describing the plan, I have already related the execution and success. But no sooner had Alexius passed the threshold of the golden gate than he trembled at his own rashness;
he paused, he deliberated, till the desperate volunteers urged
him forwards by the assurance that in retreat lay the greatest
and most inevitable danger. Whilst the Cæsar kept his
regulars in firm array, the Comans dispersed themselves on
all sides; an alarm was sounded, and the threats of fire and
pillage compelled the citizens to a decisive resolution. The
Greeks of Constantinople remembered their native sovereigns;
the Genoese merchants their recent alliance and Venetian foes;
every quarter was in arms; and the air resounded with a general acclamation of "Long life and victory to Michael and
John, the august emperors of the Romans!" Their rival, Baldwin, was awakened by the sound; but the most pressing danger
could not prompt him to draw his sword in the defence of a
city which he deserted perhaps with more pleasure than
regret: he fled from the palace to the sea-shore, where he
descried the welcome sails of the fleet returning from the
vain and fruitless attempt on Daphnusia. Constantinople was
irrecoverably lost; but the Latin emperor and the principal
families embarked on board the Venetian galleys, and steered
for the isle of Eubœa, and afterwards for Italy, where
the royal fugitive was entertained by the pope and Sicilian
king with a mixture of contempt and pity. From the loss of
Constantinople to his death he consumed thirteen years
soliciting the Catholic powers to join in his restoration: the

lesson had been familiar to his youth; nor was his last exile more indigent or shameful than his three former pilgrimages to the courts of Europe. His son Philip was the heir of an ideal empire; and the pretensions of *his* daughter Catherine were transported by her marriage to Charles of Valois, the brother of Philip the Fair, king of France. The house of Courtenay was represented in the female line by successive alliances, till the title of emperor of Constantinople, too bulky and sonorous for a private name, modestly expired in silence and oblivion.

GENERAL CONSEQUENCES OF THE CRUSADES

After this narrative of the expeditions of the Latins to Palestine and Constantinople, I cannot dismiss the subject without revolving the general consequences on the countries that were the scene, and on the nations that were the actors, of these memorable crusades. As soon as the arms of the Franks were withdrawn, the impression, though not the memory, was erased in the Mahometan realms of Egypt and Syria. The faithful disciples of the prophet were never tempted by a profane desire to study the laws or language of the idolaters; nor did the simplicity of their primitive manners receive the slightest alteration from their intercourse in peace and war with the unknown strangers of the West. The Greeks, who thought themselves proud, but who were only vain, showed a disposition somewhat less inflexible. In the efforts for the recovery of their empire they emulated the valour, discipline, and tactics of their antagonists. The modern literature of the West they might justly despise; but its free spirit would instruct them in the rights of man; and some institutions of public and private life were adopted from the French. The correspondence of Constantinople and Italy diffused the knowledge of the Latin tongue; and several of the fathers and classics were at length honoured with a Greek version. But the national and religious prejudices of the Orientals were inflamed by persecution; and the reign of the Latins confirmed the separation of the two churches.

If we compare, at the era of the crusades, the Latins of Europe with the Greeks and Arabians, their respective degrees of knowledge, industry, and art, our rude ancestors must be content with the third rank in the scale of nations. Their successive improvement and present superiority may be ascribed to a peculiar energy of character, to an active and imitative spirit, unknown to their more polished rivals, who at that time were in a stationary or retrograde state. With such a disposition the Latins should have derived the most early and essential benefits from a series of events which opened to their eyes the prospect of the world, and introduced them to a long and frequent intercourse with the more cultivated regions of the East. The first and most obvious progress was in trade and manufactures, in the arts which are strongly prompted by the thirst of wealth, the calls of necessity, and the gratification of the sense or vanity. Among the crowd of unthinking fanatics a captive or a pilgrim might sometimes observe the superior refinements of Cairo and Constantinople: the first importer of windmills was the benefactor of nations; and if such blessings are enjoyed without any grateful remembrance, history has condescended to notice the more apparent luxuries of silk and sugar, which were transported into Italy from Greece and Egypt. But the intellectual wants of the Latins were more slowly felt and supplied; the ardour of studious curiosity was awakened in Europe by different causes and more recent events; and, in the age of the crusades, they viewed with careless indifference the literature of the Greeks and Arabians. Some rudiments of mathematical and medicinal knowledge might be imparted in practice and in figures; necessity might produce some interpreters for the grosser business of merchants and soldiers; but the commerce of the Orientals had not diffused the study and knowledge of their languages in the schools of Europe. If a similar principle of religion repulsed the idiom of the Koran, it should have excited their patience and curiosity to understand the original text of the Gospel; and the same grammar would have unfolded the sense of Plato and the beauties of Homer. Yet, in a reign of sixty years, the Latins of Constantinople disdained the speech and learning of their subjects; and the manuscripts were the only treasures which the natives might enjoy without rapine or envy. Aristotle was indeed the oracle of the Western universities, but it was a barbarous Aristotle; and, instead of ascending to the fountain head, his Latin votaries humbly accepted a corrupt and remote version from the Jews and Moors of Andalusia. The principle of the crusades was a savage fanaticism; and the most important

effects were analogous to the cause. Each pilgrim was ambitious to return with his sacred spoils, the relics of Greece
and Palestine; and each relic was preceded and followed by
a train of miracles and visions. The belief of the Catholics
was corrupted by new legends, their practice by new superstitions; and the establishment of the inquisition, the mendicant
orders of monks and friars, the last abuse of indulgences,
and the final progress of idolatry, flowed from the baleful
fountain of the holy war. The active spirit of the Latins
preyed on the vitals of their reason and religion; and if the
ninth and tenth centuries were the times of darkness, the
thirteenth and fourteenth were the age of absurdity and fable.

In the profession of Christianity, in the cultivation of a
fertile land, the northern conquerors of the Roman empire
insensibly mingled with the provincials and rekindled the
embers of the arts of antiquity. Their settlements about the
age of Charlemagne had acquired some degree of order and
stability, when they were overwhelmed by new swarms of invaders, the Normans, Saracens, and Hungarians, who re-
plunged the western countries of Europe into their former
state of anarchy and barbarism. About the eleventh century
the second tempest had subsided by the expulsion or conversion of the enemies of Christendom: the tide of civilisation,
which had so long ebbed, began to flow with a steady and
accelerated course; and a fairer prospect was opened to the
hopes and efforts of the rising generations. Great was the increase, and rapid the progress, during the two hundred years
of the crusades; and some philosophers have applauded the
propitious influence of these holy wars, which appear to me
to have checked rather than forwarded the maturity of
Europe.[1] The lives and labours of millions which were buried
in the East would have been more profitably employed in
the improvement of their native country: the accumulated
stock of industry and wealth would have overflowed in
navigation and trade; and the Latins would have been enriched
and enlightened by a pure and friendly correspondence with
the climates of the East. In one respect I can indeed perceive
the accidental operation of the crusades, not so much in
producing a benefit as in removing an evil. The larger portion

---

[1] On this interesting subject, the progress of society in Europe, a strong
ray of philosophic light has broke from Scotland in our own times; and it
is with private, as well as public regard, that I repeat the names of Hume,
Robertson, and Adam Smith.

of the inhabitants of Europe was chained to the soil, without freedom, or property, or knowledge; and the two orders of ecclesiastics and nobles, whose numbers were comparatively small, alone deserved the name of citizens and men. This oppressive system was supported by the arts of the clergy and the swords of the barons. The authority of the priests operated in the darker ages as a salutary antidote: they prevented the total extinction of letters, mitigated the fierceness of the times, sheltered the poor and defenceless, and preserved or revived the peace and order of civil society. But the independence, rapine, and discord of the feudal lords were unmixed with any semblance of good; and every hope of industry and improvement was crushed by the iron weight of the martial aristocracy. Among the causes that undermined that Gothic edifice, a conspicuous place must be allowed to the crusades. The estates of the barons were dissipated, and their race was often extinguished, in these costly and perilous expeditions. Their poverty extorted from their pride those charters of freedom which unlocked the fetters of the slave, secured the farm of the peasant and the shop of the artificer, and gradually restored a substance and a soul to the most numerous and useful part of the community. The conflagration which destroyed the tall and barren trees of the forest gave air and scope to the vegetation of the smaller and nutritive plants of the soil.

In A.D. 1261 the Greeks recovered Constantinople and enthroned Michael Palæologus, the first Emperor of what was to be the last Byzantine dynasty. In the second half of the 13th century the city was beset by Mogul invaders under the successors of Genghis Khan. As the Mogul power waned, the Ottoman Turks established themselves in Asia Minor and gained a footing in Europe. Gibbon describes these developments in the following three chapters, cc. 62–64.

The End of the Roman Empire

65.

SIEGE OF CONSTANTINOPLE BY AMURATH II. DISCIPLINE OF THE TURKS. INVENTION OF GUNPOWDER

In 1402 imminent danger from the Ottoman Turks was relieved by Timour (or Tamerlaine), who captured the Ottoman ruler Bajazet II. The Ottoman power, however, revived under Amurath II and the doom of Constantinople was certain.

SIEGE OF CONSTANTINOPLE BY AMURATH II

IN THESE CONFLICTS the wisest Turks, and indeed the body of the nation, were strongly attached to the unity of the empire; and Romania and Anatolia, so often torn asunder by private ambition, were animated by a strong and invincible tendency of cohesion. Their efforts might have instructed the Christian powers; and had they occupied, with a confederate fleet, the straits of Gallipoli, the Ottomans, at least in Europe, must have been speedily annihilated. But the schism of the West, and the factions and wars of France and England, diverted the Latins from this generous enterprise: they enjoyed the present respite, without a thought of futurity; and were often tempted by a momentary interest to serve the common enemy of their religion. A colony of Genoese, which had been planted at Phocæa on the Ionian coast, was enriched by the lucrative monopoly of alum; and their tranquillity, under the Turkish empire, was secured by the annual payment of tribute. In the last civil war of the Ottomans, the Genoese governor, Adorno, a bold and ambitious youth, embraced the party of Amurath; and undertook, with seven stout galleys, to transport him from Asia to Europe. The sultan and five hundred guards embarked on board the admiral's ship; which was manned by eight hundred of the bravest Franks. His life and liberty were in their hands; nor can we, without reluctance, applaud the fidelity of Adorno, who, in the midst of the passage, knelt before him, and gratefully accepted a discharge of his arrears of tribute. They landed in sight of Mustapha and Gallipoli; two thousand Italians, armed with lances and battle-axes, attended Amurath to the conquest of Adrianople; and this venal service was soon repaid by the ruin of the commerce and colony of Phocæa.

If Timour had generously marched at the request, and to the relief, of the Greek emperor, he might be entitled to the praise and gratitude of the Christians. But a Musulman who carried into Georgia the sword of persecution, and respected the holy warfare of Bajazet, was not disposed to pity or succour the *idolaters* of Europe. The Tartar followed the impulse of ambition; and the deliverance of Constantinople was the accidental consequence. When Manuel abdicated the government, it was his prayer, rather than his hope, that the ruin of the church and state might be delayed beyond his unhappy days; and after his return from a western pilgrimage, he expected every hour the news of the sad catastrophe. On a sudden he was astonished and rejoiced by the intelligence of the retreat, the overthrow, and the captivity of the Ottoman. Manuel immediately sailed from Modon in the Morea; ascended the throne of Constantinople, and dismissed his blind competitor to an easy exile in the isle of Lesbos. The ambassadors of the son of Bajazet were soon introduced to his presence; but their pride was fallen, their tone was modest: they were awed by the just apprehension lest the Greeks should open to the Moguls the gates of Europe. Soliman saluted the emperor by the name of father; solicited at his hands the government or gift of Romania; and promised to deserve his favour by inviolable friendship, and the restitution of Thessalonica, with the most important places along the Strymon, the Propontis, and the Black Sea. The alliance of Soliman exposed the emperor to the enmity and revenge of Mousa: the Turks appeared in arms before the gates of Constantinople; but they were repulsed by sea and land; and unless the city was guarded by some foreign mercenaries, the Greeks must have wondered at their own triumph. But, instead of prolonging the division of the Ottoman powers, the policy or passion of Manuel was tempted to assist the most formidable of the sons of Bajazet. He concluded a treaty with Mahomet, whose progress was checked by the insuperable barrier of Gallipoli: the sultan and his troops were transported over the Bosphorus; he was hospitably entertained in the capital; and his successful sally was the first step to the conquest of Romania. The ruin was suspended by the prudence and moderation of the conqueror: he faithfully discharged his own obligations and those of Soliman; respected the laws of gratitude and peace; and left the emperor guardian of his two younger sons, in the vain hope of saving them from the jealous cruelty of their brother Amurath. But the execution of his last testament would have offended the national honour and religion; and the divan unanimously pronounced that the royal youths should never be abandoned to the custody and education of a Christian dog. On this refusal the Byzantine councils were divided: but the age and caution of Manuel yielded to the presumption of his son John; and they unsheathed a dangerous weapon of revenge, by dismissing the true or false Mustapha, who had long been detained as a captive and hostage, and for whose maintenance they received an annual pension of three hundred thousand aspers. At the door of his prison, Mustapha subscribed to every proposal; and the keys of Gallipoli, or rather of Europe, were stipulated as the price of his deliverance. But no sooner was he seated on the throne of Romania than he dismissed the Greek ambassadors with a smile of contempt, declaring, in a pious tone, that, at the day of judgment, he would rather answer for the violation of an oath, than for the surrender of a Musulman city into the hands of the infidels. The emperor was at once the enemy of the two rivals, from whom he had sustained, and to whom he had offered, an injury; and the victory of Amurath was followed, in the ensuing spring, by the siege of Constantinople.

The religious merit of subduing the city of the Cæsars attracted from Asia a crowd of volunteers, who aspired to the crown of martyrdom; their military ardour was inflamed by the promise of rich spoils and beautiful females; and the sultan's ambition was consecrated by the presence and prediction of Seid Bechar, a descendant of the prophet, who arrived in the camp, on a mule, with a venerable train of five hundred disciples. But he might blush, if a fanatic could blush, at the failure of his assurances. The strength of the walls resisted an army of two hundred thousand Turks: their assaults were repelled by the sallies of the Greeks and their foreign mercenaries; the old resources of defence were opposed to the new engines of attack; and the enthusiasm of the dervish, who was snatched to heaven in visionary converse with Mahomet, was answered by the credulity of the Christians, who *beheld* the Virgin Mary, in a violet garment, walking on the rampart and animating their courage. After a siege of two months Amurath was recalled to Boursa by a domestic revolt, which had been kindled by Greek treachery, and was soon extinguished by the death of a guiltless brother. While he led his Janizaries to new conquests in Europe and Asia, the Byzantine empire was indulged in a servile and precarious respite of thirty years. Manuel sank into the grave; and John Palæologus was permitted to reign, for an annual tribute of three hundred thousand aspers, and the dereliction of almost all that he held beyond the suburbs of Constantinople.

DISCIPLINE OF THE TURKS

In the establishment and restoration of the Turkish empire the first merit must doubtless be assigned to the personal qualities of the sultans; since, in human life, the most important scenes will depend on the character of a single actor. By some shades of wisdom and virtue they may be discriminated from each other; but, except in a single instance, a period of nine reigns, and two hundred and sixty-five years, is occupied, from the elevation of Othman to the death of Soliman, by a rare series of warlike and active princes, who impressed their subjects with obedience and their enemies with terror. Instead of the slothful luxury of the seraglio, the heirs of royalty were educated in the council and the field: from early youth they were entrusted by their fathers with the command of provinces and armies; and this manly institution, which was often productive of civil war, must have essentially contributed to the discipline and vigour of the monarchy. The Ottomans cannot style themselves, like the Arabian caliphs, the descendants or successors of the apostle of God; and the kindred which they claim with the Tartar khans of the house of Zingis appears to be founded in flattery rather than in truth. Their origin is obscure; but their sacred and indefeasible right, which no time can erase, and no violence can infringe, was soon and unalterably implanted in the minds of their subjects. A weak or vicious sultan may be deposed and strangled; but his inheritance devolves to an infant or an idiot; nor has the most daring rebel presumed to ascend the throne of his lawful sovereign. While the transient dynasties of Asia have been continually subverted by a crafty vizir in the palace or a victorious general in the camp, the Ottoman succession has been confirmed by the practice of five centuries, and is now incorporated with the vital principle of the Turkish nation.

To the spirit and constitution of that nation a strong and singular influence may however be ascribed. The primitive subjects of Othman were the four hundred families of wandering Turkmans who had followed his ancestors from the Oxus to the Sangar; and the plains of Anatolia are still covered with the white and black tents of their rustic brethren. But this original drop was dissolved in the mass of voluntary and vanquished subjects, who, under the name of Turks, are united by the common ties of religion, language, and manners. In the cities from Erzeroum to Belgrade, that national appellation is common to all the Moslems, the first and most honourable inhabitants; but they have abandoned, at least in Romania, the villages and the cultivation of the land to the Christian peasants. In the vigorous age of the Ottoman government the Turks were themselves excluded from all civil and military honours; and a servile class, an artificial people, was raised by the discipline of education to obey, to conquer, and to command. From the time of Orchan and the first Amurath the sultans were persuaded that a government of the sword must be renewed in each generation with new soldiers; and that such soldiers must be sought, not in effeminate Asia, but among the hardy and warlike natives of Europe. The provinces of Thrace, Macedonia, Albania, Bulgaria, and Servia became the perpetual seminary of the Turkish army; and when the royal fifth of the captives was diminished by conquest, an inhuman tax of the fifth child, or of every fifth year, was rigorously levied on the Christian families. At the age of twelve or fourteen years the most robust youths were torn from their parents; their names were enrolled in a book; and from that moment they were clothed, taught, and maintained for the public service. According to the promise of

their appearance, they were selected for the royal schools of
Boursa, Pera, and Adrianople, entrusted to the care of the
bashaws, or dispersed in the houses of the Anatolian peas-
antry. It was the first care of their masters to instruct them
in the Turkish language: their bodies were exercised by every
labour that could fortify their strength; they learned to
wrestle, to leap, to run, to shoot with the bow, and afterwards
with the musket; till they were drafted into the chambers and
companies of the Janizaries, and severely trained in the military or monastic discipline of the order. The youths most
conspicuous for birth, talents, and beauty, were admitted into
the inferior class of *Agiamoglans,* or the more liberal rank of
Ichoglans, of whom the former were attached to the palace,
and the latter to the person of the prince. In four successive
schools, under the rod of the white eunuchs, the arts of horse-
manship and of darting the javelin were their daily exercise,
while those of a more studious cast applied themselves to the
study of the Koran, and the knowledge of the Arabic and
Persian tongues. As they advanced in seniority and merit,
they were gradually dismissed to military, civil, and even
ecclesiastical employments: the longer their stay, the higher
was their expectation; till, at a mature period, they were
admitted into the number of the forty agas, who stood before
the sultan, and were promoted by his choice to the government
of provinces and the first honours of the empire. Such a mode
of institution was admirably adapted to the form and spirit
of a despotic monarchy. The ministers and generals were, in
the strictest sense, the slaves of the emperor, to whose bounty
they were indebted for their instruction and support. When
they left the seraglio, and suffered their beards to grow as
the symbol of enfranchisement, they found themselves in an
important office, without faction or friendship, without parents
and without heirs, dependent on the hand which had raised
them from the dust, and which, on the slightest displeasure,
could break in pieces these statues of glass, as they are
aptly termed by the Turkish proverb. In the slow and painful
steps of education, their characters and talents were unfolded
to a discerning eye: the *man,* naked and alone, was reduced
to the standard of his personal merit; and, if the sovereign
had wisdom to choose, he possessed a pure and boundless
liberty of choice. The Ottoman candidates were trained by
the virtues of abstinence to those of action; by the habits

of submission to those of command. A similar spirit was
diffused among the troops; and their silence and sobriety,
their patience and modesty, have extorted the reluctant
praise of their Christian enemies. Nor can the victory appear
doubtful, if we compare the discipline and exercise of the
Janizaries with the pride of birth, the independence of chivalry,
the ignorance of the new levies, the mutinous temper of the
veterans, and the vices of intemperance and disorder which
so long contaminated the armies of Europe.

INVENTION OF GUNPOWDER

The only hope of salvation for the Greek empire and the
adjacent kingdoms would have been some more powerful
weapon, some discovery in the art of war, that should give
them a decisive superiority over their Turkish foes. Such a
weapon was in their hands; such a discovery had been made
in the critical moment of their fate. The chemists of China
or Europe had found, by casual or elaborate experiments, that
a mixture of saltpetre, sulphur, and charcoal produces, with
a spark of fire, a tremendous explosion. It was soon observed
that, if the expansive force were compressed in a strong
tube, a ball of stone or iron might be expelled with irresistible
and destructive velocity. The precise era of the invention
and application of gunpowder is involved in doubtful traditions and equivocal language; yet we may clearly discern that
it was known before the middle of the fourteenth century,
and that before the end of the same the use of artillery in
battles and sieges by sea and land was familiar to the states
of Germany, Italy, Spain, France, and England. The priority
of nations is of small account; none could derive any exclusive
benefit from their previous or superior knowledge; and in
the common improvement they stood on the same level of
relative power and military science. Nor was it possible to
circumscribe the secret within the pale of the church; it was
disclosed to the Turks by the treachery of apostates and the
selfish policy of rivals; and the sultans had sense to adopt, and
wealth to reward, the talents of a Christian engineer. The
Genoese, who transported Amurath into Europe, must be
accused as his preceptors; and it was probably by their hands
that his cannon was cast and directed at the siege of Constantinople. The first attempt was indeed unsuccessful; but

in the general warfare of the age the advantage was on *their* side who were most commonly the assailants; for a while the proportion of the attack and defence was suspended, and this thundering artillery was pointed against the walls and towers which had been erected only to resist the less potent engines of antiquity. By the Venetians the use of gunpowder was communicated without reproach to the sultans of Egypt and Persia, their allies against the Ottoman power; the secret was soon propagated to the extremities of Asia; and the advantage of the European was confined to his easy victories over the savages of the new world. If we contrast the rapid progress of this mischievous discovery with the slow and laborious advances of reason, science, and the arts of peace, a philosopher, according to his temper, will laugh or weep at the folly of mankind.

66.

GREEK APPEALS TO THE WEST. VISIT OF
JOHN PALÆOLOGUS TO ROME. VISIT OF MANUEL TO
ITALY, FRANCE, AND ENGLAND. EXPEDITION OF JOHN
PALÆOLOGUS II. TEMPORARY UNION OF THE GREEKS
AND LATINS. REVIVAL OF GREEK LEARNING IN ITALY.
POPE NICHOLAS V. USE AND ABUSE OF
ANCIENT LEARNING

IN THE FOUR last centuries of the Greek emperors, their
friendly or hostile aspect towards the pope and the Latins
may be observed as the thermometer of their prosperity or
distress—as the scale of the rise and fall of the barbarian
dynasties. When the Turks of the house of Seljuk pervaded
Asia, and threatened Constantinople, we have seen at the
council of Placentia the suppliant ambassadors of Alexius imploring the protection of the common father of the Christians.
No sooner had the arms of the French pilgrims removed the
sultan from Nice to Iconium than the Greek princes resumed,
or avowed, their genuine hatred and contempt for the schismatics of the West, which precipitated the first downfall of
their empire. The date of the Mogul invasion is marked in
the soft and charitable language of John Vataces. After the
recovery of Constantinople the throne of the first Palæologus
was encompassed by foreign and domestic enemies: as long
as the sword of Charles was suspended over his head he
basely courted the favour of the Roman pontiff, and sacrificed
to the present danger his faith, his virtue, and the affection
of his subjects. On the decease of Michael the prince and
people asserted the independence of their church and the
purity of their creed: the elder Andronicus neither feared nor
loved the Latins; in his last distress pride was the safeguard
of superstition; nor could he decently retract in his age the
firm and orthodox declarations of his youth. His grandson,
the younger Andronicus, was less a slave in his temper and
situation; and the conquest of Bithynia by the Turks admon-

ished him to seek a temporal and spiritual alliance with the
Western princes. After a separation and silence of fifty years a
secret agent, the monk Barlaam, was despatched to Pope
Benedict the Twelfth; and his artful instructions appear to
have been drawn by the master-hand of the great domestic.
"Most holy father," was he commissioned to say, "the emperor
is not less desirous than yourself of an union between the
two churches; but in this delicate transaction he is obliged to
respect his own dignity and the prejudices of his subjects.
The ways of union are twofold, force and persuasion. Of
force, the inefficacy has been already tried, since the Latins
have subdued the empire without subduing the minds of the
Greeks. The method of persuasion, though slow, is sure and
permanent. A deputation of thirty or forty of our doctors
would probably agree with those of the Vatican in the love
of truth and the unity of belief; but on their return, what
would be the use, the recompense, of such agreement? the
scorn of their brethren, and the reproaches of a blind and
obstinate nation. Yet that nation is accustomed to reverence
the general councils which have fixed the articles of our faith;
and if they reprobate the decrees of Lyons, it is because the
Eastern churches were neither heard nor represented in that
arbitrary meeting. For this salutary end it will be expedient,
and even necessary, that a well-chosen legate should be sent
into Greece to convene the patriarchs of Constantinople, Alexandria, Antioch, and Jerusalem, and with their aid to prepare
a free and universal synod. But at this moment," continued
the subtle agent, "the empire is assaulted and endangered by
the Turks, who have occupied four of the greatest cities of
Anatolia. The Christian inhabitants have expressed a wish of
returning to their allegiance and religion; but the forces and
revenues of the emperor are insufficient for their deliverance:
and the Roman legate must be accompanied or preceded by
an army of Franks to expel the infidels, and open a way to
the holy sepulchre." If the suspicious Latins should require
some pledge, some previous effect of the sincerity of the
Greeks, the answers of Barlaam were perspicuous and rational.
"1. A general synod can alone consummate the union of the
churches; nor can such a synod be held till the three Oriental
patriarchs and a great number of bishops are enfranchised
from the Mahometan yoke. 2. The Greeks are alienated by
a long series of oppression and injury: they must be recon-

ciled by some act of brotherly love, some effectual succour, which may fortify the authority and arguments of the emperor and the friends of the union. 3. If some difference of faith or ceremonies should be found incurable, the Greeks however are the disciples of Christ, and the Turks are the common enemies of the Christian name. The Armenians, Cyprians, and Rhodians are equally attacked; and it will become the piety of the French princes to draw their swords in the general defence of religion. 4. Should the subjects of Andronicus be treated as the worst of schismatics, of heretics, of pagans, a judicious policy may yet instruct the powers of the West to embrace a useful ally, to uphold a sinking empire, to guard the confines of Europe, and rather to join the Greeks against the Turks than to expect the union of the Turkish arms with the troops and treasures of captive Greece." The reasons, the offers, and the demands of Andronicus were eluded with cold and stately indifference. The kings of France and Naples declined the dangers and glory of a crusade: the pope refused to call a new synod to determine old articles of faith; and his reward for the obsolete claims of the Latin emperor and clergy engaged him to use an offensive superscription,—"To the *moderator* of the Greeks, and the persons who style themselves the patriarchs of the Eastern churches." For such an embassy a time and character less propitious could not easily have been found. Benedict the Twelfth was a dull peasant, perplexed with scruples, and immersed in sloth and wine: his pride might enrich with a third crown the papal tiara, but he was alike unfit for the regal and the pastoral office.

After the decease of Andronicus, while the Greeks were distracted by intestine war, they could not presume to agitate a general union of the Christians. But as soon as Cantacuzene had subdued and pardoned his enemies, he was anxious to justify, or at least to extenuate, the introduction of the Turks into Europe and the nuptials of his daughter with a Musulman prince. Two officers of state, with a Latin interpreter, were sent in his name to the Roman court, which was transplanted to Avignon, on the banks of the Rhône, during a period of seventy years: they represented the hard necessity which had urged him to embrace the alliance of the miscreants, and pronounced by his command the specious and edifying sounds of union and crusade. Pope Clement the Sixth, the successor of Benedict, received them with hospitality and honour, acknowledged the innocence of their sovereign, excused his distress, applauded his magnanimity, and displayed a clear knowledge of the state and revolutions of the Greek empire, which he had imbibed from the honest accounts of a Savoyard lady, an attendant of the empress Anne. If Clement was ill endowed with the virtues of a priest, he possesed however the spirit and magnificence of a prince whose liberal hand distributed benefices and kingdoms with equal facility. Under his reign Avignon was the seat of pomp and pleasure: in his youth he had surpassed the licentiousness of a baron; and the palace, nay the bedchamber of the pope, was adorned, or polluted, by the visits of his female favourites. The wars of France and England were adverse to the holy enterprise; but his vanity was amused by the splendid idea; and the Greek ambassadors returned with two Latin bishops, the ministers of the pontiff. On their arrival at Constantinople the emperor and the nuncios admired each other's piety and eloquence; and their frequent conferences were filled with mutual praises and promises, by which both parties were amused, and neither could be deceived. "I am delighted," said the devout Cantacuzene, "with the project of our holy war, which must redound to my personal glory as well as to the public benefit of Christendom. My dominions will give a free passage to the armies of France: my troops, my galleys, my treasures, shall be consecrated to the common cause; and happy would be my fate could I deserve and obtain the crown of martyrdom. Words are insufficient to express the ardour with which I sigh for the reunion of the scattered members of Christ. If my death could avail, I would gladly present my sword and my neck: if the spiritual phœnix could arise from my ashes, I would erect the pile and kindle the flame with my own hands." Yet the Greek emperor presumed to observe that the articles of faith which divided the two churches had been introduced by the pride and precipitation of the Latins: he disclaimed the servile and arbitrary steps of the first Palæologus, and firmly declared that he would never submit his conscience unless to the decrees of a free and universal synod. "The situation of the times," continued he, "will not allow the pope and myself to meet either at Rome or Constantinople; but some maritime city may be chosen on the verge of the two empires, to unite the bishops, and to instruct the faithful of the East and West." The nuncios seemed content with the proposition; and Cantacuzene affects to deplore the failure of his hopes, which were soon overthrown by the death of Clement, and the different temper of his successor. His own life was prolonged, but it was prolonged in a cloister; and, except by his prayers, the humble monk was incapable of directing the counsels of his pupil or the state.

VISIT OF JOHN PALÆOLOGUS TO ROME

Yet of all the Byzantine princes, that pupil, John Palæologus, was the best disposed to embrace, to believe, and to obey the shepherd of the West. His mother, Anne of Savoy, was baptized in the bosom of the Latin church: her marriage with Andronicus imposed a change of name, of apparel, and of worship, but her heart was still faithful to her country and religion: she had formed the infancy of her son, and she governed the emperor after his mind, or at least his stature, was enlarged to the size of man. In the first year of his deliverance and restoration the Turks were still masters of the Hellespont; the son of Cantacuzene was in arms at Adrianople, and Palæologus could depend neither on himself nor on his people. By his mother's advice, and in the hope of foreign aid, he abjured the rights both of the church and state; and the act of slavery, subscribed in purple ink, and sealed with the *golden* bull, was privately intrusted to an Italian agent. The first article of the treaty is an oath of fidelity and obedience to Innocent the Sixth and his successors, the supreme pontiffs of the Roman and Catholic church. The emperor promises to entertain with due reverence their legates and nuncios, to assign a palace for their residence and a temple for their worship, and to deliver his second son Manuel as the hostage of his faith. For these condescensions he requires a prompt succour of fifteen galleys, with five hundred men-at-arms and a thousand archers, to serve against his Christian and Musulman enemies. Palæologus engages to impose on his clergy and people the same spiritual yoke; but as the resistance of the Greeks might be justly foreseen, he adopts the two effectual methods of corruption and education. The legate was empowered to distribute the vacant benefices among the ecclesiasticals who should subscribe the creed of the Vatican: three schools were instituted

to instruct the youth of Constantinople in the language and
doctrine of the Latins; and the name of Andronicus, the heir
of the empire, was enrolled as the first student. Should he fail
in the measures of persuasion or force, Palæologus declares
himself unworthy to reign, transfers to the pope all regal and
paternal authority, and invests Innocent with full power to
regulate the family, the government, and the marriage of his
son and successor. But this treaty was neither executed nor
published: the Roman galleys were as vain and imaginary as
the submission of the Greeks; and it was only by the secrecy
that their sovereign escaped the dishonour of this fruitless
humiliation.

The tempest of the Turkish arms soon burst on his head;
and after the loss of Adrianople and Romania he was enclosed in his capital, the vassal of the haughty Amurath,
with the miserable hope of being the last devoured by the
savage. In this abject state Palæologus embraced the resolution of embarking for Venice, and casting himself at the feet
of the pope: he was the first of the Byzantine princes who had
ever visited the unknown regions of the West, yet in them
alone he could seek consolation or relief; and with less
violation of his dignity he might appear in the sacred college
than at the Ottoman *Porte*. After a long absence the Roman
pontiffs were returning from Avignon to the banks of the
Tiber: Urban the Fifth, of a mild and virtuous character, encouraged or allowed the pilgrimage of the Greek prince, and,
within the same year, enjoyed the glory of receiving in the
Vatican the two Imperial shadows who represented the
majesty of Constantine and Charlemagne. In this suppliant
visit the emperor of Constantinople, whose vanity was lost
in his distress, gave more than could be expected of empty
sounds and formal submissions. A previous trial was imposed;
and in the presence of four cardinals he acknowledged, as
a true Catholic, the supremacy of the pope, and the double
procession of the Holy Ghost. After this purification he was
introduced to a public audience in the church of St. Peter:
Urban, in the midst of the cardinals, was seated on his
throne; the Greek monarch, after three genuflexions, devoutly
kissed the feet, the hands, and at length the mouth of the holy
father, who celebrated high mass in his presence, allowed him
to lead the bridle of his mule, and treated him with a
sumptuous banquet in the Vatican. The entertainment of

Palæologus was friendly and honourable, yet some difference was observed between the emperors of the East and West; nor could the former be entitled to the rare privilege of chanting the Gospel in the rank of a deacon. In favour of his proselyte, Urban strove to rekindle the zeal of the French king and the other powers of the West; but he found them cold in the general cause, and active only in their domestic quarrels. The last hope of the emperor was in an English mercenary, John Hawkwood, or Acuto, who, with a band of adventurers, the White Brotherhood, had ravaged Italy from the Alps to Calabria, sold his services to the hostile states, and incurred a just excommunication by shooting his arrows against the papal residence. A special licence was granted to negotiate with the outlaw, but the forces, or the spirit, of Hawkwood were unequal to the enterprise: and it was for the advantage perhaps of Palæologus to be disappointed of a succour that must have been costly, that could not be effectual, and which might have been dangerous. The disconsolate Greek prepared for his return, but even his return was impeded by a most ignominious obstacle. On his arrival at Venice he had borrowed large sums at exorbitant usury; but his coffers were empty, his creditors were impatient, and his person was detained as the best security for the payment. His eldest son Andronicus, the regent of Constantinople, was repeatedly urged to exhaust every resource, and even by stripping the churches, to extricate his father from captivity and disgrace. But the unnatural youth was insensible of the disgrace, and secretly pleased with the captivity of the emperor: the state was poor, the clergy was obstinate; nor could some religious scruple be wanting to excuse the guilt of his indifference and delay. Such undutiful neglect was severely reproved by the piety of his brother Manuel, who instantly sold or mortgaged all that he possessed, embarked for Venice, relieved his father, and pledged his own freedom to be responsible for the debt. On his return to Constantinople the parent and king distinguished his two sons with suitable rewards; but the faith and manners of the slothful Palæologus had not been improved by his Roman pilgrimage; and his apostasy or conversion, devoid of any spiritual or temporal effects, was speedily forgotten by the Greeks and Latins.

VISIT OF MANUEL TO ITALY, FRANCE, AND ENGLAND

Thirty years after the return of Palæologus, his son and successor Manuel, from a similar motive, but on a larger scale, again visited the countries of the West. In a preceding chapter I have related his treaty with Bajazet, the violation of that treaty, the siege or blockade of Constantinople, and the French succour under the command of the gallant Boucicault. By his ambassadors Manuel had solicited the Latin powers; but it was thought that the presence of a distressed monarch would draw tears and supplies from the hardest barbarians, and the marshal who advised the journey prepared the reception of the Byzantine prince. The land was occupied by the Turks; but the navigation of Venice was safe and open: Italy received him as the first, or at least the second, of the Christian princes; Manuel was pitied as the champion and confessor of the faith, and the dignity of his behaviour prevented that pity from sinking into contempt. From Venice he proceeded to Padua and Pavia; and even the duke of Milan, a secret ally of Bajazet, gave him safe and honourable conduct to the verge of his dominions. On the confines of France the royal officers undertook the care of his person, journey, and expenses; and two thousand of the richest citizens, in arms and on horseback, came forth to meet him as far as Charenton, in the neighbourhood of the capital. At the gates of Paris he was saluted by the chancellor and the parliament; and Charles the Sixth, attended by his princes and nobles, welcomed his brother with a cordial embrace. The successor of Constantine was clothed in a robe of white silk and mounted on a milk-white steed, a circumstance, in the French ceremonial, of singular importance: the white colour is considered as the symbol of sovereignty; and in a late visit the German emperor, after an haughty demand and a peevish refusal, had been reduced to content himself with a black courser. Manuel was lodged in the Louvre: a succession of feasts and balls, the pleasures of the banquet and the chase, were ingeniously varied by the politeness of the French to display their magnificence and amuse his grief; he was indulged in the liberty of his chapel, and the doctors of the Sorbonne were astonished, and possibly scandalised, by the language, the rites, and the vestments of his Greek clergy.

But the slightest glance on the state of the kingdom must teach him to despair of any effectual assistance. The unfortunate Charles, though he enjoyed some lucid intervals, continually relapsed into furious or stupid insanity; the reins of government were alternately seized by his brother and uncle, the dukes of Orleans and Burgundy, whose factious competition prepared the miseries of civil war. The former was a gay youth, dissolved in luxury and love: the latter was the father of John, count of Nevers, who had so lately been ransomed from Turkish captivity; and, if the fearless son was ardent to revenge his defeat, the more prudent Burgundy was content with the cost and peril of the first experiment. When Manuel had satiated the curiosity, and perhaps fatigued the patience of the French, he resolved on a visit to the adjacent island. In his progress from Dover he was entertained at Canterbury with due reverence by the prior and monks of St. Austin, and, on Blackheath, king Henry the Fourth, with the English court, saluted the Greek hero (I copy our old historian), who, during many days, was lodged and treated in London as emperor of the East. But the state of England was still more adverse to the design of the holy war. In the same year the hereditary sovereign had been deposed and murdered: the reigning prince was a successful usurper, whose ambition was punished by jealousy and remorse; nor could Henry of Lancaster withdraw his person or forces from the defence of a throne incessantly shaken by conspiracy and rebellion. He pitied, he praised, he feasted, the emperor of Constantinople; but if the English monarch assumed the cross, it was only to appease his people, and perhaps his conscience, by the merit or semblance of this pious intention. Satisfied, however, with gifts and honours, Manuel returned to Paris; and, after a residence of two years in the West, shaped his course through Germany and Italy, embarked at Venice, and patiently expected, in the Morea, the moment of his ruin or deliverance. Yet he had escaped the ignominious necessity of offering his religion to public or private sale. The Latin church was distracted by the great schism: the kings, the nations, the universities of Europe, were divided in their obedience between the popes of Rome and Avignon; and the emperor, anxious to conciliate the friendship of both parties, abstained from any correspondence with the indigent and unpopular rivals. His journey coincided with the year of

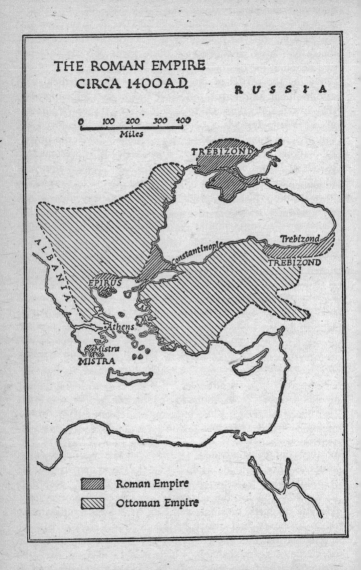

THE ROMAN EMPIRE
CIRCA 1400 A.D.

RUSSIA

0   100   200   300   400
          Miles

TREBIZOND

ALBANIA

Constantinople

Trebizond

TREBIZOND

EPIRUS

Athens

Mistra
MISTRA

Roman Empire

Ottoman Empire

the jubilee; but he passed through Italy without desiring or deserving the plenary indulgence which abolished the guilt or penance of the sins of the faithful. The Roman pope was offended by this neglect, accused him of irreverence to an image of Christ, and exhorted the princes of Italy to reject and abandon the obstinate schismatic.

During the period of the crusades the Greeks beheld with astonishment and terror the perpetual stream of emigration that flowed, and continued to flow, from the unknown climates of the West. The visits of their last emperors removed the veil of separation, and they disclosed to their eyes the powerful nations of Europe, whom they no longer presumed to brand with the name of barbarians. The observations of Manuel and his more inquisitive followers have been preserved by a Byzantine historian of the times: his scattered ideas I shall collect and abridge; and it may be amusing enough, perhaps instructive, to contemplate the rude pictures of Germany, France, and England, whose ancient and modern state are so familiar to *our* minds. I. GERMANY (says the Greek Chalcondyles) is of ample latitude from Vienna to the Ocean, and it stretches (a strange geography) from Prague, in Bohemia, to the river Tartessus and the Pyrenæan mountains. The soil, except in figs and olives, is sufficiently fruitful; the air is salubrious, the bodies of the natives are robust and healthy, and these cold regions are seldom visited with the calamities of pestilence or earthquakes. After the Scythians or Tartars, the Germans are the most numerous of nations: they are brave and patient, and, were they united under a single head, their force would be irresistible. By the gift of the pope, they have acquired the privilege of choosing the Roman emperor; nor is any people more devoutly attached to the faith and obedience of the Latin patriarch. The greatest part of the country is divided among the princes and prelates; but Strassburg, Cologne, Hamburg, and more than two hundred free cities, are governed by sage and equal laws, according to the will and for the advantage of the whole community. The use of duels, or single combats on foot, prevails among them in peace and war; their industry excels in all the mechanic arts; and the Germans may boast of the invention of gunpowder and cannon, which is now diffused over the greatest part of the world. II. The kingdom of FRANCE is spread above fifteen or twenty days' journey from Germany to

Spain, and from the Alps to the British Ocean, containing many flourishing cities, and among these Paris, the seat of the king, which surpasses the rest in riches and luxury. Many princes and lords alternately wait in his palace and acknowledge him as their sovereign: the most powerful are the dukes of Bretagne and Burgundy, of whom the latter possesses the wealthy province of Flanders, whose harbours are frequented by the ships and merchants of our own and the more remote seas. The French are an ancient and opulent people, and their language and manners, though somewhat different, are not dissimilar from those of the Italians. Vain of the Imperial dignity of Charlemagne, of their victories over the Saracens, and of the exploits of their heroes Oliver and Rowland, they esteem themselves the first of the western nations; but this foolish arrogance has been recently humbled by the unfortunate events of their wars against the English, the inhabitants of the British island. III. BRITAIN, in the ocean and opposite to the shores of Flanders, may be considered either as one or as three islands; but the whole is united by a common interest, by the same manners, and by a similar government. The measure of its circumference is five thousand stadia: the land is overspread with towns and villages; though destitute of wine, and not abounding in fruit-trees, it is fertile in wheat and barley, in honey and wool, and much cloth is manufactured by the inhabitants. In populousness and power, in riches and luxury, London, the metropolis of the isle, may claim a pre-eminence over all the cities of the West. It is situate on the Thames, a broad and rapid river, which at the distance of thirty miles falls into the Gallic Sea; and the daily flow and ebb of the tide affords a safe entrance and departure to the vessels of commerce. The king is the head of a powerful and turbulent aristocracy: his principal vassals hold their estates by a free and unalterable tenure, and the laws define the limits of his authority and their obedience. The kingdom has been often afflicted by foreign conquest and domestic sedition; but the natives are bold and hardy, renowned in arms and victorious in war. The form of their shields or targets is derived from the Italians, that of their swords from the Greeks; the use of the long bow is the peculiar and decisive advantage of the English. Their language bears no affinity to the idioms of the continent: in the habits of domestic life they are not easily distinguished from their neighbours of France; but the most singular circumstance of their manners is their disregard of conjugal honour and of female chastity. In their mutual visits, as the first act of hospitality, the guest is welcomed in the embraces of their wives and daughters: among friends they are lent and borrowed without shame; nor are the islanders offended at this strange commerce and its inevitable consequences. Informed as we are of the customs of old England, and assured of the virtue of our mothers, we may smile at the credulity, or resent the injustice, of the Greek, who must have confounded a modest salute[1] with a criminal embrace. But his credulity and injustice may teach an important lesson, to distrust the accounts of foreign and remote nations, and to suspend our belief of every tale that deviates from the laws of nature and the character of man.

After his return, and the victory of Timour, Manuel reigned many years in prosperity and peace. As long as the sons of Bajazet solicited his friendship and spared his dominions, he was satisfied with the national religion; and his leisure was employed in composing twenty theological dialogues for its defence. The appearance of the Byzantine ambassadors at the council of Constance announces the restoration of the Turkish power, as well as of the Latin church: the conquest of the sultans, Mahomet and Amurath, reconciled the emperor to the Vatican; and the siege of Constantinople almost tempted him to acquiesce in the double procession of the Holy Ghost. When Martin the Fifth ascended without a rival the chair of St. Peter, a friendly intercourse of letters and embassies was revived between the East and West. Ambition on one side, and distress on the other, dictated the same decent language of charity and peace: the artful Greek expressed a desire of marrying his six sons to Italian princesses; and the Roman, not less artful, despatched the daughter of the marquis of Montferrat, with a company of noble virgins, to soften, by their charms, the obstinacy of the schismatics. Yet under this mask of zeal a discerning eye will perceive that all was hollow and insincere in the court and church of Constantinople. According to the vicissitudes of danger and repose, the emperor advanced or retreated; alternately instructed and dis-

---

[1] Erasmus has a pretty passage on the English fashion of kissing strangers on their arrival and departure, from whence, however, he draws no scandalous inferences.

avowed his ministers; and escaped from an importunate pressure by urging the duty of inquiry, the obligation of collecting the sense of his patriarchs and bishops, and the impossibility of convening them at a time when the Turkish arms were at the gates of his capital. From a review of the public transactions it will appear that the Greeks insisted on three successive measures, a succour, a council, and a final reunion, while the Latins eluded the second, and only promised the first as a consequential and voluntary reward of the third. But we have an opportunity of unfolding the most secret intentions of Manuel, as he explained them in a private conversation without artifice or disguise. In his declining age the emperor had associated John Palæologus, the second of the name, and the eldest of his sons, on whom he devolved the greatest part of the authority and weight of government. One day, in the presence only of the historian Phranza, his favourite chamberlain, he opened to his colleague and successor the true principle of his negociations with the pope. "Our last resource," said Manuel, "against the Turks is their fear of our union with the Latins, of the warlike nations of the West, who may arm for our relief and for their destruction. As often as you are threatened by the miscreants, present this danger before their eyes. Propose a council; consult on the means; but ever delay and avoid the convocation of an assembly, which cannot tend either to our spiritual or temporal emolument. The Latins are proud; the Greeks are obstinate; neither party will recede or retract; and the attempt of a perfect union will confirm the schism, alienate the churches, and leave us, without hope or defence, at the mercy of the barbarians." Impatient of this salutary lesson, the royal youth arose from his seat and departed in silence; and the wise monarch (continues Phranza), casting his eyes on me, thus resumed his discourse: "My son deems himself a great and heroic prince; but, alas! our miserable age does not afford scope for heroism or greatness. His daring spirit might have suited the happier times of our ancestors; but the present state requires not an emperor, but a cautious steward of the last relics of our fortunes. Well do I remember the lofty expectations which he built on our alliance with Mustapha; and much do I fear that his rash courage will urge the ruin of our house, and that even religion may precipitate our downfall." Yet the experience and authority of Manuel preserved the peace and eluded the council; till, in the seventy-eighth year of his age, and in the habit of a monk, he terminated his career, dividing his precious moveables among his children and the poor, his physicians and his favourite servants. Of his six sons, Andronicus the Second was invested with the principality of Thessalonica, and died of a leprosy soon after the sale of that city to the Venetians and its final conquest by the Turks. Some fortunate incidents had restored Peloponnesus, or the Morea, to the empire: and in his more prosperous days, Manuel had fortified the narrow isthmus of six miles with a stone wall and one hundred and fifty-three towers. The wall was overthrown by the first blast of the Ottomans; the fertile peninsula might have been sufficient for the four younger brothers, Theodore and Constantine, Demetrius and Thomas; but they wasted in domestic contests the remains of their strength; and the least successful of the rivals were reduced to a life of dependence in the Byzantine palace.

EXPEDITION OF JOHN PALÆOLOGUS II

The eldest of the sons of Manuel, John Palæologus the Second, was acknowledged, after his father's death, as the sole emperor of the Greeks. He immediately proceeded to repudiate his wife, and to contract a new marriage with the princess of Trebizond: beauty was in his eyes the first qualification of an empress; and the clergy had yielded to his firm assurance, that, unless he might be indulged in a divorce, he would retire to a cloister and leave the throne to his brother Constantine. The first, and in truth the only victory of Palæologus, was over a Jew, whom, after a long and learned dispute, he converted to the Christian faith; and this momentous conquest is carefully recorded in the history of the times. But he soon resumed the design of uniting the East and West; and, regardless of his father's advice, listened, as it should seem with sincerity, to the proposal of meeting the pope in a general council beyond the Adriatic. This dangerous project was encouraged by Martin the Fifth, and coldly entertained by his successor Eugenius, till, after a tedious negociation, the emperor received a summons from a Latin assembly of a new character, the independent prelates of

Basil, who styled themselves the representatives and judges of the Cátholic church.

The Roman pontiff had fought and conquered in the cause of ecclesiastical freedom; but the victorious clergy were soon exposed to the tyranny of their deliverer; and his sacred character was invulnerable to those arms which they found so keen and effectual against the civil magistrate. Their great charter, the right of election, was annihilated by appeals, evaded by trusts or commendams, disappointed by reversionary grants, and superseded by previous and arbitrary reservations. A public auction was instituted in the court of Rome: the cardinals and favourites were enriched with the spoils of nations; and every country might complain that the most important and valuable benefices were accumulated on the heads of aliens and absentees. During their residence at Avignon the ambition of the popes subsided in the meaner passions of avarice[1] and luxury: they rigorously imposed on the clergy the tributes of first-fruits and tenths; but they freely tolerated the impunity of vice, disorder, and corruption. These manifold scandals were aggravated by the great schism of the West, which continued above fifty years. In the furious conflicts of Rome and Avignon, the vices of the rivals were mutually exposed; and their precarious situation degraded their authority, relaxed their discipline, and multiplied their wants and exactions. To heal the wounds, and restore the monarchy, of the church, the synods of Pisa and Constance were successively convened; but these great assemblies, conscious of their strength, resolved to vindicate the privileges of the Christian aristocracy. From a personal sentence against two pontiffs whom they rejected, and a third, their acknowledged sovereign, whom they deposed, the fathers of Constance proceeded to examine the nature and limits of the Roman supremacy; nor did they separate till they had established the authority, above the pope, of a general council. It was enacted, that, for the government and reformation of the church, such assemblies should be held at regular intervals; and that each synod, before its dissolution, should appoint the time and place of the subsequent meeting. By the influence of the

---

[1] Pope John XXII (in 1334) left behind him, at Avignon, eighteen millions of gold florins, and the value of seven millions more in plate and jewels. See the Chronicle of John Villani, whose brother received the account from the papal treasurers. A treasure of six or eight millions sterling in the xivth century is enormous, and almost incredible.

court of Rome, the next convocation at Sienna was easily eluded; but the bold and vigorous proceedings of the council of Basel had almost been fatal to the reigning pontiff, Eugenius the Fourth. A just suspicion · of his design prompted the fathers to hasten the promulgation of their first decree, that the representatives of the church-militant on earth were invested with a divine and spiritual jurisdiction over all Christians, without excepting the pope; and that a general council could not be dissolved, prorogued, or transferred, unless by their free deliberation and consent. On the notice that Eugenius had fulminated a bull for that purpose, they ventured to summon, to admonish, to threaten, to censure, the contumacious successor of St. Peter. After many delays, to allow time for repentance, they finally declared, that, unless he submitted within the term of sixty days, he was suspended from the exercise of all temporal and ecclesiastical authority. And to mark their jurisdiction over the prince as well as the priest, they assumed the government of Avignon, annulled the alienation of the sacred patrimony, and protected Rome from the imposition of new taxes. Their boldness was justified, not only by the general opinion of the clergy, but by the support and power of the first monarchs of Christendom: the emperor Sigismond declared himself the servant and protector of the synod; Germany and France adhered to their cause; the duke of Milan was the enemy of Eugenius; and he was driven from the Vatican by an insurrection of the Roman people. Rejected at the same time by his temporal and spiritual subjects, submission was his only choice: by a most humiliating bull, the pope repealed his own acts, and ratified those of the council; incorporated his legates and cardinals with that venerable body; and *seemed* to resign himself to the decrees of the supreme legislature. Their fame pervaded the countries of the East: and it was in their presence that Sigismond received the ambassadors of the Turkish sultan, who laid at his feet twelve large vases filled with robes of silk and pieces of gold. The fathers of Basel aspired to the glory of reducing the Greeks, as well as the Bohemians, within the pale of the church; and their deputies invited the emperor and patriarch of Constantinople to unite with an assembly which possessed the confidence of the Western nations. Palæologus was not averse to the proposal; and his ambassadors were introduced with due honours into the Catholic senate. But the choice of the place appeared to be an insuperable obstacle, since he refused to pass the Alps, or the sea of Sicily, and positively required that the synod should be adjourned to some convenient city in Italy, or at least on the Danube. The other articles of this treaty were more readily stipulated: it was agreed to defray the travelling expenses of the emperor, with a train of seven hundred persons, to remit an immediate sum of eight thousand ducats for the accommodation of the Greek clergy; and in his absence to grant a supply of ten thousand ducats, with three hundred archers and some galleys, for the protection of Constantinople. The city of Avignon advanced the funds for the preliminary expenses; and the embarkation was prepared at Marseilles with some difficulty and delay.

In his distress the friendship of Palæologus was disputed by the ecclesiastical powers of the West; but the dexterous activity of a monarch prevailed over the slow debates and inflexible temper of a republic. The decrees of Basel continually tended to circumscribe the despotism of the pope, and to erect a supreme and perpetual tribunal in the church. Eugenius was impatient of the yoke; and the union of the Greeks might afford a decent pretence for translating a rebellious synod from the Rhine to the Po. The independence of the fathers was lost if they passed the Alps: Savoy or Avignon, to which they acceded with reluctance, were described at Constantinople as situate far beyond the Pillars of Hercules; the emperor and his clergy were apprehensive of the dangers of a long navigation; they were offended by an haughty declaration, that, after suppressing the *new* heresy of the Bohemians, the council would soon eradicate the *old* heresy of the Greeks. On the side of Eugenius all was smooth, and yielding, and respectful; and he invited the Byzantine monarch to heal by his presence the schism of the Latin, as well as of the Eastern, church. Ferrara, near the coast of the Adriatic, was proposed for their amicable interview: and with some indulgence of forgery and theft, a surreptitious decree was procured, which transferred the synod, with its own consent, to that Italian city. Nine galleys were equipped for this service at Venice and in the isle of Candia; their diligence anticipated the slower vessels of Basel: the Roman admiral was commissioned to burn, sink, and destroy; and these priestly squadrons might have encountered each other in the same seas where Athens and Sparta had formerly contended for the pre-eminence of glory. Assaulted by the importunity of the factions, who were ready to fight for the possession of his person, Palæologus hesitated before he left his palace and country on a perilous experiment. His father's advice still dwelt on his memory; and reason must suggest, that, since the Latins were divided among themselves, they could never unite in a foreign cause. Sigismond dissuaded the unseasonable adventure; his advice was impartial, since he adhered to the council; and it was enforced by the strange belief that the German Cæsar would nominate a Greek his heir and successor in the empire of the West. Even the Turkish sultan was a counsellor whom it might be unsafe to trust, but whom it was dangerous to offend. Amurath was unskilled in the disputes, but he was apprehensive of the union, of the Christians. From his own treasures he offered to relieve the wants of the Byzantine court; yet he declared with seeming magnanimity that Constantinople should be secure and inviolate in the absence of her sovereign. The resolution of Palæologus was decided by the most splendid gifts and the most specious promises: he wished to escape for a while from a scene of danger and distress; and after dismissing with an ambiguous answer the messengers of the council, he declared his intention of embarking in the Roman galleys. The age of the patriarch Joseph was more susceptible of fear than of hope; he trembled at the perils of the sea, and expressed his apprehension that his feeble voice, with thirty perhaps of his orthodox brethren, would be oppressed in a foreign land by the power and numbers of a Latin synod. He yielded to the royal mandate, to the flattering assurance that he would be heard as the oracle of nations, and to the secret wish of learning from his brother of the West to deliver the church from the yoke of kings. The five *crossbearers,* or dignitaries, of St. Sophia, were bound to attend his person; and one of these, the great ecclesiarch or preacher, Sylvester Syropulus, has composed a free and curious history of the *false* union. Of the clergy that reluctantly obeyed the summons of the emperor and the patriarch, submission was the first duty, and patience the most useful virtue. In a chosen list of twenty bishops we discover the metropolitan titles of Heraclea and Cyzicus, Nice and Nicomedia, Ephesus and Trebizond, and the personal merit of Mark and Bessarion, who, in the confidence of their learning and eloquence, were promoted to the episcopal rank.

Some monks and philosophers were named to display the science and sanctity of the Greek church; and the service of the choir was performed by a select band of singers and musicians. The patriarchs of Alexandria, Antioch, and Jerusalem, appeared by their genuine or fictitious deputies; the primate of Russia represented a national church, and the Greeks might contend with the Latins in the extent of their spiritual empire. The precious vases of St. Sophia were exposed to the winds and waves, that the patriarch might officiate with becoming splendour: whatever gold the emperor could procure was expended in the massy ornaments of his bed and chariot; and while they affected to maintain the prosperity of their ancient fortune, they quarrelled for the division of fifteen thousand ducats, the first alms of the Roman pontiff. After the necessary preparations, John Palæologus, with a numerous train, accompanied by his brother Demetrius and the most respectable persons of the church and state, embarked in eight vessels with sails and oars, which steered through the Turkish straits of Gallipoli to the Archipelago, the Morea, and the Adriatic Gulf.

TEMPORARY UNION OF THE GREEKS AND LATINS

After a tedious and troublesome navigation of seventy-seven days, this religious squadron cast anchor before Venice; and their reception proclaimed the joy and magnificence of that powerful republic. In the command of the world the modest Augustus had never claimed such honours from his subjects as were paid to his feeble successor by an independent state. Seated on the poop, on a lofty throne, he received the visit, or, in the Greek style, the *adoration*, of the doge and senators. They sailed in the Bucentaur, which was accompanied by twelve stately galleys: the sea was overspread with innumerable gondolas of pomp and pleasure; the air resounded with music and acclamations; the mariners, and even the vessels, were dressed in silk and gold; and in all the emblems and pageants the Roman eagles were blended with the lions of St. Mark. The triumphal procession, ascending the great canal, passed under the bridge of the Rialto; and the Eastern strangers gazed with admiration on the palaces, the churches, and the populousness of a city that seems to float on the bosom of the waves. They sighed to behold the spoils and trophies with which it had been decorated after the sack of Constantinople. After an hospitable entertainment of fifteen days, Palæologus pursued his journey by land and water from Venice to Ferrara; and on this occasion the pride of the Vatican was tempered by policy to indulge the ancient dignity of the emperor of the East. He made his entry on a *black* horse; but a milk-white steed, whose trappings were embroidered with golden eagles, was led before him; and the canopy was borne over his head by the princes of Este, the sons or kinsmen of Nicholas, marquis of the city, and a sovereign more powerful than himself. Palæologus did not alight till he reached the bottom of the staircase: the pope advanced to the door of the apartment; refused his proffered genuflexion; and, after a paternal embrace, conducted the emperor to a seat on his left hand. Nor would the patriarch descend from his galley till a ceremony, almost equal, had been stipulated between the bishops of Rome and Constantinople. The latter was saluted by his brother with a kiss of union and charity; nor would any of the Greek ecclesiastics submit to kiss the feet of the Western primate. On the opening of the synod, the place of honour in the centre was claimed by the temporal and ecclesiastical chiefs;. and it was only by alleging that his predecessors had not assisted in person at Nice or Chalcedon that Eugenius could evade the ancient precedents of Constantine and Marcian. After much debate it was agreed that the right and left sides of the church should be occupied by the two nations; that the solitary chair of St. Peter should be raised the first of the Latin line; and that the throne of the Greek emperor, at the head of his clergy, should be equal and opposite to the second place, the vacant seat of the emperor of the West.[1]

But as soon as festivity and form had given place to a more serious treaty, the Greeks were dissatisfied with their journey, with themselves, and with the pope. The artful pencil of his emissaries had painted him in a prosperous state, at the head of the princes and prelates of Europe, obedient at his voice to believe and to arm. The thin appearance of the universal synod of Ferrara betrayed his weakness; and the Latins opened

---

[1] The Latin vulgar was provoked to laughter at the strange dresses of the Greeks, and especially the length of their garments, their sleeves, and their beards; nor was the emperor distinguished, except by the purple colour, and his diadem or tiara with a jewel on the top. Yet another spectator confesses that the Greek fashion was più grave e più degna than the Italian.

the first session with only five archbishops, eighteen bishops, and ten abbots, the greatest part of whom were the subjects or countrymen of the Italian pontiff. Except the duke of Burgundy, none of the potentates of the West condescended to appear in person, or by their ambassadors; nor was it possible to suppress the judicial acts of Basel against the dignity and person of Eugenius, which were finally concluded by a new election. Under these circumstances a truce or delay was asked and granted, till Palæologus could expect from the consent of the Latins some temporal reward for an unpopular union; and, after the first session, the public proceedings were adjourned above six months. The emperor, with a chosen band of his favourites and *Janizaries,* fixed his summer residence at a pleasant spacious monastery, six miles from Ferrara; forgot, in the pleasures of the chase, the distress of the church and state; and persisted in destroying the game, without listening to the just complaints of the marquis or the husbandman. In the meanwhile his unfortunate Greeks were exposed to all the miseries of exile and poverty; for the support of each stranger a monthly allowance was assigned of three or four gold florins, and, although the entire sum did not amount to seven hundred florins, a long arrear was repeatedly incurred by the indigence or policy of the Roman court.[1] They sighed for a speedy deliverance, but their escape was prevented by a triple chain; a passport from their superiors was required at the gates of Ferrara; the government of Venice had engaged to arrest and send back the fugitives, and inevitable punishment awaited them at Constantinople; excommunication, fines, and a sentence, which did not respect the sacerdotal dignity, that they should be stripped naked and publicly whipped. It was only by the alternative of hunger or dispute that the Greeks could be persuaded to open the first conference, and they yielded with extreme reluctance to attend from Ferrara to Florence the rear of a flying synod. This new translation was urged by inevitable necessity: the city was

---

[1] The Greeks obtained, with much difficulty, that, instead of provisions, money should be distributed, four florins *per* month to the persons of honourable rank, and three florins to their servants, with an addition of thirty more to the emperor, twenty-five to the patriarch, and twenty to the prince, or despot, Demetrius. The payment of the first month amounted to 691 florins, a sum which will not allow us to reckon above 200 Greeks of every condition. On the 20th October, 1438, there was an arrear of four months; in April, 1439, of three; and of five and a half in July, at the time of the union.

visited by the plague; the fidelity of the marquis might be suspected; the mercenary troops of the duke of Milan were at the gates, and, as they occupied Romagna, it was not without difficulty and danger that the pope, the emperor, and the bishops explored their way through the unfrequented paths of the Apennine.

Yet all these obstacles were surmounted by time and policy. The violence of the fathers of Basel rather promoted than injured the cause of Eugenius: the nations of Europe abhorred the schism, and disowned the election, of Felix the Fifth, who was successively a duke of Savoy, an hermit, and a pope; and the great princes were gradually reclaimed by his competitor to a favourable neutrality and a firm attachment. The legates, with some respectable members, deserted to the Roman army, which insensibly rose in numbers and reputation; the council of Basel was reduced to thirty-nine bishops and three hundred of the inferior clergy; while the Latins of Florence could produce the subscriptions of the pope himself, eight cardinals, two patriarchs, eight archbishops, fifty-two bishops, and forty-five abbots or chiefs of religious orders. After the labour of nine months and the debates of twenty-five sessions, they attained the advantage and glory of the reunion of the Greeks. Four principal questions had been agitated between the two churches: 1. The use of unleavened bread in the communion of Christ's body. 2. The nature of purgatory. 3. The supremacy of the pope. And, 4. The single or double procession of the Holy Ghost. The cause of either nation was managed by ten theological champions: the Latins were supported by the inexhaustible eloquence of Cardinal Julian, and Mark of Ephesus and Bessarion of Nice were the bold and able leaders of the Greek forces. We may bestow some praise on the progress of human reason, by observing that the first of these questions was *now* treated as an immaterial rite, which might innocently vary with the fashion of the age and country. With regard to the second, both parties were agreed in the belief of an intermediate state of purgation for the venial sins of the faithful; and whether their souls were purified by elemental fire was a doubtful point, which in a few years might be conveniently settled on the spot by the disputants. The claims of supremacy appeared of a more weighty and substantial kind, yet by the Orientals the Roman bishop had ever been respected as the first of the five patriarchs; nor did they scruple to admit that his jurisdiction should be exercised agreeably to the holy canons: a vague allowance, which might be defined or eluded by occasional convenience. The procession of the Holy Ghost from the Father alone, or from the Father and the Son, was an article of faith which had sunk much deeper into the minds of men; and in the sessions of Ferrara and Florence the Latin addition of *filioque* was subdivided into two questions, whether it were legal, and whether it were orthodox. Perhaps it may not be necessary to boast on this subject of my own impartial indifference: but I must think that the Greeks were strongly supported by the prohibition of the council of Chalcedon against adding any article whatsoever, to the creed of Nice, or rather of Constantinople.[1] In earthly affairs it is not easy to conceive how an assembly of legislators can bind their successors invested with powers equal to their own. But the dictates of inspiration must be true and unchangeable; nor should a private bishop or a provincial synod have presumed to innovate against the judgment of the Catholic church. On the substance of the doctrine the controversy was equal and endless; reason is confounded by the procession of a deity; the Gospel, which lay on the altar, was silent; the various texts of the fathers might be corrupted by fraud or entangled by sophistry; and the Greeks were ignorant of the characters and writings of the Latin saints.[2] Of this at least we may be sure, that neither side could be convinced by the arguments of their opponents. Prejudice may be enlightened by reason, and a superficial glance may be rectified by a clear and more perfect view of an object adopted to our faculties. But the bishops and monks had been taught from their infancy to repeat a form of mysterious words: their national and personal honour depended on the repetition of the same sounds, and their narrow minds were hardened and inflamed by the acrimony of a public dispute.

While they were lost in a cloud of dust and darkness, the pope and emperor were desirous of a seeming union, which

---

[1] The Greeks, who disliked the union, were unwilling to sally from this strong fortress. The shame of the Latins was aggravated by their producing an old MS. of the second council of Nice, with *filioque* in the Nicene creed. A palpable forgery!

[2] "When I go into a Latin church, I do not bow to the saints there because I do not know any of them." [Translation of a remark by Syropulus quoted by Gibbon in Greek.]

could alone accomplish the purposes of their interview; and
the obstinacy of public dispute was softened by the arts of
private and personal negotiation. The patriarch Joseph had
sunk under the weight of age and infirmities; his dying voice
breathed the counsels of charity and concord, and his vacant
benefice might tempt the hopes of the ambitious clergy. The
ready and active obedience of the archbishops of Russia and
Nice, of Isidore and Bessarion, was prompted and recompensed by their speedy promotion to the dignity of cardinals.
Bessarion, in the first debates, had stood forth the most strenuous and eloquent champion of the Greek church; and if the
apostate, the bastard, was reprobated by his country, he
appears in ecclesiastical story a rare example of a patriot who
was recommended to court favour by loud opposition and
well-timed compliance. With the aid of his two spiritual coadjutors, the emperor applied his arguments to the general situation and personal characters of the bishops, and each was
successively moved by authority and example. Their revenues
were in the hands of the Turks, their persons in those of the
Latins; an episcopal treasure, three robes and forty ducats,
was soon exhausted; the hopes of their return still depended
on the ships of Venice and the alms of Rome; and such was
their indigence, that their arrears, the payment of a debt,
would be accepted as a favour, and might operate as a bribe.
The danger and relief of Constantinople might excuse some
prudent and pious dissimulation; and it was insinuated that
the obstinate heretics who should resist the consent of the
East and West would be abandoned in a hostile land to the
revenge or justice of the Roman pontiff. In the first private
assembly of the Greeks the formulary of union was approved
by twenty-four, and rejected by twelve, members; but the five
crossbearers of St. Sophia, who aspired to represent the patriarch, were disqualified by ancient discipline, and their right
of voting was transferred to an obsequious train of monks,
grammarians, and profane laymen. The will of the monarch
produced a false and servile unanimity, and no more than two
patriots had courage to speak their own sentiments and those
of their country. Demetrius, the emperor's brother, retired
to Venice, that he might not be witness of the union; and
Mark of Ephesus, mistaking perhaps his pride for his conscience, disclaimed all communion with the Latin heretics,
and avowed himself the champion and confessor of the or-

thodox creed.[1] In the treaty between the two nations several
forms of consent were proposed, such as might satisfy the
Latins without dishonouring the Greeks; and they weighed the
scruples of words and syllables till the theological balance
trembled with a slight preponderance in favour of the Vatican.
It was agreed (I must entreat the attention of the reader) that
the Holy Ghost proceeds from the Father *and* the Son, as
from one principle and one substance; that he proceeds *by* the
Son, being of the same nature and substance; and that he
proceeds from the Father *and* the Son, by one *spiration* and
production. It is less difficult to understand the articles of the
preliminary treaty: that the pope should defray all the expenses of the Greeks in their return home; that he should
annually maintain two galleys and three hundred soldiers for
the defence of Constantinople; that all the ships which transported pilgrims to Jerusalem should be obliged to touch at
port; that as often as they were required, the pope should
furnish ten galleys for a year, or twenty for six months; and
that he should powerfully solicit the princes of Europe, if
the emperor had occasion for land-forces.

The same year, and almost the same day, were marked by
the deposition of Eugenius at Basel, and, at Florence, by his
reunion of the Greeks and Latins. In the former synod (which
he styled indeed an assembly of dæmons) the pope was branded with the guilt of simony, perjury, tyranny, heresy, and
schism; and declared to be incorrigible in his vices, unworthy
of any title, and incapable of holding any ecclesiastical office.
In the latter he was revered as the true and holy vicar of
Christ, who, after a separation of six hundred years, had reconciled the Catholics of the East and West in one fold, and
under one shepherd. The act of union was subscribed by the
pope, the emperor, and the principal members of both
churches; even by those who, like Syropulus, had been deprived of the right of voting. Two copies might have sufficed
for the East and West; but Eugenius was not satisfied unless
four authentic and similar transcripts were signed and attested
as the monuments of his victory. On a memorable day, the
sixth of July, the successors of St. Peter and Constantine
ascended their thrones; the two nations assembled in the

---

[1] I had forgot another popular and orthodox protester: a favourite hound,
who usually lay quiet on the foot-cloth of the emperor's throne, but who
barked most furiously while the act of union was reading, without being
silenced by the soothing or the lashes of the royal attendants.

cathedral of Florence; their representatives, Cardinal Julian, and Bessarion archbishop of Nice, appeared in the pulpit, and, after reading in the respective tongues the act of union, they mutually embraced in the name and the presence of their applauding brethren. The pope and his ministers then officiated according to the Roman liturgy; the creed was chanted with the addition of *filioque;* the acquiescence of the Greeks was poorly excused by their ignorance of the harmonious but inarticulate sounds; and the more scrupulous Latins refused any public celebration of the Byzantine rite. Yet the emperor and his clergy were not totally unmindful of national honour. The treaty was ratified by their consent: it was tacitly agreed that no innovation should be attempted in their creed or ceremonies; they spared and secretly respected the generous firmness of Mark of Ephesus, and, on the decease of the patriarch, they refused to elect his successor, except in the cathedral of St. Sophia. In the distribution of public and private rewards the liberal pontiff exceeded their hopes and his promises: the Greeks, with less pomp and pride, returned by the same road of Ferrara and Venice; and their reception at Constantinople was such as will be described in the following chapter. The success of the first trial encouraged Eugenius to repeat the same edifying scenes, and the deputies of the Armenians, the Maronites, the Jacobites of Syria and Egypt, the Nestorians, and the Ethiopians, were successively introduced to kiss the feet of the Roman pontiff, and to announce the obedience and the orthodoxy of the East. These Oriental embassies, unknown in the countries which they presumed to represent, diffused over the West the fame of Eugenius; and a clamour was artfully propagated against the remnant of a schism in Switzerland and Savoy which alone impeded the harmony of the Christian world. The vigour of opposition was succeeded by the lassitude of despair; the council of Basel was silently dissolved; and Felix, renouncing the tiara, again withdrew to the devout or delicious hermitage of Ripaille. A general peace was secured by mutual acts of oblivion and indemnity: all ideas of reformation subsided; the popes continued to exercise and abuse their ecclesiastical despotism; nor has Rome been since disturbed by the mischiefs of a contested election.

REVIVAL OF GREEK LEARNING IN ITALY

The journeys of three emperors were unavailing for their temporal, or perhaps their spiritual, salvation; but they were productive of a beneficial consequence, the revival of the Greek learning in Italy, from whence it was propagated to the last nations of the West and North. In their lowest servitude and depression, the subjects of the Byzantine throne were still possessed of a golden key that could unlock the treasures of antiquity, of a musical and prolific language that gives a soul to the objects of sense, and a body to the abstractions of philosophy. Since the barriers of the monarchy, and even of the capital, had been trampled under foot, the various barbarians had doubtless corrupted the form and substance of the national dialect; and ample glossaries have been composed, to interpret a multitude of words, of Arabic, Turkish, Sclavonian, Latin, or French origin. But a purer idiom was spoken in the court and taught in the college, and the flourishing state of the language is described, and perhaps embellished, by a learned Italian, who, by a long residence and noble marriage, was naturalised at Constantinople about thirty years before the Turkish conquest. "The vulgar speech," said Philelphus, "has been depraved by the people, and infected by the multitude of strangers and merchants, who every day flock to the city and mingle with the inhabitants. It is from the disciples of such a school that the Latin language received the versions of Aristotle and Plato, so obscure in sense, and in spirit so poor. But the Greeks, who have escaped the contagion, are those whom *we* follow, and they alone are worthy of our imitation. In familiar discourse they still speak the tongue of Aristophanes and Euripides, of the historians and philosophers of Athens; and the style of their writings is still more elaborate and correct. The persons who, by their birth and offices, are attached to the Byzantine court, are those who maintain, with the least alloy, the ancient standard of elegance and purity; and the native graces of language most conspicuously shine among the noble matrons, who are excluded from all intercourse with foreigners. With foreigners do I say? They live retired and sequestered from the eyes of their fellow-citizens. Seldom are they seen in the streets; and when they leave their houses, it is in the dusk of evening, on visits to the churches and their nearest kindred. On these occasions they are on horseback, covered with a veil, and encompassed by their parents, their husbands, or their servants."

Among the Greeks a numerous and opulent clergy was dedicated to the service of religion; their monks and bishops have ever been distinguished by the gravity and austerity of their manners, nor were they diverted, like the Latin priests, by the pursuits and pleasures of a secular and even military life. After a large deduction for the time and talents that were lost in the devotion, the laziness, and the discord of the church and cloister, the more inquisitive and ambitious minds would explore the sacred and profane erudition of their native language. The ecclesiastics presided over the education of youth: the schools of philosophy and eloquence were perpetuated till the fall of the empire; and it may be affirmed that more books and more knowledge were included within the walls of Constantinople than could be dispersed over the extensive countries of the West. But an important distinction has been already noticed: the Greeks were stationary or retrograde, while the Latins were advancing with a rapid and progressive motion. The nations were excited by the spirit of independence and emulation; and even the little world of the Italian states contained more people and industry than the decreasing circle of the Byzantine empire. In Europe the lower ranks of society were relieved from the yoke of feudal servitude; and freedom is the first step to curiosity and knowledge. The use, however rude and corrupt, of the Latin tongue had been preserved by superstition; the universities, from Bologna to Oxford,[1] were peopled with thousands of scholars; and their misguided ardour might be directed to more liberal and manly studies. In the resurrection of science Italy was the first that cast away her shroud; and the eloquent Petrarch, by his lessons and his example, may justly be applauded as the first harbinger of day. A purer style of composition, a more generous and rational strain of sentiment, flowed from the study and imitation of the writers of ancient Rome; and the disciples of Cicero and Virgil approached, with reverence and love, the

---

[1] At the end of the xvth century there existed in Europe about fifty universities, and of these the foundation of ten or twelve is prior to the year 1300. They were crowded in proportion to their scarcity. Bologna contained 10,000 students, chiefly of the civil law. In the year 1357 the number at Oxford had decreased from 30,000 to 6000 scholars. Yet even this decrease is much superior to the present list of the members of the university.

sanctuary of their Grecian masters. In the sack of Constantinople the French, and even the Venetians, had despised and destroyed the works of Lysippus and Homer; the monuments of art may be annihilated by a single blow, but the immortal mind is renewed and multiplied by the copies of the pen, and such copies it was the ambition of Petrarch and his friends to possess and understand. The arms of the Turks undoubtedly pressed the flight of the Muses: yet we may tremble at the thought that Greece might have been overwhelmed, with her schools and libraries, before Europe had emerged from the deluge of barbarism; that the seeds of science might have been scattered by the winds before the Italian soil was prepared for their cultivation.

The most learned Italians of the fifteenth century have confessed and applauded the restoration of Greek literature, after a long oblivion of many hundred years. Yet in that country, and beyond the Alps, some names are quoted; some profound scholars who, in the darker ages, were honourably distinguished by their knowledge of the Greek tongue; and national vanity has been loud in the praise of such rare examples of erudition. Without scrutinising the merit of individuals, truth must observe that their science is without a cause and without an effect; that it was easy for them to satisfy themselves and their more ignorant contemporaries; and that the idiom, which they had so marvellously acquired, was transcribed in few manuscripts, and was not taught in any university of the West. In a corner of Italy it faintly existed as the popular, or at least as the ecclesiastical, dialect. The first impression of the Doric and Ionic colonies has never been completely erased; the Calabrian churches were long attached to the throne of Constantinople; and the monks of St. Basil pursued their studies in Mount Athos and the schools of the East. Calabria was the native country of Barlaam, who has already appeared as a sectary and an ambassador; and Barlaam was the first who revived, beyond the Alps, the memory, or at least the writings, of Homer. He is described, by Petrarch and Boccace, as a man of diminutive stature, though truly great in the measure of learning and genius: of a piercing discernment, though of a slow and painful elocution. For many ages (as they affirm) Greece had not produced his equal in the knowledge of history, grammar, and philosophy; and his merit was celebrated in the attestations of the princes and doctors of Constantinople. One of these attestations is still extant; and the emperor Cantacuzene, the protector of his adversaries, is forced to allow that Euclid, Aristotle, and Plato were familiar to that profound and subtle logician. In the court of Avignon he formed an intimate connection with Petrarch, the first of the Latin scholars; and the desire of mutual instruction was the principle of their literary commerce. The Tuscan applied himself with eager curiosity and assiduous diligence to the study of the Greek language; and in a laborious struggle with the dryness and difficulty of the first rudiments he began to reach the sense, and to feel the spirit, of poets and philosophers whose minds were congenial to his own. But he was soon deprived of the society and lessons of this useful assistant; Barlaam relinquished his fruitless embassy, and, on his return to Greece, he rashly provoked the swarms of fanatic monks, by attempting to substitute the light of reason to that of their navel. After a separation of three years the two friends again met in the court of Naples; but the generous pupil renounced the fairest occasion of improvement; and by his recommendation Barlaam was finally settled in a small bishopric of his native Calabria. The manifold avocations of Petrarch, love and friendship, his various correspondence and frequent journeys, the Roman laurel, and his elaborate compositions in prose and verse, in Latin and Italian, diverted him from a foreign idiom; and as he advanced in life the attainment of the Greek language was the object of his wishes rather than of his hopes. When he was about fifty years of age, a Byzantine ambassador, his friend and a master of both tongues, presented him with a copy of Homer, and the answer of Petrarch is at once expressive of his eloquence, gratitude, and regret. After celebrating the generosity of the donor, and the value of a gift more precious in his estimation than gold or rubies, he thus proceeds:—"Your present of the genuine and original text of the divine poet, the fountain of all invention, is worthy of yourself and of me; you have fulfilled your promise, and satisfied my desires. Yet your liberality is still imperfect: with Homer you should have given me yourself; a guide who could lead me into the fields of light, and disclose to my wondering eyes the specious miracles of the Iliad and Odyssey. But, alas! Homer is dumb, or I am deaf; nor is it in my power to enjoy the beauty which I possess. I have seated him by the side of Plato, the prince of poets near the prince

of philosophers, and I glory in the sight of my illustrious
guests. Of their immortal writings, whatever had been translated into the Latin idiom I had already acquired; but if there
be no profit, there is some pleasure, in beholding these venerable Greeks in their proper and national habit. I am delighted
with the aspect of Homer; and as often as I embrace the
silent volume, I exclaim with a sigh, Illustrious bard! with
what pleasure should I listen to thy song, if my sense of hearing were not obstructed and lost by the death of one friend,
and in the much lamented absence of another! Nor do I yet
despair, and the example of Cato suggests some comfort and
hope, since it was in the last period of age that he attained
the knowledge of the Greek letters."

The prize which eluded the efforts of Petrarch was obtained
by the fortune and industry of his friend Boccace, the father
of the Tuscan prose. That popular writer, who derives his
reputation from the Decameron, an hundred novels of pleasan-
try and love, may aspire to the more serious praise of restoring
in Italy the study of the Greek language. In the year one
thousand three hundred and sixty a disciple of Barlaam,
whose name was Leo or Leontius Pilatus, was detained in
his way to Avignon by the advice and hospitality of Boccace,
who lodged the stranger in his house, prevailed on the republic of Florence to allow him an annual stipend, and devoted
his leisure to the first Greek professor, who taught that language in the Western countries of Europe. The appearance of
Leo might disgust the most eager disciple: he was clothed
in the mantle of a philosopher or a mendicant; his countenance
was hideous; his face was overshadowed with black hair;
his beard long and uncombed; his deportment rustic; his
temper gloomy and inconstant; nor could he grace his discourse with the ornaments or even the perspicuity of Latin
elocution. But his mind was stored with a treasure of Greek
learning: history and fable, philosophy and grammar, were
alike at his command; and he read the poems of Homer in
the schools of Florence. It was from his explanation that Boccace composed and transcribed a literal prose version of the
Iliad and Odyssey, which satisfied the thirst of his friend
Petrarch, and which, perhaps in the succeeding century, was
clandestinely used by Laurentius Valla, the Latin interpreter.
It was from his narratives that the same Boccace collected
the materials for his treatise on the genealogy of the heathen

gods, a work, in that age, of stupendous erudition, and which he ostentatiously sprinkled with Greek characters and passages, to excite the wonder and applause of his more ignorant readers. The first steps of learning are slow and laborious; no more than ten votaries of Homer could be enumerated in all Italy, and neither Rome, nor Venice, nor Naples, could add a single name to this studious catalogue. But their numbers would have multiplied, their progress would have been accelerated, if the inconstant Leo, at the end of three years, had not relinquished an honourable and beneficial station. In his passage Petrarch entertained him at Padua a short time: he enjoyed the scholar, but was justly offended with the gloomy and unsocial temper of the man. Discontented with the world and with himself, Leo depreciated his present enjoyments, while absent persons and objects were dear to his imagination. In Italy he was a Thessalian, in Greece a native of Calabria; in the company of the Latins he disdained their language, religion, and manners; no sooner was he landed at Constantinople than he again sighed for the wealth of Venice and the elegance of Florence. His Italian friends were deaf to his importunity: he depended on their curiosity and indulgence, and embarked on a second voyage; but on his entrance into the Adriatic the ship was assailed by a tempest, and the unfortunate teacher, who like Ulysses had fastened himself to the mast, was struck dead by a flash of lightning. The humane Petrarch dropped a tear on his disaster; but he was most anxious to learn whether some copy of Euripides or Sophocles might not be saved from the hands of the mariners.

But the faint rudiments of Greek learning, which Petrarch had encouraged and Boccace had planted, soon withered and expired. The succeeding generation was content for a while with the improvement of Latin eloquence; nor was it before the end of the fourteenth century that a new and perpetual flame was rekindled in Italy. Previous to his own journey, the emperor Manuel despatched his envoys and orators to implore the compassion of the Western princes. Of these envoys the most conspicuous, or the most learned, was Manuel Chrysoloras, of noble birth, and whose Roman ancestors are supposed to have migrated with the great Constantine. After visiting the courts of France and England, where he obtained some contributions and more promises, the envoy was invited to assume the office of a professor; and Florence had again

the honour of this second invitation. By his knowledge, not
only of the Greek but of the Latin tongue, Chrysoloras deserved the stipend and surpassed the expectation of the republic. His school was frequented by a crowd of disciples of
every rank and age; and one of these, in a general history, has
described his motives and his success. "At that time," said
Leonard Aretin, "I was a student of the civil law; but my soul
was inflamed with the love of letters, and I bestowed some
application on the sciences of logic and rhetoric. On the
arrival of Manuel I hesitated whether I should desert my legal
studies or relinquish this golden opportunity; and thus, in the
ardour of youth, I communed with my own mind—Wilt thou
be wanting to thyself and thy fortune? Wilt thou refuse to
be introduced to a familiar converse with Homer, Plato, and
Demosthenes? with those poets, philosophers, and orators,
of whom such wonders are related, and who are celebrated
by every age as the great masters of human science? Of professors and scholars in civil law, a sufficient supply will always
be found in our universities; but a teacher, and such a teacher
of the Greek language, if he once be suffered to escape, may
never afterwards be retrieved. Convinced by these reasons,
I gave myself to Chrysoloras, and so strong was my passion,
that the lessons which I had imbibed in the day were the constant subject of my nightly dreams." At the same time and
place the Latin classics were explained by John of Ravenna,
the domestic pupil of Petrarch: the Italians, who illustrated
their age and country, were formed in this double school, and
Florence became the fruitful seminary of Greek and Roman
erudition. The presence of the emperor recalled Chrysoloras
from the college to the court; but he afterwards taught at
Pavia and Rome with equal industry and applause. The remainder of his life, about fifteen years, was divided between
Italy and Constantinople, between embassies and lessons. In
the noble office of enlightening a foreign nation, the grammarian was not unmindful of a more sacred duty to his prince
and country; and Manuel Chrysoloras died at Constance on
a public mission from the emperor to the council.

After his example, the restoration of the Greek letters in
Italy was prosecuted by a series of emigrants, who were destitute of fortune and endowed with learning, or at least with
language. From the terror or oppression of the Turkish arms,
the natives of Thessalonica and Constantinople escaped to a

land of freedom, curiosity, and wealth. The synod introduced into Florence the lights of the Greek church and the oracles of the Platonic philosophy; and the fugitives who adhered to the union had the double merit of renouncing their country, not only for the Christian but for the Catholic cause. A patriot, who sacrifices his party and conscience to the allurements of favour, may be possessed however of the private and social virtues: he no longer hears the reproachful epithets of slave and apostate, and the consideration which he acquires among his new associates will restore in his own eyes the dignity of his character. The prudent conformity of Bessarion was rewarded with the Roman purple: he fixed his residence in Italy, and the Greek cardinal, the titular patriarch of Constantinople, was respected as the chief and protector of his nation: his abilities were exercised in the legations of Bologna, Venice, Germany, and France; and his election to the chair of St. Peter floated for a moment on the uncertain breath of a conclave.[1] His ecclesiastical honours diffused a splendour and pre-eminence over his literary merit and service; his palace was a school; as often as the cardinal visited the Vatican he was attended by a learned train of both nations; of men applauded by themselves and the public, and whose writings, now overspread with dust, were popular and useful in their own times. I shall not attempt to enumerate the restorers of Grecian literature in the fifteenth century; and it may be sufficient to mention with gratitude the names of Theodore Gaza, of George of Trebizond, of John Argyropulus, and Demetrius Chalcondyles, who taught their native language in the schools of Florence and Rome. Their labours were not inferior to those of Bessarion, whose purple they revered, and whose fortune was the secret object of their envy. But the lives of these grammarians were humble and obscure; they had declined the lucrative paths of the church; their dress and manners secluded them from the commerce of the world; and since they were confined to the merit, they might be content with the rewards of learning. From this character Janus Lascaris will deserve an exception. His eloquence, politeness, and Imperial descent, recommended him to the French monarchs; and in the same cities he was alternately employed to

---

[1] The cardinals knocked at his door, but his conclavist refused to interrupt the studies of Bessarion; "Nicholas," said he, "thy respect has cost thee an hat, and me the tiara."

teach and to negociate. Duty and interest prompted them to cultivate the study of the Latin language, and the most successful attained the faculty of writing and speaking with fluency and elegance in a foreign idiom. But they ever retained the inveterate vanity of their country: their praise, or at least their esteem, was reserved for the national writers to whom they owed their fame and subsistence; and they sometimes betrayed their contempt in licentious criticism or satire on Virgil's poetry and the oratory of Tully. The superiority of these masters arose from the familiar use of a living language; and their first disciples were incapable of discerning how far they had degenerated from the knowledge and even the practice of their ancestors. A vicious pronunciation,[1] which they introduced, was banished from the schools by the reason of the succeeding age. Of the power of the Greek accents they were ignorant; and those musical notes, which, from an Attic tongue and to an Attic ear, must have been the secret soul of harmony, were to their eyes, as to our own, no more than mute and unmeaning marks, in prose superfluous and troublesome in verse. The art of grammar they truly possessed; the valuable fragments of Apollonius and Herodian were transfused into their lessons; and their treatises of syntax and etymology, though devoid of philosophic spirit, are still useful to the Greek student. In the shipwreck of the Byzantine libraries each fugitive seized a fragment of treasure, a copy of some author, who, without his industry, might have perished: the transcripts were multiplied by an assiduous and sometimes an elegant pen, and the text was corrected and explained by their own comments or those of the elder scholiasts. The sense, though not the spirit, of the Greek classics was interpreted to the Latin world: the beauties of style evaporate in a version; but the judgment of Theodore Gaza selected the more solid works of Aristotle and Theophrastus, and their natural

---

[1] Manuel Chrysoloras and his colleagues are accused of ignorance, envy, or avarice. The modern Greeks pronounce the β as a V consonant, and confound three vowels ⟨η ι υ⟩ and several diphthongs. Such was the vulgar pronunciation which the stern Gardiner maintained by penal statutes in the university of Cambridge; but the monosyllable βη represented to an Attic ear the bleating of sheep, and a bellwether is better evidence than a bishop or a chancellor. The treatises of those scholars, particularly Erasmus, who asserted a more classical pronunciation, are collected in the Sylloge of Havercamp; but it is difficult to paint sounds by words; and, in their reference to modern use, they can be understood only by their respective countrymen. We may observe that our peculiar pronunciation of the θ, th, is approved by Erasmus.

histories of animals and plants opened a rich fund of genuine and experimental science.

Yet the fleeting shadows of metaphysics were pursued with more curiosity and ardour. After a long oblivion, Plato was revived in Italy by a venerable Greek,[1] who taught in the house of Cosmo of Medicis. While the synod of Florence was involved in theological debate, some beneficial consequences might flow from the study of his elegant philosophy: his style is the purest standard of the Attic dialect, and his sublime thoughts are sometimes adapted to familiar conversation, and sometimes adorned with the richest colours of poetry and eloquence. The dialogues of Plato are a dramatic picture of life and death of a sage; and, as often as he descends from the clouds, his moral system inculcates the love of truth, of our country, and of mankind. The precept and examples of Socrates recommended a modest doubt and liberal inquiry; and if the Platonists, with blind devotion, adored the visions and errors of their divine master, their enthusiasm might correct the dry, dogmatic method of the Peripatetic school. So equal, yet so opposite, are the merits of Plato and Aristotle, that they may be balanced in endless controversy, but some spark of freedom may be produced by the collision of adverse servitude. The modern Greeks were divided between the two sects: with more fury than skill they fought under the banner of their leaders, and the field of battle was removed in their flight from Constantinople to Rome. But this philosophical debate soon degenerated into an angry and personal quarrel of grammarians; and Bessarion, though an advocate for Plato, protected the national honour by interposing the advice and authority of a mediator. In the gardens of the Medici the academical doctrine was enjoyed by the polite and learned; but their philosophic society was quickly dissolved; and if the writings of the Attic sage were perused in the closet, the more powerful Stagyrite continued to reign the oracle of the church and school.

POPE NICHOLAS V

I have fairly represented the literary merits of the Greeks; yet it must be confessed that they were seconded and sur-

---

[1] George Gemistus Pletho, a various and voluminous writer, the master of Bessarion, and all the Platonists of the times. He visited Italy in his old age, and soon returned to end his days in Peloponnesus.

passed by the ardour of the Latins. Italy was divided into many independent states; and at that time it was the ambition of princes and republics to vie with each other in the encouragement and reward of literature. The fame of Nicholas the Fifth has not been adequate to his merits. From a plebeian origin he raised himself by his virtue and learning: the character of the man prevailed over the interest of the pope, and he sharpened those weapons which were soon pointed against the Roman church. He had been the friend of the most eminent scholars of the age: he became their patron; and such was the humility of his manners, that the change was scarcely discernible either to them or to himself. If he pressed the acceptance of a liberal gift, it was not as the measure of desert, but as the proof of benevolence; and when modest merit declined his bounty, "Accept it," would he say, with a consciousness of his own worth: "you will not always have a Nicholas among ye." The influence of the holy see pervaded Christendom; and he exerted that influence in the search, not of benefices, but of books. From the ruins of the Byzantine libraries, from the darkest monasteries of Germany and Britain, he collected the dusty manuscripts of the writers of antiquity; and wherever the original could not be removed, a faithful copy was transcribed and transmitted for his use. The Vatican, the old repository for bulls and legends, for superstition and forgery, was daily replenished with more precious furniture; and such was the industry of Nicholas, that in a reign of eight years he formed a library of five thousand volumes. To his munificence the Latin world was indebted for the versions of Xenophon, Diodorus, Polybius, Thucydides, Herodotus, and Appian; of Strabo's Geography, of the Iliad, of the most valuable works of Plato and Aristotle, of Ptolemy and Theophrastus, and of the fathers of the Greek church. The example of the Roman pontiff was preceded or imitated by a Florentine merchant, who governed the republic without arms and without a title. Cosmo of Medicis was the father of a line of princes whose name and age are almost synonymous with the restoration of learning: his credit was ennobled into fame; his riches were dedicated to the service of mankind; he corresponded at once with Cairo and London; and a cargo of Indian spices and Greek books was often imported in the same vessel. The genius and education of his grandson Lorenzo rendered him not only a patron but a judge and candidate in the literary race. In his palace, distress was entitled to relief, and merit to reward: his leisure hours were delightfully spent in the Platonic academy; he encouraged the emulation of Demetrius Chalcondyles and Angelo Politian; and his active missionary Janus Lascaris returned from the East with a treasure of two hundred manuscripts, fourscore of which were as yet unknown in the libraries of Europe. The rest of Italy was animated by a similar spirit, and the progress of the nation repaid the liberality of her princes. The Latins held the exclusive property of their own literature; and these disciples of Greece were soon capable of transmitting and improving the lessons which they had imbibed. After a short succession of foreign teachers, the tide of emigration subsided; but the language of Constantinople was spread beyond the Alps, and the natives of France, Germany, and England [1] imparted to their country the sacred fire which they had kindled in the schools of Florence and Rome. In the productions of the mind, as in those of the soil, the gifts of nature are excelled by industry and skill: the Greek authors, forgotten on the banks of the Ilissus, have been illustrated on those of the Elbe and the Thames; and Bessarion or Gaza might have envied the superior science of the barbarians, the accuracy of Budæus, the taste of Erasmus, the copiousness of Stephens, the erudition of Scaliger, the discernment of Reiske or of Bentley. On the side of the Latins the discovery of printing was a casual advantage; but this useful art has been applied by Aldus and his innumerable successors to perpetuate and multiply the works of antiquity.[2] A single manuscript imported from Greece is revived in ten thousand copies, and each copy is fairer than the original. In this form Homer and Plato would peruse with more satis-

---

[1] The Greek language was introduced into the university of Oxford in the last years of the xvth century by Grocyn, Linacer, and Latimer, who had all studied at Florence under Demetrius Chalcondyles. See Dr. Knight's curious Life of Erasmus. Although a stout academical patriot, he is forced to acknowledge that Erasmus learned Greek at Oxford, and taught it at Cambridge.

[2] The press of Aldus Manutius, a Roman, was established at Venice about the year 1494: he printed above sixty considerable works of Greek literature, almost all for the first time; several containing different treatises and authors, and of several authors two, three, or four editions. Yet his glory must not tempt us to forget that the first Greek books, the Grammar of Constantine Lascaris, was printed at Milan in 1476, and that the Florence Homer of 1488 displays all the luxury of the typographical art. See the Annales Typographici of Maittaire, and the Bibliographie Instructive of De Bure, a knowing bookseller of Paris.

faction their own writings; and their scholiasts must resign
the prize to the labours of our Western editors.

USE AND ABUSE OF ANCIENT LEARNING

Before the revival of classic literature the barbarians in
Europe were immersed in ignorance; and their vulgar tongues
were marked with the rudeness and poverty of their manners.
The students of the more perfect idioms of Rome and Greece
were introduced to a new world of light and science; to the
society of the free and polished nations of antiquity; and to
a familiar converse with those immortal men who spoke the
sublime language of eloquence and reason. Such an intercourse must tend to refine the taste and to elevate the genius
of the moderns; and yet, from the first experiment, it might
appear that the study of the ancients had given fetters, rather
than wings, to the human mind. However laudable, the spirit
of imitation is of a servile cast; and the first disciples of the
Greeks and Romans were a colony of strangers in the midst
of their age and country. The minute and laborious diligence
which explored the antiquities of remote times might have
improved or adorned the present state of society; the critic
and metaphysician were the slaves of Aristotle; the poets,
historians, and orators were proud to repeat the thoughts
and words of the Augustan age: the works of nature were
observed with the eyes of Pliny and Theophrastus; and some
Pagan votaries professed a secret devotion to the gods of
Homer and Plato.[1] The Italians were oppressed by the strength
and number of their ancient auxiliaries: the century after the
deaths of Petrarch and Boccace was filled with a crowd of
Latin imitators, who decently repose on our shelves; but in
that era of learning it will not be easy to discern a real discovery of science, a work of invention or eloquence, in the
popular language of the country. But as soon as it had been

---

[1] I will select three singular examples of this classic enthusiasm. 1. At the
synod of Florence, Gemistus Pletho said, in familiar conversation, to George
of Trebizond, that in a short time mankind would unanimously renounce the
Gospel and the Koran for a religion similar to that of the Gentiles. 2. Paul
II. persecuted the Roman academy, which had been founded by Pomponius
Lætus; and the principal members were accused of heresy, impiety, and
paganism. 3. In the next century some scholars and poets in France celebrated
the success of Jodelle's tragedy of Cleopatra by a festival of Bacchus, and, as
it is said, by the sacrifice of a goat. Yet the spirit of bigotry might often
discern a serious impiety in the sportive play of fancy and learning.

deeply saturated with the celestial dew, the soil was quickened into vegetation and life; the modern idioms were refined; the classics of Athens and Rome inspired a pure taste and a generous emulation; and in Italy, as afterwards in France and England, the pleasing reign of poetry and fiction was succeeded by the light of speculative and experimental philosophy: Genius may anticipate the season of maturity; but in the education of a people, as in that of an individual, memory must be exercised before the powers of reason and fancy can be expanded: nor may the artist hope to equal or surpass, till he has learned to imitate, the works of his predecessors.

The Union of the churches achieved at the Council of Florence was soon followed by the final schism of the Greek church (1440–1448). The operations of Ladislaus king of Poland and Hungary and the revolts of John Huniades and Scanderbeg hampered the Turks but could not hold off the final issue. Constantine Palæologus became, as it proved, the last Roman emperor in Constantinople, from 1448–1453. These events are described by Gibbon in Chapter 67.

68.

CHARACTER AND REIGN OF MAHOMET II. HIS SIEGE
AND CAPTURE OF CONSTANTINOPLE. HIS ENTRY INTO
THE CITY. GRIEF AND TERROR OF EUROPE

THE SIEGE of Constantinople by the Turks attracts our first
attention to the person and character of the great destroyer.
Mahomet the Second was the son of the second Amurath;
and though his mother has been decorated with the titles of
Christian and princess, she is more probably confounded with
the numerous concubines who peopled from every climate
the harem of the sultan. His first education and sentiments
were those of a devout Musulman; and as often as he con-
versed with an infidel he purified his hands and face by the
legal rites of ablution. Age and empire appear to have relaxed
this narrow bigotry: his aspiring genius disdained to acknowledge a power above his own; and in his looser hours he presumed (it is said) to brand the prophet of Mecca as a robber
and impostor. Yet the sultan persevered in a decent reverence
for the doctrine and discipline of the Koran: his private indiscretion must have been sacred from the vulgar ear; and
we should suspect the credulity of strangers and sectaries, so
prone to believe that a mind which is hardened against truth
must be armed with superior contempt for absurdity and
error. Under the tuition of the most skilful masters Mahomet
advanced with an early and rapid progress in the paths of
knowledge; and besides his native tongue it is affirmed that
he spoke or understood five languages, the Arabic, the Persian,
the Chaldæan or Hebrew, the Latin, and the Greek. The
Persian might indeed contribute to his amusement, and the
Arabic to his edification; and such studies are familiar to
the Oriental youth. In the intercourse of the Greeks and
Turks a conqueror might wish to converse with the people
over whom he was ambitious to reign: his own praises in
Latin poetry or prose might find a passage to the royal ear;

but what use or merit could recommend to the statesman or the scholar the uncouth dialect of his Hebrew slaves? The history and geography of the world were familiar to his memory: the lives of the heroes of the East, perhaps of the West, excited his emulation: his skill in astrology is excused by the folly of the times, and supposes some rudiments of mathematical science; and a profane taste for the arts is betrayed in his liberal invitation and reward of the painters of Italy.[1] But the influences of religion and learning were employed without effect on his savage and licentious nature. I will not transcribe, nor do I firmly believe, the stories of his fourteen pages whose bellies were ripped open in search of a stolen melon, or of the beauteous slave whose head he severed from her body to convince the Janizaries that their master was not the votary of love.[2] His sobriety is attested by the silence of the Turkish annals, which accuse three, and three only, of the Ottoman line of the vice of drunkenness.[3] But it cannot be denied that his passions were at once furious and inexorable; that in the palace, as in the field, a torrent of blood was spilt on the slightest provocation; and that the noblest of the captive youth were often dishonoured by his unnatural lust. In the Albanian war he studied the lessons, and soon surpassed the example, of his father; and the conquest of two empires, twelve kingdoms, and two hundred cities, a vain and flattering account, is ascribed to his invincible sword. He was doubtless a soldier, and possibly a general; Constantinople has sealed his glory; but if we compare the means, the obstacles, and the achievements, Mahomet the Second must blush to sustain a parallel with Alexander or Timour. Under his command the Ottoman forces were always more numerous than their enemies, yet their progress was bounded by the Euphrates and the Adriatic, and his arms were checked by Huniades and Scanderbeg, by the Rhodian knights, and by the Persian king.

In the reign of Amurath he twice tasted of royalty, and

---

[1] The famous Gentile Bellino, whom he had invited from Venice, was dismissed with a chain and collar of gold and a purse of 300 ducats. With Voltaire I laugh at the foolish story of a slave purposely beheaded to instruct the painter in the action of the muscles.

[2] Dr. Johnson's *Irene* is founded on this story. Gibbon's doubts have been confirmed by later writers. Bury points out the story is found in Seneca's (b. 55 B.C.) *Controversiæ*, x. 5.—D.M.L.

[3] These Imperial drunkards were Soliman I., Selim II., and Amurath IV. The sophis of Persia can produce a more regular succession; and in the last age our European travellers were the witnesses and companions of their revels.

twice descended from the throne: his tender age was incapable of opposing his father's restoration, but never could he forgive the vizirs who had recommended that salutary measure. His nuptials were celebrated with the daughter of a Turkman emir; and, after a festival of two months, he departed from Adrianople with his bride to reside in the government of Magnesia. Before the end of six weeks he was recalled by a sudden message from the divan which announced the decease of Amurath and the mutinous spirit of the Janizaries. His speed and vigour commanded their obedience: he passed the Hellespont with a chosen guard: and at the distance of a mile from Adrianople the vizirs and emirs, the imams and cadhis, the soldiers and the people, fell prostrate before the new sultan. They affected to weep, they affected to rejoice: he ascended the throne at the age of twenty-one years, and removed the cause of sedition by the death, the inevitable death, of his infant brothers. The ambassadors of Europe and Asia soon appeared to congratulate his accession and solicit his friendship, and to all he spoke the language of moderation and peace. The confidence of the Greek emperor was revived by the solemn oaths and fair assurances with which he sealed the ratification of the treaty: and a rich domain on the banks of the Strymon was assigned for the annual payment of three hundred thousand aspers, the pension of an Ottoman prince who was detained at his request in the Byzantine court. Yet the neighbours of Mahomet might tremble at the severity with which a youthful monarch reformed the pomp of his father's household: the expenses of luxury were applied to those of ambition, and an useless train of seven thousand falconers was either dismissed from his service or enlisted in his troops. In the first summer of his reign he visited with an army the Asiatic provinces; but after humbling the pride Mahomet accepted the submission of the Caramanian, that he might not be diverted by the smallest obstacle from the execution of his great design.

Mahomet built a fortress at Asomaton on the Bosphorus and made preparations for the siege of Constantinople. A cannon was constructed of tremendous power. Meanwhile the emperor Constantine Palæologus tried unsuccessfully to attract help from the West.

THE SIEGE OF CONSTANTINOPLE

Of the triangle which composes the figure of Constantinople the two sides along the sea were made inaccessible to an enemy; the Propontis by nature, and the harbour by art. Between the two waters, the basis of the triangle, the land side was protected by a double wall and a deep ditch of the depth of one hundred feet. Against this line of fortification, which Phranza, an eye-witness, prolongs to the measure of six miles, the Ottomans directed their principal attack; the emperor, after distributing the service and command of the most perilous stations, undertook the defence of the external wall. In the first days of the siege the Greek soldiers descended into the ditch, or sallied into the field; but they soon discovered that, in the proportion of their numbers, one Christian was of more value than twenty Turks: and, after these bold preludes, they were prudently content to maintain the rampart with their missile weapons. Nor should this prudence be accused of pusillanimity. The nation was indeed pusillanimous and base; but the last Constantine deserves the name of an hero: his noble band of volunteers was inspired with Roman virtue; and the foreign auxiliaries supported the honour of the Western chivalry. The incessant volleys of lances and arrows were accompanied with the smoke, the sound, and the fire of their musketry and cannon. Their small arms discharged at the same time either five, or even ten, balls of lead, of the size of a walnut; and, according to the closeness of the ranks and the force of the powder, several breastplates and bodies were transpierced by the same shot. But the Turkish approaches were soon sunk in trenches or covered with ruins. Each day added to the science of the Christians; but their inadequate stock of gunpowder was wasted in the operations of each day. Their ordnance was not powerful either in size or number; and if they possessed some heavy cannon, they feared to plant them on the walls, lest the aged structure should be shaken and overthrown by the explosion. The same destructive secret had been revealed to the Moslems; by whom it was employed with the superior energy of zeal, riches, and despotism. The great cannon of Mahomet has been separately noticed; an important and visible object in the history of the times: but that enormous engine was flanked by two fellows almost of equal magnitude: the long order of the Turkish artillery was pointed against the walls; fourteen batteries thundered at once on the most accessible places; and of one of these it is ambiguously expressed that it was mounted with one hundred and thirty guns, or that it discharged one hundred and thirty bullets. Yet in the power and activity of the sultan we may discern the infancy of the new science. Under a master who counted the moments the great cannon could be loaded and fired no more than seven times in one day. The heated metal unfortunately burst; several workmen were destroyed; and the skill of an artist was admired who bethought himself of preventing the danger and the accident, by pouring oil, after each explosion, into the mouth of the cannon.

The first random shots were productive of more sound than effect; and it was by the advice of a Christian that the engineers were taught to level their aim against the two opposite sides of the salient angles of a bastion. However imperfect, the weight and repetition of the fire made some impression on the walls; and the Turks, pushing their approaches to the edge of the ditch, attempted to fill the enormous chasm and to build a road to the assault. Innumerable fascines, and hogsheads, and trunks of trees, were heaped on each other; and such was the impetuosity of the throng, that the foremost and the weakest were pushed headlong down the precipice and instantly buried under the accumulated mass. To fill the ditch was the toil of the besiegers; to clear away the rubbish was the safety of the besieged; and, after a long and bloody conflict, the web that had been woven in the day was still unravelled in the night. The next resource of Mahomet was the practice of mines; but the soil was rocky; in every attempt he was stopped and undermined by the Christian engineers; nor had the art been yet invented of replenishing those subterraneous passages with gunpowder and blowing whole towers and cities into the air. A circumstance that distinguishes the siege of Constantinople is the reunion of the ancient and modern artillery. The cannon were intermingled with the mechanical engines for casting stones and darts; the bullet and the battering-ram were directed against the same walls; nor had the discovery of gunpowder superseded the use of the liquid and unextinguishable fire. A wooden turret of the largest size was advanced on rollers:

this portable magazine of ammunition and fascines was protected by a threefold covering of bulls' hides; incessant volleys
were securely discharged from the loopholes; in the front
three doors were contrived for the alternate sally and retreat
of the soldiers and workmen. They ascended by a staircase to
the upper platform, and, as high as the level of that platform,
a scaling-ladder could be raised by pulleys to form a bridge
and grapple with the adverse rampart. By these various arts
of annoyance, some as new as they were pernicious to the
Greeks, the tower of St. Romanus was at length overturned:
after a severe struggle the Turks were repulsed from the
breach and interrupted by darkness; but they trusted that
with the return of light they should renew the attack with
fresh vigour and decisive success. Of this pause of action,
this interval of hope, each moment was improved by the
activity of the emperor and Justiniani, who passed the night
on the spot, and urged the labours which involved the safety
of the church and city. At the dawn of day the impatient sultan perceived, with astonishment and grief, that his wooden
turret had been reduced to ashes: the ditch was cleared and
restored, and the tower of St. Romanus was again strong and
entire. He deplored the failure of his design, and uttered a
profane exclamation, that the word of the thirty-seven thousand prophets should not have compelled him to believe that
such a work, in so short a time, could have been accomplished by the infidels.

The generosity of the Christian princes was cold and tardy;
but in the first apprehension of a siege Constantine had
negotiated, in the isles of the Archipelago, the Morea, and
Sicily, the most indispensable supplies. As early as the beginning of April, five great ships, equipped for merchandise
and war, would have sailed from the harbour of Chios, had
not the wind blown obstinately from the north. One of these
ships bore the Imperial flag; the remaining four belonged
to the Genoese; and they were laden with wheat and barley,
with wine, oil, and vegetables, and, above all, with soldiers
and mariners, for the service of the capital. After a tedious
delay a gentle breeze, and on the second day a strong gale
from the south, carried them through the Hellespont and the
Propontis; but the city was already invested by sea and land,
and the Turkish fleet, at the entrance of the Bosphorus, was
stretched from shore to shore, in the form of a crescent, to

intercept, or at least to repel, these bold auxiliaries. The reader
who has present to his mind the geographical picture of Constantinople will conceive and admire the greatness of the
spectacle. The five Christian ships continued to advance
with joyful shouts, and a full press both of sails and oars,
against an hostile fleet of three hundred vessels; the rampart,
the camp, the coasts of Europe and Asia, were lined with
innumerable spectators, who anxiously awaited the event of
this momentous succour. At the first view that event could
not appear doubtful; the superiority of the Moslems was
beyond all measure or account, and, in a calm, their numbers
and valour must inevitably have prevailed. But their hasty
and imperfect navy had been created, not by the genius of
the people, but by the will of the sultan: in the height of
their prosperity the Turks have acknowledged that, if God
had given them the earth, he had left the sea to the infidels;
and a series of defeats, a rapid progress of decay, has established the truth of their modest confession. Except eighteen
galleys of some force, the rest of their fleet consisted of open
boats, rudely constructed and awkwardly managed, crowded
with troops, and destitute of cannon; and since courage arises
in a great measure from the consciousness of strength, the
bravest of the Janizaries might tremble on a new element. In
the Christian squadron five stout and lofty ships were guided
by skilful pilots, and manned with the veterans of Italy and
Greece, long practised in the arts and perils of the sea. Their
weight was directed to sink or scatter the weak obstacles that
impeded their passage: their artillery swept the waters; their
liquid fire was poured on the heads of the adversaries, who,
with the design of boarding, presumed to approach them;
and the winds and waves are always on the side of the ablest
navigators. In this conflict the Imperial vessel, which had
been almost overpowered, was rescued by the Genoese; but
the Turks, in a distant and a closer attack, were twice repulsed
with considerable loss. Mahomet himself sat on horseback on
the beach, to encourage their valour by his voice and presence,
by the promise of reward, and by fear more potent than the
fear of the enemy. The passions of his soul, and even the
gestures of his body, seemed to imitate the actions of the
combatants; and, as if he had been the lord of nature, he
spurred his horse with a fearless and impotent effort into the
sea. His loud reproaches, and the clamours of the camp,

urged the Ottomans to a third attack, more fatal and bloody than the two former; and I must repeat, though I cannot credit, the evidence of Phranza, who affirms, from their own mouth, that they lost above twelve thousand men in the slaughter of the day. They fled in disorder to the shores of Europe and Asia, while the Christian squadron, triumphant and unhurt, steered along the Bosphorus, and securely anchored within the chain of the harbour. In the confidence of victory, they boasted that the whole Turkish power must have yielded to their arms; but the admiral, or captain bashaw, found some consolation for a painful wound in his eye, by representing that accident as the cause of his defeat. Baltha Ogli was a renegade of the race of the Bulgarian princes: his military character was tainted with the unpopular vice of avarice; and under the despotism of the prince or people, misfortune is a sufficient evidence of guilt. His rank and services were annihilated by the displeasure of Mahomet. In the royal presence, the captain bashaw was extended on the ground by four slaves, and received one hundred strokes with a golden rod: his death had been pronounced, and he adored the clemency of the sultan, who was satisfied with the milder punishment of confiscation and exile. The introduction of this supply revived the hopes of the Greeks, and accused the supineness of their Western allies. Amidst the deserts of Anatolia and the rocks of Palestine, the millions of the crusades had buried themselves in a voluntary and inevitable grave; but the situation of the Imperial city was strong against her enemies, and accessible to her friends; and a rational and moderate armament of the maritime states might have saved the relics of the Roman name, and maintained a Christian fortress in the heart of the Ottoman empire. Yet this was the sole and feeble attempt for the deliverance of Constantinople: the more distant powers were insensible of its danger; and the ambassador of Hungary, or at least of Huniades, resided in the Turkish camp, to remove the fears and to direct the operations of the sultan.

It was difficult for the Greeks to penetrate the secret of the divan; yet the Greeks are persuaded that a resistance so obstinate and surprising had fatigued the perseverance of Mahomet. He began to meditate a retreat; and the siege would have been speedily raised, if the ambition and jealousy of the second vizir had not opposed the perfidious advice of

Calil Bashaw, who still maintained a secret correspondence
with the Byzantine court. The reduction of the city appeared
to be hopeless, unless a double attack could be made from
the harbour as well as from the land; but the harbour was
inaccessible: an impenetrable chain was now defended by
eight large ships, more than twenty of a smaller size, with
several galleys and sloops; and, instead of forcing this barrier,
the Turks might apprehend a naval sally and a second encounter in the open sea. In this perplexity the genius of
Mahomet conceived and executed a plan of a bold and
marvellous cast, of transporting by land his lighter vessels
and military stores from the Bosphorus into the higher part
of the harbour. The distance is about ten miles; the ground
is uneven, and was overspread with thickets; and, as the road
must be opened behind the suburb of Galata, their free passage or total destruction must depend on the option of the
Genoese. But these selfish merchants were ambitious of the
favour of being the last devoured, and the deficiency of art
was supplied by the strength of obedient myriads. A level
way was covered with a broad platform of strong and solid
planks; and to render them more slippery and smooth, they
were anointed with the fat of sheep and oxen. Fourscore
light galleys and brigantines of fifty and thirty oars were
disembarked on the Bosphorus shore, arranged successively
on rollers, and drawn forwards by the power of men and
pulleys. Two guides or pilots were stationed at the helm and
the prow of each vessel: the sails were unfurled to the winds,
and the labour was cheered by song and acclamation. In the
course of a single night this Turkish fleet painfully climbed
the hill, steered over the plain, and was launched from the
declivity into the shallow waters of the harbour, far above
the molestation of the deeper vessels of the Greeks. The
real importance of this operation was magnified by the consternation and confidence which it inspired; but the notorious,
unquestionable fact was displayed before the eyes, and is
recorded by the pens, of the two nations. A similar stratagem
had been repeatedly practised by the ancients; the Ottoman galleys (I must again repeat) should be considered as
large boats; and, if we compare the magnitude and the
distance, the obstacles and the means, the boasted miracle
has perhaps been equalled by the industry of our own times.
As soon as Mahomet had occupied the upper harbour with

a fleet and army, he constructed in the narrowest part a bridge, or rather mole, of fifty cubits in breadth and one hundred in length: it was formed of casks and hogsheads, joined with rafters, linked with iron, and covered with a solid floor. On this floating battery he planted one of his largest cannon, while the fourscore galleys, with troops and scaling-ladders, approached the most accessible side, which had formerly been stormed by the Latin conquerors. The indolence of the Christians has been accused for not destroying these unfinished works; but their fire, by a superior fire, was controlled and silenced; nor were they wanting in a nocturnal attempt to burn the vessels as well as the bridge of the sultan. His vigilance prevented their approach: their foremost galliots were sunk or taken; forty youths, the bravest of Italy and Greece, were inhumanly massacred at his command; nor could the emperor's grief be assuaged by the just though cruel retaliation of exposing from the walls the heads of two hundred and sixty Musulman captives. After a siege of forty days the fate of Constantinople could no longer be averted. The diminutive garrison was exhausted by a double attack: the fortifications, which had stood for ages against hostile violence, were dismantled on all sides by the Ottoman cannon; many breaches were opened, and near the gate of St. Romanus four towers had been levelled with the ground. For the payment of his feeble and mutinous troops, Constantine was compelled to despoil the churches with the promise of a fourfold restitution; and his sacrilege offered a new reproach to the enemies of the union. A spirit of discord impaired the remnant of the Christian strength: the Genoese and Venetian auxiliaries asserted the pre-eminence of their respective service; and Justiniani and the great duke, whose ambition was not extinguished by the common danger, accused each other of treachery and cowardice.

During the siege of Constantinople the words of peace and capitulation had been sometimes pronounced; and several embassies had passed between the camp and the city. The Greek emperor was humbled by adversity; and would have yielded to any terms compatible with religion and royalty. The Turkish sultan was desirous of sparing the blood of his soldiers; still more desirous of securing for his own use the Byzantine treasures; and he accomplished a sacred duty in presenting to the *Gabours* the choice of circumcision, of

tribute, or of death. The avarice of Mahomet might have
been satisfied with an annual sum of one hundred thousand
ducats; but his ambition grasped the capital of the East: to
the prince he offered a rich equivalent, to the people a free
toleration, or a safe departure: but after some fruitless treaty,
he declared his resolution of finding either a throne or a
grave under the walls of Constantinople. A sense of honour,
and the fear of universal reproach, forbade Palæologus to
resign the city into the hands of the Ottomans; and he determined to abide the last extremities of war. Several days
were employed by the sultan in the preparations of the assault; and a respite was granted by his favourite science of
astrology, which had fixed on the twenty-ninth of May as the
fortunate and fatal hour. On the evening of the twenty-seventh
he issued his final orders; assembled in his presence the
military chiefs; and dispersed his heralds through the camp
to proclaim the duty and the motives of the perilous enterprise. Fear is the first principle of a despotic government;
and his menaces were expressed in the Oriental style, that
the fugitives and deserters, had they the wings of a bird,
should not escape from his inexorable justice. The greatest
part of his bashaws and Janizaries were the offspring of
Christian parents: but the glories of the Turkish name were
perpetuated by successive adoption; and in the gradual
change of individuals, the spirit of a legion, a regiment, or an
oda, is kept alive by imitation and discipline. In this holy
warfare the Moslems were exhorted to purify their minds
with prayer, their bodies with seven ablutions; and to abstain from food till the close of the ensuing day. A crowd
of dervishes visited the tents, to instil the desire of martyrdom,
and the assurance of spending an immortal youth amidst the
rivers and gardens of paradise, and in the embraces of the
black-eyed virgins. Yet Mahomet principally trusted to the
efficacy of temporal and visible rewards. A double pay was
promised to the victorious troops; "The city and the buildings," said Mahomet, "are mine; but I resign to your valour
the captives and the spoil, the treasures of gold and beauty;
be rich and be happy. Many are the provinces of my empire:
the intrepid soldier who first ascends the walls of Constantinople shall be rewarded with the government of the fairest and
most wealthy; and my gratitude shall accumulate his honours
and fortunes above the measure of his own hopes." Such

various and potent motives diffused among the Turks a general ardour, regardless of life and impatient for action: the camp re-echoed with the Moslem shouts of "God is God: there is but one God," and "Mahomet is the apostle of God"; and the sea and land, from Galata to the seven towers, were illuminated by the blaze of their nocturnal fires.

Far different was the state of the Christians, who, with loud and impotent complaints, deplored the guilt, or the punishment, of their sins. The celestial image of the Virgin had been exposed in solemn procession; but their divine patroness was deaf to their entreaties: they accused the obstinacy of the emperor for refusing a timely surrender; anticipated the horrors of their fate; and sighed for the repose and security of Turkish servitude. The noblest of the Greeks, and the bravest of the allies, were summoned to the palace, to prepare them, on the evening of the twenty-eighth, for the duties and dangers of the general assault. The last speech of Palæologus was the funeral oration of the Roman empire: he promised, he conjured, and he vainly attempted to infuse the hope which was extinguished in his own mind. In this world all was comfortless and gloomy; and neither the Gospel nor the church have proposed any conspicuous recompense to the heroes who fall in the service of their country. But the example of their prince, and the confinement of a siege, had armed these warriors with the courage of despair; and the pathetic scene is described by the feelings of the historian Phranza, who was himself present at this mournful assembly. They wept, they embraced: regardless of their families and fortunes, they devoted their lives; and each commander, departing to his station, maintained all night a vigilant and anxious watch on the rampart. The emperor, and some faithful companions, entered the dome of St. Sophia, which in a few hours was to be converted into a mosque; and devoutly received, with tears and prayers, the sacrament of the holy communion. He reposed some moments in the palace, which resounded with cries and lamentations; solicited the pardon of all whom he might have injured; and mounted on horseback to visit the guards, and explore the motions of the enemy. The distress and fall of the last Constantine are more glorious than the long prosperity of the Byzantine Cæsars.

THE CAPTURE OF CONSTANTINOPLE

In the confusion of darkness an assailant may sometimes
succeed; but in this great and general attack, the military
judgment and astrological knowledge of Mahomet advised
him to expect the morning, the memorable twenty-ninth of
May, in the fourteen hundred and fifty-third year of the
Christian era. The preceding night had been strenuously
employed: the troops, the cannon, and the fascines were
advanced to the edge of the ditch, which in many parts
presented a smooth and level passage to the breach; and his
fourscore galleys almost touched, with the prows and their
scaling ladders, the less defensible walls of the harbour.
Under pain of death, silence was enjoined; but the physical
laws of motion and sound are not obedient to discipline or
fear: each individual might suppress his voice and measure
his footsteps; but the march and labour of thousands must
inevitably produce a strange confusion of dissonant clamours,
which reached the ears of the watchmen of the towers. At
daybreak, without the customary signal of the morning gun,
the Turks assaulted the city by sea and land; and the
similitude of a twined or twisted thread has been applied to
the closeness and continuity of their line of attack. The foremost ranks consisted of the refuse of the host, a voluntary
crowd who fought without order or command; of the feeble-
ness of age or childhood, of peasants and vagrants, and of
all who had joined the camp in the blind hope of plunder
and martyrdom. The common impulse drove them onwards
to the wall; the most audacious to climb were instantly
precipitated; and not a dart, not a bullet, of the Christians,
was idly wasted on the accumulated throng. But their strength
and ammunition were exhausted in this laborious defence: the
ditch was filled with the bodies of the slain; they supported
the footsteps of their companions; and of this devoted vanguard the death was more serviceable than the life. Under
their respective bashaws and sanjaks, the troops of Anatolia
and Romania were successively led to the charge: their
progress was various and doubtful; but, after a conflict of
two hours, the Greeks still maintained and improved their
advantage; and the voice of the emperor was heard, encourag-
ing his soldiers to achieve, by a last effort, the deliverance

of their country. In that fatal moment the Janizaries arose, fresh, vigorous, and invincible. The sultan himself on horseback, with an iron mace in his hand, was the spectator and judge of their valour; he was surrounded by ten thousand of his domestic troops, whom he reserved for the decisive occasion; and the tide of battle was directed and impelled by his voice and eye. His numerous ministers of justice were posted behind the line, to urge, to restrain, and to punish; and if danger was in the front, shame and inevitable death were in the rear, of the fugitives. The cries of fear and of pain were drowned in the martial music of drums, trumpets, and attaballs; and experience has proved that the mechanical operation of sounds, by quickening the circulation of the blood and spirits, will act on the human machine more forcibly than the eloquence of reason and honour. From the lines, the galleys, and the bridge, the Ottoman artillery thundered on all sides; and the camp and city, the Greeks and the Turks, were involved in a cloud of smoke, which could only be dispelled by the final deliverance or destruction of the Roman empire. The single combats of the heroes of history or fable amuse our fancy and engage our affections: the skilful evolutions of war may inform the mind, and improve a necessary, though pernicious, science. But in the uniform and odious pictures of a general assault, all is blood, and horror, and confusion; nor shall I strive, at the distance of three centuries and a thousand miles, to delineate a scene of which there could be no spectators, and of which the actors themselves were incapable of forming any just or adequate idea.

The immediate loss of Constantinople may be ascribed to the bullet or arrow, which pierced the gauntlet of John Justiniani. The sight of his blood, and the exquisite pain, appalled the courage of the chief, whose arms and counsels were the firmest rampart of the city. As he withdrew from his station in quest of a surgeon, his flight was perceived and stopped by the indefatigable emperor. "Your wound," exclaimed Palæologus, "is slight; the danger is pressing: your presence is necessary; and whither will you retire?"— "I will retire," said the trembling Genoese, "by the same road which God has opened to the Turks"; and at these words he hastily passed through one of the breaches of the inner wall. By this pusillanimous act he stained the honours

of a military life and the few days which he survived in
Galata, or the isle of Chios, were embittered by his own and
the public reproach. His example was imitated by the greatest
part of the Latin auxiliaries, and the defence began to slacken
when the attack was pressed with redoubled vigour. The
number of the Ottomans was fifty, perhaps a hundred, times
superior to that of the Christians; the double walls were reduced by the cannon to a heap of ruins: in a circuit of
several miles some places must be found more easy of access,
or more feebly guarded; and if the besiegers could penetrate
in a single point, the whole city was irrecoverably lost. The
first who deserved the sultan's reward was Hassan the
Janizary, of gigantic stature and strength. With his scimitar
in one hand and his buckler in the other, he ascended the
outward fortification: of the thirty Janizaries who were
emulous of his valour, eighteen perished in the bold adventure.
Hassan and his twelve companions had reached the summit:
the giant was precipitated from the rampart: he rose on one
knee, and was again oppressed by a shower of darts and
stones. But his success had proved that the achievement was
possible: the walls and towers were instantly covered with
a swarm of Turks; and the Greeks, now driven from the
vantage ground, were overwhelmed by increasing multitudes.
Amidst these multitudes, the emperor,[1] who accomplished
all the duties of a general and a soldier, was long seen and
finally lost. The nobles, who fought round his person, sustained, till their last breath, the honourable names of Palæologus and Cantacuzene: his mournful exclamation was
heard, "Cannot there be found a Christian to cut off my
head?" and his last fear was that of falling alive into the
hands of the infidels. The prudent despair of Constantine
cast away the purple: amidst the tumult he fell by an unknown hand, and his body was buried under a mountain of
the slain. After his death resistance and order were no more:

---

[1] Ducas kills him with two blows of Turkish soldiers; Chalcondyles wounds
him in the shoulder, and then tramples him in the gate. The grief of
Phranza, carrying him among the enemy, escapes from the precise image
of his death; but we may, without flattery, apply these noble lines of
Dryden:—

> As to Sebastian, let them search the field;
> And, where they find a mountain of the slain,
> Send one to climb, and, looking down beneath,
> There they will find him at his manly length,
> With his face up to heaven, in that red monument
> Which his good sword had digg'd.

the Greeks fled towards the city; and many were pressed and stifled in the narrow pass of the gate of St. Romanus. The victorious Turks rushed through the breaches of the inner wall; and as they advanced into the streets, they were soon joined by their brethren, who had forced the gate Phenar on the side of the harbour. In the first heat of the pursuit about two thousand Christians were put to the sword; but avarice soon prevailed over cruelty; and the victors acknowledged that they should immediately have given quarter, if the valour of the emperor and his chosen bands had not prepared them for a similar opposition in every part of the capital. It was thus, after a siege of fifty-three days, that Constantinople, which had defied the power of Chosroes, the Chagan, and the caliphs, was irretrievably subdued by the arms of Mahomet the Second. Her empire only had been subverted by the Latins: her religion was trampled in the dust by the Moslem conquerors.

The tidings of misfortune fly with a rapid wing; yet such was the extent of Constantinople, that the more distant quarters might prolong, some moments, the happy ignorance of their ruin. But in the general consternation, in the feelings of selfish or social anxiety, in the tumult and thunder of the assault, a *sleepless* night and morning must have elapsed; nor can I believe that many Grecian ladies were awakened by the Janizaries from a sound and tranquil slumber. On the assurance of the public calamity, the houses and convents were instantly deserted; and the trembling inhabitants flocked together in the streets, like a herd of timid animals, as if accumulated weakness could be productive of strength, or in the vain hope that amid the crowd each individual might be safe and invisible. From every part of the capital they flowed into the church of St. Sophia: in the space of an hour, the sanctuary, the choir, the nave, the upper and lower galleries, were filled with the multitudes of fathers and husbands, of women and children, of priests, monks, and religious virgins: the doors were barred on the inside, and they sought protection from the sacred dome which they had so lately abhorred as a profane and polluted edifice. Their confidence was founded on the prophecy of an enthusiast or impostor, that one day the Turks would enter Constantinople, and pursue the Romans as far as the column of Constantine

in the square before St. Sophia: but that this would be the
term of their calamities; that an angel would descend from
heaven with a sword in his hand, and would deliver the
empire, with that celestial weapon, to a poor man seated at
the foot of the column. "Take this sword," would he say,
"and avenge the people of the Lord." At these animating
words the Turks would instantly fly, and the victorious
Romans would drive them from the West, and from all
Anatolia, as far as the frontiers of Persia. It is on this occasion that Ducas, with some fancy and much truth, up-
braids the discord and obstinacy of the Greeks. "Had that
angel appeared," exclaims the historian, "had he offered to
exterminate your foes if you would consent to the union
of the church, even then, in that fatal moment, you would
have rejected your safety, or have deceived your God."

While they expected the descent of the tardy angel, the
doors were broken with axes; and as the Turks encountered
no resistance, their bloodless hands were employed in select-
ing and securing the multitude of their prisoners. Youth,
beauty, and the appearance of wealth, attracted their choice;
and the right of property was decided among themselves by
a prior seizure, by personal strength, and by the authority of
command. In the space of an hour the male captives were
bound with cords, the females with their veils and girdles.
The senators were linked with their slaves; the prelates with
the porters of the church; and young men of a plebeian class
with noble maids whose faces had been invisible to the sun
and their nearest kindred. In this common captivity the
ranks of society were confounded; the ties of nature were
cut asunder; and the inexorable soldier was careless of the
father's groans, the tears of the mother, and the lamentations
of the children. The loudest in their wailings were the nuns,
who were torn from the altar with naked bosoms, outstretched
hands, and dishevelled hair; and we should piously believe
that few could be tempted to prefer the vigils of the harem
to those of the monastery. Of these unfortunate Greeks, of
these domestic animals, whole strings were rudely driven
through the streets; and as the conquerors were eager to return for more prey, their trembling pace was quickened with
menaces and blows. At the same hour a similar rapine was
exercised in all the churches and monasteries, in all the
palaces and habitations, of the capital; nor could any place,

however sacred or sequestered, protect the persons or the property of the Greeks. Above sixty thousand of this devoted people were transported from the city to the camp and fleet; exchanged or sold according to the caprice or interest of their masters, and dispersed in remote servitude through the provinces of the Ottoman empire. Among these we may notice some remarkable characters. The historian Phranza, first chamberlain and principal secretary, was involved with his family in the common lot. After suffering four months the hardships of slavery, he recovered his freedom: in the ensuing winter he ventured to Adrianople, and ransomed his wife from the *mir bashi*, or master of the horse; but his two children, in the flower of youth and beauty, had been seized for the use of Mahomet himself. The daughter of Phranza died in the seraglio, perhaps a virgin: his son, in the fifteenth year of his age, preferred death to infamy, and was stabbed by the hand of the royal lover. A deed thus inhuman cannot surely be expiated by the taste and liberality with which he released a Grecian matron and her two daughters, on receiving a Latin ode from Philelphus, who had chosen a wife in that noble family. The pride or cruelty of Mahomet would have been most sensibly gratified by the capture of a Roman legate; but the dexterity of Cardinal Isidore eluded the search, and he escaped from Galata in a plebeian habit. The chain and entrance of the outward harbour was still occupied by the Italian ships of merchandise and war. They had signalised their valour in the siege: they embraced the moment of retreat, while the Turkish mariners were dissipated in the pillage of the city. When they hoisted sail, the beach was covered with a suppliant and lamentable crowd; but the means of transportation were scanty; the Venetians and Genoese selected their countrymen; and, notwithstanding the fairest promises of the sultan, the inhabitants of Galata evacuated their houses, and embarked with their most precious effects.

In the fall and the sack of great cities an historian is condemned to repeat the tale of uniform calamity: the same effects must be produced by the same passions; and when those passions may be indulged without control, small, alas! is the difference between civilised and savage man. Amidst the vague exclamations of bigotry and hatred, the Turks are not accused of a wanton or immoderate effusion of Christian

blood: but according to their maxims (the maxims of antiquity), the lives of the vanquished were forfeited; and the
legitimate reward of the conqueror was derived from the
service, the sale, or the ransom of his captives of both sexes.
The wealth of Constantinople had been granted by the
sultan to his victorious troops; and the rapine of an hour is
more productive than the industry of years. But as no regular
division was attempted of the spoil, the respective shares were
not determined by merit; and the rewards of valour were
stolen away by the followers of the camp, who had declined
the toil and danger of the battle. The narrative of their
depredations could not afford either amusement or instruction: the total amount, in the last poverty of the empire, has
been valued at four millions of ducats; and of this sum a
small part was the property of the Venetians, the Genoese,
the Florentines, and the merchants of Ancona. Of these
foreigners the stock was improved in quick and perpetual
circulation: but the riches of the Greeks were displayed in
the idle ostentation of palaces and wardrobes, or deeply buried
in treasures of ingots and old coin, lest it should be demanded
at their hands for the defence of their country. The profana-
tion and plunder of the monasteries and churches excited
the most tragic complaints. The dome of St. Sophia itself,
the earthly heaven, the second firmament, the vehicle of the
cherubim, the throne of the glory of God, was despoiled
of the oblations of ages; and the gold and silver, the pearls
and jewels, the vases and sacerdotal ornaments, were most
wickedly converted to the service of mankind. After the
divine images had been stripped of all that could be valuable
to a profane eye, the canvas, or the wood, was torn, or
broken, or burnt, or trod under foot, or applied, in the stables
or the kitchen, to the vilest uses. The example of sacrilege
was imitated, however, from the Latin conquerors of Constantinople; and the treatment which Christ, the Virgin, and
the saints had sustained from the guilty Catholic, might be
inflicted by the zealous Musulman on the monuments of
idolatry. Perhaps, instead of joining the public clamour, a
philosopher will observe that in the decline of the arts the
workmanship could not be more valuable than the work, and
that a fresh supply of visions and miracles would speedily
be renewed by the craft of the priest and the credulity of the
people. He will more seriously deplore the loss of the Byzan-

tine libraries, which were destroyed or scattered in the general confusion: one hundred and twenty thousand manuscripts are said to have disappeared; ten volumes might be purchased for a single ducat; and the same ignominious price, too high perhaps for a shelf of theology, included the whole works of Aristotle and Homer, the noblest productions of the science and literature of ancient Greece. We may reflect with pleasure that an inestimable portion of our classic treasures was safely deposited in Italy; and that the mechanics of a German town had invented an art which derides the havoc of time and barbarism.

THE ENTRY OF MAHOMET II

From the first hour of the memorable twenty-ninth of May, disorder and rapine prevailed in Constantinople till the eighth hour of the same day, when the sultan himself passed in triumph through the gate of St. Romanus. He was attended by his viziers, bashaws, and guards, each of whom (says a Byzantine historian) was robust as Hercules, dexterous as Apollo, and equal in battle to any ten of the race of ordinary mortals. The conqueror gazed with satisfaction and wonder on the strange though splendid appearance of the domes and palaces, so dissimilar from the style of Oriental architecture. In the hippodrome, or *atmeidan*, his eye was attracted by the twisted column of the three serpents; and, as a trial of his strength, he shattered with his iron mace or battle-axe the under jaw of one of these monsters, which in the eyes of the Turks were the idols or talismans of the city. At the principal door of St. Sophia he alighted from his horse and entered the dome; and such was his jealous regard for that monument of his glory, that, on observing a zealous Musulman in the act of breaking the marble pavement, he admonished him with his scimitar that, if the spoil and captives were granted to the soldiers, the public and private buildings had been reserved for the prince. By his command the metropolis of the Eastern church was transformed into a mosque: the rich and portable instruments of superstition had been removed; the crosses were thrown down; and the walls, which were covered with images and mosaics, were washed and purified, and restored to a state of naked simplicity. On the same day, or on the ensuing Friday, the *muezin*, or crier,

ascended the most lofty turret, and proclaimed the *ezan,* or
public invitation, in the name of God and his prophet; the
imam preached; and Mahomet the Second performed the
namaz of prayer and thanksgiving on the great altar, where
the Christian mysteries had so lately been celebrated before
the last of the Cæsars. From St. Sophia he proceeded to the
august but desolate mansion of an hundred successors of the
great Constantine, but which in a few hours had been stripped
of the pomp of royalty. A melancholy reflection on the
vicissitudes of human greatness forced itself on his mind,
and he repeated an elegant distich of Persian poetry: "The
spider has wove his web in the Imperial palace, and the owl
hath sung her watch-song on the towers of Afrasiab."

Yet his mind was not satisfied, nor did the victory seem
complete, till he was informed of the fate of Constantine—
whether he had escaped, or been made prisoner, or had fallen
in the battle. Two Janizaries claimed the honour and reward
of his death: the body, under a heap of slain, was discovered
by the golden eagles embroidered on his shoes; the Greeks
acknowledged with tears the head of their late emperor;
and, after exposing the bloody trophy, Mahomet bestowed on
his rival the honours of a decent funeral. After his decease
Lucas Notaras, great duke and first minister of the empire,
was the most important prisoner. When he offered his person
and his treasures at the foot of the throne, "And why," said
the indignant sultan, "did you not employ these treasures in
the defence of your prince and country?"—"They were
yours," answered the slave; "God had reserved them for your
hands."—"If he reserved them for me," replied the despot,
"how have you presumed to withhold them so long by a
fruitless and fatal resistance?" The great duke alleged the
obstinacy of the strangers, and some secret encouragement
from the Turkish vizir; and from this perilous interview he
was at length dismissed with the assurance of pardon and
protection. Mahomet condescended to visit his wife, a venerable princess oppressed with sickness and grief; and his
consolation for her misfortunes was in the most tender strain
of humanity and filial reverence. A similar clemency was extended to the principal officers of state, of whom several
were ransomed at his expense; and during some days he
declared himself the friend and father of the vanquished
people. But the scene was soon changed, and before his de-

parture the hippodrome streamed with the blood of his noblest captives. His perfidious cruelty is execrated by the Christians: they adorn with the colours of heroic martyrdom the execution of the great duke and his two sons, and his death is ascribed to the generous refusal of delivering his children to the tyrant's lust. Yet a Byzantine historian has dropped an unguarded word of conspiracy, deliverance, and Italian succour: such treason may be glorious; but the rebel who bravely ventures, has justly forfeited his life; nor should we blame a conqueror for destroying the enemies whom he can no longer trust. On the eighteenth of June the victorious sultan returned to Adrianople, and smiled at the base and hollow embassies of the Christian princes, who viewed their approaching ruin in the fall of the Eastern empire.

Constantinople had been left naked and desolate, without a prince or a people. But she could not be despoiled of the incomparable situation which marks her for the metropolis of a great empire; and the genius of the place will ever triumph over the accidents of time and fortune. Boursa and Adrianople, the ancient seats of the Ottomans, sunk into provincial towns; and Mahomet the Second established his own residence and that of his successors on the same commanding spot which had been chosen by Constantine. The fortifications of Galata, which might afford a shelter to the Latins, were prudently destroyed; but the damage of the Turkish cannon was soon repaired, and before the month of August great quantities of lime had been burnt for the restoration of the walls of the capital. As the entire property of the soil and buildings, whether public or private, or profane or sacred, was now transferred to the conqueror, he first separated a space of eight furlongs from the point of the triangle for the establishment of his seraglio or palace. It is here, in the bosom of luxury, that the *Grand Signor* (as he has been emphatically named by the Italians) appears to reign over Europe and Asia; but his person on the shores of the Bosphorus may not always be secure from the insults of an hostile navy. In the new character of a mosque, the cathedral of St. Sophia was endowed with an ample revenue, crowned with lofty minarets, and surrounded with groves and fountains for the devotion and refreshment of the Moslems. The same model was imitated in the *jami*, or royal mosques; and the first of these was built by Mahomet himself, on the ruins of the church of the holy apostles and the tombs of the Greek emperors. On the third day after the conquest the grave of Abou Ayub, or Job, who had fallen in the first siege of the Arabs, was revealed in a vision; and it is before the sepulchre of the martyr that the new sultans are girded with the sword of empire. Constantinople no longer appertains to the Roman historian; nor shall I enumerate the civil and religious edifices that were profaned or erected by its Turkish masters: the population was speedily renewed, and before the end of September five thousand families of Anatolia and Romania had obeyed the royal mandate, which enjoined them, under pain of death, to occupy their new habitations in the capital. The throne of Mahomet was guarded by the numbers and fidelity of his Moslem subjects; but his rational policy aspired to collect the remnant of the Greeks, and they returned in crowds as soon as they were assured of their lives, their liberties, and the free exercise of their religion. In the election and investiture of a patriarch the ceremonial of the Byzantine court was revived and imitated. With a mixture of satisfaction and horror, they beheld the sultan on his throne, who delivered into the hands of Gennadius the crosier or pastoral staff, the symbol of his ecclesiastical office; who conducted the patriarch to the gate of the seraglio, presented him with a horse richly caparisoned, and directed the vizirs and bashaws to lead him to the palace which had been allotted for his residence. The churches of Constantinople were shared between the two religions: their limits were marked; and, till it was infringed by Selim, the grandson of Mahomet, the Greeks enjoyed above sixty years the benefit of this equal partition. Encouraged by the ministers of the divan, who wished to elude the fanaticism of the sultan, the Christian advocates presumed to allege that this division had been an act, not of generosity, but of justice; not a concession, but a compact; and that, if one-half of the city had been taken by storm, the other moiety had surrendered on the faith of a sacred capitulation. The original grant had indeed been consumed by fire; but the loss was supplied by the testimony of three aged Janizaries who remembered the transaction, and their venal oaths are of more weight in the opinion of Cantemir than the positive and unanimous consent of the history of the times.

The remaining fragments of the Greek kingdom in Europe

and Asia I shall abandon to the Turkish arms; but the final
extinction of the two last dynasties which have reigned in
Constantinople should terminate the decline and fall of the
Roman empire in the East. The despots of the Morea, Demetrius and Thomas, the two surviving brothers of the name
of PALÆOLOGUS, were astonished by the death of the emperor
Constantine and the ruin of the monarchy. Hopeless of defence, they prepared, with the noble Greeks who adhered
to their fortune, to seek a refuge in Italy, beyond the reach
of the Ottoman thunder. Their first apprehensions were dispelled by the victorious sultan, who contented himself with
a tribute of twelve thousand ducats; and while his ambition
explored the continent and the islands in search of prey, he
indulged the Morea in a respite of seven years. But this
respite was a period of grief, discord, and misery. The
hexamilion, the rampart of the isthmus, so often raised and
so often subverted, could not long be defended by three
hundred Italian archers: the keys of Corinth were seized by
the Turks; they returned from their summer excursions with
a train of captives and spoil, and the complaints of the injured Greeks were heard with indifference and disdain. The
Albanians, a vagrant tribe of shepherds and robbers, filled
the peninsula with rapine and murder: the two despots implored the dangerous and humiliating aid of a neighbouring
bashaw; and when he had quelled the revolt, his lessons
inculcated the rule of their future conduct. Neither the ties
of blood, nor the oaths which they repeatedly pledged in the
communion and before the altar, nor the stronger pressure
of necessity, could reconcile or suspend their domestic quarrels. They ravaged each other's patrimony with fire and
sword; the alms and succours of the West were consumed in
civil hostility, and their power was only exerted in savage
and arbitrary executions. The distress and revenge of the
weaker rival invoked their supreme lord; and, in the season
of maturity and revenge, Mahomet declared himself the
friend of Demetrius, and marched into the Morea with an
irresistible force. When he had taken possession of Sparta,
"You are too weak," said the sultan, "to control this turbulent province; I will take your daughter to my bed, and you
shall pass the remainder of your life in security and honour."
Demetrius sighed and obeyed; surrendered his daughter and
his castles, followed to Adrianople his sovereign and son,

and received for his own maintenance and that of his followers a city in Thrace, and the adjacent isles of Imbros,
Lemnos, and Samothrace. He was joined the next year by a
companion of misfortune, the last of the Comnenian race,
who, after the taking of Constantinople by the Latins, had
founded a new empire on the coast of the Black Sea. In
the progress of his Anatolian conquests, Mahomet invested
with a fleet and army the capital of David, who presumed to
style himself emperor of Trebizond; and the negotiation was
comprised in a short and peremptory question, "Will you
secure your life and treasures by resigning your kingdom?
or had you rather forfeit your kingdom, your treasures, and
your life?" The feeble Comnenus was subdued by his own
fears, and the example of a Musulman neighbour, the prince
of Sinope, who, on a similar summons, had yielded a fortified
city with four hundred cannon and ten or twelve thousand
soldiers. The capitulation of Trebizond was faithfully performed, and the emperor, with his family, was transported to
a castle in Romania; but on a slight suspicion of corresponding
with the Persian king, David, and the whole Comnenian race,
were sacrificed to the jealousy or avarice of the conqueror.
Nor could the name of father long protect the unfortunate
Demetrius from exile and confiscation: his abject submission
moved the pity and contempt of the sultan; his followers
were transplanted to Constantinople, and his poverty was
alleviated by a pension of fifty thousand aspers, till a monastic
habit and a hardy death released Palæologus from an earthly
master. It is not easy to pronounce whether the servitude of
Demetrius, or the exile of his brother Thomas, be the most
inglorious. On the conquest of the Morea the despot escaped
to Corfu, and from thence to Italy, with some naked adherents: his name, his sufferings, and the head of the apostle
St. Andrew, entitled him to the hospitality of the Vatican;
and his misery was prolonged by a pension of six thousand
ducats from the pope and cardinals. His two sons, Andrew
and Manuel, were educated in Italy; but the eldest, contemptible to his enemies and burdensome to his friends, was
degraded by the baseness of his life and marriage. A title
was his sole inheritance; and that inheritance he successively
sold to the kings of France and Arragon. During his transient
prosperity, Charles the Eighth was ambitious of joining the
empire of the East with the kingdom of Naples: in a public

festival he assumed the appellation and the purple of *Augustus;* the Greeks rejoiced, and the Ottoman already trembled, at the approach of the French chivalry. Manuel Palæologus, the second son, was tempted to revisit his native country: his return might be grateful, and could not be dangerous, to the Porte; he was maintained at Constantinople in safety and ease, and an honourable train of Christians and Moslems attended him to the grave. If there be some animals of so generous a nature that they refuse to propagate in a domestic state, the last of the Imperial race must be ascribed to an inferior kind: he accepted from the sultan's liberality two beautiful females, and his surviving son was lost in the habit and religion of a Turkish slave.

GRIEF AND TERROR OF EUROPE

The importance of Constantinople was felt and magnified in its loss: the pontificate of Nicholas the Fifth, however peaceful and prosperous, was dishonoured by the fall of the Eastern empire; and the grief and terror of the Latins revived, or seemed to revive, the old enthusiasm of the crusades. In one of the most distant countries of the West, Philip duke of Burgundy entertained, at Lisle in Flanders, an assembly of his nobles; and the pompous pageants of the feast were skilfully adapted to their fancy and feelings. In the midst of the banquet a gigantic Saracen entered the hall, leading a fictitious elephant with a castle on his back: a matron in a mourning robe, the symbol of religion, was seen to issue from her castle: she deplored her oppression, and accused the slowness of her champions: the principal herald of the golden fleece advanced, bearing on his fist a live pheasant, which, according to the rites of chivalry, he presented to the duke. At this extraordinary summons, Philip, a wise and aged prince, engaged his person and powers in the holy war against the Turks: his example was imitated by the barons and knights of the assembly: they swore to God, the Virgin, the ladies, and the *pheasant;* and their particular vows were not less extravagant than the general sanction of their oath. But the performance was made to depend on some future and foreign contingency; and during twelve years, till the last hour of his life, the duke of Burgundy might be scrupulously, and perhaps sincerely, on the eve of his de-

parture. Had every breast glowed with the same ardour;
had the union of the Christians corresponded with their
bravery; had every country from Sweden to Naples supplied
a just proportion of cavalry and infantry, of men and money,
it is indeed probable that Constantinople would have been
delivered, and that the Turks might have been chased beyond
the Hellespont or the Euphrates. But the secretary of the
emperor, who composed every epistle, and attended every
meeting, Æneas Sylvius, a statesman and orator, describes
from his own experience the repugnant state and spirit of
Christendom. "It is a body," says he, "without a head; a
republic without laws or magistrates. The pope and the
emperor may shine as lofty titles, as splendid images; but *they*
are unable to command, and none are willing to obey: every
state has a separate prince, and every prince has a separate
interest. What eloquence could unite so many discordant and
hostile powers under the same standard? Could they be assembled in arms, who would dare to assume the office of
general? What order could be maintained?—what military
discipline? Who would undertake to feed such an enormous
multitude? Who would understand their various languages,
or direct their stranger and incompatible manners? What
mortal could reconcile the English with the French, Genoa
with Arragon, the Germans with the natives of Hungary
and Bohemia? If a small number enlisted in the holy war,
they must be overthrown by the infidels: if many, by their
own weight and confusion." Yet the same Æneas, when he
was raised to the papal throne, under the name of Pius the
Second, devoted his life to the prosecution of the Turkish
war. In the council of Mantua he excited some sparks of a
false or feeble enthusiasm; but when the pontiff appeared at
Ancona, to embark in person with the troops, engagements
vanished in excuses; a precise day was adjourned to an indefinite term; and his effective army consisted of some German
pilgrims, whom he was obliged to disband with indulgences
and alms. Regardless of futurity, his successors and the powers
of Italy were involved in the schemes of present and domestic
ambition; and the distance or proximity of each object determined in their eyes its apparent magnitude. A more enlarged view of their interest would have taught them to
maintain a defensive and naval war against the common
enemy; and the support of Scanderbeg and his brave Albanians

might have prevented the subsequent invasion of the kingdom of Naples. The siege and sack of Otranto by the Turks diffused a general consternation; and Pope Sixtus was preparing to fly beyond the Alps, when the storm was instantly dispelled by the death of Mahomet the Second, in the fifty-first year of his age. His lofty genius aspired to the conquest of Italy: he was possessed of a strong city and a capacious harbour; and the same reign might have been decorated with the trophies of the NEW and the ANCIENT ROME.

Two results of the appeal for help to the West (see summary, p. 1058) require a mention here. One was the despatch of two thousand Genoese soldiers led by Justiniani (Giustiniani); the other was a mission with Cardinal Isidore, as papal legate. The account of Justiniani's conduct on p. 1069 is neither historical nor fair. The immediate cause of the city's capture was the entry of some Turks through a postern which Justiniani had opened for a sally. Isidore's mission served only to increase the Greeks' enmity towards the Latins. Someone remarked that he would rather see a Mahomet's turban in the city than a cardinal's hat. After the Latin rites had been used in St. Sophia, the church was deserted, and "a vast and gloomy silence prevailed in that venerable dome." This explains the reference to pollution on p. 1071.

The Epilogue: Medieval Rome and the Dawn of the Renaissance

69.

IN THE FIRST AGES of the decline and fall of the Roman empire our eye is invariably fixed on the royal city, which had given laws to the fairest portion of the globe. We contemplate her fortunes, at first with admiration, at length with pity, always with attention; and when that attention is diverted from the Capitol to the provinces, they are considered as so many branches which have been successively severed from the Imperial trunk. The foundation of a second Rome, on the shores of the Bosphorus, has compelled the historian to follow the successors of Constantine; and our curiosity has been tempted to visit the most remote countries of Europe and Asia, to explore the causes and the authors of the long decay of the Byzantine monarchy. By the conquests of Justinian we have been recalled to the banks of the Tiber, to the deliverance of the ancient metropolis; but that deliverance was a change, or perhaps an aggravation, of servitude. Rome had been already stripped of her trophies, her gods, and her Cæsars; nor was the Gothic dominion more inglorious and oppressive than the tyranny of the Greeks. In the eighth century of the Christian era a religious quarrel, the worship of images, provoked the Romans to assert their independence: their bishop became the temporal, as well as the spiritual, father of a free people; and of the Western empire, which was restored by Charlemagne, the title and image still decorate the singular constitution of modern Germany. The name of Rome must yet command our involuntary respect: the climate (whatsoever may be its influence) was no longer the same: the purity of blood had been contaminated through a thousand channels; but the venerable aspect of her ruins, and the memory of past greatness, rekindled a spark of the national character. The darkness of the middle ages exhibits some scenes not unworthy of our notice. Nor shall I dismiss the present work till I have reviewed the state and revolutions of the ROMAN CITY, which acquiesced under the absolute dominion of the popes about the same time that Constantinople was enslaved by the Turkish arms.

In the beginning of the twelfth century,[1] the era of the first crusade, Rome was revered by the Latins as the metropolis of the world, as the throne of the pope and the emperor, who, from the eternal city, derived their title, their honours, and the right or exercise of temporal dominion. After so long an interruption it may not be useless to repeat that the successors of Charlemagne and the Othos were chosen beyond the Rhine in a national diet; but that these princes were content with the humble names of kings of Germany and Italy till they had passed the Alps and the Apennine, to seek their Imperial crown on the banks of the Tiber. At some distance from the city their approach was saluted by a long procession of the clergy and people with palms and crosses; and the terrific emblems of wolves and lions, of dragons and eagles, that floated in the military banners, represented the departed legions and cohorts of the republic. The royal oath to maintain the liberties of Rome was thrice reiterated, at the bridge, the gate, and on the stairs of the Vatican; and the distribution of a customary donative feebly imitated the magnificence of the first Cæsars. In the church of St. Peter the coronation was performed by his successor: the voice of God was confounded with that of the people; and the public consent was declared in the acclamations of "Long life and victory to our lord the pope! long life and victory to our lord the emperor! long life and victory to the Roman and Teutonic armies!" The names of Cæsar and Augustus, the laws of Constantine and Justinian, the example of Charlemagne and Otho, established the supreme dominion of the emperors: their title and image was engraved on the papal coins; and their jurisdiction was marked by the sword

---

[1] The reader has been so long absent from Rome that I would advise him to recollect or review the 49th chapter of this History.

of justice, which they delivered to the prefect of the city. But every Roman prejudice was awakened by the name, the language, and the manners of a barbarian lord. The Cæsars of Saxony or Franconia were the chiefs of a feudal aristocracy; nor could they exercise the discipline of civil and military power, which alone secures the obedience of a distant people, impatient of servitude, though perhaps incapable of freedom. Once, and once only, in his life, each emperor, with an army of Teutonic vassals, descended from the Alps. I have described the peaceful order of his entry and coronation; but that order was commonly disturbed by the clamour and sedition of the Romans, who encountered their sovereign as a foreign invader: his departure was always speedy, and often shameful; and, in the absence of a long reign, his authority was insulted and his name was forgotten. The progress of independence in Germany and Italy undermined the foundations of the Imperial sovereignty, and the triumph of the popes was the deliverance of Rome.

Of her two sovereigns, the emperor had precariously reigned by the right of conquest; but the authority of the pope was founded on the soft though more solid basis of opinion and habit. The removal of a foreign influence restored and endeared the shepherd to his flock. Instead of the arbitrary or venal nomination of a German court, the vicar of Christ was freely chosen by the college of cardinals, most of whom were either natives or inhabitants of the city. The applause of the magistrates and people confirmed his election; and the ecclesiastical power that was obeyed in Sweden and Britain had been ultimately derived from the suffrage of the Romans. The same suffrage gave a prince, as well as a pontiff, to the capital. It was universally believed that Constantine had invested the popes with the temporal dominion of Rome; and the boldest civilians, the most profane sceptics, were satisfied with disputing the right of the emperor and the validity of his gift. The truth of the fact, the authenticity of his donation, was deeply rooted in the ignorance and tradition of four centuries; and the fabulous origin was lost in the real and permanent effects. The name of *Dominus*, or Lord, was inscribed on the coin of the bishops: their title was acknowledged by acclamations and oaths of allegiance, and, with the free or reluctant consent of the German Cæsars, they had long exercised a supreme or subordinate jurisdiction over the city and patrimony of St. Peter. The reign of the popes, which gratified the prejudices, was not incompatible with the liberties of Rome; and a more critical inquiry would have revealed a still nobler source of their power—the gratitude of a nation whom they had rescued from the heresy and oppression of the Greek tyrant. In an age of superstition it should seem that the union of the royal and sacerdotal characters would mutually fortify each other, and that the keys of Paradise would be the surest pledge of earthly obedience. The sanctity of the office might indeed be degraded by the personal vices of the man. But the scandals of the tenth century were obliterated by the austere and more dangerous virtues of Gregory the Seventh and his successors; and in the ambitious contests which they maintained for the rights of the church, their sufferings or their success must equally tend to increase the popular veneration. They sometimes wandered in poverty and exile, the victims of persecution; and the apostolic zeal with which they offered themselves to martyrdom must engage the favour and sympathy of every Catholic breast. And sometimes, thundering from the Vatican, they created, judged, and deposed the kings of the world; nor could the proudest Roman be disgraced by submitting to a priest whose feet were kissed and whose stirrup was held by the successors of Charlemagne. Even the temporal interest of the city should have protected in peace and honour the residence of the popes, from whence a vain and lazy people derived the greatest part of their subsistence and riches. The fixed revenue of the popes was probably impaired: many of the old patrimonial estates, both in Italy and the provinces, had been invaded by sacrilegious hands; nor could the loss be compensated by the claim, rather than the possession, of the more ample gifts of Pepin and his descendants. But the Vatican and Capitol were nourished by the incessant and increasing swarms of pilgrims and suppliants: the pale of Christianity was enlarged, and the pope and cardinals were overwhelmed by the judgment of ecclesiastical and secular causes. A new jurisprudence had established in the Latin church the right and practice of appeals; and from the North and West the bishops and abbots were invited or summoned to solicit, to complain, to accuse, or to justify, before the threshold of the apostles. A rare prodigy is once recorded, that two horses, belonging to the archbishops of Maintz and

Cologne, repassed the Alps, yet laden with gold and silver;
but it was soon understood that the success, both of the pilgrims and clients, depended much less on the justice of their
cause than on the value of their offering. The wealth and
piety of these strangers were ostentatiously displayed, and
their expenses, sacred or profane, circulated in various
channels for the emolument of the Romans.

Such powerful motives should have firmly attached the
voluntary and pious obedience of the Roman people to their
spiritual and temporal father. But the operation of prejudice
and interest is often disturbed by the sallies of ungovernable
passion. The Indian who fells the tree that he may gather
the fruit, and the Arab who plunders the caravans of commerce, are actuated by the same impulse of savage nature,
which overlooks the future in the present, and relinquishes
for momentary rapine the long and secure possession of the
most important blessings. And it was thus that the shrine of
St. Peter was profaned by the thoughtless Romans, who pillaged the offerings and wounded the pilgrims, without computing the number and value of similar visits, which they
prevented by their inhospitable sacrilege. Even the influence
of superstition is fluctuating and precarious; and the slave,
whose reason is subdued, will often be delivered by his
avarice or pride. A credulous devotion for the fables and
oracles of the priesthood most powerfully acts on the mind
of a barbarian; yet such a mind is the least capable of pre-
ferring imagination to sense, of sacrificing to a distant motive,
to an invisible, perhaps an ideal object, the appetites and
interests of the present world. In the vigour of health and
youth, his practice will perpetually contradict his belief, till
the pressure of age, or sickness, or calamity, awakens his
terrors, and compels him to satisfy the double debt of piety
and remorse. I have already observed that the modern times
of religious indifference are the most favourable to the peace
and security of the clergy. Under the reign of superstition
they had much to hope from the ignorance, and much to
fear from the violence, of mankind. The wealth, whose constant increase must have rendered them the sole proprietors
of the earth, was alternately bestowed by the repentant father
and plundered by the rapacious son: their persons were
adored or violated; and the same idol, by the hands of the
same votaries, was placed on the altar or trampled in the

dust. In the feudal system of Europe, arms were the title of distinction and the measure of allegiance; and amidst their tumult the still voice of law and reason was seldom heard or obeyed. The turbulent Romans disdained the yoke and insulted the impotence of their bishop; nor would his education or character allow him to exercise, with decency or effect, the power of the sword. The motives of his election and the frailties of his life were exposed to their familiar observation; and proximity must diminish the reverence which his name and his decrees impressed on a barbarous world. This difference has not escaped the notice of our philosophic historian: "Though the name and authority of the court of Rome were so terrible in the remote countries of Europe, which were sunk in profound ignorance and were entirely unacquainted with its character and conduct, the pope was so little revered at home, that his inveterate enemies surrounded the gates of Rome itself, and even controlled his government in that city; and the ambassadors, who from a distant extremity of Europe carried to him the humble, or rather abject, submissions of the greatest potentate of the age, found the utmost difficulty to make their way to him and to throw themselves at his feet." [1]

Since primitive times the popes had had to contend with opposition, insult, and violence. In the middle of the twelfth century a movement to restore the republic was started by Arnold of Brescia. Arnold was expelled from Rome by Adrian IV (the English pope) and the emperor Frederic Barbarossa, and subsequently burnt alive. But a form of republican government, which included the office of Senator, was established.

METHODS OF PAPAL ELECTION

Ambition is a weed of quick and early vegetation in the vineyard of Christ. Under the first Christian princes the chair of St. Peter was disputed by the votes, the venality, the vio-

---

[1] Hume's History of England, vol. i. p. 419. The same writer has given us from Fitz-Stephen a singular act of cruelty perpetrated on the clergy by Goeffrey, the father of Henry II. "When he was master of Normandy the chapter of Seez presumed, without his consent, to proceed to the election of a bishop: upon which he ordered all of them, with the bishop elect, to be castrated, and made all their testicles be brought him in a platter." Of the pain and danger they might justly complain; yet, since they had vowed chastity, he deprived them of a superfluous treasure.

lence, of a popular election: the sanctuaries of Rome were
polluted with blood; and, from the third to the twelfth century, the church was distracted by the mischief of frequent
schisms. As long as the final appeal was determined by the
civil magistrate, these mischiefs were transient and local; the
merits were tried by equity or favour; nor could the unsuccessful competitor long disturb the triumph of his rival. But
after the emperors had been divested of their prerogatives,
after a maxim had been established that the vicar of Christ
is amenable to no earthly tribunal, each vacancy of the holy
see might involve Christendom in controversy and war. The
claims of the cardinals and inferior clergy, of the nobles and
people, were vague and litigious: the freedom of choice was
overruled by the tumults of a city that no longer owned or
obeyed a superior. On the decease of a pope, two factions
proceeded in different churches to a double election: the
number and weight of votes, the priority of time, the merit
of the candidates, might balance each other: the most respectable of the clergy were divided; and the distant princes,
who bowed before the spiritual throne, could not distinguish
the spurious from the legitimate idol. The emperors were
often the authors of the schism, from the political motive of
opposing a friendly to an hostile pontiff; and each of the
competitors was reduced to suffer the insults of his enemies,
who were not awed by conscience, and to purchase the support of his adherents, who were instigated by avarice or ambition. A peaceful and perpetual succession was ascertained
by Alexander the Third, who finally abolished the tumultuary
votes of the clergy and people, and defined the right of election in the sole college of cardinals. The three orders of
bishops, priests, and deacons, were assimilated to each other
by this important privilege; the parochial clergy of Rome obtained the first rank in the hierarchy: they were indifferently
chosen among the nations of Christendom; and the possession of the richest benefices, of the most important bishoprics,
was not incompatible with their title and office. The senators
of the Catholic church, the coadjutors and legates of the
supreme pontiff, were robed in purple, the symbol of martyrdom or royalty; they claimed a proud equality with kings;
and their dignity was enhanced by the smallness of their
number, which, till the reign of Leo the Tenth, seldom exceeded twenty or twenty-five persons. By this wise regulation

all doubt and scandal were removed, and the root of schism was so effectually destroyed, that in a period of six hundred years a double choice has only once divided the unity of the sacred college. But as the concurrence of two-thirds of the votes had been made necessary, the election was often delayed by the private interest and passions of the cardinals; and while they prolonged their independent reign, the Christian world was left destitute of a head. A vacancy of almost three years had preceded the elevation of Gregory the Tenth, who resolved to prevent the future abuse; and his bull, after some opposition, has been consecrated in the code of the canon law. Nine days are allowed for the obsequies of the deceased pope, and the arrival of the absent cardinals; on the tenth, they are imprisoned, each with one domestic, in a common apartment or *conclave*, without any separation of walls or curtains; a small window is reserved for the introduction of necessaries; but the door is locked on both sides, and guarded by the magistrates of the city, to seclude them from all correspondence with the world. If the election be not consummated in three days, the luxury of their table is contracted to a single dish at dinner and supper; and after the eighth day they are reduced to a scanty allowance of bread, water, and wine. During the vacancy of the holy see the cardinals are prohibited from touching the revenues, or assuming, unless in some rare emergency, the government of the church: all agreements and promises among the electors are formally annulled; and their integrity is fortified by their solemn oath and the prayers of the Catholics. Some articles of inconvenient or superfluous rigour have been gradually relaxed, but the principle of confinement is vigorous and entire: they are still urged, by the personal motives of health and freedom, to accelerate the moment of their deliverance; and the improvement of ballot or secret votes has wrapped the struggles of the conclave in the silky veil of charity and politeness. By these institutions the Romans were excluded from the election of their prince and bishop; and in the fever of wild and precarious liberty, they seemed insensible of the loss of this inestimable privilege. The emperor Lewis of Bavaria revived the example of the great Otho. After some negotiation with the magistrates, the Roman people was assembled in the square before St. Peter's: the pope of Avignon, John the Twenty-second, was deposed: the

choice of his successor was ratified by their consent and applause. They freely voted for a new law, that their bishop
should never be absent more than three months in the year,
and two days' journey from the city; and that, if he neglected to return on the third summons, the public servant
should be degraded and dismissed. But Lewis forgot his own
debility and the prejudices of the times: beyond the precincts
of a German camp, his useless phantom was rejected; the
Romans despised their own workmanship; the antipope implored the mercy of his lawful sovereign; and the exclusive
right of the cardinals was more firmly established by this unseasonable attack.

MIGRATION OF THE POPES TO AVIGNON

Had the election been always held in the Vatican, the
rights of the senate and people would not have been violated
with impunity. But the Romans forgot, and were forgotten,
in the absence of the successors of Gregory the Seventh, who
did not keep as a divine precept their ordinary residence in
the city and diocese. The care of that diocese was less important than the government of the universal church; nor
could the popes delight in a city in which their authority was
always opposed, and their person was often endangered.
From the persecution of the emperors, and the wars of Italy,
they escaped beyond the Alps into the hospitable bosom of
France; from the tumults of Rome they prudently withdrew
to live and die in the more tranquil stations of Anagni,
Perugia, Viterbo, and the adjacent cities. When the flock was
offended or impoverished by the absence of the shepherd,
they were recalled by a stern admonition, that St. Peter had
fixed his chair, not in an obscure village, but in the capital of
the world; by a ferocious menace that the Romans would
march in arms to destroy the place and people that should
dare to afford them a retreat. They returned with timorous
obedience, and were saluted with the account of a heavy
debt, of all the losses which their desertion had occasioned,
the hire of lodgings, the sale of provisions, and the various
expenses of servants and strangers who attended the court.
After a short interval of peace, and perhaps of authority,
they were again banished by new tumults, and again summoned by the imperious or respectful invitation of the senate.

In these occasional retreats the exiles and fugitives of the Vatican were seldom long, or far, distant from the metropolis; but in the beginning of the fourteenth century the apostolic throne was transported, as it might seem for ever, from the Tiber to the Rhône; and the cause of the transmigration may be deduced from the furious contest between Boniface the Eighth and the king of France. The spiritual arms of excommunication and interdict were repulsed by the union of the three estates, and the privileges of the Gallican church; but the pope was not prepared against the carnal weapons which Philip the Fair had courage to employ. As the pope resided at Anagni, without the suspicion of danger, his palace and person were assaulted by three hundred horse, who had been secretly levied by William of Nogaret, a French minister, and Sciarra Colonna, of a noble but hostile family of Rome. The cardinals fled; the inhabitants of Anagni were seduced from their allegiance and gratitude; but the dauntless Boniface, unarmed and alone, seated himself in his chair, and awaited, like the conscript fathers of old, the swords of the Gauls. Nogaret, a foreign adversary, was content to execute the orders of his master: by the domestic enmity of Colonna, he was insulted with words and blows; and during a confinement of three days his life was threatened by the hardships which they inflicted on the obstinacy which they provoked. Their strange delay gave time and courage to the adherents of the church, who rescued him from sacrilegious violence; but his imperious soul was wounded in a vital part; and Boniface expired at Rome in a frenzy of rage and revenge. His memory is stained with the glaring vices of avarice and pride; nor has the courage of a martyr promoted this ecclesiastical champion to the honours of a saint; a magnanimous sinner (say the chronicles of the times), who entered like a fox, reigned like a lion, and died like a dog. He was succeeded by Benedict the Eleventh, the mildest of mankind. Yet he excommunicated the impious emissaries of Philip, and devoted the city and people of Anagni by a tremendous curse, whose effects are still visible to the eyes of superstition.

After his decease, the tedious and equal suspense of the conclave was fixed by the dexterity of the French faction. A specious offer was made and accepted, that, in the term of forty days, they would elect one of the three candidates who should be named by their opponents. The archbishop of Bor-

deaux, a furious enemy of his king and country, was the first
on the list; but his ambition was known; and his conscience
obeyed the calls of fortune and the commands of a benefactor, who had been informed by a swift messenger that the
choice of a pope was now in his hands. The terms were regulated in a private interview; and with such speed and secrecy
was the business transacted, that the unanimous conclave
applauded the elevation of Clement the Fifth. The cardinals
of both parties were soon astonished by a summons to attend
him beyond the Alps; from whence, as they soon discovered,
they must never hope to return. He was engaged by promise
and affection to prefer the residence of France; and, after
dragging his court through Poitou and Gascony, and devour-
ing, by his expense, the cities and convents on the road, he
finally reposed at Avignon, which flourished above seventy
years the seat of the Roman pontiff and the metropolis of
Christendom. By land, by sea, by the Rhône, the position of
Avignon was on all sides accessible; the southern provinces of
France do not yield to Italy itself; new palaces arose for the
accommodation of the pope and cardinals; and the arts of
luxury were soon attracted by the treasures of the church.
They were already possessed of the adjacent territory, the
Venaissin county, a populous and fertile spot; and the sovereignty of Avignon was afterwards purchased from the youth
and distress of Jane, the first queen of Naples and countess of
Provence, for the inadequate price of fourscore thousand
florins. Under the shadow of the French monarchy, amidst
an obedient people, the popes enjoyed an honourable and
tranquil state, to which they long had been strangers: but
Italy deplored their absence; and Rome, in solitude and
poverty, might repent of the ungovernable freedom which had
driven from the Vatican the successor of St. Peter. Her repentance was tardy and fruitless: after the death of the old
members, the sacred college was filled with French cardinals,
who beheld Rome and Italy with abhorrence and contempt,
and perpetuated a series of national, and even provincial,
popes, attached by the most indissoluble ties to their native
country.

INSTITUTION OF THE JUBILEE, OR HOLY YEAR

The progress of industry had produced and enriched the Italian republics: the era of their liberty is the most flourishing period of population and agriculture, of manufactures and commerce; and their mechanic labours were gradually refined into the arts of elegance and genius. But the position of Rome was less favourable, the territory less fruitful: the character of the inhabitants was debased by indolence and elated by pride; and they fondly conceived that the tribute of subjects must for ever nourish the metropolis of the church and empire. This prejudice was encouraged in some degree by the resort of pilgrims to the shrines of the apostles; and the last legacy of the popes, the institution of the HOLY YEAR, was not less beneficial to the people than to the clergy. Since the loss of Palestine, the gift of plenary indulgences, which had been applied to the crusades, remained without an object; and the most valuable treasure of the church was sequestered above eight years from public circulation. A new channel was opened by the diligence of Boniface the Eighth, who reconciled the vices of ambition and avarice; and the pope had sufficient learning to recollect and revive the secular games which were celebrated in Rome at the conclusion of every century. To sound without danger the depth of popular credulity, a sermon was seasonably pronounced, a report was artfully scattered, some aged witnesses were produced; and on the first of January of the year thirteen hundred the church of St. Peter was crowded with the faithful, who demanded the *customary* indulgence of the holy time. The pontiff, who watched and irritated their devout impatience, was soon persuaded by ancient testimony of the justice of their claim; and he proclaimed a plenary absolution to all Catholics who, in the course of that year, and at every similar period, should respectfully visit the apostolic churches of St. Peter and St. Paul. The welcome sound was propagated through Christendom; and at first from the nearest provinces of Italy, and at length from the remote kingdoms of Hungary and Britain, the highways were thronged with a swarm of pilgrims who sought to expiate their sins in a journey, however costly or laborious, which was exempt from the perils of military service. All exceptions of rank or sex, of age or infirmity,

were forgotten in the common transport; and in the streets
and churches many persons were trampled to death by the
eagerness of devotion. The calculation of their numbers could
not be easy nor accurate; and they have probably been magnified by a dexterous clergy, well apprised of the contagion
of example: yet we are assured by a judicious historian, who
assisted at the ceremony, that Rome was never replenished
with less than two hundred thousand strangers; and another
spectator has fixed at two millions the total concourse of the
year. A trifling oblation from each individual would accumulate a royal treasure; and two priests stood night and day,
with rakes in their hands, to collect, without counting, the
heaps of gold and silver that were poured on the altar of St.
Paul. It was fortunately a season of peace and plenty; and if
forage was scarce, if inns and lodgings were extravagantly
dear, an inexhaustible supply of bread and wine, of meat and
fish, was provided by the policy of Boniface and the venal
hospitality of the Romans. From a city without trade or industry all casual riches will speedily evaporate: but the
avarice and envy of the next generation solicited Clement the
Sixth to anticipate the distant period of the century. The
gracious pontiff complied with their wishes; afforded Rome
this poor consolation for his loss; and justified the change by
the name and practice of the Mosaic Jubilee. His summons
was obeyed; and the number, zeal, and liberality of the pilgrims did not yield to the primitive festival. But they encountered the triple scourge of war, pestilence, and famine:
many wives and virgins were violated in the castles of Italy;
and many strangers were pillaged or murdered by the savage
Romans, no longer moderated by the presence of their bishop.
To the impatience of the popes we may ascribe the successive
reduction to fifty, thirty-three, and twenty-five years; although
the second of these terms is commensurate with the life of
Christ. The profusion of indulgences, the revolt of the Protestants, and the decline of superstition, have much diminished the value of the jubilee; yet even the nineteenth and
last festival was a year of pleasure and profit to the Romans;
and a philosophic smile will not disturb the triumph of the
priest or the happiness of the people.

THE ROMAN NOBILITY

In the beginning of the eleventh century Italy was exposed to the feudal tyranny, alike oppressive to the sovereign and the people. The rights of human nature were vindicated by her numerous republics, who soon extended their liberty and dominion from the city to the adjacent country. The sword of the nobles was broken; their slaves were enfranchised; their castles were demolished; they assumed the habits of society and obedience; their ambition was confined to municipal honours; and in the proudest aristocracy of Venice or Genoa, each patrician was subject to the laws. But the feeble and disorderly government of Rome was unequal to the task of curbing her rebellious sons, who scorned the authority of the magistrate within and without the walls. It was no longer a civil contention between the nobles and plebeians for the government of the state: the barons asserted in arms their personal independence; their palaces and castles were fortified against a siege; and their private quarrels were maintained by the numbers of their vassals and retainers. In origin and affection they were aliens to their country: and a genuine Roman, could such have been produced, might have renounced these haughty strangers, who disdained the appellation of citizens, and proudly styled themselves the princes of Rome. After a dark series of revolutions all records of pedigree were lost; the distinction of surnames was abolished; the blood of the nations was mingled in a thousand channels; and the Goths and Lombards, the Greeks and Franks, the Germans and Normans, had obtained the fairest possessions by royal bounty, or the prerogative of valour. These examples might be readily presumed; but the elevation of a Hebrew race to the rank of senators and consuls is an event without a parallel in the long captivity of these miserable exiles. In the time of Leo the Ninth a wealthy and learned Jew was converted to Christianity; and honoured at his baptism with the name of his godfather, the reigning pope. The zeal and courage of Peter the son of Leo were signalised in the cause of Gregory the Seventh, who entrusted his faithful adherent with the government of Hadrian's mole, the tower of Crescentius, or, as it is now called, the castle of St. Angelo. Both the father and the son were the

parents of a numerous progeny: their riches, the fruits of
usury, were shared with the noblest families of the city; and
so extensive was their alliance, that the grandson of the
proselyte was exalted by the weight of his kindred to the
throne of St. Peter. A majority of the clergy and people supported his cause: he reigned several years in the Vatican;
and it is only the eloquence of St. Bernard, and the final triumph of Innocent the Second, that has branded Anacletus
with the epithet of antipope. After his defeat and death the
posterity of Leo is no longer conspicuous; and none will be
found of the modern nobles ambitious of descending from a
Jewish stock. It is not my design to enumerate the Roman
families which have failed at different periods, or those which
are continued in different degrees of splendour to the present
time. The old consular line of the *Frangipani* discover their
name in the generous act of *breaking* or dividing bread in a
time of famine; and such benevolence is more truly glorious
than to have enclosed, with their allies the *Corsi,* a spacious
quarter of the city in the chains of their fortifications; the
Savelli, as it should seem a Sabine race, have maintained
their original dignity; the obsolete surname of the *Capizucchi*
is inscribed on the coins of the first senators; the *Conti* preserve the honour, without the estate, of the counts of Signia;
and the *Annibaldi* must have been very ignorant, or very
modest, if they had not descended from the Carthaginian
hero.

But among, perhaps above, the peers and princes of the
city, I distinguish the rival houses of Colonna and Ursini,
whose private story is an essential part of the annals of modern Rome. I. The name and arms of Colonna have been the
theme of much doubtful etymology; nor have the orators
and antiquarians overlooked either Trajan's pillar, or the
columns of Hercules, or the pillar of Christ's flagellation, or
the luminous column that guided the Israelites in the desert.
Their first historical appearance in the year eleven hundred
and four attests the power and antiquity, while it explains the
simple meaning, of the name. By the usurpation of Cavæ the
Colonna provoked the arms of Paschal the Second; but they
lawfully held in the Campagna of Rome the hereditary fiefs
of Zagarola and *Colonna;* and the latter of these towns was
probably adorned with some lofty pillar, the relic of a villa
or temple. They likewise possessed one moiety of the neigh-

bouring city of Tusculum; a strong presumption of their
descent from the counts of Tusculum, who in the tenth century were the tyrants of the apostolic see. According to their
own and the public opinion, the primitive and remote source
was derived from the banks of the Rhine; and the sovereigns
of Germany were not ashamed of a real or fabulous affinity
with a noble race, which in the revolutions of seven hundred
years has been often illustrated by merit and always by fortune. About the end of the thirteenth century the most powerful branch was composed of an uncle and six brothers, all
conspicuous in arms or in the honours of the church. Of
these, Peter was elected senator of Rome, introduced to the
Capitol in a triumphant car, and hailed in some vain acclamations with the title of Cæsar; while John and Stephen
were declared marquis of Ancona and count of Romagna, by
Nicholas the Fourth, a patron so partial to their family, that
he has been delineated in satirical portraits, imprisoned as it
were in a hollow pillar. After his decease their haughty behaviour provoked the displeasure of the most implacable of
mankind. The two cardinals, the uncle and the nephew, denied the election of Boniface the Eighth; and the Colonna
were oppressed for a moment by his temporal and spiritual
arms. He proclaimed a crusade against his personal enemies;
their estates were confiscated; their fortresses on either side
of the Tiber were besieged by the troops of St. Peter and
those of the rival nobles; and after the ruin of Palestrina or
Præneste, their principal seat, the ground was marked with
a ploughshare, the emblem of perpetual desolation. Degraded,
banished, proscribed, the six brothers, in disguise and danger, wandered over Europe without renouncing the hope of
deliverance and revenge. In this double hope the French
court was their surest asylum: they prompted and directed
the enterprise of Philip; and I should praise their magnanimity had they respected the misfortune and courage of the
captive tyrant. His civil acts were annulled by the Roman
people, who restored the honours and possessions of the
Colonna; and some estimate may be formed of their wealth
by their losses, of their losses by the damages of one hundred thousand gold florins which were granted them against
the accomplices and heirs of the deceased pope. All the spiritual censures and disqualifications were abolished by his
prudent successors; and the fortune of the house was more

firmly established by this transient hurricane. The boldness of Sciarra Colonna was signalised in the captivity of Boniface, and long afterwards in the coronation of Lewis of Bavaria; and by the gratitude of the emperor the pillar in their arms was encircled with a royal crown. But the first of the family in fame and merit was the elder Stephen, whom Petrarch loved and esteemed as a hero superior to his own times and not unworthy of ancient Rome. Persecution and exile displayed to the nations his abilities in peace and war; in his distress he was an object, not of pity but of reverence; the aspect of danger provoked him to avow his name and country; and when he was asked, "Where is now your fortress?" he laid his hand on his heart, and answered, "Here." He supported with the same virtue the return of prosperity; and, till the ruin of his declining age, the ancestors, the character, and the children of Stephen Colonna exalted his dignity in the Roman republic and at the court of Avignon. II. The Ursini migrated from Spoleto; the sons of Ursus, as they are styled in the twelfth century, from some eminent person who is only known as the father of their race. But they were soon distinguished among the nobles of Rome by the number and bravery of their kinsmen, the strength of their towers, the honours of the senate and sacred college, and the elevation of two popes, Celestin the Third and Nicholas the Third, of their name and lineage. Their riches may be accused as an early abuse of nepotism: the estates of St. Peter were alienated in their favour by the liberal Celestin; and Nicholas was ambitious for their sake to solicit the alliance of monarchs; to found new kingdoms in Lombardy and Tuscany; and to invest them with the perpetual office of senators of Rome. All that has been observed of the greatness of the Colonna will likewise redound to the glory of the Ursini, their constant and equal antagonists in the long hereditary feud which distracted above two hundred and fifty years the ecclesiastical state. The jealousy of pre-eminence and power was the true ground of their quarrel; but as a specious badge of distinction, the Colonna embraced the name of Ghibelines and the party of the empire; the Ursini espoused the title of Guelphs and the cause of the church. The eagle and the keys were displayed in their adverse banners; and the two factions of Italy most furiously raged when the origin and nature of the dispute were long since forgotten. After the retreat of the popes to Avignon they disputed in arms the vacant republic; and the mischiefs of discord were perpetuated by the wretched compromise of electing each year two rival senators. By their private hostilities the city and country were desolated, and the fluctuating balance inclined with their alternate success. But none of either family had fallen by the sword till the most renowned champion of the Ursini was surprised and slain by the younger Stephen Colonna. His triumph is stained with the reproach of violating the truce; their defeat was basely avenged by the assassination, before the church door, of an innocent boy and his two servants. Yet the victorious Colonna, with an annual colleague, was declared senator of Rome during the term of five years. And the muse of Petrarch inspired a wish, a hope, a prediction, that the generous youth, the son of his venerable hero, would restore Rome and Italy to their pristine glory; that his justice would extirpate the wolves and lions, the serpents and *bears*, who laboured to subvert the eternal basis of the marble COLUMN.

70.

PETRARCH. RIENZI AND THE RESTORATION OF THE *GOOD
ESTATE*. PROSPERITY OF THE ROMAN REPUBLIC.
KNIGHTHOOD, CORONATION, AND FOLLIES OF RIENZI.
RETURN OF THE POPES TO ROME. GREAT SCHISM
OF THE WEST. GOVERNMENT OF ROME IN THE
FIFTEENTH CENTURY. ECCLESIASTICAL GOVERNMENT

IN THE APPREHENSION of modern times Petrarch is the Italian
songster of Laura and love. In the harmony of his Tuscan
rhymes Italy applauds, or rather adores, the father of her
lyric poetry; and his verse, or at least his name, is repeated
by the enthusiasm or affection of amorous sensibility. Whatever may be the private taste of a stranger, his slight and
superficial knowledge should humbly acquiesce in the taste
of a learned nation; yet I may hope or presume that the
Italians do not compare the tedious uniformity of sonnets
and elegies with the sublime compositions of their epic muse,
the original wildness of Dante, the regular beauties of Tasso,
and the boundless variety of the incomparable Ariosto. The
merits of the lover I am still less qualified to appreciate: nor
am I deeply interested in a metaphysical passion for a nymph
so shadowy, that her existence has been questioned; for a
matron so prolific, that she was delivered of eleven legitimate
children, while her amorous swain sighed and sung at the
fountain of Vaucluse. But in the eyes of Petrarch and those
of his graver contemporaries his love was a sin, and Italian
verse a frivolous amusement. His Latin works of philosophy,
poetry, and eloquence established his serious reputation which
was soon diffused from Avignon over France and Italy: his
friends and disciples were multiplied in every city; and if the
ponderous volume of his writings be now abandoned to a long
repose, our gratitude must applaud the man who, by precept
and example, revived the spirit and study of the Augustan
age. From his earliest youth Petrarch aspired to the poetic
crown. The academical honours of the three faculties had in-

troduced a royal degree of master or doctor in the art of poetry; and the title of poet-laureat, which custom, rather than vanity, perpetuates in the English court, was first invented by the Cæsars of Germany. In the musical games of antiquity a prize was bestowed on the victor: the belief that Virgil and Horace had been crowned in the Capitol inflamed the emulation of a Latin bard; and the laurel was endeared to the lover by a verbal resemblance with the name of his mistress. The value of either object was enhanced by the difficulties of the pursuit; and if the virtue or prudence of Laura was inexorable, he enjoyed, and might boast of enjoying, the nymph of poetry. His vanity was not of the most delicate kind, since he applauds the success of his own *labours;* his name was popular; his friends were active; the open or secret opposition of envy and prejudice was surmounted by the dexterity of patient merit. In the thirty-sixth year of his age he was solicited to accept the object of his wishes; and on the same day, in the solitude of Vaucluse, he received a similar and solemn invitation from the senate of Rome and the university of Paris. The learning of a theological school, and the ignorance of a lawless city, were alike unqualified to bestow the ideal though immortal wreath which genius may obtain from the free applause of the public and of posterity: but the candidate dismissed this troublesome reflection; and, after some moments of complacency and suspense, preferred the summons of the metropolis of the world.

The ceremony of his coronation was performed in the Capitol, by his friend and patron the supreme magistrate of the republic. Twelve patrician youths were arrayed in scarlet; six representatives of the most illustrious families, in green robes, with garlands of flowers, accompanied the procession; in the midst of the princes and nobles, the senator, count of Anguillara, a kinsman of the Colonna, assumed his throne; and at the voice of a herald Petrarch arose. After discoursing on a text of Virgil, and thrice repeating his vows for the prosperity of Rome, he knelt before the throne and received from the senator a laurel crown, with a more precious declaration, "This is the reward of merit." The people shouted, "Long life to the Capitol and the poet!" A sonnet in praise of Rome was accepted as the effusion of genius and gratitude; and after the whole procession had visited the Vatican the

profane wreath was suspended before the shrine of St. Peter.
In the act or diploma which was presented to Petrarch, the
title and prerogatives of poet-laureat are revived in the Capitol after the lapse of thirteen hundred years; and he receives
the perpetual privilege of wearing, at his choice, a crown of
laurel, ivy, or myrtle, of assuming the poetic habit, and of
teaching, disputing, interpreting, and composing, in all places
whatsoever, and on all subjects of literature. The grant was
ratified by the authority of the senate and people; and the
character of citizen was the recompense of his affection for
the Roman name. They did him honour, but they did him
justice. In the familiar society of Cicero and Livy he had
imbibed the ideas of an ancient patriot; and his ardent fancy
kindled every idea to a sentiment, and every sentiment to a
passion. The aspect of the seven hills and their majestic ruins
confirmed these lively impressions; and he loved a country
by whose liberal spirit he had been crowned and adopted.
The poverty and debasement of Rome excited the indignation and pity of her grateful son: he dissembled the faults of
his fellow-citizens; applauded with partial fondness the last
of their heroes and matrons; and in the remembrance of the
past, in the hope of the future, was pleased to forget the
miseries of the present time. Rome was still the lawful mistress of the world; the pope and the emperor, her bishop and
general, had abdicated their station by an inglorious retreat
to the Rhône and the Danube; but if she could resume her
virtue, the republic might again vindicate her liberty and
dominion. Amidst the indulgence of enthusiasm and eloquence, Petrarch, Italy, and Europe were astonished by a
revolution which realised for a moment his most splendid
visions. The rise and fall of the tribune Rienzi will occupy
the following pages: the subject is interesting, the materials
are rich, and the glance of a patriot bard will sometimes
vivify the copious, but simple, narrative of the Florentine,
and more especially of the Roman, historian.

RIENZI AND THE RESTORATION OF THE *GOOD ESTATE*

In a quarter of the city which was inhabited only by mechanics and Jews, the marriage of an innkeeper and a washer-
woman produced the future deliverer of Rome. From such
parents Nicholas Rienzi Gabrini could inherit neither dignity

nor fortune; and the gift of a liberal education, which they painfully bestowed, was the cause of his glory and untimely end. The study of history and eloquence, the writings of Cicero, Seneca, Livy, Cæsar, and Valerius Maximus, elevated above his equals and contemporaries the genius of the young plebeian: he perused with indefatigable diligence the manuscripts and marbles of antiquity; loved to dispense his knowledge in familiar language, and was often provoked to exclaim, "Where are now these Romans? their virtue, their justice, their power? why was I not born in those happy times?" When the republic addressed to the throne of Avignon an embassy of the three orders, the spirit and eloquence of Rienzi recommended him to a place among the thirteen deputies of the commons. The orator had the honour of haranguing Pope Clement the Sixth, and the satisfaction of conversing with Petrarch, a congenial mind; but his aspiring hopes were chilled by disgrace and poverty, and the patriot was reduced to a single garment and the charity of the hospital. From this misery he was relieved by the sense of merit or the smile of favour; and the employment of apostolic notary afforded him a daily stipend of five gold florins, a more honourable and extensive connection, and the right of contrasting, both in words and actions, his own integrity with the vices of the state. The eloquence of Rienzi was prompt and persuasive: the multitude is always prone to envy and censure: he was stimulated by the loss of a brother and the impunity of the assassins; nor was it possible to excuse or exaggerate the public calamities. The blessings of peace and justice, for which civil society has been instituted, were banished from Rome: the jealous citizens, who might have endured every personal or pecuniary injury, were most deeply wounded in the dishonour of their wives and daughters; they were equally oppressed by the arrogance of the nobles and the corruption of the magistrates; and the abuse of arms or of laws was the only circumstance that distinguished the lions from the dogs and serpents of the Capitol. These allegorical emblems were variously repeated in the pictures which Rienzi exhibited in the streets and churches; and while the spectators gazed with curious wonder, the bold and ready orator unfolded the meaning, applied the satire, inflamed their passions, and announced a distant hope of comfort and deliverance. The privileges of Rome, her eternal sovereignty over

her princes and provinces, was the theme of his public and
private discourse; and a monument of servitude became in
his hands a title and incentive of liberty. The decree of the
senate, which granted the most ample prerogatives to the
emperor Vespasian, had been inscribed on a copper-plate
still extant in the choir of the church of St. John Lateran. A
numerous assembly of nobles and plebeians was invited to this
political lecture, and a convenient theatre was erected for
their reception. The notary appeared in a magnificent and
mysterious habit, explained the inscription by a version and
commentary, and descanted with eloquence and zeal on the
ancient glories of the senate and people, from whom all legal
authority was derived. The supine ignorance of the nobles was
incapable of discerning the serious tendency of such repre-
sentations: they might sometimes chastise with words and
blows the plebeian reformer; but he was often suffered in
the Colonna palace to amuse the company with his threats
and predictions; and the modern Brutus was concealed under
the mask of folly and the character of a buffoon. While they
indulged their contempt, the restoration of the *good estate*,
his favourite expression, was entertained among the people
as a desirable, a possible, and at length as an approaching,
event; and while all had the disposition to applaud, some had
the courage to assist, their promised deliverer.

A prophecy, or rather a summons, affixed on the church
door of St. George, was the first public evidence of his designs; a nocturnal assembly of an hundred citizens on Mount
Aventine, the first step to their execution. After an oath of
secrecy and aid, he represented to the conspirators the importance and facility of their enterprise; that the nobles, without union or resources, were strong only in the fear of their
imaginary strength; that all power, as well as right, was in
the hands of the people; that the revenues of the apostolical
chamber might relieve the public distress; and that the pope
himself would approve their victory over the common enemies of government and freedom. After securing a faithful
band to protect his first declaration, he proclaimed through
the city, by sound of trumpet, that on the evening of the following day all persons should assemble without arms before
the church of St. Angelo, to provide for the re-establishment
of the good estate. The whole night was employed in the
celebration of thirty masses of the Holy Ghost; and in the

morning Rienzi, bareheaded, but in complete armour, issued from the church, encompassed by the hundred conspirators. The pope's vicar, the simple bishop of Orvieto, who had been persuaded to sustain a part in this singular ceremony, marched on his right hand, and three great standards were borne aloft as the emblems of their design. In the first, the banner of *liberty,* Rome was seated on two lions, with a palm in one hand and a globe in the other; St. Paul, with a drawn sword, was delineated in the banner of *justice;* and in the third, St. Peter held the keys of *concord* and *peace.* Rienzi was encouraged by the presence and applause of an innumerable crowd, who understood little and hoped much; and the procession slowly rolled forwards from the castle of St. Angelo to the Capitol. His triumph was disturbed by some secret emotions which he laboured to suppress: he ascended without opposition, and with seeming confidence, the citadel of the republic; harangued the people from the balcony, and received the most flattering confirmation of his acts and laws. The nobles, as if destitute of arms and counsels, beheld in silent consternation this strange revolution; and the moment had been prudently chosen when the most formidable, Stephen Colonna, was absent from the city. On the first rumour he returned to his palace, affected to despise this plebeian tumult, and declared to the messenger of Rienzi that at his leisure he would cast the madman from the windows of the Capitol. The great bell instantly rang an alarm, and so rapid was the tide, so urgent was the danger, that Colonna escaped with precipitation to the suburb of St. Laurence: from thence, after a moment's refreshment, he continued the same speedy career till he reached in safety his castle of Palestrina, lamenting his own imprudence, which had not trampled the spark of this mighty conflagration. A general and peremptory order was issued from the Capitol to all the nobles that they should peaceably retire to their estates: they obeyed, and their departure secured the tranquillity of the free and obedient citizens of Rome.

But such voluntary obedience evaporates with the first transports of zeal; and Rienzi felt the importance of justifying his usurpation by a regular form and a legal title. At his own choice, the Roman people would have displayed their attachment and authority by lavishing on his head the names of senator or consul, of king or emperor: he preferred the

ancient and modest appellation of tribune; the protection of
the commons was the essence of that sacred office, and they
were ignorant that it had never been invested with any share
in the legislative or executive powers of the republic. In this
character, and with the consent of the Romans, the tribune
enacted the most salutary laws for the restoration and maintenance of the good estate. By the first he fulfils the wish of
honesty and inexperience, that no civil suit should be protracted beyond the term of fifteen days. The danger of frequent perjury might justify the pronouncing against a false
accuser the same penalty which his evidence would have inflicted: the disorders of the times might compel the legislator
to punish every homicide with death and every injury with
equal retaliation. But the execution of justice was hopeless
till he had previously abolished the tyranny of the nobles. It
was formally provided that none, except the supreme magistrate, should possess or command the gates, bridges, or towers
of the state; that no private garrisons should be introduced
into the towns or castles of the Roman territory; that none
should bear arms or presume to fortify their houses in the
city or country; that the barons should be responsible for
the safety of the highways and the free passage of provisions;
and that the protection of malefactors and robbers should
be expiated by a fine of a thousand marks of silver. But these
regulations would have been impotent and nugatory, had
not the licentious nobles been awed by the sword of the civil
power. A sudden alarm from the bell of the Capitol could
still summon to the standard above twenty thousand volunteers: the support of the tribune and the laws required a
more regular and permanent force. In each harbour of the
coast a vessel was stationed for the assurance of commerce:
a standing militia of three hundred and sixty horse and
thirteen hundred foot was levied, clothed, and paid in the
thirteen quarters of the city; and the spirit of a commonwealth may be traced in the grateful allowance of one hundred florins, or pounds, to the heirs of every soldier who
lost his life in the service of his country. For the maintenance of the public defence, for the establishment of gran-
aries, for the relief of widows, orphans, and indigent convents, Rienzi applied, without fear of sacrilege, the revenues
of the apostolic chamber: the three branches of hearth-
money, the salt-duty, and the customs, were each of the an-

nual produce of one hundred thousand florins; and scandalous were the abuses, if in four or five months the amount of
the salt-duty could be trebled by his judicious economy.
After thus restoring the forces and finances of the republic,
the tribune recalled the nobles from their solitary independence, required their personal appearance in the Capitol, and
imposed an oath of allegiance to the new government, and of
submission to the laws of the good estate. Apprehensive for
their safety, but still more apprehensive of the danger of a
refusal, the princes and barons returned to their houses at
Rome in the garb of simple and peaceful citizens: the Colonna and Ursini, the Savelli and Frangipani, were confounded before the tribunal of a plebeian, of the vile buffoon
whom they had so often derided, and their disgrace was
aggravated by the indignation which they vainly struggled to
disguise. The same oath was successively pronounced by the
several orders of society, the clergy and gentlemen, the judges
and notaries, the merchants and artisans, and the gradual
descent was marked by the increase of sincerity and zeal.
They swore to live and die with the republic and the church,
whose interest was artfully united by the nominal association
of the bishop of Orvieto, the pope's vicar, to the office of
tribune. It was the boast of Rienzi that he had delivered the
throne and patrimony of St. Peter from a rebellious aristocracy; and Clement the Sixth, who rejoiced in its fall, affected to believe the professions, to applaud the merits, and to
confirm the title of his trusty servant. The speech, perhaps
the mind, of the tribune, was inspired with a lively regard for
the purity of the faith: he insinuated his claim to a super-
natural mission from the Holy Ghost; enforced by a heavy
forfeiture the annual duty of confession and communion;
and strictly guarded the spiritual as well as temporal welfare
of his faithful people.

PROSPERITY OF THE ROMAN REPUBLIC

Never perhaps has the energy and effect of a single mind
been more remarkably felt than in the sudden, though transient, reformation of Rome by the tribune Rienzi. A den of
robbers was converted to the discipline of a camp or convent: patient to hear, swift to redress, inexorable to punish,
his tribunal was always accessible to the poor and stranger;

nor could birth, or dignity, or the immunities of the church, protect the offender or his accomplices. The privileged houses, the private sanctuaries in Rome, on which no officer of justice would presume to trespass, were abolished; and he applied the timber and iron of their barricades in the fortifications of the Capitol. The venerable father of the Colonna was exposed in his own palace to the double shame of being desirous and of being unable to protect a criminal. A mule, with a jar of oil, had been stolen near Capranica; and the lord of the Ursini family was condemned to restore the damage and to discharge a fine of four hundred florins for his negligence in guarding the highways. Nor were the persons of the barons more inviolate than their lands or houses; and, either from accident or design, the same impartial rigour was exercised against the heads of the adverse factions. Peter Agapet Colonna, who had himself been senator of Rome, was arrested in the street for injury or debt; and justice was appeased by the tardy execution of Martin Ursini, who, among his various acts of violence and rapine, had pillaged a shipwrecked vessel at the mouth of the Tiber. His name, the purple of two cardinals, his uncles, a recent marriage, and a mortal disease, were disregarded by the inflexible tribune, who had chosen his victim. The public officers dragged him from his palace and nuptial bed: his trial was short and satisfactory; the bell of the Capitol convened the people: stripped of his mantle, on his knees, with his hands bound behind his back, he heard the sentence of death, and, after a brief confession, Ursini was led away to the gallows. After such an example, none who were conscious of guilt could hope for impunity, and the flight of the wicked, the licentious, and the idle, soon purified the city and territory of Rome. In this time (says the historian) the woods began to rejoice that they were no longer infested with robbers; the oxen began to plough; the pilgrims visited the sanctuaries; the roads and inns were replenished with travellers; trade, plenty, and good faith were restored in the markets; and a purse of gold might be exposed without danger in the midst of the highway. As soon as the life and property of the subject are secure, the labours and rewards of industry spontaneously revive: Rome was still the metropolis of the Christian world, and the fame and fortunes of the tribune were diffused in every country by the strangers who had enjoyed the blessings of his government.

The deliverance of his country inspired Rienzi with a vast and perhaps visionary idea of uniting Italy in a great federative republic, of which Rome should be the ancient and lawful head, and the free cities and princes the members and associates. His pen was not less eloquent than his tongue, and his numerous epistles were delivered to swift and trusty messengers. On foot, with a white wand in their hand, they traversed the forests and mountains; enjoyed, in the most hostile states, the sacred security of ambassadors; and reported, in the style of flattery or truth, that the highways along their passage were lined with kneeling multitudes, who implored Heaven for the success of their undertaking. Could passion have listened to reason, could private interest have yielded to the public welfare, the supreme tribunal and confederate union of the Italian republic might have healed their intestine discord, and closed the Alps against the barbarians of the North. But the propitious season had elapsed; and if Venice, Florence, Sienna, Perugia, and many inferior cities, offered their lives and fortunes to the good estate, the tyrants of Lombardy and Tuscany must despise or hate the plebeian author of a free constitution. From them, however, and from every part of Italy, the tribune received the most friendly and respectful answers: they were followed by the ambassadors of the princes and republics; and in this foreign conflux, on all the occasions of pleasure or business, the low-born notary could assume the familiar or majestic courtesy of a sovereign.[1] The most glorious circumstance of his reign was an appeal to his justice from Lewis king of Hungary, who complained that his brother and her husband had been perfidiously strangled by Jane queen of Naples: her guilt or innocence was pleaded in a solemn trial at Rome; but after hearing the advocates, the tribune adjourned this weighty and invidious cause, which was soon determined by the sword of the Hungarian. Beyond the Alps, more especially at Avignon, the revolution was the theme of curiosity, wonder, and applause. Petrarch had been the private friend, perhaps the secret coun-

---

[1] It was thus that Oliver Cromwell's old acquaintance, who remembered his vulgar and ungracious entrance into the House of Commons, were astonished at the ease and majesty of the Protector on his throne. The consciousness of merit and power will sometimes elevate the manners to the station.

sellor, of Rienzi: his writings breathe the most ardent spirit of patriotism and joy; and all respect for the pope, all gratitude for the Colonna, was lost in the superior duties of a Roman citizen. The poet-laureat of the Capitol maintains the act, applauds the hero, and mingles with some apprehension and advice the most lofty hopes of the permanent and rising greatness of the republic.

KNIGHTHOOD, CORONATION, AND FOLLIES OF RIENZI

While Petrarch indulged these prophetic visions, the Roman hero was fast declining from the meridian of fame and power; and the people, who had gazed with astonishment on the ascending meteor, began to mark the irregularity of its course, and the vicissitudes of light and obscurity. More eloquent than judicious, more enterprising than resolute, the faculties of Rienzi were not balanced by cool and commanding reason; he magnified in a tenfold proportion the objects of hope and fear; and prudence, which could not have erected, did not presume to fortify, his throne. In the blaze of prosperity, his virtues were insensibly tinctured with the adjacent vices; justice with cruelty, liberality with profusion, and the desire of fame with puerile and ostentatious vanity. He might have learned that the ancient tribunes, so strong and sacred in the public opinion, were not distinguished in style, habit, or appearance, from an ordinary plebeian; and that, as often as they visited the city on foot, a single viator, or beadle, attended the exercise of their office. The Gracchi would have frowned or smiled, could they have read the sonorous titles and epithets of their successor,—"NICHOLAS, SEVERE AND MERCIFUL; DELIVERER OF ROME; DEFENDER OF ITALY; FRIEND OF MANKIND, AND OF LIBERTY, PEACE, AND JUSTICE; TRIBUNE AUGUST": his theatrical pageants had prepared the revolution; but Rienzi abused, in luxury and pride, the political maxim of speaking to the eyes, as well as the understanding, of the multitude. From nature he had received the gift of an handsome person, till it was swelled and disfigured by intemperance: and his propensity to laughter was corrected in the magistrate by the affectation of gravity and sternness. He was clothed, at least on public occasions, in a parti-coloured robe of velvet or satin, lined with fur, and embroidered with gold: the rod of justice, which he carried in his hand, was a sceptre of polished steel, crowned with a globe and cross of gold, and enclosing a small fragment of the true and holy wood. In his civil and religious processions through the city, he rode on a white steed, the symbol of royalty: the great banner of the republic, a sun with a circle of stars, a dove with an olive-branch, was displayed over his head; a shower of gold and silver was scattered among the populace; fifty guards with halberds encompassed his person; a troop of horse preceded his march; and their tymbals and trumpets were of massy silver.

The ambition of the honours of chivalry betrayed the meanness of his birth and degraded the importance of his office; and the equestrian tribune was not less odious to the nobles, whom he adopted, than to the plebeians, whom he deserted. All that yet remained of treasure, or luxury, or art, was exhausted on that solemn day. Rienzi led the procession from the Capitol to the Lateran; the tediousness of the way was relieved with decorations and games; the ecclesiastical, civil, and miltary orders marched under their various banners; the Roman ladies attended his wife; and the ambassadors of Italy might loudly applaud or secretly deride the novelty of the pomp. In the evening, when they had reached the church and palace of Constantine, he thanked and dismissed the numerous assembly, with an invitation to the festival of the ensuing day. From the hands of a venerable knight he received the order of the Holy Ghost; the purification of the bath was a previous ceremony; but in no step of his life did Rienzi excite such scandal and censure as by the profane use of the porphyry vase in which Constantine (a foolish legend) had been healed of his leprosy by Pope Sylvester. With equal presumption the tribune watched or reposed within the consecrated precincts of the baptistery; and the failure of his state-bed was interpreted as an omen of his approaching downfall. At the hour of worship he showed himself to the returning crowds in a majestic attitude, with a robe of purple, his sword, and gilt spurs; but the holy rites were soon interrupted by his levity and insolence. Rising from his throne, and advancing towards the congregation, he proclaimed in a loud voice, "We summon to our tribunal Pope Clement, and command him to reside in his diocese of Rome: we also summon the sacred college of cardinals. We again summon the two pretenders, Charles of Bohemia and Lewis of Bavaria, who style themselves emperors: we likewise summon all the electors of Germany to inform us on what pretence they have usurped the inalienable right of the Roman people, the ancient and lawful sovereigns of the empire." Unsheathing his maiden sword, he thrice brandished it to the three parts of the world, and thrice repeated the extravagant declaration, "And this too is mine!" The pope's vicar, the bishop of Orvieto, attempted to check this career of folly; but his feeble protest was silenced by martial music; and instead of withdrawing from the assembly, he consented to dine with his brother tribune at a table which had hitherto been reserved for the supreme pontiff. A banquet, such as the Cæsars had given, was prepared for the Romans. The apartments, porticoes, and courts of the Lateran were spread with innumerable tables for either sex and every condition; a stream of wine flowed from the nostrils of Constantine's brazen horse; no complaint, except of the scarcity of water, could be heard; and the licentiousness of the multitude was curbed by discipline and fear. A subsequent day was appointed for the coronation of Rienzi; seven crowns of different leaves or metals were successively placed on his head by the most eminent of the Roman clergy; they represented the seven gifts of the Holy Ghost; and he still professed to imitate the example of the ancient tribunes. These extraordinary spectacles might deceive or flatter the people; and their own vanity was gratified in the vanity of their leader. But in his private life he soon deviated from the strict rule of frugality and abstinence; and the plebeians, who were awed by the splendour of the nobles, were provoked by the luxury of their equal. His wife, his son, his uncle (a barber in name and profession) exposed the contrast of vulgar manners and princely expense; and without acquiring the majesty, Rienzi degenerated into the vices, of a king.

In 1347 Rienzi was degraded from office and forced into exile. After seven years he returned to Rome with the title of Senator but was murdered four months later, September, 1354.

RETURN OF THE POPES TO ROME

The first and most generous wish of Petrarch was the restoration of a free republic; but after the exile and death of his plebeian hero, he turned his eyes from the tribune to the king of the Romans. The Capitol was yet stained with the blood of Rienzi when Charles the Fourth descended from the Alps to obtain the Italian and Imperial crowns. In his passage through Milan he received the visit, and repaid the flattery, of the poet-laureat; accepted a medal of Augustus; and promised, without a smile, to imitate the founder of the Roman monarchy. A false application of the names and maxims of antiquity was the source of the hopes and disappointments of Petrarch; yet he could not overlook the difference of times and characters; the immeasurable distance between the first Cæsars and a Bohemian prince, who by the favour of the clergy had been elected the titular head of the German aristocracy. Instead of restoring to Rome her glory and her provinces, he had bound himself by a secret treaty with the pope to evacuate the city on the day of his coronation; and his shameful retreat was pursued by the reproaches of the patriot bard.

After the loss of liberty and empire, his third and more humble wish was to reconcile the shepherd with his flock; to recall the Roman bishop to his ancient and peculiar diocese. In the fervour of youth, with the authority of age, Petrarch addressed his exhortations to five successive popes, and his eloquence was always inspired by the enthusiasm of sentiment and the freedom of language. The son of a citizen of Florence invariably preferred the country of his birth to that of his education; and Italy, in his eyes, was the queen and garden of the world. Amidst her domestic factions she was doubtless superior to France both in art and science, in wealth and politeness; but the difference could scarcely support the epithet of barbarous, which he promiscuously bestows on the countries beyond the Alps. Avignon, the mystic Babylon, the sink of vice and corruption, was the object of his hatred and contempt; but he forgets that her scandalous vices were not the growth of the soil, and that in every residence they would adhere to the power and luxury of the papal court. He confesses that the successor of St. Peter is the bishop of the universal church; yet it was not on the banks of the Rhône, but of the Tiber, that the apostle had fixed his everlasting throne: and while every city in the Christian world was blessed with a bishop, the metropolis alone was desolate and forlorn. Since the removal of the

Holy See the sacred buildings of the Lateran and the Vatican, their altars and their saints, were left in a state of poverty and decay; and Rome was often painted under the image of a disconsolate matron, as if the wandering husband could be reclaimed by the homely portrait of the age and infirmities of his weeping spouse. But the cloud which hung over the seven hills would be dispelled by the presence of their lawful sovereign: eternal fame, the prosperity of Rome, and the peace of Italy, would be the recompense of the pope who should dare to embrace this generous resolution. Of the five whom Petrarch exhorted, the three first, John the Twenty-second, Benedict the Twelfth, and Clement the Sixth, were importuned or amused by the boldness of the orator; but the memorable change which had been attempted by Urban the Fifth was finally accomplished by Gregory the Eleventh. The execution of their design was opposed by weighty and almost insuperable obstacles. A king of France, who has deserved the epithet of wise, was unwilling to release them from a local dependence: the cardinals, for the most part his subjects, were attached to the language, manners, and climate of Avignon; to their stately palaces; above all, to the wines of Burgundy. In their eyes Italy was foreign or hostile; and they reluctantly embarked at Marseilles, as if they had been sold or banished into the land of the Saracens. Urban the Fifth resided three years in the Vatican with safety and honour; his sanctity was protected by a guard of two thousand horse; and the king of Cyprus, the queen of Naples, and the emperors of the East and West, devoutly saluted their common father in the chair of St. Peter. But the joy of Petrarch and the Italians was soon turned into grief and indignation. Some reasons of public or private moment, his own impatience or the prayers of the cardinals, recalled Urban to France; and the approaching election was saved from the tyrannic patriotism of the Romans. The powers of heaven were interested in their cause: Bridget of Sweden, a saint and pilgrim, disapproved the return, and foretold the death, of Urban the Fifth; the migration of Gregory the Eleventh was encouraged by St. Catherine of Sienna, the spouse of Christ and ambassadress of the Florentines; and the popes themselves, the great masters of human credulity, appear to have listened to these visionary females. Yet those celestial admonitions were supported by some arguments of temporal policy. The residence of Avignon had been invaded by hostile violence: at the head of thirty thousand robbers an hero had extorted ransom and absolution from the vicar of Christ and the sacred college; and the maxim of the French warriors, to spare the people and plunder the church, was a new heresy of the most dangerous import. While the pope was driven from Avignon, he was strenuously invited to Rome. The senate and people acknowledged him as their lawful sovereign, and laid at his feet the keys of the gates, the bridges, and the fortresses; of the quarter at least beyond the Tiber. But this loyal offer was accompanied by a declaration that they could no longer suffer the scandal and calamity of his absence; and that his obstinacy would finally provoke them to revive and assert the primitive right of election. The abbot of Mount Cassino had been consulted whether he would accept the triple crown from the clergy and people: "I am a citizen of Rome," replied that venerable ecclesiastic, "and my first law is the voice of my country."

If superstition will interpret an untimely death; if the merit of counsels be judged from the event; the heavens may seem to frown on a measure of such apparent reason and propriety. Gregory the Eleventh did not survive above fourteen months his return to the Vatican; and his decease was followed by the great schism of the West, which distracted the Latin church above forty years. The sacred college was then composed of twenty-two cardinals: six of these had remained at Avignon; eleven Frenchmen, one Spaniard, and four Italians, entered the conclave in the usual form. Their choice was not yet limited to the purple; and their unanimous votes acquiesced in the archbishop of Bari, a subject of Naples, conspicuous for his zeal and learning, who ascended the throne of St. Peter under the name of Urban the Sixth. The epistle of the sacred college affirms his free and regular election, which had been inspired as usual by the Holy Ghost; he was adored, invested, and crowned, with the customary rites; his temporal authority was obeyed at Rome and Avignon, and his ecclesiastical supremacy was acknowledged in the Latin world. During several weeks the cardinals attended their new master with the fairest professions of attachment and loyalty, till the summer heats permitted a decent escape from the city. But as soon as they were united at Anagni and Fundi, in a place of security, they cast aside

the mask, accused their own falsehood and hypocrisy, excommunicated the apostate and antichrist of Rome, and proceeded to a new election of Robert of Geneva, Clement the
Seventh, whom they announced to the nations as the true and
rightful vicar of Christ. Their first choice, an involuntary and
illegal act, was annulled by the fear of death and the menaces of the Romans; and their complaint is justified by the
strong evidence of probability and fact. The twelve French
cardinals, above two-thirds of the votes, were masters of the
election; and whatever might be their provincial jealousies, it
cannot fairly be presumed that they would have sacrificed
their right and interest to a foreign candidate, who would
never restore them to their native country. In the various,
and often inconsistent, narratives, the shades of popular
violence are more darkly or faintly coloured: but the licentiousness of the seditious Romans was inflamed by a sense
of their privileges, and the danger of a second emigration.
The conclave was intimidated by the shouts, and encompassed by the arms, of thirty thousand rebels; the bells of
the Capitol and St. Peter's rang an alarm; "Death, or an
Italian pope!" was the universal cry; the same threat was
repeated by the twelve bannerets or chiefs of the quarters, in
the form of charitable advice; some preparations were made
for burning the obstinate cardinals; and had they chosen a
Transalpine subject, it is probable that they would never have
departed alive from the Vatican. The same constraint imposed
the necessity of dissembling in the eyes of Rome and of the
world; the pride and cruelty of Urban presented a more inevitable danger; and they soon discovered the features of the
tyrant, who could walk in his garden and recite his breviary
while he heard from an adjacent chamber six cardinals groan-
ing on the rack. His inflexible zeal, which loudly censured
their luxury and vice, would have attached them to the stations and duties of their parishes at Rome; and had he not
fatally delayed a new promotion, the French cardinals would
have been reduced to a helpless minority in the sacred college.
For these reasons, and in the hope of repassing the Alps, they
rashly violated the peace and unity of the church; and the
merits of their double choice are yet agitated in the Catholic
schools. The vanity, rather than the interest of the nation, determined the court and clergy of France. The states of Savoy,
Sicily, Cyprus, Arragon, Castile, Navarre, and Scotland, were

inclined by their example and authority to the obedience of
Clement the Seventh, and, after his decease, of Benedict the
Thirteenth. Rome and the principal states of Italy, Germany,
Portugal, England, the Low Countries, and the kingdoms of
the North, adhered to the prior election of Urban the Sixth,
who was succeeded by Boniface the Ninth, Innocent the
Seventh, and Gregory the Twelfth.

GREAT SCHISM OF THE WEST

From the banks of the Tiber and the Rhône the hostile
pontiffs encountered each other with the pen and the sword:
the civil and ecclesiastical order of society was disturbed; and
the Romans had their full share of the mischiefs of which
they may be arraigned as the primary authors. They had
vainly flattered themselves with the hope of restoring the seat
of the ecclesiastical monarchy, and of relieving their poverty
with the tributes and offerings of the nations; but the separation of France and Spain diverted the stream of lucrative devotion; nor could the loss be compensated by the two jubilees
which were crowded into the space of ten years. By the avocations of the schism, by foreign arms, and popular tumults,
Urban the Sixth and his three successors were often compelled
to interrupt their residence in the Vatican. The Colonna and
Ursini still exercised their deadly feuds: the bannerets of
Rome asserted and abused the privileges of a republic: the
vicars of Christ, who had levied a military force, chastised
their rebellion with the gibbet, the sword, and the dagger; and,
in a friendly conference, eleven deputies of the people were
perfidiously murdered and cast into the street. Since the invasion of Robert the Norman, the Romans had pursued their
domestic quarrels without the dangerous interposition of a
stranger. But in the disorders of the schism, an aspiring neighbour, Ladislaus king of Naples, alternately supported and
betrayed the pope and the people; by the former he was declared *gonfalonier*, or general of the church, while the latter
submitted to his choice the nomination of their magistrates.
Besieging Rome by land and water, he thrice entered the
gates as a barbarian conqueror; profaned the altars, violated
the virgins, pillaged the merchants, performed his devotions
at St. Peter's, and left a garrison in the castle of St. Angelo.
His arms were sometimes unfortunate, and to a delay of three

days he was indebted for his life and crown: but Ladislaus
triumphed in his turn; and it was only his premature death
that could save the metropolis and the ecclesiastical state
from the ambitious conqueror, who had assumed the title,
or at least the powers of King of Rome.

I have not undertaken the ecclesiastical history of the
schism; but Rome, the object of these last chapters, is deeply interested in the disputed succession of her sovereigns. The
first counsels for the peace and union of Christendom arose
from the university of Paris, from the faculty of the Sorbonne,
whose doctors were esteemed, at least in the Gallican church,
as the most consummate masters of theological science. Prudently waiving all invidious inquiry into the origin and merits
of the dispute, they proposed, as a healing measure, that the
two pretenders of Rome and Avignon should abdicate at the
same time, after qualifying the cardinals of the adverse factions to join in a legitimate election; and that the nations
should *subtract* their obedience, if either of the competitors
preferred his own interest to that of the public. At each vacancy these physicians of the church deprecated the mischiefs
of a hasty choice; but the policy of the conclave and the ambition of its members were deaf to reason and entreaties; and
whatsoever promises were made, the pope could never be
bound by the oaths of the cardinal. During fifteen years the
pacific designs of the university were eluded by the arts of
the rival pontiffs, the scruples or passions of their adherents,
and the vicissitudes of French factions, that ruled the insanity of Charles the Sixth. At length a vigorous resolution was
embraced; and a solemn embassy, of the titular patriarch of
Alexandria, two archbishops, five bishops, five abbots, three
knights, and twenty doctors, was sent to the courts of Avignon
and Rome, to require, in the name of the church and king,
the abdication of the two pretenders, of Peter de Luna, who
styled himself Benedict the Thirteenth, and of Angelo Cor-
rario, who assumed the name of Gregory the Twelfth. For
the ancient honour of Rome, and the success of their commission, the ambassadors solicited a conference with the
magistrates of the city, whom they gratified by a positive
declaration that the most Christian king did not entertain a
wish of transporting the holy see from the Vatican, which
he considered as the genuine and proper seat of the successor
of St. Peter. In the name of the senate and people, an eloquent

Roman asserted their desire to co-operate in the union of the church, deplored the temporal and spiritual calamities of the long schism, and requested the protection of France against the arms of the king of Naples. The answers of Benedict and Gregory were alike edifying and alike deceitful; and, in evading the demand of their abdication, the two rivals were animated by a common spirit. They agreed on the necessity of a previous interview; but the time, the place, and the manner, could never be ascertained by mutual consent. "If the one advances," says a servant of Gregory, "the other retreats; one appears an animal fearful of the land, the other a creature apprehensive of the water. And thus, for a short remnant of life and power, will these aged priests endanger the peace and salvation of the Christian world."

The Christian world was at length provoked by their obstinacy and fraud: they were deserted by their cardinals, who embraced each other as friends and colleagues; and their revolt was supported by a numerous assembly of prelates and ambassadors. With equal justice, the council of Pisa deposed the popes of Rome and Avignon; the conclave was unanimous in the choice of Alexander the Fifth, and his vacant seat was soon filled by a similar election of John the Twenty-third, the most profligate of mankind. But instead of extinguishing the schism, the rashness of the French and Italians had given a third pretender to the chair of St. Peter. Such new claims of the synod and conclave were disputed; three kings, of Germany, Hungary, and Naples, adhered to the cause of Gregory the Twelfth: and Benedict the Thirteenth, himself a Spaniard, was acknowledged by the devotion and patriotism of that powerful nation. The rash proceedings of Pisa were corrected by the council of Constance; the emperor Sigismond acted a conspicuous part as the advocate or protector of the Catholic church; and the number and weight of civil and ecclesiastical members might seem to constitute the states-general of Europe. Of the three popes, John the Twenty-third was the first victim: he fled and was brought back a prisoner: the most scandalous charges were suppressed; the vicar of Christ was only accused of piracy, murder, rape, sodomy, and incest; and after subscribing his own condemnation, he expiated in prison the imprudence of trusting his person to a free city beyond the Alps. Gregory the Twelfth, whose obedience was reduced to the narrow precincts of

Rimini, descended with more honour from the throne; and his ambassador convened the session in which he renounced the title and authority of lawful pope. To vanquish the obstinacy of Benedict the Thirteenth or his adherents, the emperor in person undertook a journey from Constance to Perpignan. The kings of Castile, Arragon, Navarre, and Scotland, obtained an equal and honourable treaty: with the concurrence of the Spaniards, Benedict was deposed by the council; but the harmless old man was left in a solitary castle to excommunicate twice each day the rebel kingdoms which had deserted his cause. After thus eradicating the remains of the schism, the synod of Constance proceeded with slow and cautious steps to elect the sovereign of Rome and the head of the church. On this momentous occasion the college of twenty-three cardinals was fortified with thirty deputies; six of whom were chosen in each of the five great nations of Christendom, —the Italian, the German, the French, the Spanish, and the *English:* the interference of strangers was softened by their generous preference of an Italian and a Roman; and the hereditary, as well as personal, merit of Otho Colonna recommended him to the conclave. Rome accepted with joy and obedience the noblest of her sons; the ecclesiastical state was defended by his powerful family; and the elevation of Martin the Fifth is the era of the restoration and establishment of the popes in the Vatican.

THE GOVERNMENT OF ROME IN THE FIFTEENTH CENTURY

A citizen has remarked, with pride and pleasure, that the king of the Romans, after passing with a slight salute the cardinals and prelates who met him at the gate, distinguished the dress and person of the senator of Rome; and in this last farewell, the pageants of the empire and the republic were clasped in a friendly embrace. According to the laws of Rome her first magistrate was required to be a doctor of laws, an alien, of a place at least forty miles from the city, with whose inhabitants he must not be connected in the third canonical degree of blood or alliance. The election was annual: a severe scrutiny was instituted into the conduct of the departing senator; nor could he be recalled to the same office till after the expiration of two years. A liberal salary of three thousand florins was assigned for his expense and reward; and his

public appearance represented the majesty of the republic.
His robes were of gold brocade or crimson velvet, or in the
summer season of a lighter silk: he bore in his hand an ivory
sceptre; the sounds of trumpets announced his approach; and
his solemn steps were preceded at least by four lictors or attendants, whose red wands were enveloped with bands or
streamers of the golden colour or livery of the city. His oath
in the Capitol proclaims his right and duty, to observe and
assert the laws, to control the proud, to protect the poor, and
to exercise justice and mercy within the extent of his jurisdiction. In these useful functions he was assisted by three
learned strangers; the two *collaterals* and the judge of criminal
appeals: their frequent trials of robberies, rapes, and murders
are attested by the laws; and the weakness of these laws con-
nives at the licentiousness of private feuds and armed associa-
tions for mutual defence. But the senator was confined to the
administration of justice: the Capitol, the treasury, and the
government of the city and its territory were entrusted to the
three *conservators*, who were changed four times in each
year: the militia of the thirteen regions assembled under the
banners of their respective chiefs, or *caporioni;* and the first
of these was distinguished by the name and dignity of the
prior. The popular legislature consisted of the secret and the
common councils of the Romans. The former was composed
of the magistrates and their immediate predecessors, with
some fiscal and legal officers, and three classes of thirteen,
twenty-six, and forty counsellors; amounting in the whole to
about one hundred and twenty persons. In the common council all male citizens had a right to vote; and the value of their
privilege was enhanced by the care with which any foreigners
were prevented from usurping the title and character of
Romans. The tumult of a democracy was checked by wise
and jealous precautions: except the magistrates, none could
propose a question; none were permitted to speak, except
from an open pulpit or tribunal; all disorderly acclamations
were suppressed; the sense of the majority was decided by a
secret ballot; and their decrees were promulgated in the
venerable name of the Roman senate and people. It would
not be easy to assign a period in which this theory of government has been reduced to accurate and constant practice,
since the establishment of order has been gradually connected with the decay of liberty. But in the year one thousand

five hundred and eighty the ancient statutes were collected, methodised in three books, and adapted to present use, under the pontificate, and with the approbation, of Gregory the Thirteenth: this civil and criminal code is the modern law of the city; and, if the popular assemblies have been abolished, a foreign senator, with the three conservators, still resides in the palace of the Capitol. The policy of the Cæsars has been repeated by the popes; and the bishop of Rome affected to maintain the form of a republic, while he reigned with the absolute powers of a temporal, as well as spiritual, monarch.

ECCLESIASTICAL GOVERNMENT

The spiritual thunders of the Vatican depend on the force of opinion; and if that opinion be supplanted by reason or passion, the sound may idly waste itself in the air; and the helpless priest is exposed to the brutal violence of a noble or a plebeian adversary. But after their return from Avignon, the keys of St. Peter were guarded by the sword of St. Paul. Rome was commanded by an impregnable citadel: the use of cannon is a powerful engine against popular seditions: a regular force of cavalry and infantry was enlisted under the banners of the pope: his ample revenues supplied the resources of war; and, from the extent of his domain, he could bring down on a rebellious city an army of hostile neighbours and loyal subjects. Since the union of the duchies of Ferrara and Urbino, the ecclesiastical state extends from the Mediterranean to the Adriatic, and from the confines of Naples to the banks of the Po; and as early as the sixteenth century the greater part of that spacious and fruitful country acknowledged the lawful claims and temporal sovereignty of the Roman pontiffs. Their claims were readily deduced from the genuine or fabulous donations of the darker ages: the successive steps of their final settlement would engage us too far in the transactions of Italy, and even of Europe; the crimes of Alexander the Sixth, the martial operations of Julius the Second, and the liberal policy of Leo the Tenth, a theme which has been adorned by the pens of the noblest historians of the times. In the first period of their conquests, till the expedition of Charles the Eighth, the popes might successfully wrestle with the adjacent princes and states, whose military force was equal or inferior to their own. But as soon

as the monarchs of France, Germany, and Spain contended
with gigantic arms for the dominion of Italy, they supplied
with art the deficiency of strength, and concealed, in a laby-
rinth of wars and treaties, their aspiring views and the immortal hope of chasing the barbarians beyond the Alps. The
nice balance of the Vatican was often subverted by the soldiers of the North and West, who were united under the
standard of Charles the Fifth: the feeble and fluctuating
policy of Clement the Seventh exposed his person and dominions to the conqueror; and Rome was abandoned seven
months to a lawless army, more cruel and rapacious than
the Goths and Vandals. After this severe lesson the popes
contracted their ambition, which was almost satisfied, resumed
the character of a common parent, and abstained from all
offensive hostilities, except in an hasty quarrel, when the
vicar of Christ and the Turkish sultan were armed at the
same time against the kingdom of Naples. The French and
Germans at length withdrew from the field of battle: Milan,
Naples, Sicily, Sardinia, and the sea-coast of Tuscany, were
firmly possessed by the Spaniards; and it became their interest
to maintain the peace and dependence of Italy, which continued almost without disturbance from the middle of the
sixteenth to the opening of the eighteenth century. The Vatican was swayed and protected by the religious policy of the
Catholic king: his prejudice and interest disposed him in
every dispute to support the prince against the people; and
instead of the encouragement, the aid, and the asylum which
they obtained from the adjacent states, the friends of liberty
or the enemies of law were enclosed on all sides within the
iron circle of despotism. The long habits of obedience and
education subdued the turbulent spirit of the nobles and commons of Rome. The barons forgot the arms and factions of
their ancestors, and insensibly became the servants of luxury
and government. Instead of maintaining a crowd of tenants
and followers, the produce of their estates was consumed in
the private expenses which multiply the pleasures and diminish
the power of the lord. The Colonna and Ursini vied with
each other in the decoration of their palaces and chapels; and
their antique splendour was rivalled or surpassed by the sudden opulence of the papal families. In Rome the voice of
freedom and discord is no longer heard; and, instead of the

foaming torrent, a smooth and stagnant lake reflects the image of idleness and servitude.

A Christian, a philosopher, and a patriot, will be equally scandalised by the temporal kingdom of the clergy; and the local majesty of Rome, the remembrance of her consuls and triumphs, may seem to embitter the sense and aggravate the shame of her slavery. If we calmly weigh the merits and defects of the ecclesiastical government, it may be praised in its present state as a mild, decent, and tranquil system, exempt from the dangers of a minority, the sallies of youth, the expenses of luxury, and the calamities of war. But these advantages are overbalanced by a frequent, perhaps a septennial, election of a sovereign, who is seldom a native of the country: the reign of a *young* statesman of threescore, in the decline of his life and abilities, without hope to accomplish, and without children to inherit, the labours of his transitory reign. The successful candidate is drawn from the church, and even the convent; from the mode of education and life the most adverse to reason, humanity, and freedom. In the trammels of servile faith he has learned to believe because it is absurd, to revere all that is contemptible, and to despise whatever might deserve the esteem of a rational being; to punish error as a crime, to reward mortification and celibacy as the first of virtues; to place the saints of the calendar above the heroes of Rome and the sages of Athens; and to consider the missal, or the crucifix, as more useful instruments than the plough or the loom. In the office of nuncio, or the rank of cardinal, he may acquire some knowledge of the world; but the primitive stain will adhere to his mind and manners: from study and experience he may suspect the mystery of his profession; but the sacerdotal artist will imbibe some portion of the bigotry which he inculcates. The genius of Sixtus the Fifth burst from the gloom of a Franciscan cloister. In a reign of five years he exterminated the outlaws and banditti, abolished the *profane* sanctuaries of Rome, formed a naval and military force, restored and emulated the monuments of antiquity, and, after a liberal use and large increase of the revenue, left five millions of crowns in the castle of St. Angelo. But his justice was sullied with cruelty, his activity was prompted by the ambition of conquest: after his decease the abuses revived; the treasure was dissipated; he entailed on posterity thirty-five new taxes and the venality of offices; and, after his death, his statue was demolished by an ungrateful or an injured people. The wild and original character of Sixtus the Fifth stands alone in the series of the pontiffs: the maxims and effects of their temporal government may be collected from the positive and comparative view of the arts and philosophy, the agriculture and trade, the wealth and population, of the ecclesiastical state. For myself, it is my wish to depart in charity with all mankind, nor am I willing, in these last moments, to offend even the pope and clergy of Rome.

71.

POGGIO'S DISCOURSE ON THE RUINS OF ROME IN
THE FIFTEENTH CENTURY. FOUR CAUSES OF RUIN.
THE COLISEUM. RESTORATION OF THE CITY. FINAL
REFLECTIONS ON THE DECLINE AND FALL OF THE
ROMAN EMPIRE

IN THE LAST DAYS of Pope Eugenius the Fourth,[1] two of his
servants, the learned Poggio and a friend, ascended the Capi-
toline hill, reposed themselves among the ruins of columns
and temples, and viewed from that commanding spot the
wide and various prospects of desolation. The place and the
object gave ample scope for moralising on the vicissitudes of
fortune, which spares neither man nor the proudest of his
works, which buries empires and cities in a common grave;
and it was agreed that, in proportion to her former greatness,
the fall of Rome was the more awful and deplorable. "Her
primæval state, such as she might appear in a remote age,
when Evander entertained the stranger of Troy, has been
delineated by the fancy of Virgil. This Tarpeian rock was
then a savage and solitary thicket: in the time of the poet
it was crowned with the golden roofs of a temple; the temple
is overthrown, the gold has been pillaged, the wheel of fortune has accomplished her revolution, and the sacred ground
is again disfigured with thorns and brambles. The hill of the
Capitol, on which we sit, was formerly the head of the Roman
empire, the citadel of the earth, the terror of kings; illustrated by the footsteps of so many triumphs, enriched with the
spoils and tributes of so many nations. This spectacle of the
world, how is it fallen! how changed! how defaced! the path
of victory is obliterated by vines, and the benches of the
senators are concealed by a dunghill. Cast your eyes on the
Palatine hill, and seek among the shapeless and enormous

---

[1] This seems to be a slip for Pope Martin the Fifth. In note 51 to Chapter
65 Gibbon points out that Poggio's dialogue *De Varietate Fortunæ* was
composed shortly before Martin's death about the end of 1430. Milman
comments on this; Bury passes it over.—D.M.L.

fragments the marble theatre, the obelisks, the colossal statues, the porticoes of Nero's palace: survey the other hills of the city, the vacant space is interrupted only by ruins and gardens. The forum of the Roman people, where they assembled to enact their laws and elect their magistrates, is now enclosed for the cultivation of potherbs, or thrown open for the reception of swine and buffaloes. The public and private edifices, that were founded for eternity, lie prostrate, naked, and broken, like the limbs of a mighty giant; and the ruin is the more visible, from the stupendous relics that have survived the injuries of time and fortune."

These relics are minutely described by Poggio, one of the first who raised his eyes from the monuments of legendary to those of classic superstition. 1. Besides a bridge, an arch, a sepulchre, and the pyramid of Cestius, he could discern, of the age of the republic, a double row of vaults in the salt-office of the Capitol, which were inscribed with the name and munificence of Catulus. 2. Eleven temples were visible in some degree, from the perfect form of the Pantheon to the three arches and a marble column of the temple of Peace, which Vespasian erected after the civil wars and the Jewish triumph. 3. Of the number, which he rashly defines, of seven *thermæ*, or public baths, none were sufficiently entire to represent the use and distribution of the several parts; but those of Diocletian and Antoninus Caracalla still retained the titles of the founders, and astonished the curious spectator, who, in observing their solidity and extent, the variety of marbles, the size and multitude of the columns, compared the labour and expense with the use and importance. Of the baths of Constantine, of Alexander, of Domitian, or rather of Titus, some vestige might yet be found. 4. The triumphal arches of Titus, Severus, and Constantine, were entire, both the structure and the inscriptions: a falling fragment was honoured with the name of Trajan; and two arches, then extant, in the Flaminian way, have been ascribed to the baser memory of Faustina and Gallienus. 5. After the wonder of the Coliseum, Poggio might have overlooked a small amphitheatre of brick, most probably for the use of the prætorian camp: the theatres of Marcellus and Pompey were occupied in a great measure by public and private buildings; and in the Circus, Agonalis and Maximus, little more than the situation and the form could be investigated. 6. The columns of Trajan and Antonine were

still erect; but the Egyptian obelisks were broken or buried.
A people of gods and heroes, the workmanship of art, was
reduced to one equestrian figure of gilt brass and to five
marble statues, of which the most conspicuous were the two
horses of Phidias and Praxiteles. 7. The two mausoleums or
sepulchres of Augustus and Hadrian could not totally be lost;
but the former was only visible as a mound of earth, and the
latter, the castle of St. Angelo, had acquired the name and
appearance of a modern fortress. With the addition of some
separate and nameless columns, such were the remains of
the ancient city; for the marks of a more recent structure
might be detected in the walls, which formed a circumference
of ten miles, included three hundred and seventy-nine turrets,
and opened into the country by thirteen gates.

This melancholy picture was drawn above nine hundred
years after the fall of the Western empire, and even of the
Gothic kingdom of Italy. A long period of distress and anarchy, in which empire, and arts, and riches had migrated
from the banks of the Tiber, was incapable of restoring or
adorning the city; and, as all that is human must retrograde
if it do not advance, every successive age must have hastened
the ruin of the works of antiquity. To measure the progress
of decay, and to ascertain, at each era, the state of each
edifice, would be an endless and a useless labour; and I shall
content myself with two observations, which will introduce a
short inquiry into the general causes and effects. 1. Two hundred years before the eloquent complaint of Poggio, an
anonymous writer composed a description of Rome. His ignorance may repeat the same objects under strange and fabulous names. Yet this barbarous topographer had eyes and
ears; he could observe the visible remains; he could listen to
the tradition of the people; and he distinctly enumerates seven
theatres, eleven baths, twelve arches, and eighteen palaces,
of which many had disappeared before the time of Poggio.
It is apparent that many stately monuments of antiquity survived till a late period, and that the principles of destruction
acted with vigorous and increasing energy in the thirteenth
and fourteenth centuries. 2. The same reflection must be
applied to the three last ages; and we should vainly seek the
Septizonium of Severus, which is celebrated by Petrarch and
the antiquarians of the sixteenth century. While the Roman
edifices were still entire, the first blows, however weighty and

impetuous, were resisted by the solidity of the mass and the harmony of the parts; but the slightest touch would precipitate the fragments of arches and columns, that already nodded to their fall.

FOUR CAUSES OF DESTRUCTION

After a diligent inquiry I can discern four principal causes of the ruin of Rome, which continued to operate in a period of more than a thousand years. I. The injuries of time and nature. II. The hostile attacks of the barbarians and Christians. III. The use and abuse of the materials. And, IV. The domestic quarrels of the Romans.

I. The art of man is able to construct monuments far more permanent than the narrow span of his own existence: yet these monuments, like himself, are perishable and frail; and in the boundless annals of time his life and his labours must equally be measured as a fleeting moment. Of a simple and solid edifice it is not easy however to circumscribe the duration. As the wonders of ancient days, the pyramids attracted the curiosity of the ancients: a hundred generations, the leaves of autumn, have dropped into the grave, and after the fall of the Pharaohs and Ptolemies, the Cæsars and Caliphs, the same pyramids stand erect and unshaken above the floods of the Nile. A complex figure of various and minute parts is more accessible to injury and decay; and the silent lapse of time is often accelerated by hurricanes and earthquakes, by fires and inundations. The air and earth have doubtless been shaken; and the lofty turrets of Rome have tottered from their foundations; but the seven hills do not appear to be placed on the great cavities of the globe; nor has the city, in any age, been exposed to the convulsions of nature, which, in the climate of Antioch, Lisbon, or Lima, have crumbled in a few moments the works of ages into dust. Fire is the most powerful agent of life and death: the rapid mischief may be kindled and propagated by the industry or negligence of mankind; and every period of the Roman annals is marked by the repetition of similar calamities. A memorable conflagration, the guilt or misfortune of Nero's reign, continued, though with unequal fury, either six or nine days. Innumerable buildings, crowded in close and crooked streets, supplied perpetual fuel for the flames; and when they ceased, four only of the four-

teen regions were left entire; three were totally destroyed,
and seven were deformed by the relics of smoking and lacer-
ated edifices. In the full meridian of empire the metropolis
arose with fresh beauty from her ashes; yet the memory of
the old deplored their irreparable losses, the arts of Greece,
the trophies of victory, the monuments of primitive or fabulous antiquity. In the days of distress and anarchy every
wound is mortal, every fall irretrievable; nor can the damage
be restored either by the public care of government, or the
activity of private interest. Yet two causes may be alleged
which render the calamity of fire more destructive to a
flourishing than a decayed city. 1. The more combustible
materials of brick, timber, and metals, are first melted or
consumed; but the flames may play without injury or effect on
the naked walls and massy arches that have been despoiled
of their ornaments. 2. It is among the common and plebeian
habitations that a mischievous spark is most easily blown to
a conflagration; but as soon as they are devoured, the greater
edifices which have resisted or escaped are left as so many
islands in a state of solitude and safety. From her situation,
Rome is exposed to the danger of frequent inundations. Without excepting the Tiber, the rivers that descend from either
side of the Apennine have a short and irregular course; a
shallow stream in the summer heats; an impetuous torrent
when it is swelled in the spring or winter, by the fall of rain
and the melting of the snows. When the current is repelled
from the sea by adverse winds, when the ordinary bed is inadequate to the weight of waters, they rise above the banks,
and overspread, without limits or control, the plains and
cities of the adjacent country. Soon after the triumph of the
first Punic war the Tiber was increased by unusual rains; and
the inundation, surpassing all former measure of time and
place, destroyed all the buildings that were situate below the
hills of Rome. According to the variety of ground, the same
mischief was produced by different means; and the edifices
were either swept away by the sudden impulse, or dissolved
and undermined by the long continuance, of the flood. Under
the reign of Augustus the same calamity was renewed: the
lawless river overturned the palaces and temples on its banks;
and, after the labours of the emperor in cleansing and widen-
ing the bed that was encumbered with ruins, the vigilance of
his successors was exercised by similar dangers and designs.

The project of diverting into new channels the Tiber itself, or some of the dependent streams, was long opposed by superstition and local interests; nor did the use compensate the toil and cost of the tardy and imperfect execution. The servitude of rivers is the noblest and most important victory which man has obtained over the licentiousness of nature; and if such were the ravages of the Tiber under a firm and active government, what could oppose, or who can enumerate, the injuries of the city after the fall of the Western empire? A remedy was at length produced by the evil itself: the accumulation of rubbish and the earth that has been washed down from the hills is supposed to have elevated the plain of Rome fourteen or fifteen feet, perhaps, above the ancient level; and the modern city is less accessible to the attacks of the river.

II. The crowd of writers of every nation, who impute the destruction of the Roman monuments to the Goths and the Christians, have neglected to inquire how far they were animated by an hostile principle, and how far they possessed the means and the leisure to satiate their enmity. In the preceding volumes of this History I have described the triumph of barbarism and religion; and I can only résumé, in a few words, their real or imaginary connection with the ruin of ancient Rome. Our fancy may create, or adopt, a pleasing romance, that the Goths and Vandals sallied from Scandinavia, ardent to avenge the flight of Odin;[1] to break the chains, and to chastise the oppressors, of mankind; that they wished to burn the records of classic literature, and to found their national architecture on the broken members of the Tuscan and Corinthian orders. But in simple truth, the northern conquerors were neither sufficiently savage, nor sufficiently refined, to entertain such aspiring ideas of destruction and revenge. The shepherds of Scythia and Germany had been educated in the armies of the empire, whose discipline they acquired, and whose weakness they invaded: with the familiar use of the Latin tongue they had learned to reverence the name and titles of Rome; and, though incapable of emulating, they were more inclined to admire than to abolish the arts and studies of a brighter period. In the transient possession

---

[1] I take this opportunity of declaring that, in the course of twelve years, I have forgotten, or renounced, the flight of Odin from Azoph to Sweden, which I never very seriously believed. The Goths are apparently Germans; but all beyond Cæsar and Tacitus is darkness or fable in the antiquities of Germany.

of a rich and unresisting capital, the soldiers of Alaric and
Genseric were stimulated by the passions of a victorious army;
amidst the wanton indulgence of lust or cruelty, portable
wealth was the object of their search: nor could they derive
pride or pleasure from the unprofitable reflection that they
had battered to the ground the works of the consuls and
Cæsars. Their moments were indeed precious: the Goths
evacuated Rome on the sixth, the Vandals on the fifteenth
day; and, though it be far more difficult to build than to
destroy, their hasty assault would have made a slight impression on the solid piles of antiquity. We may remember that
both Alaric and Genseric affected to spare the buildings of
the city; that they subsisted in strength and beauty under the
auspicious government of Theodoric; and that the momentary
resentment of Totila was disarmed by his own temper and
the advice of his friends and enemies. From these innocent
barbarians the reproach may be transferred to the Catholics
of Rome. The statues, altars, and houses of the dæmons were
an abomination in their eyes; and in the absolute command
of the city, they might labour with zeal and perseverance to
erase the idolatry of their ancestors. The demolition of the
temples in the East affords to *them* an example of conduct,
and to us an argument of belief; and it is probable that a
portion of guilt or merit may be imputed with justice to the
Roman proselytes. Yet their abhorrence was confined to the
monuments of heathen superstition; and the civil structures
that were dedicated to the business or pleasure of society
might be preserved without injury or scandal. The change of
religion was accomplished, not by a popular tumult, but by
the decrees of the emperor, of the senate, and of time. Of
the Christian hierarchy, the bishops of Rome were commonly
the most prudent and least fanatic; nor can any positive
charge be opposed to the meritorious act of saving and converting the majestic structure of the Pantheon.

III. The value of any object that supplies the wants or
pleasures of mankind is compounded of its substance and its
form, of the materials and the manufacture. Its price must
depend on the number of persons by whom it may be acquired
and used; on the extent of the market; and consequently on the
ease or difficulty of remote exportation, according to the nature
of the commodity, its local situation, and the temporary circumstances of the world. The barbarian conquerors of Rome

usurped in a moment the toil and treasure of successive ages;
but, except the luxuries of immediate consumption, they must
view without desire all that could not be removed from the
city in the Gothic waggons or the fleet of the Vandals. Gold
and silver were the first objects of their avarice; as in every
country, and in the smallest compass, they represent the most
ample command of the industry and possessions of mankind.
A vase or a statue of those precious metals might tempt
the vanity of some barbarian chief; but the grosser multitude,
regardless of the form, was tenacious only of the substance;
and the melted ingots might be readily divided and stamped
into the current coin of the empire. The less active or less
fortunate robbers were reduced to the baser plunder of brass,
lead, iron, and copper: whatever had escaped the Goths and
Vandals was pillaged by the Greek tyrants; and the emperor
Constans, in his rapacious visit, stripped the bronze tiles from
the roof of the Pantheon. The edifices of Rome might be
considered as a vast and various mine: the first labour of
extracting the materials was already performed; the metals
were purified and cast; the marbles were hewn and polished;
and after foreign and domestic rapine had been satiated, the
remains of the city, could a purchaser have been found, were
still venal. The monuments of antiquity had been left naked
of their precious ornaments; but the Romans would demolish
with their own hands the arches and walls, if the hope of
profit could surpass the cost of the labour and exportation.
If Charlemagne had fixed in Italy the seat of the Western
empire, his genius would have aspired to restore, rather than
to violate, the works of the Cæsars; but policy confined the
French monarch to the forests of Germany; his taste could be
gratified only by destruction; and the new palace of Aix la
Chapelle was decorated with the marbles of Ravenna and
Rome. Five hundred years after Charlemagne, a king of
Sicily, Robert, the wisest and most liberal sovereign of the
age, was supplied with the same materials by the easy navigation of the Tiber and the sea; and Petrarch sighs an indignant complaint, that the ancient capital of the world should
adorn from her own bowels the slothful luxury of Naples.
But these examples of plunder or purchase were rare in the
darker ages; and the Romans, alone and unenvied, might
have applied to their private or public use the remaining structures of antiquity, if in their present form and situation they

had not been useless in a great measure to the city and its inhabitants. The walls still described the old circumference, but the city had descended from the seven hills into the Campus Martius; and some of the noblest monuments which had braved the injuries of time were left in a desert far remote from the habitations of mankind. The palaces of the senators were no longer adapted to the manners or fortunes of their indigent successors: the use of baths and porticoes was forgotten: in the sixth century the games of the theatre, amphitheatre, and circus had been interrupted: some temples were devoted to the prevailing worship; but the Christian churches preferred the holy figure of the cross; and fashion, or reason, had distributed after a peculiar model the cells and offices of the cloister. Under the ecclesiastical reign the number of these pious foundations was enormously multiplied; and the city was crowded with forty monasteries of men, twenty of women, and sixty chapters and colleges of canons and priests, who aggravated, instead of relieving, the depopulation of the tenth century. But if the forms of ancient architecture were disregarded by a people insensible of their use and beauty, the plentiful materials were applied to every call of necessity or superstition; till the fairest columns of the Ionic and Corinthian orders, the richest marbles of Paros and Numidia, were degraded, perhaps to the support of a convent or a stable. The daily havoc which is perpetrated by the Turks in the cities of Greece and Asia may afford a melancholy example; and in the gradual destruction of the monuments of Rome, Sixtus the Fifth may alone be excused for employing the stones of the Septizonium in the glorious edifice of St. Peter's. A fragment, a ruin, howsoever mangled or profaned, may be viewed with pleasure and regret; but the greater part of the marble was deprived of substance, as well as of place and proportion; it was burnt to lime for the purpose of cement. Since the arrival of Poggio the temple of Concord and many capital structures had vanished from his eyes; and an epigram of the same age expresses a just and pious fear that the continuance of this practice would finally annihilate all the monuments of antiquity. The smallness of their numbers was the sole check on the demands and depredations of the Romans. The imagination of Petrarch might create the presence of a mighty people; and I hesitate to believe that, even in the fourteenth century, they could be reduced to a con-

temptible list of thirty-three thousand inhabitants. From that
period to the reign of Leo the Tenth, if they multiplied to
the amount of eighty-five thousand, the increase of citizens
was in some degree pernicious to the ancient city.

IV. I have reserved for the last the most potent and forci-
ble cause of destruction, the domestic hostilities of the Romans
themselves. Under the dominion of the Greek and French
emperors the peace of the city was disturbed by accidental,
though frequent, seditions: it is from the decline of the latter,
from the beginning of the tenth century, that we may date the
licentiousness of private war, which violated with impunity
the laws of the Code and the Gospel, without respecting the
majesty of the absent sovereign, or the presence and person
of the vicar of Christ. In a dark period of five hundred years
Rome was perpetually afflicted by the sanguinary quarrels
of the nobles and the people, the Guelphs and Ghibelines, the
Colonna and Ursini; and if much has escaped the knowledge,
and much is unworthy of the notice, of history, I have exposed
in the two preceding chapters the causes and effects of the
public disorders. At such a time, when every quarrel was
decided by the sword, and none could trust their lives or
properties to the impotence of law, the powerful citizens were
armed for safety, or offence, against the domestic enemies
whom they feared or hated. Except Venice alone, the same
dangers and designs were common to all the free republics
of Italy; and the nobles usurped the prerogative of fortifying
their houses, and erecting strong towers that were capable of
resisting a sudden attack. The cities were filled with these
hostile edifices; and the example of Lucca, which contained
three hundred towers; her law, which confined their height
to the measure of fourscore feet, may be extended with suitable latitude to the more opulent and populous states. The
first step of the senator Brancaleone in the establishment of
peace and justice was to demolish (as we have already seen)
one hundred and forty of the towers of Rome; and, in the
last days of anarchy and discord, as late as the reign of Martin
the Fifth, forty-four still stood in one of the thirteen or
fourteen regions of the city. To this mischievous purpose
the remains of antiquity were most readily adapted: the temples and arches afforded a broad and solid basis for the new
structures of brick and stone; and we can name the modern

turrets that were raised on the triumphal monuments of Julius
Cæsar, Titus, and the Antonines. With some slight alterations,
an amphitheatre, a mausoleum, was transformed into a strong
and spacious citadel. I need not repeat that the mole of
Hadrian had assumed the title and form of the castle of St.
Angelo; the Septizonium of Severus was capable of standing
against a royal army; the sepulchre of Metella has sunk under
its outworks; the theatres of Pompey and Marcellus were
occupied by the Savelli and Ursini families; and the rough
fortress has been gradually softened to the splendour and elegance of an Italian palace. Even the churches were encompassed with arms and bulwarks, and the military engines on
the roof of St. Peter's were the terror of the Vatican and the
scandal of the Christian world. Whatever is fortified will be
attacked; and whatever is attacked may be destroyed. Could
the Romans have wrested from the popes the castle of St.
Angelo, they had resolved by a public decree to annihilate
that monument of servitude. Every building of defence was
exposed to a siege; and in every siege the arts and engines of
destruction were laboriously employed. After the death of
Nicholas the Fourth, Rome, without a sovereign or a senate,
was abandoned six months to the fury of civil war. "The
houses," says a cardinal and poet of the times, "were crushed
by the weight and velocity of enormous stones; the walls
were perforated by the strokes of the battering-ram; the
towers were involved in fire and smoke; and the assailants
were stimulated by rapine and revenge." The work was consummated by the tyranny of the laws; and the factions of
Italy alternately exercised a blind and thoughtless vengeance
on their adversaries, whose houses and castles they razed to
the ground. In comparing the *days* of foreign with the *ages*
of domestic hostility, we must pronounce that the latter have
been far more ruinous to the city; and our opinion is confirmed by the evidence of Petrarch. "Behold," says the laureat,
"the relics of Rome, the image of her pristine greatness!
neither time nor the barbarian can boast the merit of this
stupendous destruction: it was perpetrated by her own citizens,
by the most illustrious of her sons; and your ancestors (he
writes to a noble Annibaldi) have done with the battering-
ram what the Punic hero could not accomplish with the
sword." The influence of the two last principles of decay
must in some degree be multiplied by each other; since the

houses and towers which were subverted by civil war required a new and perpetual supply from the monuments of antiquity.

THE COLISEUM

These general observations may be separately applied to the amphitheatre of Titus, which has obtained the name of the COLISEUM, either from its magnitude, or from Nero's colossal statue: an edifice, had it been left to time and nature, which might perhaps have claimed an eternal duration. The curious antiquaries, who have computed the numbers and seats, are disposed to believe that above the upper row of stone steps the amphitheatre was encircled and elevated with several stages of wooden galleries, which were repeatedly consumed by fire, and restored by the emperors. Whatever was precious, or portable, or profane, the statues of gods and heroes, and the costly ornaments of sculpture, which were cast in brass, or overspread with leaves of silver and gold, became the first prey of conquest or fanaticism, of the avarice of the barbarians or the Christians. In the massy stones of the Coliseum many holes are discerned; and the two most probable conjectures represent the various accidents of its decay. These stones were connected by solid links of brass or iron, nor had the eye of rapine overlooked the value of the baser metals; the vacant space was converted into a fair or market; the artisans of the Coliseum are mentioned in an ancient survey; and the chasms were perforated or enlarged to receive the poles that supported the shops or tents of the mechanic trades. Reduced to its naked majesty, the Flavian amphitheatre was contemplated with awe and admiration by the pilgrims of the North; and their rude enthusiasm broke forth in a sublime proverbial expression, which is recorded in the eighth century, in the fragments of the venerable Bede: "As long as the Coliseum stands, Rome shall stand; when the Coliseum falls, Rome will fall; when Rome falls, the world will fall." In the modern system of war, a situation commanded by three hills would not be chosen for a fortress, but the strength of the walls and arches could resist the engines of assault; a numerous garrison might be lodged in the enclosure; and while one faction occupied the Vatican and the Capitol, the other was entrenched in the Lateran and the Coliseum.

The abolition at Rome of the ancient games must be under-

stood with some latitude; and the carnival sports, of the Testa-
cean mount and the Circus Agonalis, were regulated by the
law or custom of the city. The senator presided with dignity
and pomp to adjudge and distribute the prizes, the gold ring,
or the *pallium,* as it was styled, of cloth or silk. A tribute on
Jews supplied the annual expense; and the races, on foot,
on horseback, or in chariots, were ennobled by a tilt and
tournament of seventy-two of the Roman youth. In the year
one thousand three hundred and thirty-two, a bull-feast, after
the fashion of the Moors and Spaniards, was celebrated in the
Coliseum itself; and the living manners are painted in a diary
of the times. A convenient order of benches was restored;
and a general proclamation, as far as Rimini and Ravenna,
invited the nobles to exercise their skill and courage in this
perilous adventure. The Roman ladies were marshalled in
three squadrons, and seated in three balconies, which on this
day, the third of September, were lined with scarlet cloth. The
fair Jacova di Rovere led the matrons from beyond the Tiber,
a pure and native race, who still represent the features and
character of antiquity. The remainder of the city was divided
as usual between the Colonna and Ursini: the two factions
were proud of the number and beauty of their female bands:
the charms of Savella Ursini are mentioned with praise; and
the Colonna regretted the absence of the youngest of their
house, who had sprained her ankle in the garden of Nero's
tower. The lots of the champions were drawn by an old and
respectable citizen; and they descended into the arena, or pit,
to encounter the wild bulls, on foot as it should seem, with a
single spear. Amidst the crowd, our annalist has selected the
names, colours, and devices of twenty of the most conspicuous knights. Several of the names are the most illustrious of
Rome and the ecclesiastical state: Malatesta, Polenta, della
Valle, Cafarello, Savelli, Capoccio, Conti, Annibaldi, Altieri,
Corsi: the colours were adapted to their taste and situation;
the devices are expressive of hope or despair, and breathe
the spirit of gallantry and arms. "I am alone, like the youngest
of the Horatii," the confidence of an intrepid stranger: "I
live disconsolate," a weeping widower: "I burn under the
ashes," a discreet lover: "I adore Lavinia, or Lucretia," the
ambiguous declaration of a modern passion: "My faith is as
pure," the motto of a white livery: "Who is stronger than
myself?" of a lion's hide: "If I am drowned in blood, what

a pleasant death!" the wish of ferocious courage. The pride or prudence of the Ursini restrained them from the field, which was occupied by three of their hereditary rivals, whose inscriptions denoted the lofty greatness of the Colonna name: "Though sad, I am strong," "Strong as I am great," "If I fall," addressing himself to the spectators, "you fall with me," intimating (says the contemporary writer) that, while the other families were the subjects of the Vatican, they alone were the supporters of the Capitol. The combats of the amphitheatre were dangerous and bloody. Every champion successively encountered a wild bull; and the victory may be ascribed to the quadrupeds, since no more than eleven were left on the field, with the loss of nine wounded and eighteen killed on the side of their adversaries. Some of the noblest families might mourn, but the pomp of the funerals, in the churches of St. John Lateran and Sta. Maria Maggiore, afforded a second holiday to the people. Doubtless it was not in such conflicts that the blood of the Romans should have been shed; yet, in blaming their rashness, we are compelled to applaud their gallantry; and the noble volunteers, who display their magnificence, and risk their lives, under the balconies of the fair, excite a more generous sympathy than the thousands of captives and malefactors who were reluctantly dragged to the scene of slaughter.

This use of the amphitheatre was a rare, perhaps a singular, festival: the demand for the materials was a daily and continual want, which the citizens could gratify without restraint or remorse. In the fourteenth century a scandalous act of concord secured to both factions the privilege of extracting stones from the free and common quarry of the Coliseum; and Poggio laments that the greater part of these stones had been burnt to lime by the folly of the Romans. To check this abuse, and to prevent the nocturnal crimes that might be perpetrated in the vast and gloomy recess, Eugenius the Fourth surrounded it with a wall; and, by a charter, long extant, granted both the ground and edifice to the monks of an adjacent convent. After his death the wall was overthrown in a tumult of the people; and had they themselves respected the noblest monument of their fathers, they might have justified the resolve that it should never be degraded to private property. The inside was damaged: but in the middle of the sixteenth century, an era of taste and learning, the exterior circumference of one thousand six hundred and twelve feet was still entire and inviolate; a triple elevation of fourscore arches, which rose to the height of one hundred and eight feet. Of the present ruin the nephews of Paul the Third are the guilty agents; and every traveller who views the Farnese palace may curse the sacrilege and luxury of these upstart princes. A similar reproach is applied to the Barberini; and the repetition of injury might be dreaded from every reign, till the Coliseum was placed under the safeguard of religion by the most liberal of the pontiffs, Benedict the Fourteenth, who consecrated a spot which persecution and fable had stained with the blood of so many Christian martyrs.

RESTORATION OF THE CITY

When Petrarch first gratified his eyes with a view of those monuments whose scattered fragments so far surpass the most eloquent descriptions, he was astonished at the supine indifference of the Romans themselves; he was humbled rather than elated by the discovery that, except his friend Rienzi, and one of the Colonna, a stranger of the Rhône was more conversant with these antiquities than the nobles and natives of the metropolis. The ignorance and credulity of the Romans are elaborately displayed in the old survey of the city which was composed about the beginning of the thirteenth century; and, without dwelling on the manifold errors of name and place, the legend of the Capitol may provoke a smile of contempt and indignation. "The Capitol," says the anonymous writer, "is so named as being the head of the world; where the consuls and senators formerly resided for the government of the city and the globe. The strong and lofty walls were covered with glass and gold, and crowned with a roof of the richest and most curious carving. Below the citadel stood a palace, of gold for the greatest part, decorated with precious stones, and whose value might be esteemed at one third of the world itself. The statues of all the provinces were arranged in order; each with a small bell suspended from its neck; and such was the contrivance of art magic, that, if the province rebelled against Rome, the statue turned round to that quarter of the heavens, the bell rang, the prophet of the Capitol reported the prodigy, and the senate was admonished of the impending danger." A second example, of less importance, though of equal absurdity, may be drawn from the two marble horses, led by two naked youths, which have since been transported from the baths of Constantine to the Quirinal hill. The groundless application of the names of Phidias and Praxiteles may perhaps be excused; but these Grecian sculptors should not have been removed above four hundred years from the age of Pericles to that of Tiberius; they should not have been transformed into two philosophers or magicians, whose nakedness was the symbol of truth and knowledge, who revealed to the emperor his most secret actions; and, after refusing all pecuniary recompense, solicited the honour of leaving this eternal monument of themselves. Thus awake to the power of magic, the Romans were insensible to the beauties of art: no more than five statues were visible to the eyes of Poggio, and of the multitudes which chance or design had buried under the ruins, the resurrection was fortunately delayed till a safer and more enlightened age. The Nile, which now adorns the Vatican, had been explored by some labourers, in digging a vineyard near the temple, or convent, of the Minerva; but the impatient proprietor, who was tormented by some visits of curiosity, restored the unprofitable marble to its former grave. The discovery of a statue of Pompey, ten feet in length, was the occasion of a lawsuit. It had been found under a partition wall: the equitable judge had pronounced that the head should be separated from the body to satisfy the claims of the contiguous owners; and the sentence would have been executed if the intercession of a cardinal, and the liberality of a pope, had not rescued the Roman hero from the hands of his barbarous countrymen.

But the clouds of barbarism were gradually dispelled; and the peaceful authority of Martin the Fifth and his successors restored the ornaments of the city as well as the order of the ecclesiastical state. The improvements of Rome, since the fifteenth century, have not been the spontaneous produce of freedom and industry. The first and most natural root of a great city is the labour and populousness of the adjacent country, which supplies the materials of subsistence, of manufactures, and of foreign trade. But the greater part of the Campagna of Rome is reduced to a dreary and desolate wilderness: the overgrown estates of the princes and the clergy are cultivated by the lazy hands of indigent and hopeless vassals; and the scanty harvests are confined or ex-

ported for the benefit of a monopoly. A second and more
artificial cause of the growth of a metropolis is the residence
of a monarch, the expense of a luxurious court, and the
tributes of dependent provinces. Those provinces and tributes
had been lost in the fall of the empire; and if some streams
of the silver of Peru and the gold of Brazil have been attracted by the Vatican, the revenues of the cardinals, the
fees of office, the oblations of pilgrims and clients, and the
remnant of ecclesiastical taxes, afford a poor and precarious
supply, which maintains, however, the idleness of the court
and city. The population of Rome, far below the measure
of the great capitals of Europe, does not exceed one hundred
and seventy thousand inhabitants; and within the spacious
enclosure of the walls, the largest portion of the seven hills
is overspread with vineyards and ruins. The beauty and
splendour of the modern city may be ascribed to the abuses
of the government, to the influence of superstition. Each reign
(the exceptions are rare) has been marked by the rapid elevation of a new family, enriched by the childless pontiff at
the expense of the church and country. The palaces of these
fortunate nephews are the most costly monuments of elegance and servitude: the perfect arts of architecture, painting,
and sculpture, have been prostituted in their service; and
their galleries and gardens are decorated with the most
precious works of antiquity, which taste or vanity has
prompted them to collect. The ecclesiastical revenues were
more decently employed by the popes themselves in the pomp
of the Catholic worship; but it is superfluous to enumerate
their pious foundations of altars, chapels, and churches,
since these lesser stars are eclipsed by the sun of the Vatican,
by the dome of St. Peter, the most glorious structure that
ever has been applied to the use of religion. The fame of
Julius the Second, Leo the Tenth, and Sixtus the Fifth, is accompanied by the superior merit of Bramante and Fontana,
of Raphael and Michael Angelo; and the same munificence
which had been displayed in palaces and temples was directed
with equal zeal to revive and emulate the labours of antiquity.
Prostrate obelisks were raised from the ground, and erected
in the most conspicuous places; of the eleven aqueducts of
the Cæsars and consuls, three were restored; the artificial
rivers were conducted over a long series of old or of new
arches, to discharge into marble basins a flood of salubrious

and refreshing waters: and the spectator, impatient to ascend the steps of St. Peter's, is detained by a column of Egyptian granite, which rises between two lofty and perpetual fountains to the height of one hundred and twenty feet. The map, the description, the monuments of ancient Rome, have been elucidated by the diligence of the antiquarian and the student; and the footsteps of heroes, the relics, not of superstition, but of empire, are devoutly visited by a new race of pilgrims from the remote and once savage countries of the North.

FINAL REFLECTIONS ON THE DECLINE AND FALL OF THE ROMAN EMPIRE

Of these pilgrims, and of every reader, the attention will be excited by an History of the Decline and Fall of the Roman Empire; the greatest, perhaps, and most awful scene in the history of mankind. The various causes and progressive effects are connected with many of the events most interesting in human annals: the artful policy of the Cæsars, who long maintained the name and image of a free republic; the disorders of military despotism; the rise, establishment, and sects of Christianity; the foundation of Constantinople; the division of the monarchy; the invasion and settlements of the barbarians of Germany and Scythia; the institutions of the civil law; the character and religion of Mahomet; the temporal sovereignty of the popes; the restoration and decay of the Western empire of Charlemagne; the crusades of the Latins in the East; the conquests of the Saracens and Turks; the ruin of the Greek empire; the state and revolutions of Rome in the middle age. The historian may applaud the importance and variety of his subject; but, while he is conscious of his own imperfections, he must often accuse the deficiency of his materials. It was among the ruins of the Capitol that I first conceived the idea of a work which has amused and exercised near twenty years of my life, and which, however inadequate to my own wishes, I finally deliver to the curiosity and candour of the public.

Lausanne,
June 27, 1787

Bibliographical Note

The Decline and Fall was originally published in 6 volumes quarto. The first appeared in 1776, the second and third in 1783, and the last three in 1788. An edition in 12 volumes octavo appeared during the author's lifetime. Allowing for some obvious errors, the text presented may be taken to be what Gibbon wrote with his own typographical arrangements of capitals, italics, etc., and with his very individual spelling.

Of the numerous later editions the most pre-eminent for scholarship is that of J. B. Bury in 7 volumes, which appeared in various issues from 1896 onwards; the best of these is the illustrated one (1900–14). Dr. William Smith's edition of Dean Milman's edition (1853–54) can still be consulted with profit, and is in several ways easier to use than Bury's.

It is no part of a work such as this to compile a bibliography. The reader who desires to study the Roman Empire in the light of modern research can be referred to the relevant volumes of the *Cambridge Ancient History* and the *Cambridge Medieval History*, in all of which also full bibliographies are to be found. The following works, some of which have appeared since the histories mentioned above, will be found useful. Most of them also contain bibliographies.

A. Stuart Jones, *The Roman Empire 29 B.C.–A.D. 476* (1908). (This is still one of the best short accounts of the period.)

Methuen's History of the Roman World. Vol. VI, by R. P. Longden. Vol. VII, by H. M. D. Parker.

A. A. Vasiliev, *History of the Byzantine Empire A.D. 324–1453* (1952).

N. H. Baynes, *The Byzantine Empire* (1925).

N. H. Baynes and H. St. L. B. Moss, *Byzantium* (1948).

Christopher Dawson, *The Making of Europe* (1932).

H. Mattingly, *Roman Imperial Civilisation* (1957).

Steven Runciman, *Byzantine Civilisation* (1935).

Steven Runciman, *A History of the Crusades* (1951–54).

J. B. Bury, *The Invasion of Europe by the Barbarians* (1928).

E. A. Thompson, *A History of Attila and the Huns* (1948).

F. W. Walbank, *The Decline of the Roman Empire in the West* (1946).

INDEX

INDEX

ABGARUS, king of Edessa, alleged correspondence of Christ with, 785

ABLAVIUS, prime minister of Constantine the Great, massacred by Constantius II, 344

ABUBEKER, collects and publishes the Koran, 848; adopts the religion of Mahomet, 856; accompanies Mahomet on his flight from Mecca, 859; chosen by Mahomet to supply his place, 874; address on Mahomet's death, 875

ABULPHARAGIUS, or Gregory Bar-Hebræus, primate of the East, his narrative of the destruction of the Alexandrian Library by Amrou examined, 884

ABU SOPHIAN, chief of the branch of Omiyah, and Prince of Mecca, meditates on death of Mahomet, 858; his caravans intercepted by Moslems, 864; fruitless siege of Medina, 866; surrenders Mecca and confesses mission of Mahomet, 869

ABU TALEB, uncle and guardian of Mahomet, 842; advises Mahomet to relinquish his mission, 857; opposes his doctrine, but protects his person, ib.

ACACIUS, master of the bears, father of the Empress Theodora, 691

ACEPHALI, Egyptian sect of, 772

ADAM, a prophet, according to the Koran, 846

ADOLPHUS, reinforces his brother-in-law, Alaric, 564; made count of the domestics to Attalus, 569; succeeds Alaric, and subsequent career, 580–1

ADRIAN I, pope, receives Charlemagne at Rome, 801–2; accepts decrees of the second Nicene Council with regard to images, 807; threatens Greek emperors with excommunication, 808; his greatness, 809

ÆDESIUS, the Platonist, initiates Julian in allegory, 445; his school at Pergamus, 447

ÆNEAS SYLVIUS, pope Pius II, on impracticability of war against Turks, 1082; attempt to conduct one, 1082–3

AËTIUS, surnamed the Atheist, account of, 395

AËTIUS, general of Placidia, battle with Count Boniface, 602; flies to Pannonia, ib.; relieves Orleans, 611; defeats Attila at Châlons, 612-3; opposes him in Italy, 620; urges marriage of his son Gaudentius with the Princess Eudoxia, 624; murdered by Valentinian III, 625

AGLAË, her passion for St. Boniface, 293

AGRICOLA, defeats the Caledonians, 9; contemplates reduction of Ireland, ib.; recalled, ib.

AGRIPPA, censor with Augustus, 42

AGRIPPINA, ambition of, 95

ALARIC, the Goth, requires hostages in security of his demands for reimbursement and a Western province, 544; marches towards Rome, ib.; blockades it, 560–1; accepts a ransom, and raises the siege, 563; marches into Tuscany, 564; reinforced, ib.; his proposals to the court of Ravenna, 565; rejected by Olympius, ib.; renewed, ib.; rage